The Social Sciences in Moder

TWENTIETH-CENTURY JAPAN:
THE EMERGENCE OF A WORLD POWER

Irwin Scheiner, Editor

The Social Sciences in Modern Japan

The Marxian and Modernist Traditions

Andrew E. Barshay

UNIVERSITY OF CALIFORNIA PRESS
Berkeley · Los Angeles · London

University of California Press
Berkeley and Los Angeles, California

University of California Press, Ltd.
London, England

First paperback printing 2007

Library of Congress Cataloging-in-Publication Data

Barshay, Andrew E.
    The social sciences in modern Japan: the marxian and
modernist traditions / Andrew E. Barshay.
        p.   cm.
    Includes bibliographical references and index.
    ISBN 978-0-520-25381-0 (pbk : alk.)
    1. Social sciences—Japan—History.
2. Intellectuals—Japan—History.   3. Socialism—
Japan—History.   4. Democracy—Japan—History.
5. Political culture—Japan—History.   I. Title.

H53.J3 B37   2004
300'.952'0904—dc21   2003014237

Manufactured in the United States of America
16 15 14 13 12 11 10 09 08 07
10 9 8 7 6 5 4 3 2 1

The paper used in this publication is both acid-free and
totally chlorine-free (TCF). It meets the minimum
requirements of ANSI/NISO Z39.48–1992 (R 1997)
(Permanence of Paper). ♾

For K and I

Contents

Preface

This book was a long time in coming. It is not entirely the one I expected to write, though I dare to hope that it is a better one. Almost twenty years ago, somewhere in the course of writing my doctoral dissertation on the "public man" in imperial Japan, I noticed that for Japan's intellectuals in the 1920s and especially after 1945, the phrase "social science" seems to have been invested with an almost magical power. If properly conceived and put into practice, social science might actually solve some of the enormous problems then facing Japan and its people. In the 1920s, these had mainly to do with poverty, inequality, and overpopulation; under the radically changed conditions brought by defeat and occupation, the tasks laid upon social science included the wholesale democratization of the political and social order itself. What was the relationship between the tasks of the 1920s and those of the early postwar era? What significance was to be attributed to the intervening war and defeat? However these questions were to be answered, there seemed little doubt that they could be, and that Japanese society would improve as a result.

What I had noticed, in short, was the self-image of social science as a uniquely powerful set of ideas and practices. Yet once examined, this image of a single Mahayana-like "great vehicle" seemed to dissolve into particulars. Social science was also "the social sciences," not one but many, fractious and territorial. Where had they come from? How did they acquire their personalities as professional disciplines? As such, what fates did they encounter? By the same token, if there were moments of critical unity, why and how did they occur? My hope was to write a synthetic history that would trace the interplay of unifying and particularizing impulses in Japanese social science, from time(s) of origin that I could identify through their development as disciplines, while tying that into the convulsed history of the society and polity in which they were embedded.

I did realize that goal, partially, as I hope the opening chapters of this book will attest. I begin by offering a historical contextualization for the professional practice of social science in general (that is, not only in Japan), and an overview of Japanese trends from the 1890s onward. The theme, broadly speaking, is that of "development" or "rationalization" and the various forms of modernity that such development has engendered. My hypothesis is that the form assumed by social science in a given national setting is closely bound up with the institutional path to modernity taken by that nation. I also argue that Japan, together with Germany and prerevolutionary Russia, represented forms of "developmental alienation" from the "Atlantic Rim" symptomatic of late-emerging empires, and that this perceived condition—of vulnerability to the cultural, or virtual, imperialism of the "advanced" world—was the primary, though not the only, determinant of the social science generated in each of these settings. I go on to present detailed treatments of two of the most powerful streams of professional social science, one associated with Marxism in its various schools, the other with what in Japan is termed "modernism," and whose most representative figure is the late Maruyama Masao. I try to show how the problematics associated with developmental alienation affected both of these currents in Japanese social science, and I argue that in succession, these two sets of thought have provided Japanese social science with those moments of unity it has thus far experienced. I see no such unity at present, and do not know what the future will bring.

I do not claim to know whether unity is always best for intellectual life. It has its price, and everything depends on the political and institutional conditions under which that unity is secured. But I also think that the achievements of writers in the Marxian and modernist traditions of Japanese social science were very considerable. This is because they sought to face the central issue of their time: the gap between the rich and poor countries of the world, and between city and country within society after society, including that of Japan, in all of their political, social, and cultural ramifications. Critiques of those achievements are vitally needed, but at least to me they have yet to reach fully the intellectual level of their target. If the account I offer here reads as a requiem for an age of intellectual heroes, if it bears traces of elegy, this judgment is the reason.

Yet more is at stake here than personal retrospection or scholarly taste. Between the beginning and the end of the 1960s, Japanese society underwent fundamental transformations. By the end of that decade, it was definitively urban and mass-based in a way it had never been. The "problem of the villages" no longer had a unifying salience in social thought. The scale of corporate dominance over the national life was also unprecedented, as was Japan's share of world trade. All of this was justified in the ideological sphere by combining a traditionalizing rhetoric of service to "community" with a post-1945 ethos of democratized equality. The latter had its basis in the actual shrinking of the gap between rich and poor, relative to prewar society; to that extent, according to some arguments from the left, the Marxists and modernists themselves must be seen as "complicit" in the formation of the postwar "social contract," no less so than the "neo-Japanists" who elevated the country to the status of industrial utopia with world-historical significance.

I find it difficult to agree completely with these provocative arguments, but that is not the point here. As the postwar social contract itself seems now to be in question, the need, not just for critique, but for an alternative vision, becomes especially pressing. Could it be that the legacy of Japanese social science contains some undervalued possibilities, some resources for the effectual understanding of the present? As Sugihara Shirō, Ōshima Mario, and others have shown, one such may be the stream of liberalism that stretches back, if not to nineteenth-century figures such as Fukuzawa Yukichi and Taguchi Ukichi, then certainly to Ishibashi Tanzan in the twentieth century; in another register, as Harry Harootunian's recent work indicates, the urban-centered "interactionist" and pragmatist sociology of the post–World War I era seems to contain a wealth of still-to-be-explored insights. Whether a concerted program of retrieval will yield a different understanding of the central issues I cannot say. But I will be gratified if the work I offer here spurs efforts of this kind. As the years go by I feel a greater empathy for thinkers who find themselves looking for resources in the past as they confront their own present. We all need allies. Still, beyond strategy, beyond the most admirable desire to intervene in an ongoing struggle, I cannot escape the thought that historical judgment awaits all that we make public, including the work presented here. It may or may not be one that we like, but this is something over which we have no control.

Acknowledgments

I owe thanks to many people for help of all kinds in writing this book. I must first mention three to whom my debt is greatest: Kimiko Nishimura, my companion in life and work; Irwin Scheiner, my colleague and friend; and the late Maruyama Masao. I may have written this book, but literally, they made it possible.

Laura Hein, Robert Bellah, Harry Harootunian, and Takashi Fujitani read the entire manuscript. My debt and gratitude to each is very great, and I hereby release them (should they so wish) from any responsibility for the result. Discussions and correspondence over the years with Ōshima Mario, Hashimoto Mitsuru, Kojima Shūichi, Shimizu Yasuhisa, Matsumoto Sannosuke, and Mark Metzler never failed to stimulate my thinking, to remind me how much there was to learn and how much I wanted to learn it. My Berkeley colleagues Yeh Wen-Hsin and Frederic Wakeman Jr. have set a standard for me in the sharing of ideas.

At a late stage, I was exceptionally fortunate to have been able to discuss aspects of the manuscript with John Dunn, Robert Albritton, Shibuya Hiroshi, Yamamoto Yoshihiko, and Thomas Sekine. I owe special thanks, additionally, to Luke Franks, who generously, and amid heavy demands on his time and attention, prepared the bibliography. Finally, I owe more than a word of thanks to James Clark, former director of the University of California Press, and to Matt Stevens, for his fine editorial work.

Over the course of research and writing, I have received support, above all, from the department of history and the Center for Japanese Studies at the University of California, Berkeley. Successive grants from the Social Science Research Council and National Endowment for the Humanities, and an invitation to the School of Social Science at the Institute for Advanced Study in Princeton gave me the chance to take a year's leave from teaching and really turn the corner toward completing the manuscript. I am grateful to Joan Scott and Clifford Geertz for giving me this opportunity at a crucial juncture. Finally, I thank the Institute of Social Science at the University of Tokyo, in particular Hiraishi Naoaki, for the offer of a visiting professorship just as the manuscript was in final revision for publication. My presentation and discussions there enabled me to think through the entire argument once more. More than is usually the case, therefore, whatever errors remain now are truly my own. For everything else, I can only record a final word of thanks.

CHAPTER I

Social Science as History

What follows is a historical study of intellectuals and the social sciences, or better, of the intellectual as social scientist, in Japan from the 1890s roughly to the present. But I wish to begin with a Russian parable based on a minor character in a novel by Leo Tolstoy.

The novel is *Anna Karenin*, the character is Sergei Ivanich Koznyshev. Koznyshev is a city intellectual, a social type of whom Tolstoy was none too fond. Unlike his half-brother Konstantin Levin, Koznyshev takes the institution of the *zemstvo* land assembly seriously, even, on occasion, upbraiding the great landowner and spiritual pilgrim for ignoring his political responsibilities. This, we are shown, is somewhat unfair to Levin. Not only does Levin write a book on the problem of Russian agriculture—synonymous, in his view, with "the question" of peasant labor—but he also attempts to carry out his ideas on his own estate lands. For his part, Levin finds himself uncomfortable at Koznyshev's presence in the country. Koznyshev regards the country, or more specifically his half-brother's estate, as no more than a "valuable antidote to the corrupt influences of town," a place where he can be lazy. Real, intellectual life is possible only in the city, or in the country to the extent that it can be made a satellite of the city.

Levin is troubled by the effects of abstract thought on the personality of the intellectual:

> Levin regarded his brother as a man of vast intellect and culture, as generous
> in the highest sense of the word and endowed with a special faculty for work-

ing for the public good. But in the depths of his heart, the older he grew and the more intimately he knew his brother, the oftener the thought struck him that this faculty for working for the public good, of which he was completely devoid, was perhaps not so much a quality as a lack . . . of the vital force, of what is called heart, of the impulse that drives a man to choose some one out of all the innumerable paths of life and to care for that one only. The better he knew his brother, the more he noticed that Koznyshev . . . had reasoned out in [his mind] that it was a right thing to take interest in public affairs, and consequently took interest in them. Levin was confirmed in this supposition by observing that his brother did not take questions affecting public welfare, or the question of the immortality of the soul, a bit more to heart than he did chess problems or the ingenious design of a new machine.[1]

Nor was this all. For the problem was more than the leveling out of what should have been a clear hierarchy of concerns. It was that a morally fatal disjunction between life and thought seemed by necessity to come with intellectual activity. This disjunction, in turn, had at least two aspects. First, a flight from genuine confrontation with spiritual matters:

Listening to his brother's conversation with the professor, [Levin] noticed that they linked . . . scientific questions with the spiritual and several times almost touched on the latter; but every time they got close to what seemed the most important point, they promptly beat a hasty retreat and plunged back into the sea of subtle distinctions, reservations, quotations, allusions, and references to authorities; and he had difficulty in understanding what they were talking about.[2]

And second, although perhaps less advanced in Koznyshev's own case, was an inability or unwillingness to undertake serious self-examination:

[Sviazhsky] was one of those people—always a source of wonder to Levin— whose very logical if unoriginal convictions find no reflection in their lives, which are most definite and stable in their direction and go their way quite independently and as a rule in diametric contradiction to their convictions.[3]

Ultimately, via this displacement of what Tolstoy regarded as genuine—spiritual—problems, and their projection onto the social plane, the intellectual life becomes its own reward. And a paltry one it is. Later in *Anna Karenin*, Tolstoy allows Koznyshev, after six years' work, to publish a modestly titled but evidently intended-to-be-magnum opus, *Sketch of a Survey of the Principles and Forms of Government in Europe and Russia*. Not unnaturally, Koznyshev expected that "the book would make a serious impression on society." "And if it did not cause a revolution in social science"—his true desire?—"it would, at any rate, make a great stir in the scientific world."

Instead, the book is an abject failure:

> But a week passed, a second, a third, without the least ripple being apparent.
> His friends, the specialists and savants, occasionally, out of a sense of polite-
> ness, alluded to it. The rest of his acquaintances, not interested in learned
> works, did not talk of it at all. And in society, just now particularly taken
> up with other things, complete indifference reigned. In the press, too, for
> a whole month, there was not a word about his book.
>   . . . [A] month went by, then another, and still there was silence.
>   Only in the *Northern Beetle*, in a humorous *feuilleton* . . . was a remark
> slipped in about Koznyshev's book, suggesting in a few contemptuous words
> that it had long ago been seen through by everybody and consigned to gen-
> eral ridicule.[4]

"At last, in the third month, a critical article appeared in a serious
review." But this turned out to be a devastating—and in Koznyshev's
view personally hostile—raking over the coals. "Dead silence, both in
print and in conversation, followed that review, and Koznyshev saw that
the labor of six years into which he had put so much love and care had
gone, leaving no trace."[5]

The placement of this episode is interesting in itself. Coming immediately after Anna's suicide, it seems meant to bring home the triviality and
futility of intellectual pursuits. Pathetically unable to shed any light on
real life as Anna had endured it, such books get what they deserve.
Koznyshev, however, does recover. As we saw, "society" was "particularly
taken up with other things" when his book appeared, "other things" referring to the Serbian struggles against the Ottomans and the "Slav question." In the public agitation over these issues, Koznyshev senses that
"the soul of the nation had become articulate" and throws himself into
work on behalf of his "co-religionists and brothers."[6] Even here, Tolstoy
is mocking his character. Koznyshev is not alone. Vronsky, Anna's lover, is
also caught up in the effort, and consoles himself after Anna has taken her
own life by joining the forces. Levin, however, is skeptical of the cause
and of the motives underlying the fevered activity on its behalf. In this
case, he is also Tolstoy's explicit vehicle.[7]

THE ABSTRACTION OF THE WORLD

In discussing Koznyshev and his book, or more precisely how Levin, and
Tolstoy through him, sees such people and their work, I mean more than
to point an ironic, mocking finger at myself and the studies that follow.
Tolstoy's treatment of Koznyshev is not ignorant ridicule. Tolstoy's own

life and thought made this impossible. Nevertheless, he looks upon intellectual activity with classical scorn. What possible relation could there be
between the pallid social science of a Koznyshev and the "real" world,
with its infinite human variety, its ceaseless moral and spiritual struggles?
Is social science real knowledge, good knowledge?

Admittedly, Koznyshev's work is trivial. No change in the condition of
the masses will result from its appearance. It is without practical—
including ideological—significance. Yet now, in the opening years of the
twenty-first century, we need to take the question of the relevance, use,
and meaning of social science further than Tolstoy would allow us to go.
In ways that Tolstoy could not have seen, or might have refused to
acknowledge, the contemporary world is not only the object, but also the
product of social scientific knowledge. Of course, earlier epochs have
seen human labor, knowledge, and vision brought to bear on the world.
The agricultural revolution, or the spread of religious systems such as
Buddhism, Christianity, and Islam, transformed human life in profound
ways. The question, the modern difference, lies in the nature of change,
and of the human agency involved in bringing it about. In conjunction
with revolutions in natural science and productive modes, the human
perception of change itself has changed; no longer providence, fate, or
experience only, it is now something to be willed, caused, and even reproduced on the basis of systematized empirical knowledge.[8] Social science
in its broadest sense prescinds from and seeks to lay hold of the process
of real world-making. To the extent that the world has been objectified in
the operations of social science, it has also been subjectified, and made
capable of conscious self-transformation. Social science has not only
explicated—or interpreted—the world, it has also transformed it, "for
good or evil," as Keynes remarked. As an individual "social scientist,"
therefore, Koznyshev may have been insignificant, but the practice of systematic social inquiry is not.

It is easy to exaggerate the transformative potential of thought as
such. In "settling accounts with [their] erstwhile philosophical conscience" (in *The German Ideology*, 1846), Marx and Engels aimed their
rhetorical artillery at the German penchant for what we may term "metaphysical determinism" in human affairs. Perhaps the power ascribed to
"pure" thought is a function of the social distance between thinkers and
the masses of people in their own cultural contexts and in the world at
large; certainly the case of Germany's metaphysicians, and more starkly
that of the Russian intelligentsia, suggests as much. Yet it is precisely such
"alienated" thought that, when realized, has reacted with volcanic force

on more than one society. In terms of our concern here with the practical significance of social science, therefore, we are still justified in taking seriously the strictures of the German poet Heinrich Heine: "Mark this, ye proud men of action," he wrote in the decade of the revolution of 1848,

> [Y]e are nothing but unconscious hodmen of the men of thought who, often in humblest stillness, have appointed you your inevitable task. Maximilian Robespierre was merely the hand of Jean Jacques Rousseau, the bloody hand that drew from the womb of time the body whose soul Rousseau had created.[9]

And what of the humble professor Kant, "who had neither life nor history," yet as the "arch destroyer in the realm of thought, far surpassed in terrorism" Robespierre himself? Comparing the two, Heine exclaims:

> But both presented in the highest degree the type of the narrow-minded citizen. Nature had destined them for weighing out coffee and sugar, but fate decided that they should weigh out other things, and into the scales of one it laid a king, into the scales of the other a God. . . . And they both gave the correct weight![10]

Admittedly, neither Rousseau nor Kant should be categorized as a "social scientist" by any contemporary standard; nor should the splenetic character of Heine's manifesto against Germany be forgotten. Three points, however, are crucial in Heine's assertions. First, he counterposes humble "men of thought" to "proud men of action." The role of the nameless masses in historical change is left ambiguous; enter Marx. Second, Heine is concerned here with those forces that have destroyed the traditional order, and not so much with the processes of realizing the new one. Finally, and of immediate relevance to our present theme, Heine observes that both Kant and Robespierre operated in their respective spheres as the "type of the narrow-minded citizen." For what is the work of the humble social scientist if not diligently, relentlessly, to translate, to systematize, to "abstract" experience, to confront the social world with its own "common sense" turned inside out? Is it merely the arrogance of social science to claim that social transformation in the modern world has at some point entailed the production and mediation of such abstractions? Or more modestly that in order to be understood, let alone changed, the world must first be made an object, and conceptually reorganized according to categories? Is it not in the sober accumulation of such categorical knowledge of the world that the work of social science consists?[11]

We must, of course, distinguish the phases of such knowledge accumulation. Initially, it may have proceeded from a personal vision and sense of mission to disclose the real workings of the social world, to return it to itself. In attacking mercantilism, for example, Adam Smith sought not to create a "new man" but to reveal him as he really was in social nature. The will to disclose, however, has been transmuted, at certain times and places—not everywhere—into a collective will to transform society, and to do so along scientific or rational lines. Why and how, where and when this transmutation has taken place is a vast historical question. The aim of this book is to show that such a transmutation took place in modern Japan, and to retrace it: but only after setting it in the global context without which its significance will remain needlessly obscured by claims of national exceptionalism.

For the moment, let it suffice to observe that social science in many ways is an expression of the uneasy mutual embrace of these two wills, to disclose and to transform. We live now with a familiar result: in the epoch of hyperspecialization, "we are forced" to know more and more, and to live with the paradoxical contradiction that the intensification both of knowledge and of the impact of its application has been accompanied by a sense of loss of personal agency.[12] In a world where "more" is in fact "less," triviality and waste are ubiquitous and inherent occupational hazards. Libraries and institutes and offices are full of unread books, and those read today may be forgotten tomorrow. It seems difficult indeed to silence Tolstoy's doubts.

But to focus on the decay of the "calling" is to risk a serious misunderstanding; to forget not only the breathtaking excitement that came with the sense of discovery in early modernity (the "will to disclose" rewarded), but also the deep impress of that initial moment, to say nothing of developments to come. Let no one forget modernity's appalling wounds—the achievement of economies of scale in officially sanctioned slaughter, the induced hatreds and ignorance, the profligate and systematic waste (and neglect) of human skills and good faith. It is an open question whether they can be healed by modern people, using the instruments of modernity alone. Perhaps these instruments—of production in all spheres, but especially the institutions and technologies of communication and representative democracy—will someday be surpassed in a postmodern revolution that enhances "local humanities," cushions societies against the vicissitudes of the market, and discloses a new form of political community beyond the simultaneously integrative and atomizing force of the contemporary state. Perhaps, one must always hope.

But what of the present? In this regard, consider the words of Father

Gapon's petition to Tsar Nicholas in 1905. Amid the current, misplaced triumphalism of capital, the rapid dissipation of predictions for a "clean sweep" of Communist personnel and groups, and a global politics whose intense conflicts are strongly resistant to ideological categorization, Gapon's call returns us to the moment of democratic resurgence that was the cynosure of post–Cold War hopes. After having addressed employers with demands reflecting the needs of workers, Gapon turned to the issue of a democratically elected constituent assembly. "This," he proclaimed, "is our chief request; in it and on it all else is based; it is . . . the only plaster for our painful wounds."[13] This aspiration to democratic dialogue, the conquest of citizenship, evokes the political revolutions of modern times, reminding us that they are not yet, and by their nature can never be, concluded. (Indeed, to whom should this generation's "requests" for representation be addressed?) And to the extent that the conquest of citizenship is a process of the conscious self-transformation of society, I suggest, social science will have its never-ending task. The Czech economist Ota Šik, writing in exile more than a decade before the Velvet Revolution of 1989, argued that

> everyday experience needs the backing of a progressive social theory. The working people know, quite simply, what they do *not* want; but alone, without the aid of theory, they cannot set new aims. That is the responsibility of the social scientists—not to think up Utopias, but to analyse the existing contradictions and conflicts in society, to discover their roots in the social system, and then to devise the remedies—therein lies the humane commitment of the social sciences.[14]

Šik's view, of course, is far from current doubts about the positive efficacy of social science and from convictions about the dangers flowing from its inevitable implication in the workings of power.[15] But one need not, perhaps, abandon all effort to practice a "humane" social science that has the general purpose of modeling and testing the "stuff" of social life: not just quantified "behavior" but even more so the words, the texts, the sub- and supratextual modes of expression that inform social discourse. It is clear that we continue to rely to a significant degree on a network of post-Enlightenment abstractions in order to speak meaningfully about the social world. Imagine talking about "what is to be done" without recourse to terms such as "class," "market," "economy," "division of labor," "society," "community," "nation," "gender," "individual," and so on, and see how far one can go. On first appearance, the world models of which social science consists may seem at best obvious or pal-

lid, partially or blatantly ideological, and at worst coercively homogenizing.[16] But, subject as they are to the crucible of testing (not only for
empirical accuracy and practical effectiveness, but for theoretical coherence), models are in fact indispensable tools for grasping any social reality, local or global. They are not meant to be embodiments of eternal
truth, but instead recede to the extent that reality itself changes. This is
not to deny "the extraordinary stability of social formations . . . the vis-
cosity that is so prominent a feature of social history" over the long
run.[17] It is to say, though, that the models social science presents to the
world are meant to be used, and are fated to be recycled, if not to decom-
pose altogether.

But there is more to the power of abstraction than this. Organized
intellectual activity in any society, at any period, involves abstraction, be
it religious, metaphysical, philosophical, aesthetic, or scientific in its center of gravity. We are concerned here, however, with "abstraction" in its
modern form. This is abstraction underlain by the conviction that the
world is a "real fiction," the product of human efforts—many of which
do not succeed, or bring unimagined, even catastrophic consequences—
at social making, unmaking, and remaking. It is a world in which change
is normal, and for which the notion of revolution—and of progress born
of revolution—provides the tropic structure of general discourse.[18]
Revolutions of all kinds—political, social, scientific, economic, intellectual—signaled the advent of this modern world. These complexes of
events do not touch every society uniformly, or for that matter every segment within those societies they do touch. At the same time they form a
dominant element in the social perception of the world. One becomes
aware of what does not change precisely because change—revolution—
is incorporated, or naturalized, into the social consciousness.[19]

It is a cliché that even laundry detergents are now described as "revolutionary" so that they will sell better; other products, such as popcorn
and lemonade, appeal more often to nostalgia. In either case, "change" is
the leading trope for the representation of the social world in which
these products are meant to be sold and consumed. Social science as discussed here is concerned with knowledge of such a postrevolutionary
world. It is knowledge not only for itself ("How is the world to be
known?"), but in answer to the question: How far can abstraction go
and still be effective? Or conversely, How effective can interventions
based on abstraction be? The key is to produce the world through objec-
tification as a map to guide social praxis. Indeed, the metaphor that sug-

gests itself here is that of a relentless recycling of knowledge via the process of abstraction and application.

But what are the specificities of modern abstraction? As Marx observed in his *Grundrisse* (1857–58), in the modern world "individuals are now controlled," not merely by "abstractions," but by abstractions derived from a determinate set of social relations and forces: those of capitalist production.[20] The economy, which in much avowedly Marxian thinking tends to be equated with production alone, becomes the very abstraction of the modern world in toto. Every social act is defined as an exchange of produced goods—commodities—and the individual as little more than a site, or node, of circulation. We become what we produce; but if the exchange value of that product happens to be low, our human value as a whole suffers.[21] A person who produces nothing is worth nothing. The process by which such value "happens" to be set low or high is paradoxical. On the one hand, it is perceived as lawlike and regular, susceptible to analysis and understanding, and, on that basis, to a range of interventions from "piecemeal social engineering" to root-and-branch transformation. On the other hand, abstractions such as the market, class, and the division of labor—in combination with the even less tractable abstractions of race and gender—have tended to be bracketed, ideologically exempted from the possibility or desirability of radical, categorical change. Not to exempt them would, minimally, threaten the system of commodity circulation and extraction of surplus value; such a world would, in a profound sense, cease to cohere. Utopians, by the same token, are those who refuse to live within brackets.

The modern world, therefore, makes two contradictory promises to those who live in it. First, its fundamental processes—processes specific to itself—can be grasped via abstraction, but second, once so grasped these processes assume license to rule over those who created them.[22] Thus the "contract" at the heart of modernity is not only between people, that is, a matter of institutional arrangements, but also between people and their own ideas. Abstraction is leviathan.

Because of its apparently self-contained and self-propelling character, the capitalist system occupies a special place in the pantheon of modern abstractions. But it is really only a part of something bigger. As Derek Sayer has noted, capitalism is the

> ground upon which other modern forms of estrangement arose, and furnishes the template for the "severance" which gives modernity's machines their terrible force. But it is this wider mechanization of human social life

itself which is the problem, and this is no longer, if it ever was, confined to those theatres within which capital rules. Mechanization is of course but a metaphor. What we are actually talking about are our own forms of sociality and subjectivity, as Karl Marx was among the first to make clear.[23]

One key to understanding modernity, then, lies in grasping not simply capitalism as a self-contained system of accumulation and reproduction, but the potency of abstraction in mobilizing social and political energies, particularly in response to the consequences of capitalism itself. "The modern world," Sayer remarks, "is uniquely conducive to the emergence of political ideologies which take as their object both the analysis and the transformation of societies as totalities, like socialism. The condition for this is precisely the abstraction of the social."[24]

It is precisely this modern form of abstraction that makes it possible to conceive the total, revolutionary transformation of society—a form of transformation very different from the effects of spiritual conversion, even that of a Tolstoy. Theorist-initiates experience the sense of having come to possess knowledge—if not yet control—of vast, even terrifyingly powerful social forces. For indeed, realized abstraction does transform the life of masses of people; it modernizes, or categorically excludes from modernization, certain significant segments of society. Such processes can create great hope, both real and delusory; they can uplift and then crush without mercy.

To become aware of the possibility of total social transformation is not necessarily to desire it.[25] A spectrum of stances for and against, not always self-consistent themselves, can be evoked: the conservatism of Tocqueville, Weber, or Karl Popper might be brought into contention with radicalism à la Fourier, Marx, or Chernyshevskii. But the objective possibility of destroying an old order and replacing it with a new one would be acknowledged: Neither the moral desire to save those who suffer, nor a metaphysically guaranteed teleology, but the systematic, "scientific" inquiry into actual society has disclosed it.

The embrace of total transformation on the basis of ostensibly irrefutable scientific insight into society is always a minority position, a limit case. It should not be imagined that it is undertaken irresponsibly. On the contrary, as with the Russian intelligentsia of the nineteenth century, it has often been driven by a sense of profound debt to, or guilt before, the masses: "Mankind," wrote P. L. Lavrov in his *Historical Letters* (1869), "has paid dearly so that a few thinkers sitting in their studies could discuss its progress." Each of their critical insights "has been bought with the blood, sufferings, or toil of millions. . . . I shall relieve myself of the bloody cost of my own development if I use this same development to diminish evil in the present and in the future."[26] There is no shrinking from the awareness, furthermore, that in order to "diminish evil in the present and in the future," compulsion and suffering will be necessary. For the sake of the masses, not only the "conscience-stricken intelligentsia," but more often the masses themselves, must at times be sacrificed.

By the same token, a strong sense of responsibility may underlie the hesitation or refusal to accept, and attempt to hold back, such movement. Not only the defense of class interest or accustomed status, but a belief in reason, order, and the common good, and an unwillingness to promote what is seen as needless suffering, may inform a conservative stance and cause it to magnify what is perceived as threatening. And in the real world, the comfort of routine, mental inertia, loss of nerve, a visceral fear, even outright betrayal may also have their part in determining which side one takes. The choice is not always clear, even though the morally charged, observed facts of injustice, ignorance, and deprivation call out for action. But what action?

Which returns us, at length, to our parable. The involvement of social scientists in the modern process of abstraction puts Tolstoy's great question—"What shall we do, and, how shall we arrange our lives?"—in a new light. Tolstoy directed it originally, with full force, to the individual moral life, and answered it in the form of a tortured world-abnegation. Max Weber, quoting Tolstoy in his "Science as a Vocation" (1918), was unwilling to take Tolstoy's path, but agreed that science as such could not answer, impersonally and collectively, the existential questions that modernity engendered. Yet he seemed to despair of finding charismatic or purely personal responses that might at the same time be capable of turning aside the relentless force of what he called "rationalization."

Not everyone shares Weber's pessimism; and it is not out of shallowness or self-delusion that Derek Sayer, for example, refuses to give up searching for a principle of hope, a means of furthering, while humanizing, the ongoing and inevitably abstract process of world transformation. Modernity has been defined by a series of sociopolitical forms that have made explicit claims to embody, or minimally to determine fundamental policies on the basis of, social science. Is it the utopian strain of these claims, or the absence of democracy in their modes of realization, that has more than once led to disaster? In any case, Tolstoy's question still remains to be applied systematically to social science, the modal form of knowledge in modern times. How are the "abstractions of the social" that so forcefully—even forcibly—"arrange" so many lives produced and disseminated? How, in turn, appropriated, translated, co-opted? How resisted, superseded, rejected? And why do so many ideas, as given shape in the vast body of social-science writing, end up in the dustbin, in utter intellectual oblivion? From another—institutional—angle, how do those who engage in and uphold the value of such production negotiate the troubled course that makes the world not only the object, but the product, of their knowledge?

It is too soon, obviously, to answer this question; that is the point of writing the book. But provisionally, we may sketch one in outline. Once more, the case of Koznyshev is illuminating. In order to carry out his work, Koznyshev must acquire practical knowledge of the processes he seeks to analyze; he must involve himself with the "state," understood here as both the authorizing agency of rationalization and enforcer of order. Koznyshev's position is that of one who is neither "married" to nor resisting the state. He is suspended between complicity and resistance, and it is within this gray existential space that he must work and strive to define some sort of independent stance. In his case, the intellectual ground for such a stance (liberalism, Marxism or populism, Christian or some other form of faith), as well as talent and nerve, is lacking; that is not always so.[27] The tendency in such situations may be to form what has been termed an "amoral liaison" with the state, one deepened by Koznyshev's convenient turn to Pan-Slavism after the failure of his *Sketch*.[28] It is not clear at all where or for what Koznyshev stands, except for this: he stands for a method.

Koznyshev, then, is typically problematic. If Kant and Robespierre, world destroyers each, operated as the "type of the narrow-minded citizen," so too, if ineffectually, does Koznyshev. He is both politically ambiguous, and, one presumes, empirically competent. On this latter score, he exemplifies the tendency to equate the "science" of social science with a narrow task-orientation. Along with nerve, Koznyshev also lacks what we might call theoretical "faith." The ineffectuality of his project flows not from incompetence, but from his agnosticism. This combination of political ambiguity and intellectual constriction means that Koznyshev, despite his ambition to enlighten society, has essentially no argument to make, theoretically, historically, or practically; perhaps this is why his work was a failure.[29]

No, it will be objected: facts are facts. It is true enough that "the provenance of a fact or idea doesn't affect its validity."[30] To "seek truth from facts," as Mao Zedong urged his comrades, is a respectable and sometimes courageous undertaking. Politicians, perhaps especially revolutionary politicians, as well as pure theorists, have reason to fear facts. On the other hand, facts and ideas do not spring up ex nihilo. They are always—and here the categorical claim is justified—mediated by language, which is a sociocognitive and material element in shaping facts and ideas, and how they happen to find their provenance in specific contexts. Facts and ideas are products of a particular discourse; in this case the discourse of social abstraction, which, I hope to have shown, is intimately tied to the broad process of modernization discussed above.

To bring home the discursive character of the social sciences, we must add one final element to the discussion. The Russian parable above focused on individual considerations. But we must somehow link, without equating, the "discourses of morality and necessity," of "ethics and causal dynamics," if we are to grasp the historical meaning of social science as discourse.[31] To do so, we must recognize that they are quintessentially embodied discourses, practiced as professional disciplines within a vast range of institutions such as universities and research institutes; state and corporate bodies; political parties and other "agenda-bearing" organizations embracing a vast spectrum of movements and causes. Moreover, the institutional positions that the social sciences occupy are the result of collective, not merely individual, struggles for intellectual legitimacy both in specific national settings and at the international level.

To use an extravagant analogy: If the productive potential of the division of labor under early capitalism may be seen at work in Adam Smith's exemplary but still autonomous and inefficient pin factory, so too early social science may be seen as the work of still essentially individual, only incipiently professionalized, thinkers. By the same token, advanced capitalism is the capitalism of the corporation, and just so, "advanced" social science is the vast collective product of an army of professionals who have been "institutionalized" both in the sense of their highly differentiated disciplines and their complex and multiple organizational affiliations.[32] If modern social science must be examined in the context of its frequent "amoral liaisons" with power, it is only because social science has successfully legitimated itself *in* the world of power. But this institutionalization was not to be taken for granted: the modes by which legitimacy is achieved, along with the price paid for it, is the stuff of histories, including this one. Having achieved it, social science is in a position to mediate its abstractions, not simply back to power, but to the public world, society in general, and to engage with its feedback as well.

Thus, inevitably, some sort of circulation of knowledge, institutionally and discursively mediated, between power and public is a salient characteristic of social science. In Japan (but not only in Japan), the state has not always regarded such circulation as useful or desirable and has taken steps to thwart it.

In any case it is here, at the point of mediation, that we feel the force of the famous concluding observations of J. M. Keynes's *General Theory* (1936):

> The ideas of economists and political philosophers, both when they are right and when they are wrong, are more powerful than is commonly understood. Indeed the world is ruled by little else. Practical men, who believe themselves to be quite exempt from any intellectual influences, are usually the slaves of some defunct economist. Madmen in authority, who hear voices in the air, are distilling their frenzy from some academic scribbler of a few years back. I am sure that the power of vested interests is vastly exaggerated compared with the gradual encroachment of ideas. Not, indeed, immediately, but after a certain interval; for in the field of economic and political philosophy there are not many who are influenced by new theories after they are twenty-five or thirty years of age, so that the ideas which civil servants and politicians and even agitators apply to current events are not likely to be the newest. But, soon or late, it is ideas, not vested interests, which are dangerous for good or evil.[33]

Keynes, it will be noted, powerfully echoes but also refines—by introducing the notion of a time (or cultural?) lag between the original generation and the acceptance of economic ideas—Heine's strictures to all "proud men of action." Like Heine, Keynes also leaves "the masses" out of consideration, those masses whose lives Tolstoy found so little touched by would-be revolutionaries in social science such as Koznyshev.

So ideas matter. Yet the ideas—the models or abstractions—to be discussed in this study are but subsets of different and overlapping languages brought to bear on the analysis of society: no language, no society. The historical task at hand is to inquire into the discursive and institutional conditions under which, and patterns by which, the comprehensibility, plausibility, motivational force, and ideological plasticity of those abstractions combine to make them socially consequential; to trace how, in other words, social science becomes social power.

SOCIAL SCIENCE AS CULTURAL DISCOURSE

I began this book by talking about social science in the most general sense as a science of institutional modernity whose originary condition was the "abstraction of the world." Embedded in the discussion were two terms and themes—*discourse* and *rationalization*—that need clarification, since together they form the organizing principles for the interpretive work that follows.

I will be treating social science in Weberian fashion, as a body of cultural discourses; as an expanding network of acts of writing and speech produced around, and in turn producing, given "objects." Discourse is about something. In this case, the "something" is the "experience," the "concrete reality," as Max Weber termed it, of institutional modernity as mediated by abstract constructs or models; these latter are worked out by methods specific to one or more disciplines—preeminently, sociology, economics, political science, anthropology, ethnology, social psychology, certain schools of historical and legal study, and so on. But what social science, for Weber at least, aspires to is the "understanding of the characteristic uniqueness of the reality in which we move." Social science is the "knowledge of reality with respect to its cultural *significance*"—that is, its relation to value ideas—"and its causal relationships." "Culture," in turn, "is a finite segment of the meaningless infinity of the world-process, a segment on which *human beings* confer meaning and significance."[34]

What distinguishes these various sciences is not the differing "realities" they investigate, but the formal processes of inquiry, the "approaches," that they develop and wrangle over. "Each of the sciences cuts into the same massive socio-historical reality with its own intentions and purposes, and orders this reality according to these intentions and purposes."[35] The exact definition and mix of social sciences varies tremendously depending on historical and national context. What they have in common, beyond struggling to express theoretical truths, and beyond the self-conscious and systematic character of their "mode of representational production," is the conviction that they *can* touch what is real. Although social facts appear as such only when mediated by method or theory, once constructed, they take on a kind of "intelligible density" that can (and must) either be confirmed, disputed, falsified, or superseded through reincorporation into theory, which changes their significance.

From another angle, now: a *discourse* about social facts. The use of the term implicitly raises the linked questions of agency and representation. To ask where discourse is occurring is also to ask, Who is talking? Who can or must talk? How, that is, to whom, and for whom? Whose are the words, the figures (that is, the metaphors), the grammars? The occupation of a position, assertion of an identity, or performance of a role in a discourse, is inseparable from questions of power: not everyone is empowered to speak, or to speak in any way he or she might desire. The constraints or conventions that make discourse and agency of any kind possible—ranging from grammatical or semantic "rules," religious sanction or canons of scholarship, to the "proper" mode of address (for example) by a tenant farmer to the landlord or the seeming niceties of party etiquette—can also become shackles. It would be historically unjust to describe the shackles of imposed silence or coerced speech as merely metaphorical. Beyond that, even in a utopia of mutual good will and communicative intent, we are all post-Babelites, and our best attempts at representation can only call attention to the ever receding object of our strivings. Yet strive we do.

Discourse, therefore, is a subset of social(ized) practice. As such it cannot be unitary, any more than the power-ridden relations of organized human life can be. Like social practice, discourse presumes division and conflict—but not only division and conflict. Solidarities are possible; fights can be won. The contest over who speaks and how, the struggle for effective representation, is no less—and no more—real than other forms of social struggle over interests, rights, or justice. Discourse, as I will use the term, is the intellectual and emotional tissue of such struggles.

Contemporary (or postindustrial) society, Alain Touraine has argued, has entered a phase in which the significant conflicts are not those of social classes over the organization of production, but rather of social movements with different stakes in the ends of production—that is, in culture. Such movements, Touraine holds, are constituted by "actor[s] who call into question the social form of historicity . . . A social movement is the action, both culturally oriented and socially conflictual, of a social class defined by its position of domination or dependency in the mode of appropriation of historicity, of the cultural models of investment, knowledge and morality, toward which the social movement is itself oriented."[36]

Leaving aside for the moment the particulars of Touraine's argument (not every society is industrial, let alone postindustrial), I would stress the suggestiveness of his notion of historicity: "the set of cultural, cognitive, economic and ethical models by means of which a collectivity sets up relations with its environment." For Touraine, it is the contest over historicity that lies at the center of society, and constitutes its "unity."[37] This is a notion that, because it places agency and action at its operational core, cuts through much potentially arid criticism that discourse theory separates language from life. For clearly, the modeling that takes place among collectivities is in a real sense both the object of social science, and an activity in which social science participates, ideologically and critically. Modeling is synonymous with the production of self-conscious, organized discourses of "society" about itself—and also, so to speak, against itself. To the extent that these models can be held up to critical scrutiny according to open rules, the model transcends ideology to become an element in social "science." It is in this sense that the world we know is both the object and product of social scientific knowledge.

"The world we know," however, is a problematic expression. It is implicitly historicist—how did "the world we know" get to be the way it is? With the passage in social thought from philosophy—history, for example, as the inexorable movement of Hegel's World Spirit—to science, a new range of structuring metaphors for imagining the world came to the fore. One could speak of historical "laws of motion" as certain as those of physics. (To quote the Abbé Mably: "Is Society, then, a branch of Physics?") One could see the "world"—society—grow, evolve, develop much as a living organism would, and suppose that it could therefore be known via an evolutionary science akin to biology. The mechanical metaphor has been particularly amenable to the expression of the transformative will discussed earlier, and for that reason seems to have assumed a position of relative dominance over the biological in social thought: it permitted human agency to intervene in the natural social process, accelerating or channeling it to some imagined end. The implications of the ascendancy of "soft" information technologies and genetic engineering for the representation of the transformative will are, if not beyond my concern, then certainly beyond my competence to discuss.

If the sketch just given captures the "objective spirit" of social science at some point in the past, does it still? In an essay on what he terms the "refiguration of social thought," Clifford Geertz suggests that it does not. Surveying the past two decades in the history of the social sciences, Geertz identifies a "culture shift" composed of three converging moments. The first is the "enormous amount of genre mixing," a "blurring of kinds," that has become general in intellectual life. Second,

> Many social scientists have turned away from a "laws and instances ideal" of explanation toward a cases and interpretations one, looking less for the sort of thing that connects planets and pendulums and more for the sort that connects chrysanthemums and swords. . . . [A]nalogies drawn from the humanities are coming to play the kind of role in sociological understanding that analogies drawn from the crafts and technology have long played in physical understanding.

Finally, and importantly, Geertz "not only think[s] these things are true, . . . they are true together." They amount to an "interpretive turn," one that has yielded a "revised style of discourse in social studies." "The instruments of reasoning," Geertz holds, "are changing."[38]

From a somewhat different but related perspective, the sociologist Zygmunt Bauman argues that over the course of the twentieth century, "intellectual praxis" in the West has undergone a shift in its dominant modes, from what he calls "legislative" to "interpretive" activity.[39] Taking as his type case the French *philosophes* of the Enlightenment and their successors in the *république des lettres,* Bauman describes the modern, general "intellectual" (a term coined only in the twentieth century) as a would-be legislator; the self-appointed task of such intellectuals consisted of

> making authoritative statements which arbitrate in controversies of opinions and which select those opinions which, having been selected, become correct and binding. The authority to arbitrate is in this case legitimized by superior (objective) knowledge to which intellectuals have a better access than the non-intellectual part of society. Access to such knowledge is better thanks to procedural rules which assure the attainment of truth, the arrival at valid moral judgment, and the selection of proper artistic taste. Such procedural rules have a universal validity, as do the products of their application. The employment of such procedural rules makes the intellectual professions (scientists, moral philosophers, aesthetes) collective owners of knowledge of direct and crucial relevance to the maintenance and perfection of the social order (4–5).

Modern intellectuals, for Bauman, "are not bound by localized, communal traditions. They are, together with their knowledge, extraterritorial. This gives them the right and duty to validate (or invalidate) beliefs which may be held in various sectors of society" (5).

The universalistic ambitions of the general intellectual—ambitions given breathtakingly full play in the revolutionary educational proposals of Destutt de Tracy, Condorcet and Robespierre—have been challenged, if not replaced, by the postmodern mode of intellectual work that for Bauman is "best characterized by the metaphor of the 'interpreter' role":

> It consists of translating statements, made within one communally based tradition, so that they can be understood within the system of knowledge based on another tradition. Instead of being orientated towards selecting the best social order, this strategy is aimed at facilitating communication between autonomous (sovereign) participants. It is concerned with preventing the distortion of meaning in the process of communication. For this purpose, it promotes the need to penetrate deeply the alien system of knowledge from

which the translation is to be made (for example, Geertz's "thick description"), and the need to maintain the delicate balance between the two conversing traditions necessary for the message to be both undistorted (regarding the meaning invested by the sender) and understood (by the recipient) (5).

In establishing these two ideal types and their activities as a "structural element within the societal figuration" (19), Bauman is careful to trace the specific, even anomalous, historical conditions in which the modern intellectual emerged and flourished and was displaced; the translation, in other words, of modernity into postmodernity. The "power-knowledge" syndrome that underwrote intellectual universalism, he argues, arose in the context of European, especially French, absolutism, in which the "advanced demise of the old ruling class, the nobility, . . . left two yawning gaps among the factors indispensable in the reproduction of social order: to fill them, a new concept of social control was needed together with a new formula for the legitimation of political authority" (25). The prototypical modern intellectuals filled this space, spearheading a "cultural crusade" against traditional (ecclesiastical) authority, popular mentalities and lifeways that enabled the state to extend its reach far more deeply into society than it had ever sought to go. The *lumières* performed a crucial task, but in doing so fated their intellectual progeny to wither away—or more accurately, to be fragmented and channeled into the deepening specialist departments of modern cultural life. They were left with a dream of untrammeled discussion leading to uncoerced consensus among the members of the immaterial republic of letters; hence the coining in the early twentieth century of the collective self-designation "intellectual" as a "rallying call, and as an attempt to resuscitate the unfulfilled claims of the past" (23). On the one hand, the state had gained such "confidence as to the efficacy of the techniques of policing, surveilling, categorizing, individualizing and other methods of modern bureaucratic administration" (106) that it hardly needed advice from generalists in controlling and *nationalizing* the masses. Beyond the specific concerns of the state, "the discourses of truth, judgment and taste" had been "taken over by other forces—by autonomous institutions of specialized research and learning" (158). "The intellectual becomes now a concept which separates the carriers of culture not just from the untutored, ignorant, primitive or otherwise uncultured, but also from many a scientist, technician and artist" (157).

Fatefully intertwined with this bureaucratization of power and culture—the emergence of what I would call "authorized society"—

Bauman points out, was the globalization of the market; and it is the dual phenomena of nationalized masses under bureaucratic states that for Bauman form the precondition of postmodernity. (Here I will leave aside an account of the spread of consumer culture.)

> It is obvious that within the context of consumer culture no room is left for the intellectual as legislator. In the market, there is no one centre of power, nor any aspiration to create one. . . . There is no site from which authoritative pronouncements could be made, and no power resources concentrated and exclusive enough to serve as levers of a massive proselytizing campaign. With that, the traditional, real or hoped for, means of "intellectual legislation" are absent. Intellectuals (like everybody else) have no control over market forces and cannot realistically expect to acquire any. Consumer culture means a kind of society very different from the one where the tradition of *les philosophes,* the historical foundation of living memory of intellectual legislation, was born and to which it was geared (167).

With their zone of activity and authority thus pared away and undermined, intellectuals assumed the role, described above, of interpreters. The world is not only pluralized, and seemingly incapable of producing "consensus on world views and values"; the market, its main integrating force, cannot even tolerate the attempt. And with states compelled, as it were, to follow the market in attempting to establish their legitimacy, the possibility of "communication across cultures becomes the major problem of our time." For intellectuals in search of a role in this new world, Bauman argues, the choice (for them and for the world) becomes: "Converse or perish" (143). Supposing that "discursive redemption" (191) of modernity is worth attempting, or at least that the impossibility of some mode of conversation between "communities" can be bracketed, the question becomes one of determining the role of the interpreter or translator between "forms of life" (144); or of "drawing the boundaries of such community as may serve as the territory for legislative practices."

Defining such roles, however, necessarily depends on a prior judgment about the sociohistorical location—if not stage—of a given national society. As Bauman points out, postmodernity and modernity continue to coexist, the former in fact "inconceivable without the continuation of the latter" (5). The *pre*condition of *post*modernity, in other words, is modernity—a global market of consumerist national cultures, politically nationalized masses, and bureaucratic states. Yet not all countries have developed these characteristics simultaneously and to the same degree. Among other things, this may mean that "postmodernity" describes a world in which one society can be studded with fragments, borne on wave after wave of commodities in circulation, taken from another whose mode of life is vastly different; and that for technological reasons, this condition of heterogeneity can now be apprehended in its simultaneity. The fact that some Somali children know who Michael Jackson is does not have the same social meaning that it would in Singapore.

A more specifically historical consideration arises from a suspicion: suppose that Bauman is exaggerating the success of the antitraditional campaigns spearheaded by the *philosophes?* Suppose that the universalizing imperatives not only of the intellectuals, but of the state as well, fell short? Suppose that even the market, the ostensible dissolver of all particularisms and of the cultural absolutism of the Enlightenment and its progeny, has not reached as deeply as Bauman argues. In many societies, especially those to which industrial modernization came "late" in world time, "modernity" has been defined by the combination of substantial continuity of old elites and rurally based patterns of social relations with the modernizing impulses associated with newer elites and other educated strata. What Ernst Bloch called "non-synchronicity" *(Ungleichzeitigkeit)* in development, moreover, is not just a matter of unconscious transmission from past to present but of its strategic perpetuation in neotraditionalist ideologies that assert the possibility of "leapfrogging" over the most disintegrative aspects of industrial modernization into a postmodernity that preserves old communitarian ways of life. (Such claims have taken both statist and populist forms.) Ultimately, of course, no national society can be wholly insulated from the world. But even so, the implications are ambiguous. On the one hand, local (that is, national and subnational) elites cannot escape the political and economic pressures of "democratized consumption" that drive deliberate non-synchronicity into the arms of unwilling simultaneity. On the other hand, the international division of labor does not necessarily require, and may even assist local elites in resisting, such drives. Although neoimperialist and dependency theorists have been known to exaggerate their claims, it is wrong to dismiss the idea that development does sometimes mean the continuation of surplus extraction from societies via the perpetuation, even the creation, of precapitalist zones or relations among their laboring populations.[40]

In terms of the sociology of social science, the discussion of Geertz and Bauman would seem to allow two inferences: First, that insofar as social science is the science of ongoing "rationalization," its legislative or interpretive character will vary with the locale, and that no locale can be anything other than some kind of composite. The historical task is to grasp the interaction of these two modes in specific contexts; to see how far those contexts condition the possibility and overall efficacy—however that is to be measured—of a legislative-versus-interpretive mode of activity. Second, as with commodities, there may at the same time be something akin to a demonstration effect in the international intellectual economy, so that certain styles of discourse, problem consciousness, and practice are adopted regardless of their seeming inapplicability to the local environment.[41] Of course, variability along a legislative-interpretive continuum may reflect not only national/cultural differences, but also disciplinary character across locales as well: some disciplines are "harder," others "softer" in their response to the interpretive turn. Indeed, were it not for disparities and conflicts within and among disciplines, there would be no continuing social science at all. A proper grasp of social science as intellectual history requires that one keep in view precisely the dual structure of (a) the local and global "historicities" that form the *object* of social science inquiry, and (b) the extent of local and global adaptability among the various *disciplines* that carry out such inquiry. The fact that I take an interpretive stance no doubt reflects some of the tendencies identified by Geertz and Bauman: I do not presume to legislate for Japanese social science, let alone for Japan. But it does not mean that my object shares that stance vis-à-vis itself. It is important not to conflate stance with object, to pour method into content. To write a history of Japanese social science is to undertake an interpretive study of a legislative discourse hegemonized for a long period by a neotraditional state and its communitarian ideological projections—and counterhegemonized by the ostensibly universal science of Marxism. But it is also to study a discourse in transformation.

SOCIAL SCIENCE AND RATIONALIZATION

For at least a half-century after the opening of their country in the 1850s, Japanese did not think in terms of "modernization" but of "Westernization," only later, once the processes had taken root, coming to speak of their own composite character as Japanese and therefore modern. Why was it that "West" formed the keynote of "modern," both in a general institutional sense and in social science inquiry?

A myriad of specifically historical, even fortuitous causes—or symptoms—of this phenomenon come quickly to mind: science, steam power, steel mills, heavy weaponry; joint-stock companies; constitutionalism, nation-states, world-girding empires. In his classic and ever-controversial analysis of modernity's genesis, Weber drew a link between the singular dynamism of the West and the formal rationality of its major economic and bureaucratic organizations. For Weber, as Derek Sayer notes,

> Rationalization . . . connotes systematicity, consistency, method: whether as a cast of mind, or as the principle on which organizations are structured, it implies the exclusion of arbitrariness and above all of what he refers to as "magic." Rationality amounts to the calculated application of rules.

Formal rationalization—what Sayer calls "the wider mechanization of human social life itself"—seems to have lain at the heart of Western power. The West, in other words, was the effective and affective Other of "magic" and tradition, not only its own but that of distant peoples (in the "East") as well.[42] For Weber, formal and substantive rationality had to be distinguished. By "formally rational" Weber meant a type of social action in which "the end, the means, and the secondary results are all rationally taken into account and weighed." But ends themselves—such as accumulation, or work for its own sake—were random and formally irrational. They might, however, be "value-rational" or "substantive": a characteristic of action that has in effect become an end unto itself insofar as it is subordinated to a higher, transcendent purpose or will. In the economic sphere, this might mean that "the provisioning of given groups of persons (no matter how delimited) with goods" is performed "under some criterion . . . of ultimate values [wertende Postulate]," variously including "elements of social justice and equality, . . . status distinctions, . . . capacity for power . . . of a political unit." Beyond these concerns with outcome, Weber notes, the "spirit" and "instruments" of economic action can also be subject to "substantive" judgments of an "ethical, ascetic, or esthetic" nature.[43]

Weber's method grew from a Nietzschean insight that modernity had turned such judgments of value into matters of choice or commitment (however noble) rather than the realization of objective virtues. He assuredly feared that in the "real" world, the very distinction that sustained his sociology was being lost: after all, when formal rationality is pursued for its own sake, that rationality is irrational. Rather than the pursuit of profit, that would seem the ultimate bureaucratic temptation. And indeed, Weber's misgivings over the likely consequences of conflating formal with value rationality deepened all the more when, as in the socialist regime that emerged in Russia toward the end of his life, a given party and state claimed to embody substantive social rationality. For

Weber, the terrible struggles among the "warring gods" who represented values and worldviews promised no more than a "polar night of icy darkness and hardness, no matter which group may triumph externally now." [44]

It was not always thus. Modernity as it developed in the West found its normative articulation in the so-called moral sciences, political economy, and history, with their triumphalist narrative of accumulated institutional achievements. These achievements included the spontaneous growth of industrial capitalism, and of a postfeudal and postabsolutist form of state, in short, a liberal order. It was, to caricature, an order populated by patriotic and reasonably religious Robinson Crusoes. "Modernization," as it would later be termed, was held to be not only irreversible but desirable, a process not only of formal but substantive rationalization as well; once so assured, social and policy scientists could and did seek to engineer social transitions accordingly. This was perhaps more the case among positivists and the quantitatively inclined; but the method of *Verstehen* was not spared transmutation into an instrument of power. "Modernization" constituted itself as a standard of world judgment no less than as a license to subjugate both proletarians and "natives." At the core of social science, then, subsisted a notion of, and belief in, growth, development, and progress that literally knew no bounds.

The very sense of boundlessness, however, when confronted with the grim realities of industrial and colonial life, provoked radical critiques within the lineage of political economy itself. Marx, for example, claimed that in England, the "classic ground" of capitalism and pioneer in industrialization, capital had arisen "dripping from head to toe, from every pore, with blood and dirt." As Barrington Moore put it, "massive violence exercised by the upper classes against the lower" had been the necessary price of gradual change.[45]

Both the traumas of early industrialization and the sometimes brutal hypocrisy attending it were fully evident to later generations of social thinkers outside of Europe, who worked from traditions and assumptions either foreign or reactive to those of classical political economy. It is well to recall that non-Western peoples were brought into contact not only with classical and "social Darwinist" justifications of Western expansionism, but also with the West's own critique, however "Western" itself, of that expansion. Even more important than that self-critique was its combination with the realization—not always comforting, and leading to widely disparate practical conclusions—that there might always be qualitative differences in the development experiences of countries, owing both to their internal character and to the global conjuncture within which development is attempted.

Like the historical process of capitalist rationalization in and through which it had its being, social science was international but far from uniform in character. If all social science is the science of institutional modernity, we may hypothesize that the form taken by social science in a given national setting depends substantially upon the institutional path to modernity taken by that nation. These paths profoundly color national views of the integrative role of the state as opposed to society or market, views of industrialization and capitalist development in general, and of models to achieve, counteract, or transcend such development. How to attain any of these goals, in short, becomes a question for social science to address, if not resolve. Although the major themes and problematics of social science have their origin in a Western "heartland," discourse as such is no longer under the control of the heartland—unless one wishes to argue that adopting the language and methods of social science itself amounts to a kind of spiritual self-colonization, regardless of the social practices that such discourse subsequently informs.

The question, then, is how to account for and assess the distinctiveness of national—in this case Japanese—forms of social science. One must ask how—as is surely the case—a network of Western discourses was made meaningful outside the West, and at what cultural price. How, in other words, was discourse translated, replicated, indigenized? One final preliminary step to this inquiry, however, remains to be taken. This is to situate Japan comparatively within the "space-time" of the transition to modernity as experienced outside the West.[46]

SOCIAL SCIENCE AND DEVELOPMENTAL ALIENATION

To speak of the transition to modernity is to speak of more than "pure" capitalism. "The most fateful force in our modern life" though it has been, it has been such in specific modalities, which have in turn shaped the social sciences into recognizable national and supranational groupings.[47] One clue to how those groupings have formed may be found in the work of Alexander Gerschenkron, widely recognized as a pioneer in the comparative study of industrialization. Gerschenkron's concern was with industrialization—not capitalism, which he was not interested in as such. Industrialization was to be understood in national sequence, and he famously spoke of a continuum leading from early developers, such as England, through intermediary cases like France to late developers or followers—Germany and Russia being two classic cases. The key variable in Gerschenkron's continuum was the degree of "deviation" from the English paradigm, and the institutional means (the factor substitutions) by which that deviation was made good: the extent and quality of large bank or state involvement in investment, nature of targeted industries, and so on. Greater state involvement was for Gerschenkron an indicator of greater "backwardness," that is, of the relative absence of the material and institutional wherewithal for industrial development that also seemed necessarily to entail strong doses of political repression. In the broadest sense, his key question asked how well a backward society is able to respond to the enormous and wrenching task of rapid industrialization, and the institutional conditions under which it is compelled to do so: a question, ultimately, of the integrity and scope of state authority itself as the chief promoter of development in all fields.

Perhaps because the Soviet experience seemed never to be far from his mind, Gerschenkron attached considerable importance to ideology in cases of latecomers and minimized its importance (along with that of the state) in the English case:

> Ricardo is not known to have inspired anyone to change "God Save the King" into "God Save Industry." No one would want to detract from the force of John Bright's eloquence, but in an advanced country rational arguments in favor of industrialization policies need not be supplemented by a quasi-religious fervor [as was the case for Saint-Simon]. Buckle was not far wrong when in a famous passage in his *History* he presented the conversion of public opinion in England to free trade as achieved by the force of incontrovertible logic. In a backward country the great and sudden industrialization effort requires a New Deal in emotions.[48]

To be sure, there were major differences between the ideologies of industrialization in England, Saint-Simonian France, and a newly unified Germany, in which the national organicist theories of Friedrich List provided "a much more suitable ideology." Of Russia, where "conditions of 'absolute' backwardness" held sway, Gerschenkron made the significant observation that:

> Nothing reconciled the . . . intelligentsia more to the advent of capitalism in the country and to the destruction of its old faith in the *mir* and the *artel* than a system of ideas which presented the capitalist industrialization of the country as the result of an iron law of historical development. It is this connection which largely explains the power wielded by Marxist thought in Russia when it extended to men . . . whose Weltanschauung was altogether alien to the ideas of Marxian socialism.

"The institutional gradations of backwardness," Gerschenkron concluded, "seem to find their counterpart in men's thinking about backwardness and the way in which it can be abolished."[49]

As suggestive and acute as Gerschenkron's observations are, they are clearly limited. As Sidney Pollard notes, Gerschenkron worked almost exclusively within a national frame, occluding in the process the conjunctural, or contemporaneous, dimension of industrial development. The abundance or otherwise of historical "factor endowments" of various national societies was obviously significant in determining how (gradually or rapidly) and when (early or late) they sought to industrialize, but no less so was the force exerted by the surrounding world at the time development programs were launched. Time was no mere "efflux-ion"; it was "full," and the world was changing, presenting different and daunting structural obstacles, compulsions, and opportunities to each new latecomer not encountered by those who had come earlier. It is this, Pollard argues, that yields what he terms the "differential of contemporaneousness": the radically different consequences "that may arise when the same historical phenomenon"—such as the building of railroads, or military modernization—"reaches more or less simultaneously economies which are themselves at very different stages in their development." It was perhaps the effects of such a differential that in turn produced the sequencing—in other words the phenomenon of lag and spurt, the jerkiness of development—to which Gerschenkron repeatedly called attention. It is to be noted that Pollard, working from the history of European industrialization, sees this differential (or *Gefälle*) as a feature not only of a given national society or state relative to others, but of regions within nations that may extend across borders; and of course Europe itself was a highly variegated region par excellence. As such, Pollard suggests, it had some peripheral zones in the east that, in attempting to pursue industrialization projects in a severely unfavorable conjuncture, actually fell even further behind.[50]

Thanks to this awareness, and though it is not an integral concern of his analysis, Pollard also addresses another dimension missing from Gerschenkron's perspective: the existence of the colonized world. With the partial exception of Ottoman Bulgaria, Gerschenkron dealt exclusively with the gradations of "backwardness" among former imperialists, including France, Germany, Italy, and preeminently, Tsarist Russia and the (late) Soviet Union. Colonial backwardness, in all its variety, and the possibility that it might represent something of a qualitatively different nature from the former type, lay beyond his ken. If Russia's backwardness was absolute, still the state remained Russian: "the Russian State," as Gerschenkron put it, "was poor but strong."[51] "Rotting Tsarism," to use the idiom of Russian Marxism, was Tsarism nonetheless. By the same token, however developed the "sprouts of capitalism" may have been in prerevolutionary China, the fragmentation of political authority and semicolonial domination guaranteed that successful "late" development by a unitary national state would be impossible. In terms of ideology, especially in its ties to social science, the chief characteristic of the colonial, and decolonializing, situation must certainly lie in the perception of imperialism as a—or the—major barrier to development that should otherwise be possible.[52]

And imperialist domination was more than a barrier to material development. Domination, a fortiori in cases of "formal" colonies, but also in "semi-" or "informal" cases, was taken on both sides as a sign of cultural inferiority on the part of the dominated; successful resistance to it could vindicate those aspects of the native culture mobilized, even in retrospect, to support that resistance. When in 1949 "the Chinese people stood up," they stood up as Chinese, and then set about reconstituting a radical cultural tradition. In light of this tradition, the predominant task of Chinese social science in this century has been first to sort out a vast catalogue of social ills according to their indigenous, as opposed to foreign, genesis (in "bureaucracy" or "feudalism" vs. "imperialism"), to analyze the ways in which they have jointly shaped the stupendous problems facing successive postimperial regimes, and then to propose concrete measures for social transformation.[53]

Among the many paths to modernity, those taken by three late-developing empires—Germany, Russia, and Japan—may be grouped together for our present purposes. Whatever debilities they experienced due to their lateness as industrializers, none lost control over the state. None was colonized; to the contrary, they colonized others. Even so, for these countries, cultural, or *virtual,* imperialism on the part of the West was an acute intellectual problem and a goad to political action. Though they remained in command of their own polities and politics, their lateness or backwardness, the salience of "tradition," was an inescapable feature of their historical and cultural self-image. Neither full participants in the Western core, nor colonies of the core countries, they shared what I will call *developmental alienation:* this, I suggest, was a primary determinant of the social science that these societies generated, shaping an avowedly international, though essentially Atlantic discourse, into a national one. To understand the emergence and evolution of social

science in these major late-developing empires is to inquire into and compare the experience of late development as it was refracted and defined in
the realm of thought in three extraordinary societies, all of which, with
some degree of self- and mutual awareness, posed stark challenges to
Western (or Atlantic) notions of social order, both at the national and
international level.

Backwardness and lateness inevitably betray overtones of a cultural
judgment that is today rejected in many quarters as invidious and in some
respects empirically suspect. But from the mid-nineteenth to the mid-
twentieth century, these were the terms of art in social science, and they
were used critically to structure arguments that have not entirely lost their
cogency. As Pollard shows, the "differential of contemporaneousness"
was not entirely a matter of cultural perception. We can see now, to be
sure, that instead of backwardness, a holistic and dialectical sense of the
national, regional, and global unevenness generated by capitalism in operation may be more productive. In this perspective, unevenness is a condition, of which backwardness forms one "moment."[54] The issue of why the
less-developed zone should also have been the more vulnerable to the
form of surplus extraction imposed on it does not disappear; nor does the
problem of internal repression as a response to that vulnerability—nor
again the many instances of complicit interest on the part of the
"advanced" zone in perpetuating it. We must not repeat the error of
falsely extrapolating from one domain—that of industrial "success"—a
set of totalistic judgments of value that amount to no more than self-
flattery. At the same time, we are bound to spare thinkers whose work
was shaped by the "differential of contemporaneousness" the condescension of our improved vantage point: we stand, after all, on their shoulders.

.   .   .

To turn now to Japan. The theme of Japan as the only successful modernizer or "power" in Asia has been endlessly played out since the 1890s.
Determined to resist Western domination, Japanese elites undertook a
forced march to industrialization and military strength based for some
decades on the relentless taxation of peasant production. Initially, this
effort was supported by a somewhat freewheeling Anglophilia, with the
appropriation of American and French models in various domains as
more or less significant subthemes. Social Darwinism, the theory of
progress, and an ethic of individual and national advancement formed
the keynote of systematic Westernization. Meiji's state makers under-

stood, however, that Japan could never be a pioneer in industrialization or empire building. They soon came to seek cultural self-preservation and national strength while avoiding the pitfalls that beset the pioneer: in short, effective followership. And this brought different models, particularly that of the new German empire, to the fore.

From the late 1880s onward, as the Meiji constitution (1889), Imperial Rescript on Education (1890), and Civil Code (1898) demonstrate, "success" in the great enterprise of acquiring wealth and strength was increasingly defined in terms of the continued viability of the national culture in the face of Western influence. Politicians, officials, businessmen, educators, and publicists alike claimed that the feudal values of obedience and the strong, collective consciousness found in Japan's still overwhelmingly agrarian society would serve to bind the people to the government despite the traumas of industrialization. Japan's unique tradition would act as a brake on both individualism and radical ideologies—the characteristic pathologies, in their view, of modern society—while at the same time promoting the right kind of progress. Japan, in short, had modernized through, not despite, tradition; a new, neotraditional mode of modernization had emerged on the world historical stage.

Success, however, brought frustration and anxiety. Along with neotraditional modernization, therefore, comes a counterpart theme that seems to have had an almost independent career: namely, the "Japanese road" inevitably led to, or became twisted into, fascism and external aggression. At one time fascism and total war were seen as the ineluctable consequences of "emperor-system absolutism." But in the sunnier views of post-Restoration history that have longed enjoyed currency, these products of Japanese modernity tend to appear virtually as natural disasters that "happened" to the nation.[55] At some level of human experience, of course, this was the case. To the extent that the social sciences take a historical perspective, however, the relation between Japan's "successful" late modernization and its imperialism—*someone* had to pay for this success—remains a troubled area; it is a relation so troubled, in fact, that it seems to have provided a warrant for avoiding just such a historical perspective. For a study such as this one, however, avoidance is not an option, and a provisional statement of views on the question seems in order here.[56]

Japan's entry into the international order came on terms dictated to a considerable degree by the West. There were "rules of the game" to be learned, and, fortunately or not, many ways of playing the game of national statehood. Some of these were deemed more relevant than others. Depending on the time and circumstances, Meiji Japan presented itself alternately to the world as a young and eager apprentice of the Victorian liberals, or as the "Prussia of the East," with still other self-presentations in succeeding eras. But there was nearly universal agreement in Japan on the need for a "rich country and strong army" *(fukoku kyōhei)*. Among the national elites there was virtually no bias against infrastructural development. Also, development as it was embodied in the powers with which Japan had significant contact included a component of overseas expansion. There was again no real bias against involvement with the outside, especially the Asian world; at question were the terms. For many Japanese, successful development required the rapid acquisition of a protective empire—either that or become a colony. Such at least was the threat held out time and again to the mass of the population—along with the idea that their own numbers were expanding too fast to be contained within the narrow islands of Japan without impoverishment and mass suffering. Opposition to expansion did exist—initially on political, economic, and, later on, moral grounds—but it was a minority position. No one was to obstruct the "sway of his gracious majesty"; Japan became a late-developing empire.[57]

At the same time, Japanese officials, publicists, journalists—and social scientists—were quick to sense and make much of the country's racial, religious, and geographic alienation from the "civilization" of the modern state system, at least as dominated by the Atlantic powers.[58] In the decade following the Versailles conference, Japan emerged as the bitter "have-not," deprived on racial grounds of its justly gained sphere of influence, and soon thereafter as the champion of Asia.

It is tempting to think that Japan, as an Asian and non-Christian society, should have felt its alienation more profoundly than other latecomer imperialists, that the sense of cultural loss exacted as the price of admission to the system of modern states should have been greater in Japan than, for example, in Russia or Germany. But was it? In Japan, historical *optimism*—the sense that its neotraditional mode of rationalization was not only successful but morally just and ethnically specific—ultimately contributed more substantially than a sense of desperation born of identity loss to the total war and total defeat that remain the pivot of Japan's modern history. The massive discontinuities associated with this experience, however, have begun to soften, at least enough to allow Japan's neotraditional values and mode of development to be seen as a model for the industrialization of other Asian societies in recent decades. Familiarity and apparent likeness, however, should not be taken for intimacy;

Japan's relations with its neighbors remain sensitive, to say the least. In its origins and development, Japanese social science provides a window on why this should be the case.

Unquestionably, elements of alienation were shared by Japanese with German and Russian thinkers, with differing inflections among the three. For Japan, Bismarck's Germany was an official model ("how to cope with developmental alienation") in ways that Russia was not; Russia provides a complex and fascinating subtheme. Imperial Japan's tutelage to a newly unified Germany covered vast areas of political administration and jurisprudence and extended deep into the sphere of expressive culture, as generations of young, future elites cut their intellectual teeth on, for example, Goethe's *Sorrows of Young Werther*. On the other hand, in nineteenth century Russia, Japanese encountered a vast, backward, predominantly agrarian empire just beginning the process of industrialization; while a regional rival, a looming threat, Russia was also seen in some ways as moving along paths parallel to Japan. In its literature, Japanese discovered a dual image: that of an exploited peasantry as a metaphor for humanity made wise by suffering, and of an intelligentsia driven to reform, or if necessary destroy, the society that had produced it. Although capitalist industrialization was in fact more advanced in Japan than in Russia, the emotional resonance in both settings of the village versus the city was genuine. As Wada Haruki has noted, the sense that the masses of both countries could be "together in suffering" constitutes one important strand in Japanese thinking about Russia, particularly in the realm of art and literature.[59]

The awareness of difference from the "advanced" West has been fabulously productive of original social thought among latecomers, from the depths of nativism, through the varieties of populism, to "reactionary modernism" and revolutionary Marxism. Among the intelligentsias of the late-developing empires, a significant segment regarded the full embrace of Western institutional and technical achievements as the vehicle of their own cultural suicide. The horrors, for some, of Manchester capitalism, for others of bureaucratization, and for still others the dual horrors of socialism and revolution drove the growth of a social science that was multivocal but profoundly ill at ease with the contemporary world. The thesis of a so-called tragic consciousness in German sociology, from Ferdinand Tönnies to Georg Simmel and Max Weber and beyond, is well known. Its basic insight has been succinctly described by Martin Jay (with reference to Simmel and the early Lukács): "The chaotic richness of life struggles to achieve coherent form, but it can do so only at the cost of what makes it alive."[60] The consciousness that flowed from this insight was tragic because it doubted whether in the long run the forces for "coherence"—that is, "civilization" or "modernity"—could be attenuated.[61] Meanwhile, the early Slavophile defense of traditional communities and of the realm of the spirit, especially in national and religious forms, ushered in a Russian conservative utopia. After the 1861 reforms it was taken up by Pan-Slavist and other ideologues of Russian reaction, finally disintegrating into great power chauvinism-cum-antisemitism.[62] In the same historical moment, the Russian intelligentsia was agonizing over its guilty relation to the "masses" and dependence on the state for the maintenance of its privileges. Out of this "guilty" relation was born populism and the vision of a village community that was preternaturally socialist. The legacy of this populism in the history of socialism, and of movements for agrarian reform, has been stupendous.

As noted, Japanese social thought shared much of this alienated perspective: the privileged alienation, be it noted, of one whose power is not fully appreciated rather than one who lacks power altogether.[63] The national organicism, exaltation of village and national community, and restraint of individualism all have their counterparts, both conservative and radical. The fascination of the Japanese since the 1880s with Russian anarchists and nihilists is well documented.[64] In the 1920s a group of Japanese agronomists sought to use A. V. Chayanov's theory of peasant household economy to analyze Japanese agriculture, seeing in it "a model for a country consisting of small peasants like Japan." But it was a poor fit.[65] It was now too late to skip over the capitalist stage, and tradition had been officially co-opted in the service of capitalism. Japanese did, despairingly or hopefully, cling to the sentiment of "going to the masses" and to the ethos of alienation from the imperial state. In any case, by the 1920s, Russia's revolutions, first in 1905, and then (twice) in 1917, had shifted the focus of both radical and conservative social thinkers to the wholly unexpected advent of socialism: How and why had it happened in backward Russia? Could it happen in Japan? What could be done, within the sphere of social science, to promote or impede the processes that might lead to a Japanese revolution?

The main line of development, however, followed tracks laid in Germany: toward heavy industrialization, a powerful bureaucracy grudgingly giving space to parliamentary (and radical) politics and cultural commodification, but with an ever more shrill whistle—in Germany of lament over lost community, in Japan of prophylactic caution—being sounded by the engine. One "official" perspective on this process in Japan was articulated by the oligarch Itō Hirobumi in 1909: that imperial Japan, as long as it held on to its character as "a vast village community" (bequeathed to it by centuries of Tokugawa isolation) would, Itō was confident, succeed in its quest for national independence and world power status.[66] Itō, in other words, was betting on neotraditional rationalization to succeed. In terms of economic and social structures (see chapters 2 and 3), this meant a bet on backwardness and its sustaining values. The wager held that rapid development of heavy industry, with its immense requirements of capital and labor, could be achieved initially on the basis of surpluses extracted from agriculture and rural-based industry. The same extractive process would also support the establishment of the empire, which, along with heavy industry itself, would eventually begin to repay the effort. Backwardness in one area was to be used to overcome it in another.

The importance of these domestic Japanese developments consists not only in their striking parallelism with other cases, but in their regional political contexts. At this point the contrasts between Japan and the other latecomers become salient. Russia, the "bastion of European reaction," could and did intervene against Westernizing revolution on its own colonial borders. It could fight modernity on its doorstep, but only at the fearful price of revolutionary upheaval in which the nature, even the identity, of revolutionary and counterrevolutionary forces was (and remains) difficult to determine.[67] Germany launched the world's first total war in the name of the "Ideas of 1914." In defeat, and facing a punitive settlement, the elites of this riven society paid for their survival by turning violently against its left, abetting, or at any rate acquiescing in, the abortion of its democracy, and inviting the triumph of technical nihilism in the name of order.

Japan, of course, was geographically remote from Europe. But in ways both direct and indirect Japan did have some purchase on continental events. In defeating Russia in 1905, Japan acted in fact as an Asian adjunct of Western modernity.[68] "The Meiji Restoration caused the Russian Revolution" is a shorthand formula that captures no small truth. Until the early 1930s, cooperation—indeed alliance—with the "Anglo-American" order was the rule. More importantly, vis-à-vis Asia, Japan presented a fateful paradox. As Japan exported its form of neotraditional rationalization to Asia, it also became a model for Asian nationalism; the invocation of "traditional" Confucian virtues went along with professions of racial solidarity: *dōbun dōshu,* "same script, same race," as the slogan had it. Chinese, Koreans, and more remotely, Vietnamese, Thais (whose country was never colonized), Burmans, and Indians could not help but see something thrilling in Japan's industrial and military achievements. Thus the Japanese empire also stoked fires of anticolonial nationalism, directed both against the West (especially Great Britain) *and against Japan.* Japanese officials and makers of opinion, however, never entirely understood the forces they had stirred up; they thought it was enough to urge Asian unity against the West and struck out with violence when this unity was turned against Japan. A brutal myopia—part and parcel of the historical optimism alluded to earlier—made its way into Japanese thinking, not least in the social sciences.

Japan, in short, took what Barrington Moore once termed the "capitalist reactionary" path to modernity. To use the formulation of the late Murakami Yasusuke, Japan established a model of "late developer conservatism." In either case, it was this Japan, the successful but uneasy late modernizer, that social science took as its object—and frequently its patron. The question for us is not, "What did these conditions do to distort 'real' social science?" But rather, "What was the 'real' social science that developed under these conditions?"

CHAPTER 2

The Social Sciences in Modern Japan

An Overview

The history of Japanese social science has unfolded in five successive "moments" or intellectual orientations that defined problems, structured analysis, drove disciplinary development, and—importantly—helped to set the terms of collective agency in public discourse: What was Japan? A nation of imperial subjects? Of classes? A single *Volk?* Of "modern" individuals?

Social science anywhere is the "science," the way(s) of knowing modernity. As such it is fatefully implicated in its political, social, and cultural context, particularly via the professional groups and institutions in which it is practiced. As will become clear, the account here is biased toward elite institutions and scholars, largely because social science in Japan, as in many late developers, grew out of state concerns and developed as an unequal contest between elite and nonelite scholarship; there was no free market of ideas. The narrative is also formalist, in that "social science" is treated in terms of the self-consciously professional activity of practitioners themselves. The fact that the origins of most disciplines and theories as such may have lain outside Japan is intellectually important, but their "history," for present purposes, begins when Japanese scholars set out to organize themselves into disciplines that they took to be locally meaningful.

The first moment is the role of an emergent social science in attempting to specify the contours, as they had formed by the 1890s, of Japan's state and society in terms of their difference from those of the Western powers that had provided Japanese elites with developmental models, and from those of the Asian societies that Japan had left behind, often contemptuously, in the quest for industrial wealth and military power.[1] This neotraditional moment, which I consider to be decisive, indeed hegemonic in the long run, was that of imperial rationalization, and saw the formation of the science of indigeneity, of particularity, of Japanese-ness itself, as embodied in the imagined linkage between the institution of the monarchy and an idealized village community. The science of indigeneity was also, to recall the concerns of our introductory considerations, the science of "developmental alienation." Second is a "liberal" or pluralizing moment, concentrated in the first three decades of the twentieth century, whose essential thrust was to challenge national particularism, arguing instead for the "normality" of Japan in comparison with its fellow modern constitutional systems; prescinding from this universalist stance was a deepening critique of that system in terms of its inherent inequities and need of social reconstruction, focusing on the conditions of Japan's urbanized workers. Combining and systematizing the critical analysis of both prior moments was a third, that of Marxism, as represented by the debate between its two contending schools over the nature, developmental process, and prospects of Japan's capitalism. This Marxist moment ended abruptly in the short term, either in state repression or the massive co-optation of its adherents into the failed totalitarian regime of the late 1930s. But in the long term, Marxism represented the only intellectual and political movement that claimed to be synonymous with social science as such, having overcome the partialities of its bourgeois form; for this reason it is given pride of place in the account offered here. Moreover, Marxism fed powerfully into the fourth, no less crucial moment, that of postwar modernism *(kindaishugi)*, which sought to appropriate much of the earlier Marxist critique of prewar state and society in the interest of constructing a new "human type," the *Homo democraticus,* in the period of postwar occupation and reconstruction. *Homo democraticus,* however, was substantially transformed by the 1960s into *Homo economicus,* as modernism became a science—and an ideology—that I term "growthism." The fifth and final moment too has a dual aspect: on the one hand the "culturalist," in which elements of the original science of indigeneity, wartime rationalization, modernism and growthism combined to form a neoexceptionalism that virtually dominated the practice of professional social science until the early 1990s. I suggest, however, that growthism itself has withered since the end of the Cold War and the collapse of the bubble economy, and that culturalism ultimately cannot survive without it. Hence, on the other hand, a de facto plurality of social scientific practice accompanied by a marked ideological confusion.

MOMENT ONE: NEOTRADITIONALISM AND THE HEGEMONY OF THE PARTICULAR

Neotraditionalism held that Japan's achievement and experience were essentially not comparable to those of other peoples; or that whatever partial similarities or comparabilities might be identified, "Japan" represented a self-contained cultural whole, and that deep communication with the world outside this whole might not be possible. As if in a self-fulfilling prophecy, and despite the enormous impact of Japan on the modern world, Japanese social science remains poorly known outside Japan. Paradoxically, "noncomparability" derived from Japan's ability, ostensibly unique, to adapt strong impulses from materially "superior" cultures without sacrificing something called the "national essence." Social science was one such impulse, imported as discrete texts already encountered during sponsored visits abroad, newly via translation, or as mediated by foreign experts working in Japan itself. In the immediate post-Restoration era, the major areas of study included most fields of law, administration, political economy, and historical science, particularly as practiced in Britain, France, Germany, and the United States. Thus modern Japan's first "social" science was dominated by the analysis of the state, which after all assumed the leading role in institutional development across the board; or at least took the state, rather than society, as its first principle.

At this early point, there was little professional organization or even disciplinary consciousness; journalistic, literary, and scholarly (or scientific) discourses for decades remained exceedingly and excitingly porous. Writers and journalists such as Fukuzawa Yukichi and Tokutomi Sohō addressed large national audiences across a number of media; the muckraking social critic Yokoyama Gennosuke was influenced directly by the writer and philosophical skeptic Futabatei Shimei; the pioneering ethnologist Yanagita Kunio had deep ties to the novelists Shimazaki Tōson and Tayama Katai. The "seeing eye" and "speaking voice" of Japanese social inquiry at this stage were hardly undisciplined, but this was the discipline exerted by canons of representation drawn from traditions other than those of Western social science. The gradual incorporation, and disciplining, of the seeing eye and speaking voice into the project of creating a new social science is a story, in the broadest sense, of creative translation. The ethos was one of urgent, even aggressive, familiarization rather than theoretical reflection or synthesis. This is no way diminishes its intellectual interest, but for present purposes such "preprofessional" activity belongs to the realm of the "prehistory" of Japanese social science.[2]

At the same time, this prehistory was vital, to begin with because it never really ended, but instead sustained the heterogeneous streams of critical consciousness that remained to check and question and enrich the more official forms of social science that took shape as the nineteenth century drew to a close. More directly, the prehistory of translation and foreign training was important to the extent that it nurtured what I term the "imperial consciousness" of Japanese social science. From its earliest practitioners onward, this entailed a sense of delegation and privilege, and of identification with a "public" good derived from its early association with the state and its leading role in the process of rationalization. What was this role? For a significant period, it was the sponsored importation and appropriation of Western systems of thought, technology, and institutional organization, and their integration with native elements. Japanese of the Meiji era did not speak of "modernization" *(kindaika)*, but of "Westernization" or "Europeanization" *(ōka)*. As indicated, these "-izations" included ways of seeing and speaking, modes of representation; indeed did not just include but in a sense privileged these modes. It was understood that thought led to action, and that to change action one had to change thought. As Alexander Gerschenkron observed, for societies developing in conditions of economic backwardness, industrialization (or by extension, rationalization) was a process in which the "stronger medicine" of ideology plays a crucial role.[3]

The second step of the process—integration with native elements—is equally important; it was the institutionalization of this process of integration that provided the condition of possibility for the emergence of a Japanese social science. When the first four decades of Japan's modern experience are viewed as a whole, native elements loom very large indeed. Explaining why and with what ramifications has been one of the main preoccupations, not to say obsessions, of Japanese social science.

Yet "native" was not then, nor can it be now, taken to refer simply to the bequest of the Tokugawa past, however dynamic that past may have been. It indicates rather a "neonative" or "invented" tradition of emperorship, familism, village communitarianism, and other such constructions for which Western experience (now well understood to contain differing, even mutually conflicting, elements) provided a legitimating frame of reference. Rapid "Westernization" had transformed the social and intellectual landscape, and there was no way to go back. Pre-Restoration terms such as "*jisei*" and "*jiun*" (force, or trend, of the times) were ubiquitous in Japanese writings on society that attempted to associate them with Western notions of social progress or evolution, and that couched their arguments in terms of universalistic theories of natural rights—Japan having now joined the march toward "Civilization." The situation changed, however, with the fragmentation and defeat of the Freedom and Popular Rights movement in the early 1880s, amid the harsh deflationary conditions associated with the policies of finance minister Matsukata Masayoshi. Talk of "natural rights" gave way to a multivalent social Darwinist discourse that came, in turn, to be recast as a national organicism. "The struggle for existence" was indeed real, and it was above all a struggle of nation against nation, race against race. It was not—or should not be—a struggle of classes or groups *within* the nation. By linking such notions of national struggle with organicism, so it was thought, the future could be constrained; modernity could be put under the discipline of a rearticulated tradition. At its core subsisted the "warm manners and beautiful customs" *(junpū bizoku)* of rural Japan, and the paternal feelings of master for man that ostensibly marked its social relations. And, at the core of the core, we find the state, during its crucial formative decades, relying on surpluses extracted, and labor drawn—along with entrepreneurial and bureaucratic talent—from the villages.

Under these conditions, the sanctioned task of social scientists was to contribute to the national progress; to guide, and only secondarily to criticize—let alone overturn—a process of imperial rationalization that made use of these idealized relations in effecting a new regime of industrial discipline. Thus, Prussian-style "state science" *(Staatslehre)* flourished in imperial Japan, while liberal or democratic theory had to struggle and assume certain sublimated forms. Laissez-faire or classical economics—à la Taguchi Ukichi, for example—became relatively marginal in favor of one derived from the Historical school. Finally, Japanese sociology placed greater normative weight on the local analogue for *Gemeinschaft (kyōdōtai)*, while its counterpart, *Gesellschaft (shakai)* had virtually pathological connotations. Running through these "ruling ideas" was a drive to integrate—invent—the nation as a rural community writ large, without any undue transfer of real wealth to rural Japan. The medium of this neotraditional integration, of course, was the modernizing state. Tradition was a function of the quest for what Ronald Dore has termed "national-communitarian" modernity.[4]

To say this much, however, is to say too little. For along with tradition as invention, and defining its specificity in the case of Japan, came rationalization as irrationalization. The salient ideological elements of the imperial system, precisely to the extent that the program of national integration succeeded, were rendered taboo. Japan's unique and peerless "national polity," its line of emperors unbroken for ten thousand generations, became more of an amulet to ward off political danger than an entity susceptible to analysis, however respectful. Japan was proclaimed to be a "family state," in which a perfectly harmonious hierarchy of concentric social units, narrowing toward the emperor at its zenith, widening through local and village levels toward a base composed of an infinitely duplicated mass of households, each with its patriarch, served as a normative model of the national community. In this model, social bonds were represented as natural, rather than purposive. Yet at the same time, "the *sentiment* of consanguinity" ruled beyond any actual blood ties. These ties were all the more powerful for being fictive, all the more easily assimilable to the national cult of loyalty to sovereign as literal paterfamilias. We have here what Maruyama Masao described as a "full-scale mobilization of irrational attachments to the primary group" as the keynote of state ideology and principle of organization. And as this happened social science was denied access to the essential processes of neotraditional rationalization on the grounds that they were too sacred to be touched with the blade of analytical reason. Irrationalization, then, was a function of rationalization.[5]

The installation of an exceptionalist hegemony in social science was clearly visible to contemporaries. The Kokka Gakkai (Association for *Staatslehre*), founded in 1887, drew its membership from officialdom and from the imperial universities, as did the Kokka Keizai Kai (Association for State and Economy), established in 1890. The concomitant privileging of Prussian-style state science drew comment—some quite critical—from Japanese observers by the 1880s, especially journalists and writers such as Taguchi Ukichi. Not only was the state enshrined at the core of "social" science. The earliest Japanese translations of *Staatslehre*—*kokkagaku*—tended to emphasize its most conservative aspects; this to the detriment of more liberal notions, such as Lorenz von Stein's idea of the "social monarchy," which reflected the size and political strength of the German working class. *Kokkagaku* was also more concerned with administrative techniques of "rule by law" than with the metaphysical underpinnings of the state and its legitimacy.[6] The latter issue had been settled by making the monarchy, with its claim to descent from the sun goddess, an analytical taboo for scholars, to chilling effect. In 1892, Kume Kunitake (1839–1931), trained by Ludwig Riess and a founder of modern Japanese historiography, lost his teaching post at the Imperial University of Tokyo after publishing an article, influenced by contemporary anthropology and comparative religion, in which he declared Shintō to be a "vestige of sky worship"—*saiten no kozoku.*

A product of the same broad movement was the supersession of lais-sez-faire or classical economics, which had been vigorously disseminated since the early 1870s. Although universities such as Keiō and later Hitotsubashi (in economics), Chūō and later Waseda (in law) continued to be associated with British approaches, Tokyo and its fellow imperial universities were firmly drawn toward the German Historical school. As with *Staatslehre,* this was no matter of mere copying. Friedrich List's *Nationale System der politischen Ökonomie* (National system of politi-cal economy, 1841), for example, was well known in Ōshima Sadamasu's translation. Ōshima (1845–1906), a founder of the Kokka Keizai Kai and translator also of Henry Thomas Buckle and Malthus, generally upheld Listian principles. But he strongly rejected List's argu-ment that European colonialism represented a natural division of world labor, and unlike List believed that small-producer agriculture, and not just industry, ought to receive state protection. Ōshima's estimation of classical political economy, moreover, was nuanced. "We were fortu-nate," he wrote in his *Jōseiron* (On the current situation, 1896)

> that it was British liberalism that first entered Japan after the opening of the country in the Ka'ei era. Had American protectionism or German eclecticism been first to arrive on the scene, these would not have been enough for us to break through our obstinacy. Without British liberal theory, we would have been insufficiently equipped to see through our confusion of those days. The smashing of our obstinacy, formed over hundreds of years, by these ideas was very much like Adam Smith rising up to overcome mercantilism. . . . Nowadays everyone has grown drunk on the beauty of the word "liberty," but should it not be recognized that liberty in politics and liberty in trade are quite different matters; that while political liberty can make the people of a country free, freedom of trade means freedom for the people of another country at the expense of the country that grants it?[7]

The turn to List and historical economics was significant also because it opened the way—none too soon, in view of the rapid industrialization of Japan's economy after 1895—for the delayed entry of *Sozialpolitik* into official and academic discourse. Established in 1896, some twenty years after its German model, and operating until 1924, the Nihon Shakai

Seisaku Gakkai (Japanese Social Policy Association) had 122 members by 1909, drawn from academic, official, and moderate labor circles. Apart from stimulating the development of academic economics and empirical social research—Japan's first genuinely "social," as opposed to "state" science—the association sought to prevent the conflict of classes that had traumatized Britain and produced radical movements there and across the continent. This stance led it to advocate protective factory legislation, earning it the enmity of elements of the business world, whose resistance to bureaucratic "interference" in the "warm relations" of employers to workers prevented its passage until 1911.[8] The association also called for state action to hold off the otherwise inevitable radicalization of workers by enacting policies that would allow potential urban migrants to remain in rural villages. Ōshima Sadamasu, List's translator, had broken with his "mentor" in advancing a similar argument. The reason was not far to seek: the so-called Matsukata deflation was widely regarded as having induced Japan's first modern depression, greatly accelerating, as noted earlier, the rate of agrarian tenancy. This chronic debility in Japan's economy was not effectively redressed until the 1940s, first with ad hoc wartime decrees and legislation, and then the more thorough and widely popular land reform under the American occupation. While it was understood that only industrial wealth would be able to sustain Japan's independence, it seemed just as clear that on the villages' social viability, or lack of it, hung the entire system of national values.

Along with advocates of social policy, the earliest professional groups of sociologists began to form shortly before the turn of the century, with university courses beginning to be taught at the same time. Like many of their social policy counterparts, sociologists met suspicions that their interest in "society"—the "lower orders" in the cities—was a matter not of study but of political advocacy.[9] In the overheated atmosphere of the Russo-Japanese War era professional sociologists felt compelled to distinguish their enterprise from the subversive work of Japan's tiny and harassed band of socialists. Takebe Tongo (1871–1945), holder of the chair in sociology at Tokyo Imperial, declared that sociology "began with Comte and culminates in Tongo," and pursued a national organicism— what he later termed a "statist view of society" *(kokka shakaikan)*—that attacked any and all manifestations of the "skeptical, negative, destructive, and transient" notions of individualism and democracy.[10] Such was the price of professionalization. Still, the pressure of new ideas, particularly those of Georg Simmel, and of new problems such as urban poverty, began to drive the discipline beyond the conservatism that enframed it. Sociologists may have been methodologically disinclined to take up the study of the countryside. But there were disincentives too. The Civil Code of 1898 had defined the *ie,* or household—rather than the individual— as the normative unit of society. Apart from former warrior households (on which the model was based) and certain great merchant houses, the closest real approximations of the ostensibly traditional household were thought to be found in the countryside. Thus the *ie* (albeit less ferociously than the monarchy) was protected from sociological scrutiny by the double mantle of law and ideology, while a highly idealized image of the "solid core" of frugal owner-farmers was held up for the entire country to emulate.

But this protection was deeply problematic on its own terms. While its extent varied region by region, rural capitalist development was irreversible, as was the state's commitment to it. Officials working within the framework of national exceptionalism saw tradition instrumentally, and had little interest in preserving local customs that they could not control. It was therefore a foreboding of loss that drove the formation of the new discipline of ethnology *(minzokugaku),* of which Yanagita Kunio (1875– 1962) was founder and overwhelmingly dominant practitioner.

Born the sixth son of a destitute rural scholar of the Chinese classics and later adopted into the family of a high-level jurist, Yanagita spent his youth in literary friendships with Shimazaki Tōson, Tayama Katai, and Kunikida Doppo, continuing to write even as he pursued a career in the Ministry of Agriculture and Commerce and beyond. Beginning with writings that claimed to record local tales and legends related to him "just as he felt them *[kanjitaru mama],* adding or deleting not a word or phrase," Yanagita sought to counter the state's massive campaign of symbolic theft from rural Japan by articulating a nativist and antibureaucratic vision of what he would come to call the *jōmin,* the "people who endure." For Yanagita, the rapid decline of rural lifeways was nothing less than "domicide," and a concern in its own right. But more was at stake. As he wrote in *Jidai to nōsei* (Agricultural administration in the current age, 1910):

> The ties between each individual and his ancestors—that is, the awareness of the existence of the household *[ie]*—in a country such as Japan represents at the same time the link between the individual and the state. Even now, we need only dig back a little into the past to find that throughout history, those who have given their loyalty to the throne—those same are our ancestors. And thus we can perceive, not in vague feelings but concretely, what their

will is [for us]. An awareness that our ancestors have lived under and served
Japan's imperial house to the utmost for hundreds of generations most
clearly creates the basis for loyalty and patriotism today. What is most
to be feared is that, with the disappearance of the house, one is hard put
to explain to oneself why one must be Japanese. When individualism thrives,
we come to look upon the history of other countries and our own as if with
the same eyes. . . . In any case, the only certainty is that, whether from the
standpoint of the nation or of individual ethics, great harm comes when the
individual treats the perpetuity of the house as a trifling matter.[11]

Yanagita's preoccupation with a threatened way of life led him to
hope—perhaps against hope—that it might be possible to counter the
"officialized" discourse of community, which was little but a functional-
ist apology for the state's exploitation of the countryside. But with what?
A community possessed of "countermemory," for which the emperor
whom the "people" served was local, preideological, and unarmed.
Counter how? By publicly opposing, as Yanagita did, the compulsory
merger of Shintō shrines as part of the Home Ministry's rural improvement campaign.[12] These concerns also led Yanagita to prodigious empirical study, including the collection, classification, and reproduction of
thousands of local legends, oral tales, pieces of dialectology, and so on;
these methods became foundational for his school, recommended not
just for urban-educated followers but for local people themselves.[13]

Yanagita's notion of an original, natural village and its communal life
was typical of prewar social science in its susceptibility to co-optation. As
cultural poetics, his work was beautifully realized—appropriately so,
given his literary background. It was a project marked by an increasingly
fantastic search for the silent and invisible "original Japanese," first
among the "mountain people" of the interior, and eventually along the
"paths of the sea" that tied Japan to Okinawa. Invoking the reconstruction of Japanese tradition by eighteenth-century scholars anxious to res-
cue Japan from the "foreign" taint of long-dominant Chinese ideas and
ideals, Yanagita ultimately described his project as a "neonativism"—
shin kokugaku. Here, Yanagita was convinced, was a "science of the
native place" that would enable Japan's "real" culture to hold its own
against the twin threats of the bureaucratic and capitalist penetration of
village life on the one hand, and Marxist notions of class struggle that
pitted against each other people who should form—and continually
reproduce—a unity based on lineage and communal ties bequeathed to
them by their ancestors. The latter threat in particular, by bringing the
notion of class to the forefront of social thought, prompted Yanagita to

produce properly methodological texts based on the practices he and his many followers had developed; their thrust was to demonstrate what might be termed the "varieties of sameness" across classes and regions.[14]

Yanagita's work left a deep and extensive imprint on interwar social science: the development of anthropology, sociology, ethnology in Japan, and of a self-consciously indigenous social science of Japan, are unimaginable without Yanagita's influence. His themes were taken up and extended by academic sociologists such as Ariga Kizaemon (1897–1979), who placed particular stress on the hierarchical "family" as the structuring principle for Japanese social relationships generally. Applied during the 1930s and 1940s to the study of Japan's colonial subjects, Yanagita's approach was also widely appropriated in the postwar years. The anthropologist Nakane Chie, in her well-known *Japanese Society* (1970), pursued the "vertical society" notion that Ariga had developed out of Yanagita's work on the family; Tsurumi Kazuko and Kamishima Jirō as well made use of Yanagita's work to identify basic patterns of adherence and resistance to authority over the course of Japan's history. In another filiation, associated with the antimodernizationist People's History *(minshūshi)* school, Yanagita's critique of the modern in the name of *jōmin* communities under threat was taken in both a Marxist and "left-populist" direction by (respectively) Yasumaru Yoshio and Irokawa Daikichi. The issue in all of these appropriations becomes, What community is threatened—Japan itself or its constituent regions and smaller populations? By what modernity—that of the "West," or of Tokyo? My own sense is that the main line of Yanagita appropriations has tended to overwrite Japan itself as a "community under threat," generalizing the issue in a manner that Yanagita himself might have found illegitimate, but one nonetheless credible within the framework he provided.[15]

MOMENT TWO: TOWARD PLURALIZATION

If in its formation Japanese social science was imbued with an imperial consciousness, it also, even if despite itself, became critical. The chief characteristic of this criticism was determined by its relation to the taboo areas sketched in above: one not of dialectic but of coexistence, and always at the sufferance of those who guarded the sacred precincts. The possibility, and necessity, of a critical social science in imperial Japan arose out of the contradictions between the family state ideology in both its local and national forms, and the actual processes of social—including intellectual—transformation set in motion by its distinctive mode of rationalization. The emergence by the 1890s of a "social problem" was marked by rising discontent among industrial (especially textile) workers, a growing and increasingly vulnerable population of agrarian tenants, the beginnings of a socialist and feminist movement, and spreading ideologies of what the oligarch Yamagata Aritomo called "social destructionism." Did the imperial regime possess the capacity to recognize these problems? What sort of response—to say nothing of resolution—might be expected? Where ought the country to look in search of models for its response? These were legitimate questions for social scientists to ask, but in asking them they all too often came to be identified, in the minds of powerful officials such as Yamagata, with the problem itself. Sociology advocated society—that is, the cause of the lower orders—and society was the root of socialism.[16] In the context of turn-of-the-century Japan, it was society that posed problems for the state rather than the other way around; put another way, society was a problem to which the state was to provide, or itself was, the solution.

Under these conditions, any critical consciousness could either compromise or fight openly, at the risk of severe political and legal disability. For the most part, the former route was preferred. The method, or strategy, was to acknowledge that social science had a duty to the nation— emperor, state, and people—but to broaden the spectrum of acceptable means for the fulfillment of that duty. It should include criticism: to criticize was not to betray.[17]

But what kind of criticism? The question points to another crucial aspect of the relation between imperial and critical consciousness: The criticism that did develop reflected a great heterogeneity of perspective and method. In part this stems from the heterogeneous origins of social criticism, which included an essayistic literary tradition of travel and social observation, more recent journalistic muckraking aimed at political and economic corruption, excess and abuse, and religious and morally based exposés of the conditions of workers, women, and the poor (both urban and rural). As already indicated in the discussion of Yanagita, these critical threads wound in and out of the social science that subsequently took shape. But it is important to recognize that in a formal sense, the "science" in Japanese social science came in with the state, its educational institutions, its bureaucracies. To refine the schematized relation introduced earlier: In its formative decades—roughly until World War I— Japanese social science developed as an attempt to introduce heterogeneity into the imperial consciousness that dominated and conditioned its existence. And that meant an attempt to reconceptualize the state as such, something of which Yanagita, however critical he might have been of state policy in its particulars, was constitutionally incapable.

Others were willing to try. As the twentieth century opened, the first courses in political science *(seijigaku)* to be conceived independently of the *Staatslehre* tradition were taught in the then College of Law at Tokyo Imperial University. For Onozuka Kiheiji (1870–1944), with whom this new trend was identified, the state was a proper and legitimate object of empirical inquiry rather than a self-activating subject or realized metaphysical principle. While he carefully abjured any political use of scholarship (in rhetoric if not in fact), Onozuka did begin to pry loose the "science" of politics from its identification with administrative technique.[18] It should be noted, however, that independent university departments of political economy were characteristic only of private institutions such as Waseda; within the imperial universities, political science was taught as a subfield within faculties of law and administration.

By the beginning of the Taishō era (1912–26), with the waning of oligarchic power and the coincident growth of the middle and working classes, movements for universal suffrage and the rights of labor set to work, buoyed by the rapid expansion and reform of education and the explosion of mass-circulation newspapers, and journals of opinion and entertainment. This impingement of society on politics—even when marked by a populist nationalism—presented a broad and diverse challenge to the hegemony of agrarian-based national exceptionalism, and to the authority of "officialized" social science focused on the exaltation of the imperial state.

Among the most significant of such challenges were the attempts to conceive a liberal polity made by Minobe Tatsukichi (1873–1948) and Yoshino Sakuzō (1878–1933)—the former a constitutional scholar, the latter a political scientist in the line of Onozuka. From their positions in the law faculty at Tokyo Imperial, both sought to broaden the capacity of the political system to "represent" the people, focusing on the Diet as the proper forum for such representation. Both were convinced that the liberation of the individual—*from* traditional constraints and *for* broader participation in society and politics—was the moving spirit of modern times, and a trend from which Japan should not, and could not, claim exemption. Yet their more theoretical contributions were strikingly at odds: Minobe's "organ theory" of the emperor was universalistic and formal in character, stressing not the historical role of the imperial institution but its necessary circumscription once Japan had in place the rationalizing instruments of modern statehood. Yoshino, arguing for "people-as-the-base-ism" *(minponshugi)*, took the opposite tack of asserting not only that the franchise could be expanded without attacking or undermining imperial sovereignty, but that such expansion was consonant with the progressive tradition of the imperial institution itself.[19] For the Christian Yoshino, politics was conducted for the popular welfare, and with the aim of restoring the proper—harmonious—relation between individual and institution.

The ideas of Minobe and Yoshino were widely accepted. Minobe's approach informed a generation of bureaucratic training, while Yoshino's spurred an ultimately successful popular movement for universal male suffrage. Taken together, they represent the limit of indigenous liberalism in prewar political thought and practice. Their significance for social science lies less in their specific conceptual contributions than in their having vindicated the notion that epochal political change could be conceived and carried out by elites working in consensus with a broad social constituency and without resort to violence; in other words, that politics by consent in a self-activating society was a real and desirable possibility. And for such a possibility to be realized, a methodologically independent, empirically grounded political science was necessary. A beginning was indeed made, but its impact was limited. Political science had to establish its independence from perspectives that would subsume political processes within those of sociology, which was outpacing the former in vigor by the 1910s.[20] And it was also possible to imagine a more pluralized polity in which the role of the representative organ was magnified. But more consequentially, independence would eventually require a direct (albeit "conceptual") confrontation with the imperial institution itself, which effectively meant denationalization. That was unthinkable.

Along with sociology, economics also acquired academic citizenship at this time. Economics became in some ways primus inter pares, the most international, quantitative (though primitively so), and scientific of the social sciences. After World War I, independent economics departments were created in major universities. Perhaps because of pressures associated with its location at the hub of the imperial state, Tokyo Imperial's was particularly prone to ideological and factional disputes, while that of Kyoto quietly assumed international stature as the home of the respected *Kyoto University Economic Review*. It also housed scholars on the order of Shibata Kei, whose 1937 refutation of the Marxian tenet of a falling profit rate is still widely cited. The faculties of the Tokyo Commercial College (later Hitotsubashi) and Keiō were and remain notable. Spurred by the emergence of Marxism as a virtual synonym for social science (a development to be discussed below), the key achievement of interwar economics was to have made the first attempts to examine the contemporary Japanese economy within a rigorous theoretical framework. Marginalists and early Keynesians took their places alongside practitioners of social policy. But certainly through the mid-1930s, Marxian economists enjoyed the clearest identity as a school—and suffered for it in due course.

Appropriately, it was an economist, Sōda Kiichirō (1881–1927), who first articulated a philosophy of social, or more precisely "cultural," science, in Japan. Resolutely cosmopolitan, Sōda was an independent scholar who moved easily between economics and philosophy after a decade of study in Europe, particularly with the neo-Kantian Heinrich Rickert. While heading the bank that bore his family name, Sōda introduced the methodological writings of Weber and Simmel to Japanese audiences. Politically, he espoused the elitist liberalism of the Reimei-kai—the Dawn Society—whose public fora on occasion drew audiences in the thousands. Sōda sought to provide liberalism with philosophical grounding in a "culturalist" system of coordinate values. As he put it in "Bunkashugi no ronri" (The logic of culturalism, 1922):

> Culturalism recoils in abhorrence from bureaucratism and military cliquism, which seek to impose on the whole of society the life outlook of a limited few; and also must reject social democracy in its attempt, under the guise of [representing] the common people in general, simply to replace one privileged class with another, albeit the majority, that has no privilege. . . . What culturalism seeks is for all personalities, in the process of realizing cultural values, to be enabled to conserve their special and unique significance, and in this sense participate in the creation of cultural goods, thereby making possible the realization . . . by each individual personality, of its absolute freedom. In this sense, culturalism is personalism.[21]

Beyond his vindication of "culture" as simultaneously a personal and universal—though evidently empty—value, Sōda's importance lies in his having articulated the neo-Kantian distinction between the knowledge of nature and culture. Nature as an actor without self-consciousness was counterposed to culture, in which the subject of knowledge and action—*ninshiki shutai*—was aware of itself as such. Thus identified and delimited, the notion of "culture" could then provide a basis for the methodological autonomy and differentiation of its constituent sciences. At the same time, neo-Kantianism—Sōda's included—was virtually innocent of the idea of society. One result was a certain barrenness in methodological debate; on the other hand, when the generation of young intellectuals who were exposed to those debates came in large numbers to embrace Marxism as social science par excellence, they tended to demand that it, too, display an appropriate rigor in matters of method. In this sense, it has been remarked, "neo-Kantianism was the dialectical premise for Marxism."[22]

Yet formalism was not without its own concrete analytical results. Following Simmel, the sociologist Yoneda Shōtarō (1873–1945) defined society as the process of mental interaction among individuals apart from the state or household, and the task of his discipline as the study of forms of sociation among such individuals. Two developments of particular interest ensued: Yoneda himself had (in 1919) identified a modern "intellectual class," largely synonymous with a new middle class, as one whose income was derived through knowledge or technical expertise. Too numerous to assimilate entirely to older elites, this class would, Yoneda ventured, eventually form ties to the proletariat. Such a "movement," he argued, was a social problem of major consequence, especially in terms of the political future of the working class itself. Yoneda's student Takata Yasuma (1883–1972), in turn, stressed not so much the forms of interaction as of the unity and the will to coexist among individuals, particularly in social classes; the unity of society, whether enforced or voluntary, was an objective fact beyond Simmel's "mental interactions" of discrete individuals. It seems plausible to see in such work, which clearly prescinded from new forms of urban social interaction, a quest for "universal" principles, and as such an implicit critique of the hegemonic "reality" of the rural community at all levels. In this sense, it fits well with the pronounced universalism of Minobe's "organ theory" of the emperor. At the same time, as Yanagita's trajectory—and Takata's own return to *Gemeinschaft* in the 1930s—shows, the rural "remainder," as articulated through the state, would sooner or later exact the price of universalization.[23]

Beyond the universities, engaged and empirical social science was being pioneered by Christian and other social reformers, as well as by academics and scholars affiliated with labor unions and institutions such as the private Ōhara Institute for Social Research. Particularly notable was the evangelist Kagawa Toyohiko (1888–1960)—among the most famous men in the world in his time—who moved to the Shinkawa slums, compiling there his surveys of Kōbe and Ōsaka and writing extensively on the need for "human construction" among the flawed and wounded personalities of those afflicted by poverty. His studies of the lumpenproletariat, including large numbers of outcastes, sought to embrace the experience of modern mass poverty, beginning with its social etiology and extending to considerations of (un)employment patterns, family forms, spending habits, diet, vices, and criminality. A handful of years prior to the Rice Riots of 1918 and the 1923 Kantō earthquake (which had been followed by a massacre of Koreans in Tokyo), Kagawa strikingly predicted that degradation would predispose individuals with a weakened capacity for self-regulation to mass violence, and this sooner rather than later.[24]

Despite his powerful support of labor, tenant, and outcaste movements, Kagawa was ultimately concerned with moral uplift, and held to a brand of optimistic evolutionism in his social analysis.[25] His concrete hopes for "human construction," along with the liberal visions of Minobe, Yoshino, and Sōda were to be disappointed. Universal male suffrage, introduced in 1925, was accompanied by legislation that criminalized the "intention" to alter the "national polity" and the institution of private property. The established parties, meanwhile, proved incapable either of responding to the economic catastrophe of the depression or countering the political juggernaut toward military-bureaucratic rule created by the Manchurian invasion of 1931. Attempts to pass social legislation in the late 1920s fell victim to the "national emergency," despite efforts by agents of the state (such as those involved in conciliating labor problems) to create a modus vivendi with the newly arisen social constituencies of that era. Ultimately, the liberal challenge to compulsory communitarianism in political and social thought ended either in sublimation or in radicalization. This is not to slight the importance of individual thinkers across a spectrum including Minobe and Yoshino but extending (chronologically) to Hasegawa Nyozekan, Ōyama Ikuo, Ishibashi Tanzan, Kawai Eijirō, Kiyosawa Kiyoshi, Yanaihara Tadao, and others; or to minimize their sometimes tragic struggles or their impact, particularly via postwar retrospect, on the social sciences. On the whole, however, there was virtually no self-sustaining liberalism in theory or in practice. Liberalism remained interstitial, a vital irritant in a communitarian environment, but lacked an independent institutional base and motivational force. Over the course of the 1930s, following the decimation of both activist and academic Marxism, liberals in the imperial universities, beginning with the legal scholar Takigawa Yukitoki, were sacrificed to the guardians of the "national polity," sometimes in the name of university autonomy itself. Writing in the late 1940s, Rōyama Masamichi (1895–1980) argued that liberal political science had been trapped between and shredded by the ideological forces of the left and right, but should not be disregarded by postwar scholars. But Rōyama, a professor of politics in the law faculty of Tokyo Imperial, was seeking to protect himself and his postwar reputation from identification with the more refined elements of that very right wing to which he had given his allegiance in the 1930s. Here, perhaps, was part of the reason that his younger colleague Maruyama Masao, in a 1947 essay that provoked Rōyama's work, argued that prewar political science had left his generation "no tradition worth reviving."[26]

MOMENT THREE: THE IMPACT AND FATE OF MARXISM

The marginalization of liberalism was due to a variety of causes that took time to manifest themselves, of which two stand out. The first is a sort of formalist sublimation, effectively exemplified in Yoshino Sakuzō's "democracy" without popular sovereignty. In this way of thinking, a given ideal is held to be potentially or actually embodied in a given institution (this is the formalism); and the proper goal of politics, as defined by the academically pedigreed, becomes the ultimate realization of harmony between ideal and institution. This mentality made for sometimes moving personal idealism, but not for institutional resilience. The second cause was political radicalization. With the weakness of such formalism in mind, and perhaps also the hard economic times that hit Japan's intelligentsia after the late 1920s, Katō Shūichi, humanist par excellence, remarked of the politics of Japan's 1920s that "in order to be consistent as a liberal, it was necessary to be a Marxist."[27] We might well add: "Or at least to approximate as far as possible a class- and conflict-driven notion of social progress without the embrace of an openly revolutionary program." As Fukuda Tokuzō, a social policy stalwart and author of a pioneering study of Japan's social development, put it: "Both socialism and social policy—no, in fact everything to which the term 'social' is attached—today at least take [class struggle] as their chief concern."[28]

This tendency to regard conflict as both society's essential problem and the key to its progress as a self-activating entity was given clear articulation by Ōyama Ikuo and his colleagues at the progressive journal *Warera,* especially Hasegawa Nyozekan; the contributors to that emblem of radical liberalism, *Kaizō;* and figures such as the sociologist and philosopher Tsuchida Kyōson. It also took expression in the Ōhara Shakai Mondai Kenkyūjo—the Ōhara Institute for Social Research, founded in 1919. The training ground for generations of experts on labor and related issues, the institute also provided a home for a number of eminent Marxian economists who had lost their academic positions.[29] For it was, in fact, extremely difficult to be a Marxist, even an academic Marxist. The political, legal, and professional penalties could be steep and long lasting. The purely intellectual challenge of maintaining a consistently and thoroughly dialectical way of thinking, with its concomitant restlessness and troubling suspension of conventional moral judgment, could sometimes be very hard to bear. This was certainly the experience of Kawakami Hajime (1879–1946), who founded Marxian economics in Japan (and eventually joined the Communist Party) while in certain important respects never committing himself to historical materialism; try as he might, Kawakami could never reject the category of spiritual experience as something irreducible to any other. Whether despite or because of these formidably unfavorable conditions, the impact of Marxism was immense, if not immeasurable, and though fiercely challenged, it conditioned the entire subsequent history of social thought in Japan.

Rōyama's apologia notwithstanding, the fact was that the power of the state was valenced in favor of the right; the contest with the left was not equal. Conceptually, the individual could not be permitted to stand in an inherently antagonistic relation to the state or community; something would have to have disturbed their presumptive natural harmony. Rōyama was correct, therefore, in identifying a new threat from the left, as the image and meaning of "society" sharpened into that of class and class struggle, particularly as embodied in Marxism.

Marxism had been introduced in the late 1890s, but it took the Russian Revolution, the Rice Riots of 1918, and related labor strikes to confirm the validity of conflict-centered notions of social progress, providing the impetus for a prolonged struggle between the anarcho-syndicalist and Marxist elements of the Japanese socialist movement. In the process, Marxism established itself as a synonym for social science, transcending its role as the ideology of a harried revolutionary movement and popularizing the term "social science" for the first time. A full translation of *Capital* appeared between 1919 and 1925; fifteen thousand sets of the Kaizōsha edition of the collected works of Marx and Engels (1927–29) sold in the first printing alone. As elsewhere, the spread of Marxism in Japan depended not only on the existence of a party-authorized, *Capital*-centered canon, but on its popularization in texts by Engels, Karl Kautsky, Lenin, and Bukharin. Kawakami Hajime was undoubtedly the crucial "apostle" to young intellectuals. His appeal lay behind the proliferation of "social science" research groups in universities and high schools (even middle schools), and their prohibition by educational officials as early as the mid-1920s. More consequentially, numerous young academics were heading for Weimar Germany for direct study of original texts and interaction with German (and German-speaking) Marxists representing the entire spectrum of positions, from positivist to revisionist to Hegelian, within the tradition. Among them were Arisawa Hiromi (1896–1988) and Uno Kōzō (1897–1977), who in their careers after 1945 represented the pinnacles, respectively, of Marxism as an instrument in economic policy making, and as an academic discipline.

Regardless of variant, Marxism was "the first *Weltanschauung* in modern Japan which compelled one intellectually to explicate the transformation of social systems in a total and coherent fashion."[30] Its power was all the greater since the various social science disciplines had developed "instrumentally" as discrete sciences, and in contrast to Europe, Japan had not experienced the crisis and collapse of evolutionary or positivist systems such as those of Spencer and Comte. Each strength in Marxism, however, brought with it a corresponding flaw. Its systematic character could degenerate into dogmatism, its putative universality recalled its foreign origin (and confirmed Japan's position as a historically backward "object" of knowledge), and its critical modus operandi often provoked infighting and organizational fragmentation.[31]

Ultimately, Marxism's claim to synonymity with social science derived from its analysis of Japanese society itself, one that reflected—but in important ways transcended—all the tensions and problems just described. Its chief contribution took the form of the "debate on Japanese capitalism" that ran from the late 1920s to the late 1930s. Occasioned by political disagreements over revolutionary goals and strategy, its task was the historical characterization of the developmental process of Japanese capitalism and the modern state. The so-called Kōza-ha, or Lectures Faction, following the position of the Comintern's 1927 and 1932 Theses on Japan, focused its analyses on the entrenched and powerful "feudal" forces that controlled the absolutist imperial regime. Japanese capitalism was "special," a kind of hybrid. Bourgeois political institutions were immature or malformed, and the entire state apparatus was underlain by a vast base of semifeudal production relations among the peasantry that had been little affected by the political events of 1868. The task of social science, therefore, was to clarify the obstacles to the completion of the democratic revolution as the necessary first step in a two-stage drive toward socialism.[32] The dissident Rōnō-ha, or Worker-

Farmer Faction, while cognizant of time lags vis-à-vis the West, took a more conjunctural view, regarding Japan as one of a number of imperialist finance capitalisms. This meant, by corollary, that prior to the Restoration, Japan's agrarian economy had already developed production relations characteristic of incipient bourgeois domination. The Meiji Restoration was Japan's bourgeois revolution; vestiges of feudalism, while still powerful, were incidental and would be swept away in a socialist revolution.

By nature, the capitalism debate could not be resolved; it ended with the arrest or silencing of its participants by 1938. Because it was bound up with the internal politics of the left, sympathetic observers often felt pressed to declare for one side or the other. This factionalism largely obscured the true significance of the debate and the split in perception that triggered it, but was not an inevitable product of Marxist ideas as such: creative solutions were possible. Uno Kōzō, for example, argued in 1935 that Japan's capitalism was best viewed as a classic case of "late development" in which the capitalist mode of production was mediated via industry rather than agriculture; this meant that both the Kōza-ha emphasis on the semifeudal peasantry, and the Rōnō faction insistence on finding evidence of rural differentiation, were misplaced.[33] But it was not until the 1960s, with the virtual disappearance of the peasantry and the supersession of the Kōza–Rōnō debate, that the structure of Japan's prewar capitalism as a whole was politically permitted to come into view.

A consequence of this enforced delay, Ōshima Mario has argued, was the dominance of the Kōza-ha over Japanese Marxism, and that of Marxism over the social sciences. In turn, a framework of "advanced Europe and backward Asia" (including Japan), which was undeniably valid in the analysis of industrialization, was accorded "unbounded validity" in social science, with baleful results. By forcing society and culture into a Procrustean bed of economic determinism based on categories of production, "Japanese Marxism deepened the consciousness of historical backwardness" in all areas of "the state, the society, and the economy (both manufacturing and agriculture)." The result was a distorted understanding both of the imperial system generally, and of the actual process by which Japan emerged as a late-developing empire.[34] Despite their emancipatory, counterhegemonic intent, works such as Yamada Moritarō's *Nihon shihonshugi bunseki* (Analysis of Japanese capitalism, 1934) should also be regarded as key texts in the "invention" of a tradition, in a dual sense (see chapter 3). The Kōza-ha gave scientific imprimatur to the notion of Japanese backwardness, among the longest standing and (whether factually adequate or not) productive ideas in the history of modern Japanese social thought. In doing so, it assumed, rather than questioned, the primacy, indeed the exceptional character, of the Japanese nation-state.[35]

In another sense, Japanese Marxists also failed doubly: both in the attempt to discover empirically and to actualize politically a social logic of revolution—that is, a theory of inevitable revolution stemming from the internal processes of Japanese society. Understandably, Marxists have been heroized as the primary victims of political persecution. But we must also recognize that the national community in crisis exerted a positive appeal—one that essentially disabled the critical impulse within Japanese social science that had taken systematic form under Marxian aegis. Social thinkers long weaned of "bourgeois" sociology and distrustful of the "rationality" of the market mechanism for its indulgence of exploitation, responded with alacrity to the call of community. Faced with a choice between an open break with the national community—imprisonment, exile, coerced silence—and some sort of compromised life, a great many chose to "return to Japan."

Return meant engagement with the state, and more concretely with avowedly reformist officials who were just hitting their stride in the late 1920s and early 1930s, and their counterparts in the military. Particularly after the invasion of Manchuria in 1931, the state and military as well as segments of academia and journalism were drawn to contemporary Italian, German, and Soviet models of industrial and economic organization. The South Manchurian Railway had long since employed thousands of researchers; at home the attempt to mold the economy for total war engaged the efforts of many more. Organizations such as the Shōwa Kenkyūkai (Shōwa Research Association) and Naikaku Kikakuin (Cabinet Planning Board) recruited both academic and government economists, including luminaries-to-be such as Arisawa Hiromi. For such scholars, the disappearance of alternative foci for their expertise and direct pressure to contribute to Japan's war effort made it extremely difficult to refuse to serve.

The intolerable strain placed on resources by spiraling military demand meant that many of these wartime economic plans came to nothing. But their failure must not be allowed to obscure the patterns of thinking that drove the planners in their efforts. The rhetoric and substance of their critique of capitalism in its liberal phase were drawn in large part (or perhaps cannibalized) from Marxism, while the determinants of their politics were the more Listian demands of national and bloc self-sufficiency. For this latter reason, at the intellectual level class tended to be transmuted into *Volk (minzoku)* as the favored agent of historical change; at the political level, the Marxist could lie down with the fascist. The career of the philosopher and social theorist Miki Kiyoshi (1897–1945), an appealing thinker of truly catholic sensibilities and talents, stands as a poignant example. Poignant, first, because Miki, after a philosophical apprenticeship in Weimar Germany, took Marxism seriously as one—crucial—moment in what he hoped would be a morally adequate philosophy of praxis that also incorporated existentialist and humanist elements. Again, his case is poignant because, in his writings on social science, Miki had gone beyond the discussion of methodology and the structure of social scientific knowledge to raise directly the issues of ideology and the sociology of knowledge.[36] And it was poignant, finally, because despite his revulsion at the "chauvinism and political servility" of then-contemporary academic thought, Miki was drawn by the demands of his own elevation of praxis into a world of compromised and degraded intellects. As a sign of that degradation, we may consider the scarcely credible claims made in his *Shin Nihon no shisō genri* (Principles of thought for a new Japan, 1939) and similarly inspired journalism. The world-historical role of Japan, Miki held, was, "speaking temporally, to solve the problem of capitalism; and spatially to bring about the unity [via the displacement of Western imperialism] of East Asia." This unity was to be based on the preexisting and shared "Asian humanism," which was *gemeinschaftlich* and valued the "relational," in contrast to the *gesellschaftlich* and individualistic humanism of the West. "The fact that the East Asian community is formed under the leadership of Japan is not due to Japan's national *[minzokuteki]* egoism, but is rather based on Japan's moral mission in the face of the present [China] Incident; it is the awakening to such a mission that is vital." By the early 1940s, Miki had disavowed this mission; true to his own philosophy of praxis, he sheltered a Communist friend who had escaped police custody, was arrested, and died under miserable conditions just days before occupation authorities ordered the release of all political prisoners of the former regime.[37] This is not to dismiss the kernel of genuine hope among Asians of Miki's era that the problem of capitalism could be solved and the region rid of imperialism. It is only to point out the grotesque disparity between ends (liberation) and means (conquest) that vitiated the project from the start.[38]

Interestingly, the defeat of the Axis in 1945 seems to have done little or nothing in Japan to discredit ideas of central planning, or at least of central coordination, as it had in Germany. This was not the lesson of the war. Imperial Japan, after all, was laid waste and occupied by a United States that must have appeared not as the symbol of individualism and the market, but of successful planning and national mobilization. The New Deal left traces all over occupied Japan. For its part, the Soviet Union had also emerged from the war as a superpower, and not yet as the embodiment of stultifying bureaucratism and brutal political formalism. Socialism was no "dead dog" in 1945. The point for the present is that, while the importance in Japan of technical expertise and planning as a form of engaged social science was enhanced by the new dispensation, it was already well established. No small role in this regard was played by academic experts, who, precisely because they were comparatively small fry, were able to step directly from wartime work into significant planning roles immediately after Japan's defeat in 1945 without fear of being purged. Arisawa Hiromi (a self-described "non-Communist Marxist") provides a singular case in point; his work on planned economy, particularly the notion of priority production, combined elements of Rōnō-ha Marxism with the German theory of total war into a model of state capitalism that was widely influential after 1945.[39] This intersection of bureaucratic and radical thought in Japanese social science was both representative and momentous: it marked the formation of a technical intelligentsia whose expertise in economic policy and planning was mobilized, without interruption, in the pursuit of recovery and growth after 1945.

MOMENT FOUR: MODERNISM AND MODERNIZATION

In late 1948, Yanaihara Tadao (1893–1961), widely viewed as Japan's foremost expert on colonial policy, was named chair of the economics department of Tokyo University (the "Imperial" had been dropped a year earlier). A follower of the "Non-Church" Christianity of Uchimura Kanzō, and bitter critic of Japan's China policy, Yanaihara had been driven from his teaching post (in the same department) in December 1937. As early as the 1920s, and consistently thereafter, he had attacked Japan's assimilationist colonial policies as counterproductive and repressive of legitimate aspirations for national self-determination. Yanaihara called instead for home rule in Taiwan and (with particular passion) in Korea, with the eventual goal of independence following a period of trusteeship and guidance. This was a position based not only on his biblical conceptions of justice, but on prodigious and highly regarded empirical studies of Korea, Manchuria, Taiwan, and the Pacific Mandate Islands.[40] In the late imperial context, Yanaihara's views went far beyond those of any other liberal expert on the colonies, including his predecessor Nitobe Inazō (1862–1933), whose moderate humanitarianism uneasily coexisted with his nationalism. Nitobe's lifelong aspiration to serve as a "bridge across the Pacific" had been destroyed with Japan's invasion of Manchuria; as a former deputy speaker of the League of Nations, Nitobe felt bound to try to mitigate the damage, but his credibility was irreparably compromised. Yanaihara, despite his greater expertise, was certainly marginalized—or marginalized himself. He had spent the war years evangelizing, preaching, writing (and publishing) against war and "idolatry"—the cult of the *kokutai*—the two, he insisted, were intimately connected. Yanaihara's household was also the base for his community of followers, a group sometimes described as having preserved the "civil society" ideal through its small-scale resistance. Yet for Yanaihara such preservation seemed to require that he exercise religious authority as a patriarch; that *Gesellschaft* be vouchsafed by *Gemeinschaft*. Returning to the university only under the condition that his academic duties not impede his religious work, Yanaihara was the first director of the newly founded Institute of Social Science; as noted he became chair of economics in 1948, and he was twice named to the presidency of the university. As a Christian and social scientist, then, Yanaihara was widely regarded as a powerful symbol of the "new Japan."[41]

Again in 1948, reflecting on Japan's role as a regional imperialist, Yanaihara identified ethnocentrism as the chief, indeed fatal, flaw of Japan's colonial policy:

Assimilationism *[dōkashugi]* in Japanese colonial policy has a different intellectual basis from that practiced by France. The latter was underlain by the universal and humanistic idea of democracy, with its associated ideas of natural rights and the equality of all. For this reason, the harm that came from the excesses of that policy was a result of the premature granting to native populations with a low level of development, of freedom they did not understand, and liberation they did not seek. Japanese assimilationism, by contrast, was an ethnic nationalism centered on the imperial house; here the excesses resulted in the enforcement of unity, and the repression of national awareness by means of absolutist power. I do not believe that Japanese colonial rule was pernicious in every respect. Economic development and the spread of elementary education, at least, brought lasting benefit to colonial society. With the new circumstances in which Japan's former colonies now find themselves, the effects of Japanese control are being argued and criticized. At least as far as Japan's policy of ideological assimilation is concerned, certainly no one among the former colonial peoples can call this to mind with favorable feelings. Regrettably, Japan's policy of assimilation lacked the foundation of a humanistic and universal idea worthy of the name.[42]

Japan's colonialism, then, was incapable of self-transcendence, and was fated to collapse upon Japan's defeat. No one among the former colonies would wish to be associated with Japan in any way. Instead, Yanaihara observes, it was now Japan's turn to be "administered" by a colonial power: the United States, which would apply to Japan the same principles of "autonomy" *(jishushugi)* and "assimilationism"—that is, "democratization"—hitherto practiced in the Philippines. He then draws an arresting analogy between areas formerly subject to Japanese rule and American-occupied Japan:

> A social experiment similar to that attempted by Japan in Korea, Taiwan, and Manchuria—that is, an experiment at rule of one ethnic nationality by another *[iminzoku tōchi no minzokuteki jikken]*—is now underway. But this time it is we ourselves who have been placed on the laboratory table.[43]

For Yanaihara, being "placed on the laboratory table" by the United States alone was an unexpectedly merciful destiny for Japan, which, unlike Germany, had been spared dismemberment. But one wonders what Korea, Taiwan, and Manchuria had done to deserve the "social experiment" so recently carried out on the "body" of their respective peoples. The fact that Yanaihara does not address this question, but instead makes the Japan-Korea analogy unself-consciously, is at the heart of the problem: the symptomatic coexistence of imperial and critical consciousness in Japanese social science is demonstrated with utter clarity. Yanaihara felt that Japanese colonialism was "unscientific." Despite advances in methodology, colonial policy was circumscribed by "irrational" political and ideological forces (those of emperorism and ethnic chauvinism) that vitiated much of the potential benefit that might have derived from a more thoroughgoing attempt at scientific application.

One could argue that Yanaihara's critique of colonialism was itself far from thoroughgoing. Today, the argument against his position (to say nothing of more open apologies for colonialism) would simply assert that the more scientific, the more inhumane and irrational colonialism is. That is, the attack would focus on the supposed delusion of scientism. But this is to miss the point. While Yanaihara did indeed attack ethnic chauvinism, he did not abandon his belief that Japan ought to exercise scientifically grounded moral leadership in Asia; the "ethnic nation" continued to frame his perspective. As long as this was the case, he would be capable of equating the position of Japan's former colonies to that of Japan vis-à-vis the United States after 1945. Even his most ardent admirers recognize that Yanaihara "lacked a profound understanding of Korean nationalism."[44]

In the end, Yanaihara was not concerned so much with science in the sense of facticity and objectivity, as with the irrational moral and political context within which scientific operations were carried out. His charge that Japanese colonial policy was "unscientific" involves elision, displacement, and ellipsis. By "unscientific," he meant "immoral." A more thoroughly critical view might have led him to understand that his vision of a Japan made moral by its abasement before a "colonial power" in fact obscured a persistent, if beneficent, imperial consciousness, at the unyielding core of which subsisted an idealist and critical nationalism. The best, perhaps, of imperial Japan's social science was encapsulated in Yanaihara's work; it certainly brought him honor following Japan's defeat. We must wonder, however, not whether Yanaihara deserved that honor, but whether in honoring him, the world of Japanese social science was to that extent also permitting itself to avert its eyes from the deeper cause of the nation's own tragedy: that the "nation" had triumphed over all other solidarities. In the wake of defeat, how would Japanese social scientists assess their own work? And how would they define their task in the postwar era?

In considering the major social science issues occasioned by the postwar settlement, we may begin where we left off: with the concern, exemplified by Yanaihara Tadao, that Japan's people be brought together in a state whose rule was both formally and substantively a break with a stained past. Yanaihara saw that form and substance in democracy; as he envisioned it for Japan, it would be at once more moral and more scientific in its operation than the ancien régime. But how to uproot that regime, which had driven Japan's people to such atrocities and to such prodigies of self-sacrifice?

Social science in the early postwar decades may be equated with what is known as modernism (kindaishugi), and with an assault on Japan's "negative distinctiveness" as a state and society. Its temporal starting point was defeat and occupation, its critical genesis a drive to expose the causes of Japan's disaster. The war and the process leading to it betokened a historical pathology: the tennōsei, Japan's imperial system, was held to be inimical to a rationally organized national life and had made Japan unable to coexist with its neighbors in the world. Along with Marxism and eventually superseding it, modernism pursued the completion of the distorted and failed first phase of Japan's modernization. Not directly political, modernism animated a democratic "enlightenment" that, while it took certain cues from the rhetoric and policies of Japan's occupiers, had its roots in prewar Marxism, some aspects of liberalism (including Christian humanism), and in the experience of war itself. (The term "modernist" itself was coined by its Marxist critics, but was widely used.) This enlightenment took both ideological and practical forms, and covered the better part of the decade and a half between 1945 and 1960. As part of this effort, the task of social science as a whole was for the first time seen as the critique of the past, and of the present to the extent that it perpetuated that past.[45] Its leitmotiv was a bitter denunciation of the "failure" of prewar social science to provide objective knowledge sufficient to prevent the debacle of war: indeed the launching of the war itself was taken as proof of the deficit in reason that afflicted Japan's state and society.[46]

To be sure, the characteristic emphasis on Japan's negative distinctiveness was challenged by prewar figures such as Yanagita and Watsuji Tetsurō. Responding to, and perhaps alarmed by, the enormous readership gained by the translation (in 1948) of Ruth Benedict's *The Chrysanthemum and the Sword* (1946), they rightly criticized its disregard of internal differentiation in Japanese society and its breathtaking generalizations. Though hailed by its publisher as "the book that saved the emperor system," Yanagita and Watsuji seem to have treated Benedict's text as a set of negative distortions to be corrected. Younger scholars, such as the Cornell-trained social psychologist Minami Hiroshi, were more willing to engage its arguments. Minami's *Nihonjin no shinri* (The psychology of the Japanese) appeared in 1953. Although it criticized Benedict's "theory-driven" approach and skewed data, it also deepens, historicizes, and in some way authenticates Benedict's famous dicta concerning Japanese groupism and the country's "culture of shame."[47]

The presence of even ambivalent affirmations of the culture (or psychology) of "the Japanese" should not obscure the larger and more salient feature of the first postwar decades. The assault on negative distinctiveness was itself a means to a positive end: the exploration and promotion, in the Japanese context, of new human possibilities that the bitter experience of repression, war, defeat, and occupation had revealed.

To open up these possibilities and translate them to a needy populace was indeed an elitist project: Japan's people were now, finally, to be made fully modern.[48]

Modernist writings of the immediate postwar period, therefore, tended necessarily to portray the war as an episode of atavistic irrationality. As noted, however, the institutional usefulness of wartime economic mobilization and various forms of rationalization, along with the indisputable trend toward social leveling, came at length to be acknowledged as elements in shaping the postwar economic regime. The importance of planning and of engaged social science was only enhanced by the new dispensation, not least owing to the presence of New Deal "cadres" in the early phase of the occupation. The issue now, many social scientists thought (or dreamed), was to determine whether a democratic Japan was to follow a capitalist or socialist path. Whichever it was to be (as the government itself recognized), the basic work of data collection and problem definition would require the efforts of scores of economists—Marxians newly released from prison or permitted to return to academic positions, Keynesian generalists (such as Nakayama Ichirō), and policy specialists (Ōkōchi Kazuo on labor; Tōhata Seiichi on agriculture) who had chafed under wartime irrationalities, biding their time.[49]

Ultimately, there was to be no departure from the capitalist path. But the strong presence of Marxian economists in government was a striking feature of the early postwar decades, as was the extensive influence of Marxian approaches among academic economists. Though eventually overshadowed by their Americanized confrères, this "economic left"—figures such as Arisawa Hiromi and Tsuru Shigeto—made a crucial contribution to what has been termed the "soft infrastructure" or "invisible base" of postwar modernization.[50]

Yet modernism was not about effectiveness per se; nor did "postwar" merely denote straitened material conditions requiring sharpened expertise. At its heart lay the perception of, and desire to reinforce and "vivify," the discontinuity that marked Japan's recent past: at its most influential, modernism was as much a moral as a scientific orientation. Modernists were driven by a degree of collective guilt, expressed not so much toward the victims of Japan's aggression in Asia as, more abstractly, toward history itself. With this was combined a sense of victimhood as members of a generation profligately wasted by the state. The intense self-concern of this "community of contrition" draws criticism today, as does the fact that modernism very quickly lost sight of the external empire in its urgency to uproot the pathologies of the vanquished regime. But just this moral seriousness gave modernism its long staying power in its collaborative competition with Marxism.[51]

What sort of social science was modernism? We can draw a few indications from the work of Maruyama Masao (1914–1996) and Ōtsuka Hisao (1907–1996). Maruyama was the foremost historian of Japanese political thought and a practicing political scientist.[52] Ōtsuka was an economic historian of Europe and later concerned with what is now termed the "North-South" disparity. As Maruyama wrote in 1947, the task now is "to accomplish what the Meiji Restoration was unable to carry through: that of completing the democratic revolution," and "to confront the problem of human freedom itself." The bearer of freedom, however, is no longer the "citizen" of classical liberalism, "but rather . . . the broad working masses with workers and farmers at the core." Moreover, the crucial issue is not the "sensual liberation of the masses, but rather how and how thoroughly the masses are to acquire a new normative consciousness."[53]

Here we can see the heavy debt to Marxism as well as the Kantian— or neo-Kantian and Weberian—overlay that tied the modernists to the intellectual culture of the interwar era. In Maruyama, whose thought includes strong nominalist and social contractarian elements as well, modernism amounted to a drive to create a critical mass citizenry capable of resisting authority: the *Homo democraticus*. In Ōtsuka, who sought to combine Marx and Weber with textual fidelity to both, the holy grail was an ethical producer, a man of conscience working among social equals; postwar Japan, Ōtsuka argued, could no longer subsist on feudal "fairness," but had to strive for modern "equality." An interesting recent criticism of Ōtsuka finds that he is too optimistic, not Nietzschean enough; too committed a believer in the real possibility of reconstituting Japanese society along "ethically individualistic" lines to face Weber's "iron cage" prophecy head-on. Ōtsuka's ethics were insufficiently political—and drawn without acknowledgment from his wartime writings on productivity—and therefore too easily co-optable.[54]

It is one thing to find the sources of co-optation in the thought of an individual; strong modernists such as Maruyama and Ōtsuka will always have their partisans and detractors. However, unprecedented economic growth—along with the political defeat (in 1960) of activist academics seeking to end Japan's diplomatic and military subordination to the United States in favor of nonalignment—opened the way for the "structural" co-optation of modernism into the discourse of modernization *(kindaikaron)*, and for the transformation of *Homo democraticus* into *Homo economicus.* Although American pragmatism—and especially its behaviorist reduction—had begun to make its influence felt by the late 1940s, the real "Americanization" of professional social science took place after 1960, as in greater numbers Japanese scholars were able to undertake long-term study in American universities, and the ever-deepening trend toward specialization took hold.[55]

As a set of operating concepts, modernization congealed at this same juncture, following its energetic propagation in American scholarship and dissemination in "highbrow" Japanese periodicals such as *Shisō, Chūō kōron, Jiyū* and others. *Shisō,* for example, devoted an issue to the 1960 Hakone conference on modernization; and in a staged dialogue early in 1961 the economist Nakayama Ichirō and historian-diplomat Edwin Reischauer announced Japan's emergence as a model for noncommunist developing countries. Texts such as these pointed to a shift away from "national issue" politics focusing on "foreign relations, defense, and public order," and toward an emerging—and engineered— "national consensus for economic growth, doubling the national income and monthly pay" that "inaugurated the age of 'politics with economic technocrats in the lead.'"[56]

The modernization approach is now strongly associated with the rehabilitation of the Meiji and, eventually, Tokugawa eras as "forerunners" to Japan's startling run of sustained economic growth; "tradition," that is, was rediscovered as having contributed (via widespread literacy and rural commerce, for example) to the later success of industrialization. Yet Kawashima Takeyoshi (1909–1992), an eminent sociologist of law at Tokyo University and close collaborator of Ōtsuka Hisao, saw in modernization a tool for the analysis "not only of social change in the so-called 'East' and 'West,' but in the less developed countries and 'new states' as well." Indeed, he envisioned the "possibility in theoretical terms of being able to treat all these [cases] as a world-historical movement headed in the same direction via differing processes." Kawashima's hopes went beyond analytical results:

> To foresee in what direction the grand movement of contemporary world history is headed, and by what route; to search out the path by which to bring humanity true happiness more quickly—this is humanity's fervent desire and a task for social scientists of overriding importance. The approach discussed here may be seen as an effort in that direction.[57]

Kawashima himself retained much of the subjectivist agonism of early postwar modernism, seeing the task of social science as that of guiding the struggle to overcome traditional society and values via a revolutionary break—especially mental revolution. Its external referents were highly idealized representations of modernity abstracted from the history of revolutions in the West. But as the decade continued, modernization came to place preponderant value in the smoothest possible continuity from stage to stage in a continuous process of national historical development that could be captured in a set of quantifiable processes culminating in the maximization of gross national product (GNP). Modernism was self-consciously ideological, and saw "value freedom" in social science as something to be struggled for in the process of liberating present reality from the distortions of traditionalistic consciousness; modernization tended to assume that value freedom, or objectivity, was assured through the identification of measurable social or behavioral indices. Its key external referent was the contemporary United States, the epitome of normality, a society "always already" modern and ostensibly freed from "ideology," particularly the ideology of class and class conflict.[58]

In the modernization approach, Japan was more than a "case"; it was with respect to Japan that the term "modernization" itself first gained credibility in analyzing the process of historical change. Japan was an exemplar, identified as such by 1961, against which the mere cases—Turkey, Russia, Iran, Mexico, Korea, and in general the "developing societies" and "new states"—were to be measured. Convergence (guaranteed Americanization) was the promise held out to all "successful" modernizers; all differences of culture were in the end no more than matters of degree along a scale of functionality. But the question remained whether such convergence was in fact the ultimate desideratum in Japanese social science. Could an approach that assumed Japan's normality—rather than a condition of crisis born of perceived backwardness—ever become hegemonic in Japanese social science?

MOMENT FIVE: FROM SCIENCE TO CULTURE

Modernization à la japonaise was composed of two elements that began to separate out by the end of the 1960s: "growthism" and "culturalism." The former combined the mantra of quantification with the valorization of industrial production for its own sake, providing an enormous stimulus to applied neoclassical and Keynesian economics (known as *kindai keizaigaku*, or "modern economics") and econometrics, and beginning to undermine the commanding position of Marxian approaches. Statistical fetishism was inescapable.

Japan's national purpose was to produce; the political question was, For whom? More fundamentally, how had postwar growth occurred, and how could it be sustained? Government and academic economists focused their cyclical and macrostructural analyses on the possibly unique circumstances created by the combination of inherited dualism in industrial structure with the impact of so-called postwar characteristics—the need to reconstruct, the legacy of occupation reforms, and so on. But over time, the "micro" sphere, the role and habitus of firms, their ostensibly traditional modes of organization and interaction, and capacity to mobilize and motivate labor, came to be recognized as crucial, engaging the efforts of both Japanese and, in increasing numbers, American researchers.

Certainly the rehabilitation of tradition from early postwar condemnation injected a needed degree of concreteness into the definition of modern or civil society in Japan. American social scientists, both specialists and comparativists, were particularly impressed with the power of corporations to gear secondary and higher education to the production of modal employees, even when only a (large) minority could hope to gain "lifetime employment" in a high-prestige firm. Attention also turned to the larger economic role of corporate networks, with their interlocking capitals and their ongoing and intimate relations to the state. In place of a generalized (Western) notion of modern society that looked to independent nonstate entities—the realm of private citizens, religious and voluntary organizations, and so forth—operating on the basis of marketized relations of social "equals," modernization in Japan was seen to have maintained and promoted "neofeudalism" in human relations. "Culture," it turned out, was the key to growth, and culture meant not convergence, but profound and significant difference.

The zenith of growthism came with the national celebration of the Meiji Centenary and Expo '70. It might have seemed that growthism and culturalism would continue to work in tandem. But the Vietnam War issued a severe check to illusions of American omnipotence, including among the casualties the notion of modernization as a measurable (and guidable) process. Japan's government and corporations, as profiteers on that conflict, were also discredited. Domestically, the costs of growthism were coming due, in the form of staggering environmental pollution, urban hypercongestion, and the sense that in Japan, corporate interest had come to justify unlimited demands for labor. Neither individual nor community life seemed to have any inherent importance.

This situation ought to have represented a golden opportunity for

Marxism.[59] To a degree this was true: In the late 1960s, Uchida Yoshi-hiko (1913–1989) and Hirata Kiyoaki (1922–1995) formulated critiques both of Japanese capitalism and Soviet-style socialism on the basis of their shared development as regimes in which the "rights of the state" predominated over those of society or individuals. Uchida had argued that:

> Contemporary Japanese capitalism has developed . . . through the association of the supermodern with the premodern, and not with the modern or civil. It is precisely the survival of premodernity itself that has permitted such a rapid development of supermodernity in Japan. From which one may conclude, paradoxical though it may seem, that in Japan capitalism has developed thanks to the weakness of civil society.[60]

For his part, Hirata took up the task (long delayed in Japanese Marxist circles, but provoked finally by the Sino-Soviet split and the Russian invasion of Czechoslovakia) of critically examining "actually existing socialism" from the point of view of Marx's own texts. Focusing on Marx's assertion that the "negation" of capitalist private property re-establishes "individual property on the basis of . . . cooperation and the possession in common . . . of the means of production produced by labor itself," Hirata argued that socialism meant nothing less than the reestablishment of individual property.[61] Together, Uchida and Hirata undertook to reconceptualize the notion of civil society, detaching it from capitalism and from the notion of private property. By restoring the unity between work and property, Marxists of the "civil society" school sought to provide the theoretical—and ethical—basis for an independent socialism.[62]

Marxism, furthermore, was institutionalized as a requirement, alongside modern economics, in many Japanese university departments. The most influential school was that associated with Uno Kōzō, whose system of political economy, along with Maruyama's political science and Ōtsuka's historical economics, has been described as one of the three main currents of postwar Japanese social science.[63] Beginning in the late 1930s, Uno had pursued a logical—Hegelian—reconstruction of Capital, developing an original framework of "basic principles" of political economy, along with a three-stage historical model of capitalist development that culminated in "analysis of current conditions." Marked by its rigorous separation of economic science from ideological activity and portrayal of capital as a "structure" of all-generative power, the Uno school represented the apotheosis of Marxism as an "objective" science of political economy. Although Uno's motivation in separating science from ideology stemmed from his revulsion against Stalinist politicization, the pitfall of his system was that if Marxism is construed as only a science, it is easily superseded by a more "effective" one.

What happened at the beginning of the 1970s, however, was more than a search for better science. As empirical research was disparaged either as an ideology of expertise for hire (not "value-free" but "value-less," its critics charged), or as quietistic, a shift in orientation from quantity to quality, from "science" to "culture," extended through the social sciences. Japanese writings on the constitution of society—in the 1970s by Nakane Chie, or a decade later by Murakami Yasusuke (1931– 1993)—took on a deeper and deeper hue of what may be termed a "supermodern" perspective: the view that it was precisely the continuity of "premodern" organizational patterns and ways of thinking that had made possible Japan's unprecedented economic growth. For these analysts, the vitality of Japanese social organizations sprang from their cultural underpinnings: rationalized dependency, corporate personalism, and collective instrumental rationality.[64] In Kōza-ha Marxism and postwar modernism, culture—and community—stood for "backwardness," a fetter on rationality. Now, no longer requiring the mediation or checking mechanism of noncorporate civil society, or the promise of convergence with other advanced industrial societies, Japan's culture defined the vanguard, not of capitalism, which along with democracy was hardly mentioned, but of a new, information- and relationally oriented "system." Japan had come to embody a future that was not only post-Marxist and postsocialist, but also postindividualist and postcapitalist as well.

Yet other visions of culture and community have also been at work in the social sciences. In the 1970s, critical economics migrated from systematic Marxism to the ad hoc milieu of the local residents' and antipollution movements. The target, as attacked in the work of academic economists including Tsuru Shigeto, Miyamoto Ken'ichi and Uzawa Hirofumi, was less capitalism than the concrete pathologies of growthism itself: the penchant for massive building projects, spiraling land values, hurried and unsound engineering, environmental and social destructiveness.[65] Implicitly or explicitly, such work argued that the test of social science lay not its contribution to growth, but in the intellectual resources it could provide a people, in their localities and as a national community, to weather the inevitable cycles of growth and decline in an advanced economy fatefully intertwined with the world.

In the long run, culturalism may not survive the decline of growthism.

The end of the Cold War coincided with the bursting of the economic "bubble," leading to the most serious downturn in a half-century. Amid external pressures for liberalization, deep political corruption, and signs of decay in the corporate personalism that has marked the upper tier of the industrial economy, the hegemony of culturalism has grown tattered. The implications for social science are ambiguous. Striking work by sociologists of religion (spurred by social traumas such as the Aum Shinrikyō incident and Hanshin earthquake), new modes of historical inquiry into the Tokugawa past, and local and minority ethnographies all suggest underlying vitality. And a provocative theoretical breakout seems underway in the analyses by Yamanouchi Yasushi, among others, of the wartime origins of contemporary Japan's "system society" that goes beyond both older notions of historical stages and cultural perennialism.[66] On the other hand, Japanese social science has no strong, urgent focus: no fictive national community, no revolutionary quest, no modern—democratic—personality in need of shaping, no growth-above-all. The Japan-West framework seems to have eroded, but it is not clear that a new social science set on a Japan-Asia axis is a realistic possibility. The history of relations in the region would seem to militate against it, to say nothing of the deepening general uncertainties of the fin de siècle. The current situation is perhaps best characterized as a plurality—though not a pluralism—of uncertain significance.

CHAPTER 3

Doubly Cruel

*Marxism and the Presence of the Past
in Japanese Capitalism*

This chapter and the two that follow pose the question: When Japanese Marxists looked at Japanese capitalism, what did they see, and how did they see it? What was the object of their gaze, and how—by what method—was that gaze itself formed?

I begin with the observation that Japan has developed a tradition of noncapitalist capitalism, a capitalism in which non-, or precapitalist values and practices are held to remain salient, indeed decisive in shaping institutional as well as personal behavior in the economic sphere. This much, of course, has been said for decades by its critics and apologists both, almost to the point of *tedium ideologicum*. Specifically, Japanese Marxists, especially those of the Comintern-associated Kōza-ha, or Lectures Faction, played a crucial role in defining the contours of a "Japanese-type" capitalism. While accepting the well-established critique of capitalism that arraigned it for justifying immorality and exploitation in the name of individual gain, they went beyond this critique to develop a theoretical analysis of Japan's "version." The exploitative mechanisms of Japanese capitalism, they insisted, combined those of the market with a persistent "semifeudalism" in the social relations of production; these relations formed the foundation of Japanese-type capitalism. This framework of uneven development and "backwardness" has been extremely tenacious in Japanese social science.

Despite these analytical achievements, the Kōza-ha perspective, as is often pointed out, ignored issues of ideology and therefore failed to grasp the real dynamic of Japanese capitalism, indeed of Japan's modernization as a whole. This lay in the invented—and strategic—character of the process through which "tradition," or the past, entered the present: via the state's systematic attempt to mobilize it in its "virtual" war for survival as an imperial power. Kōza-ha Marxism revealed the structural presence of the past, but only at the cost of effacing both past-consciousness and state-consciousness, the ideological medium through which that structural presence took on its meaning. Yet it may well be wondered whether a model of capitalism without ideology can grasp capitalism at all.

THE PRESENCE OF THE PAST IN JAPANESE CAPITALISM

At the risk of perpetuating the *tedium ideologicum* mentioned above, let me fill out briefly the notion of noncapitalist capitalism as it was first developed in the 1890s, and as it stands today. In a sense, of course, all capitalism is self-denying at some level: the invisible hand both explains the social productiveness of self-interest and provides a secular theodicy of exploitation. The capitalist unconscious is everywhere a condition of the system's success, so that the invisibility of the system, rather than being a problem, is in fact a sign of ideological normalcy. The self-image of original capitalism was that of a force akin to "the Deity working its will to direct human action into socially beneficial paths that men could not discover for themselves."[1] In Japan, the disinclination to speak of capitalism as a defining element in national identity has a specific valence. There, the invisible hand seems to cut little or no moral ice, either at the individual or collective level. To be sure, some studies of Tokugawa economy and society hint at notions of the social benefits of individual (family) "selfishness," or the equation by merchant financiers of virtue with rationally calculated profit. But it seems doubtful that these ideas ever met unqualified social acceptance, before or after 1868.[2] Rather, capitalist ideology has been understood in Japan as a license for the assertion of self-interest; self-interest has in turn been regarded as the foundation of Western civil society—"a system of desires," as Hegel put it. The ideological "operating system," so to speak, of Japanese capitalism, is different: it denies the productivity of self-interest or the necessity of any link between "civil society" and capitalism. To recall the observation of Yamada Toshio: "Paradoxical though it may seem . . . in Japan capitalism has developed thanks to the weakness of civil society."[3]

In place of the social fractiousness and calculated interpersonal coldness of civil society, and therefore of ideological appeals to the invisible hand, explanations of Japan's noncapitalist capitalism look to a collectivist dynamism that derives from Tokugawa prehistory. It is associated particularly with the *ie*, or household, and village, and with familial corporatism in agricultural, artisanal and commercial enterprises that is the supposed origin—along with *bushidō* redux—of today's corporate ethos of group competitiveness, individual self-sacrifice, and loyalty to firm. Not surprisingly, "many Japanese are not aware of the fact that Japan is a capitalist country." As long as capitalism is associated with the selfishly motivated pursuit of profit, and civil society regarded as a system committed to underwriting such selfishness, How, it would be asked, could Japan possibly be capitalist?[4] Indeed, to discuss capitalism hinted (and continues to hint) at disapproval; capitalism should be invisible. Growth, on the other hand, was unambiguously good.

If we may take the issue of capitalism beyond the current habitus of Japanese firms and project it along a historical plane at the national level, what we see is not "the business of Japan is business," but "the business of business is Japan," a Listian notion of economy as a national project, one aspect of which was the creation of economic instruments that operate in a "capitalist" mode.[5] In Japan's modern history, this project is most closely associated with the Meiji-era slogan of "rich country, strong army" *(fukoku kyōhei)*, albeit with a later admixture of *Sozialpolitik*.

Slogan, yes, but also a project realized. In terms of the development of productive forces that became the (self-imposed) yardstick for measuring progress along the road to Western-style modernity, Japan on the eve of the Meiji Restoration was a woefully backward place. This backwardness, and the military and economic vulnerability to the Great Powers that came with it, was a matter of common-sense observation. It was also intellectually and psychologically oppressive—somehow it had to be overcome. Here was a political and values problem of the first order. Capitalism as a system, however, was never seen as a goal to be attained, nor was it a prescription ever offered as such by the intellectual agents of the West to Japan. Even if it had been, could the potent but centrifugally tending values of the invisible hand be trusted to direct popular energies to the manifestly political goals of winning Western "respect" and building a strong and independent state? A liberal such as Fukuzawa Yukichi might say yes; but his high profile notwithstanding, the goals of industry and empire were understood to require the state to weld Japan's best and brightest into a self-described moral force. By the turn of the twentieth century, this most visible hand had done its work. Japan could boast of a dedicated bureaucracy with a fearsome esprit de corps, emergent heavy industry, and an empire.

"Overcoming backwardness," then, was the national project of Japan, enunciated in the Charter Oath, captured in the *fukoku kyōhei* imperative, and realized, to the amazement and discomfort of the West, by late Meiji. Accompanying these organizational triumphs, and integral to them, was the "neotraditional" turn of that era. Following the Westernizing caesura of "Civilization and Enlightenment," the past returned, both to validate the present—modernity placed under the discipline of tradition—and to constrain the future. The timing of this return can hardly have been fortuitous. The institutional completion of the modern order had generated real social traumas, and real anxieties, in Japan. For elites, as for masses, appeal to a rearticulated tradition (albeit differently defined) was one response to the modern (dis)order. For present purposes, the version advanced in 1909 by Itō Hirobumi is illuminating, in the sense that he points both to the hoped-for stabilizing effects, and to the political risks, of the traditionalizing strategy.

Itō begins with a critical evocation of the "feudal legacy" of Tokugawa. Prior, perhaps, even to feudalism, Japan was "homogeneous in race, language, religion, and sentiments"; and then, long seclusion and "the centuries-long traditions and inertia of the feudal system" did their work. Under the Tokugawa, "the family and quasi-family ties permeated and formed the essence of every social organization . . . with such moral and religious tenets as laid *undue stress* on duties of fraternal aid and mutual succor." We had, Itō declares, "unconsciously become a vast village community where cold intellect and calculation of public events were always restrained and even often hindered by warm emotions between man and man." This legacy, for Itō, brought with it both strengths and dangers. In a village community, he observes, "feelings and emotions hold a higher place than intellect, free discussion is apt to be smothered," and the "attainment and transference of power" tends to become "a family question of a powerful oligarchy." His prescription: Japan's elite should strive, not to eliminate completely, but to manipulate, feudal tendencies. On the one hand, he recognizes, "Passions and emotions have to be stopped for the sake of cool calculations of national welfare, and even the best of friends have often to be sacrificed if the best abilities and highest intellects are to guide the helm." On the other, if handled correctly, the feudal legacy may represent an enormous, unrepeatable historical opportunity. "In industry," Itō notes, "in spite of the recent enormous development of manufactures in our country, our laborers have *not yet* degenerated into spiritless machines and toiling beasts. There *still survives* the bond of patron and *protégé* between them and the capitalist employers. It is this moral and emotional factor which will, in the future, form a healthy barrier against the threatening advance of socialistic ideas."[6]

Successful because village-type social hierarchy could be brought to bear in effecting labor discipline and constraining political conflict between tenants, smallholders, and workers on the one hand and large landlords and employers on the other, the reliance on warm manners and beautiful customs *(junpū bizoku)*, in fact, constituted a wager on backwardness and its sustaining values. The wager held that rapid development of heavy industry, with its immense requirements of capital and labor, could be achieved initially on the basis of surpluses extracted from agriculture and rural-based industry and obedient workers. The same extractive process would also support the establishment of the empire, which, along with heavy industry itself, would eventually begin, at least psychologically, to repay the effort. In this way, the security, independence, and historical standing of Japan and the Japanese would be assured.

Such, at least, was the wager. But did it pay off? Was the traditionalizing strategy successful? The historiography of the abolition of backwardness—of Japan's capitalist development—is divided on this point. Itō's qualified optimism was negated by the Kōza-ha assault on backwardness, which in turn defined a historiographical tradition of its own that has extended far beyond Marxist circles. From this point of view, the Meiji achievement of *fukoku kyōhei,* far from overcoming backwardness, actually ramified it. Evoking the so-called three differences—between city and country, industry and agriculture, brain work and manual work—that were the target of rage in China's Cultural Revolution, the economist Michio Morishima observes: "The policies adopted by the Japanese government after the Meiji Revolution . . . [were] pushed ahead so as to make ever greater the . . . 'three differences.' "[7] That is, decades-long landlord dominance, smallholder weakness, and widespread—if not universal—tenant penury made for debilitating inefficiency and class resentment, but they were necessary elements of a Japanese-type capitalism that used backwardness in one area to overcome it in another. Thomas C. Smith saw things similarly a generation ago: "The peasant had to be relentlessly exploited for the modernization of the nonagricultural sector of the economy. Since this condemned the peasant to poverty and backwardness, it did much to produce the profound gulf between urban and rural worlds that is so obvious and characteristic a feature of modern Japan."[8] It is beyond my purpose here to discuss how, when, and to what extent this gulf was redressed.[9] But I would emphasize, first, that the wager on backwardness was made, and second, that the relation between agriculture and modern industry, and between industrial strata themselves, implied in that wager did largely define Japan's particularistic mode of development, perhaps through the 1960s.

I do not mean to suggest that liberalism—both economic and political—played no significant role in the development of Japanese capitalism. Of course it did. But it did so, over the long run, as an adjunct to a particularist ideology in which capitalism served as an invisible means to the end of overcoming the country's backwardness. No one saw it, in part because it was morally dubious, if not ugly. And in part because appeals to the invisible hand were difficult or impossible to disengage from liberal political notions that did not sit well with Meiji's oligarchic elites. Nevertheless, to some degree all Japanese experienced the effects of capitalism. Some were thrilled by it, seeing in its ceaseless activity part of a "struggle for existence"—national existence—that was thought desirable to wage.[10] Others, such as the youthful Kawakami Hajime, saw it as a moral disaster. But it took the combined effects of the Russian Revolution and the post–World War I bust to bring the Marxist advocates of "scientific socialism" to the forefront of social science and criticism: not until then did anyone theorize Japanese capitalism in its specificity.

Thus far I have spoken of a "commonsensical," pretheoretical, but in a political sense, highly charged project of overcoming backwardness. Marxists, whether of the "Japan-as-feudal" or "Japan-as-bourgeois" schools, took that project as a central object of their critique, but did not abandon the goal; they sought rather to revolutionize both the means of overcoming backwardness and the goal itself. And so to repeat the original question: When Japanese Marxists looked at Japan's capitalism, what did they see?

YAMADA MORITARŌ AND THE "ANALYSIS OF JAPANESE CAPITALISM"

Its militaristic, semifeudal character configured the prototype of Japanese capitalism, one formed by superimposing, on the "barbarous cruelty of . . . serfdom," the "civilized horrors of overwork."[11]

As a vehicle of inquiry into the question—What did they see?—I have chosen Yamada Moritarō's *Nihon shihonshugi bunseki* (Analysis of

Japanese capitalism, 1934). Widely regarded as the highest theoretical achievement of prewar Kōza-ha Marxism, Yamada's text was influential far beyond Marxist circles and remained a point of departure for discussions of Japanese capitalism well into the postwar period. Although it met with forceful criticisms from the moment of its first appearance, no other text in the history of Japanese social science (or Japanese capitalism) came as close as Yamada's to exposing the specificities of industrial capitalism in Japan in its prewar form, to defining Japanese capitalism as a "type among types," including British, French, German, Russian, and American variants. This typicality, as the citation from the *Analysis* given above suggests, has to do with the powerful presence of the past in shaping the social relations, and therefore (for a Marxist) the consciousness, of Japanese living under this particular regime of capital. Whether despite or because of its method of analysis and theoretical point of departure—an issue addressed in the final section of this chapter— Yamada's case for the past-in-the-present as the salient feature of Japanese capitalism was not successfully refuted on theoretical or empirical grounds by Marxist critics.[12]

It was refuted, as far as its prognostications are concerned, by developments within capitalism itself. Contrary to Yamada's expectations, Japanese capitalism survived the devastation of the country's agrarian (textile)-based export sector after 1929. Against a backdrop of stepped-up state planning, a campaign of light industrial exports provided capital for intensified heavy industrialization, which was in turn spurred on by and channeled into military expenditure and continental expansion. Clearly Yamada had missed something; he makes no mention of these forces, already at work in the industrial economy, and this not so much by oversight as by systematic exclusion from analysis. Instead he continued to emphasize, correctly enough, the enormous burden of agrarian tenancy and, implicitly, the gap between the industrial strata that made up Japan's "dual structure." The specificity and ineradicable weakness of Japanese capitalism lay, for Yamada, in the indispensability of semifeudal social relations to its entire process of development, and their depressing, distortive effects on that development. Yamada was concerned, first and last, with inherited backwardness. The presence of the past, as embodied in specific social relations and institutions, was his problem.

Along with Hirano Yoshitarō's *Nihon shihonshugi shakai no kikō* (The system of capitalist society in Japan, 1934), Yamada's *Analysis* is generally recognized as the foremost product of its enunciative moment: the debate among Japanese Marxists, beginning in the late

1920s, over the mode of capitalist development in Japan. As is well known, the controversies between the Comintern-associated Kōza-ha (Lectures Faction) and dissident Rōnō-ha (Worker-Farmer Faction) developed respectively along particularist/universalist lines. Adherents of the Kōza-ha focused their analyses on the entrenched and powerful feudal forces that controlled the absolutist imperial state. Japanese capitalism was "special," a kind of hybrid; bourgeois political institutions were immature or malformed, and a retrograde consciousness persisted among the peasantry. There was backwardness everywhere. The political task at hand, therefore, was to complete the democratic revolution as the necessary first step in a two-stage drive toward socialism. The Rōnō-ha, in dissent, argued that with the Meiji Restoration, Japan had achieved its bourgeois revolution. The task of the present, therefore, lay in making the single-stage leap to socialism; vestiges of feudalism were incidental and would be swept away as a matter of course. Rōnō-ha analyses tended to be economistic in character, and though lacking a cultural theory per se, tended generally to stress the universal character of Japan as one of a number of imperialist finance capitalisms; domestically Japan was becoming a commoditized bourgeois society.

Yamada's perspective, as should already be clear, was unambiguously particularist. What distinguished his approach from more narrative-centered work, by Noro Eitarō or Hattori Shisō for example, was its analysis of Japan's capitalist development within an explicit and rigorously elaborated framework of Marxian economic theory. Yamada not only adopted a broad materialist narrative, but abstracted it, raised (or reduced) it to a mechanistic, equilibrium-oriented analysis of components and functions within a type. But it is clear that as with Noro, the perspective of backwardness and its abolition was "ground into the lenses" with which Yamada looked at Japan.[13]

Yamada carried out this task under highly unfavorable conditions that profoundly colored his perspective. Japan was in the middle of the Great Depression; the specter of class conflict had raised elite fears of a bolshevizing revolution promoted by the external agency of the Soviet Union and Comintern. To the considerable extent that Comintern theses set the keynote for Japanese Marxist attempts to explicate the structure and tendencies of capitalism, Yamada was engaged in highly political work. This would have made his task difficult enough had those theses been self-consistent. But they were not. Comintern policy toward Japan was tied to the vagaries of its China strategy—not an area of notable success.

The Theses of 1927 and 1932 resemble each other more than they do the Draft Political Theses of 1931; their existence at all is hardly comprehensible without consideration of the revolutionary situation in China, particularly the shifts from the rural-oriented efforts of the Autumn Harvest and other uprisings of 1927–29 to the attempt at urban insurrection under the Li Lisan line, then back to a rural-centered approach after 1931. The Comintern's Japan policy replicated these shifts in miniature. Common to them both is the contradiction between the inviolable, professedly scientific, authority of the Theses and the fractiousness of the Comintern as an organization.[14] For those like Yamada, whose perspective was informed by the Comintern's Theses, especially those of 1932, theory was more than science; it was also war.[15]

Yamada was directly affected by the repression of the left that had mounted steadily since 1928. In a pattern quite common among leftist scholars of his era, Yamada was arrested and imprisoned (twice—in 1930 and 1936), and compelled to resign his position as assistant professor of economics at Tokyo Imperial University; he returned to his post in 1945. Yamada's frequent invocations in the *Analysis* of "rationality" and the need for a "rational grasp" of Japanese capitalism testify to his belief in the link, in however disguised a form, between theoretical analysis and political practice.[16] Indeed, under the conditions of the 1930s, making capitalism visible through a text was itself a form of political practice.

YAMADA'S TEXT

What sort of text is the *Analysis?* Its prose is infamous: repetitive and systematic in the extreme, it strings together interminable relative clauses in and among sentence fragments, and is studded with abstract, frequently neologistic terminology. Its repeated verbatim references to the "militaristic, semi-serflike character of Japanese-type capitalism," and to "large industry, with its sub-Indian labor wages and flesh-grinding labor conditions," have an almost incantatory quality.[17] Indeed the *Analysis* is a work of obvious moral passion, of cold anger at a system that exploited and exhausted those who worked under it, the victims not only of modern selfishness but of semifeudal cruelty. It bears the psychological scars of backwardness: time and again Yamada decries the "inverted," "deformed," "withered," and "barbaric" character of Japanese-type capitalism *(Nihon-gata shihonshugi)*. It is the skill with which this anger is sublimated into theory that has made the *Analysis* a classic of Japanese social science.

Yamada opens the *Analysis* with a typology of capitalist development in historical sequence (England, France, Germany, Russia, with the United States as a special case), and then identifies the Japanese variant in the following terms:

> The characteristics of Japan's special, inverted capitalism stemming from its world-historically low position—those characteristics being a semiserf system of petty agriculture founded on labor servitude/labor rent, semi-serflike rule of in-kind payment of land tax and a general tendency toward debt serfdom—have their basis in the Restoration reforms of 1868. These were undertaken due to the pressure exerted by the advanced capitalist countries on the despotic Tokugawa system that had been in place since the early seventeenth century, and assumed condensed structural (categorical, organizational) form in the process of definition of industrial capitalism. That Japanese capitalism represents a departure, or deviation, from a [generalized] structural grasp should be clear in view of the points just enumerated.[18]

The key feature of Japanese-type capitalism was its inversion of the relation between the departments of production (as Marx defines them). Instead of a "classic" capitalist mode emerging as a result of development of the means of consumption in textiles, in Japan the "production of the means of production"—specifically in military and state-dominated heavy industry—formed the "pivot" of a revolution in production. This feature of the system, to which Japan "had been driven by necessity" brought with it the subordination of consumption along with extremes of exploitation, both of industrial labor and of peasant agriculture. Also, and integrally, it brought the rapid—premature—acquisition of colonial holdings, on which capital was to rely for resources and markets.[19]

Backwardness, for Yamada, was not a psychological complex born of the sense of urgency felt by the leadership vis-à-vis the West, but reflected rather the control of the present by the past within Japan's production and social relations. By the mid-nineteenth century, Japan was already objectively backward, and only objective social transformation could abolish the condition. Yet importantly, this backwardness was not absolute, but relative. There was a crucial connection between the degree and quality of agricultural development and the capacity of a society to organize itself politically: "Japanese agriculture," he observed elsewhere, "from the point of view of (1) technology; and (2) farm household economy, is in a position superior to that of China and India. Indeed this fact goes a long way toward explaining why, in the face of Western expansion into Asia, the South [*nanpō*] was colonized by, and China subjected to the influence of, the Great Powers; while Japan alone managed to transform itself into a capitalist country."[20]

At the same time, the objective transformations necessary for the abolition of backwardness—that is, the transformation of feudalistic elements within the capitalist structure, to prepare the way for socialist revolution—were as yet unrealized and indeed blocked by interests in the state and society whose power rested on their preservation. To this extent, backwardness was a supremely political—and ideological—issue as well as a social fact. Yamada's own treatment of "superstructure," however, is sketchy at best; he was "deaf" to the voices of ideology.[21] To be sure, younger scholars broadly in the Kōza-ha line, such as Maruyama Masao, went beyond Yamada to define the key issue in Japanese-type capitalism not as backwardness per se but as its knowing, strategic perpetuation by elites: those who occupied the "enlightened" side of the coin of a persistent premodern peasant mentality. To this extent, they foreshadow the "invention of tradition" approach taken here. Even their focus, however, remains on the deformations caused by the continued elaboration of this productive mode—now extended to the realm, not just of politics, but of ethics and morality. For analysts in this lineage, backwardness was real, had a social foundation, and was powerful enough to "infect" elites themselves.[22]

For Yamada, the "key to the whole process" of clarifying the basic structure—the antagonisms—and prospects of Japanese capitalism lies in explicating the initial formation of industrial capitalism, roughly in the period between Japan's two successful wars, that is, between the mid-1890s and mid-1900s.[23] In that formation is subsumed the process of primitive accumulation; the simultaneous, mutually determining moments of domestic industrial revolution and the turn toward imperialism; the initial emergence of finance capital (the second, "genuine" appearance comes around 1918); and the necessary impetus toward the general crisis of the late 1920s—the latter, of course, forming the enunciative moment of the *Analysis* itself. In other words, the dissolution of industrial capitalism in Japan is immanent in its own structure, and is the condition for the—cataclysmic—general crisis that is now not only immanent, but imminent as well.

The text itself has a tripartite structure, each element focusing on a different branch of the economy in analyzing how "the reproduction process in Japanese capitalism was set underway."[24] The first, treating the incorporation of cotton weaving and silk reeling (both putting out and manufacture) into the capitalist mode of production, outlines the phase of primitive accumulation, one "complete in its essentials" by the late 1890s. Yamada strongly emphasizes the feudalistic conditions of labor, particularly prison and forced labor, and the exploitation of female labor, taking note of protests and strikes by mill workers; similarly he describes, but does not analyze, the ideological forms of control—patriotism, patriarchy, religion (including oaths to deities or *kami*)—used by labor bosses *(oyakata)* in the crucial mining industry.[25]

The second part locates the pivot of the production revolution in military organization and key industries (railroads, mining, machine works), the "decisive driving force," for Yamada, of Japan's capitalist development. The key indicator of development in this sector, he holds, is "the fulfillment of the expectation that instruments of labor can be produced," through securing both raw materials (iron, both Chinese and Manchurian) for processing and "the surpassing of world levels" in shipbuilding technology, specifically in producing "machines to make machines"—for example, lathes. Pointing to the overwhelming presence of the Yahata steel works, Yamada seeks to demonstrate the dominance of state capital over heavy industry. This was the mode of development that determined both Japan's turn to imperialism in order to secure primary material, fuels, and markets; and promoted in two "jerky" stages the emergence of finance capital. But Yamada contends that the entire heavy industrial sector, to the extent that it depends on labor drawn from villages and subject to a semifeudal labor regime in the factory, will find that its growth is socially constrained; hence the fragility of Japan's heavy industry and its industrial bourgeoisie. Thus, the attempt by heavy industry to resolve the precipitous downturn of the late 1920s via industrial rationalization—mass dismissals and intensification of labor—will provoke the general collapse of the semifeudal form of labor and related conditions.[26] Yamada does not foresee the survival of industrial capitalism, let alone its successful adaptation to a "post-semifeudal" era.

The third part, finally, treats "the base"—Japan's system of "semifeudal land tenure" and "semiserf system of petty cultivation." It is here that the worst features of the industrial economy have their source: the "sub-Indian labor wages and flesh-grinding labor conditions" of large industry made possible by the "miserably laggard" state of agriculture. As critics consistently and correctly point out, in the long run, Yamada is primarily concerned with the base, as if to echo Marx's own conviction that "the social revolution can only *seriously* begin from the bottom up; that is, with landlordism."[27] Yamada elaborates a typology of landlords, the two major types being the still pivotal Northeastern (Tōhoku) type, marked by semifeudal landlord-tenant relations whose reproduction is carried out within the village, and a combination of concentrated ownership and direct cultivation along with slow-paced parcelization of tenant holdings. To this is counterposed the "usurious and parasitical" Home Province (Kinki) type of landlordism where extensive and accelerating land parcelization is taking place in a relatively commercialized environment: reproduction of the landlord-tenant relation takes place via ties to urban markets. Taken together these represent "nothing other than two types that have emerged on the basis of a semifeudal system of land ownership—and a semi-serflike regime of parcelized cultivation—that has two strata, each with its specific type of subordination *[nisō no jūzoku kitei]*."[28]

Yamada does not extend his considerations to landlord entrepreneurship, and certainly sees no evidence from any quarter of their having performed a progressive role in the development of capitalism in Japan. For Yamada, it is only with the transformation of social relations in the countryside, through the reform of the system of land tenure, that the category of smallholder can emerge as the bearer of a home market and bourgeois consciousness. Until then, feudalistic relations will always form fetters on production and obstruct the development of genuinely proportional—healthy—demand in the economy. Japan's *idée napoléonienne*—the middling peasant *(chūnō)*—will remain an ideological mockery of a tenanted mass still subject to what Marx termed "noneconomic coercion." Concretely, this means that payment in-kind (in rice) of land rent will remain the norm—cash payments, Yamada argues, are no more than a modern mask over a feudal form—and that the village will continue, not as a true community but as a "simple addition of homologous magnitudes," whose units share no more than "identity of interest" and are devoid of unity or class consciousness.[29]

No matter where he looked, Yamada saw a structurally determined impasse in Japan's capitalism. Industrial rationalization seemed to offer no positive prospect; and no serious land reform was in the offing that could solve the problem of effective demand at the base. Thus, he concludes, "At the same time that the incorporation of the 'wretched hovels' [cottage industry] was the fundamental factor in the flourishing of Japanese capitalism—the establishment of industrial capital—it also produced the fundamental cause of its own ruin."[30]

YAMADA'S METHOD: THE ANALYSIS OF REPRODUCTION

The distinct power of Yamada's text stems from its method of combining theoretical and historical perspectives in a single analysis. But in so doing, Uchida Yoshiaki has argued, Yamada disclosed a vital tension between the two elements of his intellectual will: the "unintending" Weberian sociologist, concerned with specifying and typologizing particulars, and the orthodox Marxian economist, determined to identify the "laws of motion" of a universal process.[31] Indeed, it is this tension that generated both the light and the heat necessary for the work to be treated as a contestable classic.

As Yamada envisioned it, the *Analysis* was an attempt "to analyze the foundations of Japanese capitalism. It is the chief task of this work, by means of this analysis of fundamentals, to make clear the basic structure— that is, antagonisms *[taikō]*—and prospects of Japanese capitalism. I view this task as a problem of grasping the reproduction process in Japanese capitalism; I hope, that is, to have *concretized the reproduction schema* in Japanese capitalism."[32]

The *Analysis* was also intended as a scientific demonstration of the schema's predictive power. Japanese capitalism, because it was capitalism, was destined to generate a crisis from which Yamada, at least, hoped it would not recover. Determining when that crisis would actually occur and what its effects would be, however, required analysis of the specific conditions of reproduction in Japan.[33] It meant finding a way to relate the "visible" and "invisible" systems of Japan's modernity: agriculture, industry, and empire on the one hand, to the morally problematic "something" called capitalism on the other. Yamada had to come to terms with history.

In analyzing actually existing capitalism in Japan, Yamada began with the notion of reproduction, that is, he took as his task the explanation not simply of how capitalist production and commodity circulation took place, but how the conditions for such activity were reproduced. Yet the reproduction schemas (developed in the second volume of *Capital*) that provided Yamada's basic model were highly abstract. And particularly since he worked from the schema for simple reproduction, certain critics were led to charge that Yamada conceived capitalism in equilibrium rather than in dialectical terms.[34] By the time Yamada's articles appeared in book form as the *Analysis* in 1934, he had already published a theoretical study of reproduction that anticipated and responded, albeit unsatisfactorily for some, to the argument that the reproduction schema would harness any analysis to a Procrustean bed. Exactly so, was the reply. The reproduction schema, Yamada argued, "represents the most fundamental, most general grasp, and as such does not touch directly the particular, concrete capitalist structure of any specific country, or the structure of capitalism at any specific stage." Yet "in so far as it grasps this most fundamental dimension," the reproduction schema "assumes a concrete form that is present throughout the capitalist structure of any given country or at any given stage."[35]

At some level, yes, capitalism is the same everywhere. And, Yamada would continue, it is no less important that it does the same thing everywhere, that is, in the process of "normal" operations, the capitalist system generates crises: even under the condition of perfect proportionality between departments of the economy, "the forms of motion of the totality of the social capital" bring with them their own antagonistic contradictions. The reproduction schema, therefore, enables one to determine "the ironlike necessity for change that runs through the structure at its base."[36]

Nevertheless, the "pure" capitalism laid bare in Marx's critique of political economy (even in its historical sections) could not have provided material sufficient to produce Yamada's *Analysis*. Although he strove mightily to follow *Capital*'s reproduction schemas, in formulating his model of Japanese-type capitalism, Yamada was compelled to rely on "mediating links" derived from other instances of late development as a way of attaining the concreteness he sought. Lenin's notion of a "Prussian path" to capitalism, involving a "reconstruction from above, in which elements of a bourgeois system are incorporated into the ancien régime so as to ensure its survival in the context of a hostile international environment" offered what seemed a powerful, albeit qualified, analogy to the absolutist Japanese state. *Imperialism* (1917) provided theoretical guidance in schematizing the reproduction process in a peripheral empire such as Japan's, in which an underdeveloped home market compelled the state to turn to colonialism as a substitute.[37] By the same token, the Physiocrat François Quesnay's *Table économique* (1758), "as an embodiment of equilibrium [between feudal aristocracy and bourgeoisie], which is the basic condition of absolute monarchy," hinted at a method for analyzing what Yamada regarded as Japan's essentially precapitalist agrarian sector. Indeed Quesnay's *Table* allowed Yamada to set up a schema of capitalist reproduction that formally excluded the agricultural "base" on which capitalism rested—not because the production relations of agriculture were socially inconsequential, but because they were not, in

Yamada's view, capitalist relations. Japanese agriculture was characterized by

> land rent categories [*chidai hanchū*] that absorb all surplus labor, even eat-
> ing into necessary labor itself; that do not permit any profit to materialize.
> In cases where the position of the landowner has overwhelming primacy,
> there is no space for the formation of capitalist farm operations aimed at
> realizing a profit. Thus, so-called owners of money, rather than being man-
> agers of agricultural leaseholds, tend generally to be parasitic landlords
> whose objective is the taking of land rent. Here we have a clear indication
> of the reasons for the strengthening, in the case of the development of
> Japanese capitalism, of the category of agricultural land rents that absorb
> all surplus labor and prevent the realization of profit; and of the regime of
> semi-serflike or parasitical landlordism. It is here that the limits to the capi-
> talist transformation of Japanese agriculture are formed.[38]

CRITIQUE AND ASSESSMENT

In the process of "concretizing the reproduction schema in Japanese
capitalism," the *Analysis* forges an iron link between the "special
character"—the particularism—of Japan's capitalism, and backwardness. For Yamada, particularism *was* backwardness.

It is not hard to see why Yamada's arguments, whether on Japanese
agriculture, on capitalist development in general, or on the applicability
of the reproduction schema to a specific instance, would have been controversial both in their own moment and in ours. Characteristically or
not, he made almost no direct response to criticisms of the *Analysis*. He
did adjust his views, though not his basic approach, during the years
between 1934 and the early postwar era, chiefly in the direction of giving
much overdue attention to heavy industry in general, especially in recognizing that a shift from textiles to heavy and petrochemical industries
must have been well underway prior to 1931. Yet as of 1934, Yamada
had clearly missed something, and not by oversight. He failed to grasp
the capacity of Japanese capitalism to survive the depression, having
essentially frozen his view of production relations in industry as of the
decade between the Sino- and Russo-Japanese conflicts; he had virtually
no grasp of the role of the state, especially after World War I (his assessment of industrial rationalization was narrowly drawn and essentially
negative), no developed views of trade flows or state finance, or any conjunctural perspective more recent than that of his period of initial focus.[39]

In a sense, Yamada was too faithful a Marxist: where Marx had been
forced to stop with a mere three volumes of *Capital,* dying with the more

conjunctural aspects of his overall plan unrealized, so too Yamada stopped short of any attempt to treat the position of Japan in the capitalist world economy. Instead, his types develop within the histories of their national societies, running, as it were, in parallel circles, until they are exhausted or destroyed from outside. Indeed, criticism of Yamada's text has concentrated on the static, undialectical, and insufficiently historical character of his types. In his use of equilibrium notions as the conceptual basis—not the normative or political end point—of analysis, Yamada had followed Nikolai Bukharin, whose *Historical Materialism* (1921) was avidly read in Japan. When Bukharin himself came under attack in the Soviet Union, equilibrium analyses such as Yamada's were branded "Bukharinist" and "right deviationist." While much of this criticism (which continued into the postwar years) was stridently dogmatic, it did have a germ of validity. As Iwasaki Chikatsugu comments:

> In the "type" *[kata]* itself, there is no movement or development. As molds are manufactured and then broken—which is the case with Yamada Moritarō's theory—there is only formation and disintegration. . . . As with the theory of equilibrium that is linked to it, the standpoint of "types" is by nature one of external causation. . . . In the theory of "types"—as in Yamada's *Analysis of Japanese Capitalism*—it is possible to recognize the product of a marriage between Weber and Bukharin performed on the basis of Marxism.[40]

These are not unfair, or necessarily unfavorable, observations, though they carefully skirt the possibility that the Stalinist notion of "socialism in one country" would seem to have authorized a developmental prehistory of "capitalism in one country." We may agree with the Rōnō-ha theoretician Sakisaka Itsurō (1897–1985), author of the first substantial criticism of the *Analysis*, that Yamada's capitalism "has no development"—that it hypostatized the national past (semifeudal social relations), and refused to make any bow to the Rōnō-ha.[41] But when viewed from the perspective of the 1930s and the first half of the 1940s, it is hard to see how Sakisaka's own model of Japanese capitalism drained of its specificity—based on what Sakisaka insisted ought to have happened—would have any more explanatory power than a static, structurally overdetermined model such as Yamada's. Yamada at least had his finger on a genuine, long-term problem: the disparity between sectors, and the social and ideological consequences of that disparity. His problem was that he could find no theory that would allow him to move his finger.

Ultimately, for Yamada, the analysis of Japanese capitalism does come down to the problem of land and land rent—or, as one sympathetic critic, fed up with Yamada's penchant for nominalizations, put it, "the crisis of the land rent categories."[42] Here, of course, Yamada's views were vindicated, and therefore rendered honorable superfluities. Social scientists, if they are honest, should consider themselves lucky if their work meets such a fate. As Yamazaki Ryūzō notes, if the *Analysis* may still be regarded as a key point of departure in the analysis of Japanese capitalism, it can no longer serve as a point of arrival.[43] And yet, if read not so much in terms of its own theoretical project, or of its flawed and truncated historical analysis, but as an inverted reflection of the particularism it sought to overthrow, the *Analysis* speaks still, and with a surprisingly powerful voice. If Japan's *kokutai,* its national polity, was "peerless throughout the world" in its inherent virtuousness, its "semifeudal regime of parcelized cultivation" was likewise "peerless throughout the world . . . in its baseness and cruelty."[44] Had he been permitted to speak openly, Yamada might have concluded thus: Countrymen and comrades, do not be deceived! We live with a past already cruel enough for the masses of peasants in our society; a past now brought into and indeed indispensable to the present system of exploitation. This double cruelty speaks to us in a soothing voice of warm manners and beautiful customs, yet even now is arming itself for aggressive expansion, perhaps war; and even now I dare not even name him for whose sake our people toil and suffer.

In his *Analysis of Japanese Capitalism,* Yamada Moritarō provided a theoretical analysis that both identified particularism with backwardness, and made Japanese capitalism visible as such (that is, as capitalism) for the first time. The odd fate of this combination was that while capitalism advanced in the 1950s, it did not universalize as many analysts, whether of the Rōnō-ha, Uno school, or neoclassical lineages expected it would. Instead, backwardness metamorphosed into its obverse. This is the claim that particularism should now be linked with Japan's role as the vanguard of postmodern capitalism. Both positions share the feature of projecting back into the Tokugawa past and forward again those features of society thought to explain the present: for Yamada, the conditions of the late 1920s and early 1930s; for the upholders of Tokugawa Japan's postmodernity *avant la lettre,* the years of high growth from the mid-1960s through to the recent collapse of the bubble economy. In either case, the generality of capitalist relations remains unsupportably abstract and undeserving of cultural imprimatur, while the link with the noncapitalist past remains the explanatory master key.

But what past? That of Yamada's Marxian narrative? That of the peerless national polity and its happy and harmonious village communities? It is not enough to say that the two cancel each other out, or that they depend on one another. Yamada's Marxism may be frozen in time and, in a sense, in its social categories as well; but at least it sought universality in a comparative method that was not merely synonymous with the national history it analyzed. If it is a Eurocentric delusion to seek universality through method (or to seek it at all), is it necessarily fruitful to return to a nation *(minzoku)*-centered approach? The relation of Yamada's *Analysis* to *kokutai* orthodoxy, of critique or antimyth to myth itself, suggests otherwise: the latter is a dead end. Indeed, the notion of methodology is by definition antithetical to *kokutai*-centered history.

Nor is it enough to observe that each present invents its past, for this begs the questions: Why does it do so when it does? Why does it do so at all? Out of what strands of preexisting narrative and nonnarrative practices, and by what agents? As far as Japanese capitalism is concerned, one might say, in a twist on Barrington ("no bourgeois, no democracy") Moore: no tradition, no capitalism. I mean by this not what Yamada Moritarō did, that the past controlled and therefore in a sense created the present. Rather, while taking into account the long dominance of Kōza-ha over Rōnō-ha perspectives in Japanese Marxism, and the extensive influence of the Kōza-ha over Japanese social science generally, it is necessary to go beyond it to articulate the significance of a certain kind of past-consciousness. It was here, in the sphere of ideology and the production of meaning, that Yamada's analysis, and that of the Kōza-ha generally, was weakest—although that of the Rōnō-ha was weaker still. In this respect, neither grasped the real dynamic of Japanese capitalism, indeed of Japan's modernization as a whole. This lay in the invented—and strategic—character of the process through which tradition entered the present: not just "no tradition, no capitalism," but also "no capitalism, no tradition"—no present, no past. Rather than laying bare capitalism's ideology as part of a "total grasp," Yamada's text effaced it, and unwittingly reproduced the structure of concealment that was essential to its functioning.

The development of capitalism in Japan posed a double dilemma. It arrived, garbed in a morally problematic ideology of individual profit-seeking, and moreover in a global conjuncture in which Japan was placed at a radical disadvantage. Under these conditions, and by making maximum demands on its semiautonomous agrarian sector, Japan's leadership made its wager on backwardness. These original characteristics, in turn, were translated into the ideological virtues of national communalism and ceaseless self-sacrifice that informed and naturalized capitalism in Japan. As such, they have taken on a life of their own as normative orientations, indispensable not only for those whose interest lies in maintaining the political-economic regime, but for those who attempt to resist its powerful claims. Just as in economic analysis, where Rōnō-ha universalism has formed the subtheme to Kōza-ha particularism, in intellectual-moral discourse, globalism and individualism (two sides of the same coin) have operated under community constraint, relatively loose or tight as contemporary conditions dictate. The long, seemingly interminable economic malaise of the current Heisei era has raised demands for a fundamental national reorientation, a more liberal, market-oriented society, in which individuals and corporate groups will be allowed, even encouraged, to risk failure in the pursuit of their aspirations. Will this happen? Will the essential features of Japan's modernity be redefined? It is hard to say. It is no small thing to undo a social compact, even one whose premise of corporate communitarianism and egalitarianism has all too often served to cloak systemic corruption and a bottomless demand for unrewarded labor. Qualified though it has been by long-run transformations in Japanese capitalism and by challenges to its intellectual structure, the world of Yamada's *Analysis* has not yet passed into history.

CHAPTER 4

Thinking through *Capital*

Uno Kōzō and Marxian Political Economy

Uno Kōzō (1897–1977) stands at the head of the most influential school of postwar Japanese Marxism. Resolutely academic, indeed founded on the strict separation of political economy as a science from ideological practice, Uno's avowed project was to build a system of political economy that could provide a basis for "scientific socialism," as Uno defined that term. Political economy *(keizaigaku)* was to operate at three distinct levels, or in three dimensions. The first was the "basic principles" *(gen-ron)*, which Uno formulated by appropriating and reconstructing the contents of *Capital.* These were to provide an abstract but objective model of "pure capitalism" and its "laws of motion" that could validate what Uno regarded as the hypothesis of historical materialism, and "endorse ... the feasibility of abolishing capitalism."[1] "Stage theory" *(dankairon)*, the second level, treated the process by which the tendency of original capitalism to "purify" (thus allowing the abstraction of the basic principles to begin with) was reversed in the era of imperialism and monopoly. "Stages" were typologies of development: mercantilist, liberal, and imperialist; here, Uno was not concerned with transitions. Finally, Uno called for "analysis of current conditions" *(genjō bunseki)* that would subsume the basic principles as mediated by stage-theoretic considerations. On this foundation of conceptual disjunctions, Uno created a system that was "nowhere echoed in Western Marxism."[2]

Uno's school was fated to seek an explanation for the most significant instance of capitalist surge since 1945: the largely unexpected rise of

Japan as a regional and, ultimately, a world economic power. In the last decade of his life, Uno would speak of the "ebb tide" of Marxism; it would be up to those he had trained to carry on.[3] Could his system be used to illuminate a world economy in which Japan had assumed an unwonted dominance? Or conversely, would its adepts find themselves presiding over its decomposition as its central paradigms were over-whelmed by the "flood tide" of newer economic theories and realities? In this chapter, I trace the formation of Uno's system—including a consideration of the significance of the systematizing drive itself—and its trajectory in the Japanese academic and intellectual world. This project is necessarily biographical: Uno was a garrulous man who relished debate and left an oral autobiography entitled *Shihonron gojūnen* (Fifty years with *Capital*, 1981).[4] His intellectual life was centered on Marx's great text, and it is Uno's relation to Marx that forms the concern of this chapter.

More broadly, Uno's system and its fate may be situated within three interlinked histories. First, that of social thought in modern Japan as it has reflected on the national experience of capitalist development and how it is has been conceptualized historically. Whatever he himself may have thought, Uno's followers regard his system as the solution to the politically polarized but intellectually protean "capitalism debate" among Marxists of the 1930s.[5] Second, that of international social science: Uno argued strongly for the centrality of political economy among the social sciences, and for the ultimate knowability of society as an object of cognition. Social "laws," however, could not be put to technical use. Conversely, while "nature" permitted the technical application of its laws, in a dialectical sense it remained unfathomable. Uno's conviction that social science was essentially impossible prior to capitalism—because there was no autonomous, knowable "economic" function in society until its advent—ties in to the third history with which I am concerned. This is the history of Marxism. No longer the *explanans* of modern history, to borrow a phrase from Gareth Stedman Jones, Marxism now is an *explanandum*.[6] And, I would add, a significant *explanandum*, in part due to its reach, its ties to national development experiences far outside the original Atlantic rim. That is, there was Marxism because there was capitalism: but the relation between the two seems to depend, importantly though not uniquely, on the type of capitalism, on variations in the mode of capitalist development. Which brings us back to Japan, to Japanese social thought and social science, and to Uno himself. In what sense was Uno a Marxian thinker, and a Japanese Marxian? Why did he so determinedly seek to insulate political economy as a science from ideology, and theory from practice? What was to be gained by such separation, and by systematization? If capitalism was a self-activating and self-regulating subject, how was political practice—"countersubjectivity"?—possible, and how could it be effective?

MISE-EN-SCÈNE

An episode recounted in *Fifty Years* captures well the academic character of Uno's project. It dates from Uno's years as a professor of economic policy at Tōhoku Imperial University in Sendai, a "paradise for research on *Capital*," thanks to its distance from the hub of Japan's educational and police bureaucracies.[7] A colleague, the Hegelian philosopher Takechi Tatehito, had aimed a satirical haiku in his direction:

samidare ya	the rains of early summer come
kenkyūshitsu no	while the Marxist
marukisuto	remains in his study[8]

Since the late 1920s, waves of arrests had caught numerous Marxists in Japanese universities, both faculty and students. Headlines in the national press reported the scandal of bolshevization among Japan's young intellectual elite. Uno, with what he termed his "practice complex," remained aloof, not "really" (by his own lights) a Marxist since he was not involved in organized radical politics. The "early summer rains" that fed hopes of incipient revolution seemed not to matter. Only *Capital* was important. And yet in early 1938, Uno was arrested, having been implicated in the activities of the so-called Professors' Group of the Worker-Farmer Faction, or Rōnō-ha, the Marxists who had broken in 1927 with the Comintern-associated Japan Communist Party. Although Uno was a close and lifelong friend of the Rōnō-ha theoretician Sakisaka Itsurō (1897–1985), the evidence that Uno had violated the Peace Preservation Law was circumstantial and scanty. (He had been entrusted with certain papers, sending some on to a friend for keeping and burning others.) Released on bail after submitting an official "recantation" of mistaken views and pledging to "serve the state wholeheartedly," Uno was twice acquitted of the charges against him. But he spent some fifteen months in prison near Sendai, complaining of lice, cold, and at times of shoddy lawyering. The experience (in March 1938) occasioned the following verse:

haru asaki	as spring bestirs itself
tonari wa nani o	I wonder what
shita hito zo	my neighbor is in for[9]

This poem was itself a take-off on a verse by Bashō:

aki fukaki	deep autumn;
tonari wa nani o	my neighbor —
suru hito zo	how does he live?

Bashō's melancholic poem evokes a kind of seasonal isolation: as autumn deepens, people who live at close quarters seem more remote from one another, the sounds and smells of daily life muffled and less identifiable than in warmer times of the year. In this instance, the poet lay seriously ill, the thought of his neighbor arising unbidden amid his own pain. Uno's verse, with a change of season (from autumn to spring) and verb tense (from *suru* to *shita*), speaks of a different, stranger isolation. Does his question arise out of sympathetic curiosity toward a fellow prisoner, or fear of an unknown, possibly dangerous neighbor? The testimony of Uno's own student is that he wrote out of concern and sympathy.[10] While Uno himself was not subject to physical abuse, a number of students arrested in the case seem to have been. He did lose his faculty position (despite a departmental vote to reinstate him after his final acquittal), later recalling his disgust at the thought of trying to pursue work on political economy "in a country like this." Uno spent the war years in private research institutes; at the time of the surrender he was doing economic research for Mitsubishi.[11] After a year back in Sendai, Uno moved in 1947 to the new Institute of Social Science at the University of Tokyo, which he headed from 1949 through 1952. In these years, Uno began to publish widely, including some prewar writings but, with astonishing speed, much new material that made up the first two levels of his system — and a great deal besides. With the appearance in particular of *Keizai genron* (Principles of political economy, whose two-volume first edition of 1950–52 sold some fifty thousand copies), Uno's star was fixed in the social science firmament.[12]

"THE ESSENCE OF 'CAPITAL'"

But what, after all, did capitalism mean to Uno Kōzō, and how did it come to mean what it did? What was it that led him to live and describe his life as one spent "together with *Capital*"? Let us start with one of Uno's more striking formulations of his position:

A colleague of mine from my days at Sendai, a specialist in Japanese religious history, once told me this story: how the venerable Hōnen, having read the entire Tripitaka for the fourth or fifth time, hit upon the *nenbutsu,* the invocation of Amida Buddha — "Namu Amida Butsu," or "Hail to thee, Amitabha Buddha." Though I personally have no sense of the preciousness of invoking the Name, the fact that Hōnen, out of this enormous text, found its heart in these six characters struck me as interesting, and I've never forgotten it. Not that I regard *Capital* as a sutra, to be chanted as my morning devotion. The first time I read *Capital* was also the only time I read it from beginning to end, slogging through and with little understanding of what I read. But since then, from time to time as occasion arose, I've reread it, eventually going through it entirely a number of times, and discovering its essence in the notion of the "commodification of labor power." And this has been the central consideration of everything — books, essays — that I've published since the war ended.

The "commodification of labor power" was for Uno the sine qua non of capitalism, an essence that he had drawn from *Capital.* And it was from that essence that Uno elaborated his system. Commodity exchange became capitalism, that is, a distinct, self-regulating, and self-perpetuating system and form of society, when and as the process of production itself was colonized; when and as labor power, without which production of any kind could not happen, itself became a commodity. As with any commodity, labor power embodied a contradiction between use value and value, one that could not be resolved through circulation by means of money. On the contrary, "with the production of commodities by commodities, use value produces value," and the endless reproduction of that contradiction was the "foundation for the movement of commodity economy in toto." At the same time, capital was unable to produce labor power directly, and this was "simultaneously its indispensable, fundamental condition and its basic weakness."[13]

Uno did not come to this position quickly or lightly. The self-comparison to Hōnen — though Uno was loath to claim Hōnen's powers of insight as a reader — is apt, and has implications that are worth drawing out. For Uno, the phrase "commodification of labor power" *(rōdō-ryoku shōhinka)* represented an intellectual breakthrough made possible only after years of arduous effort: as he was fond of saying, it was the *nenbutsu* of *Capital.* Dare we say that this was a form of "grace" merited by his willingness to humble himself, to say, again and again, "I do not understand"? In any case, it seems to have spurred him to an appropriative, rather than exegetical, reading of the text: to read "so as to make it [his] own," rather than seek to understand it as Marx might have intended, or as might be dictated by a notion of original context as finally and inelastically determinative. Such an ideology of authenticity was foreign to Uno. By the same token, he professed to write, not with the "gang in Tokyo" in mind, but "for the world."[14]

The commodification of labor power, in short, was for Uno something "really real" or "concrete" in the same sense that Marx (in the *Grundrisse*) defined it, as "the concentration of many determinations." It was the precipitate of a process of ever closer specifications that worked through dialectic: capitalism was the "set of material relations X"; it was also not-X (something other than X). Dialectic in this sense was not infinite: It could eventually attain the essential, that object which was both concrete and universal. As such, it was the proper, and only, foundation for a "science" of political economy whose essence was captured in *Capital*—because that text had captured what was essential, "really real," about capitalism itself.[15]

FROM SOCIALISM TO MARXISM

As was typical for intellectuals of his vintage, Uno's engagement with *Capital* was preceded by a strong curiosity about socialism in general; for most, Marxism had barely appeared on the horizon. Uno Kōzō was born in 1897 in the merchant town of Kurashiki, into a family best described as petty bourgeois; life in Kurashiki inevitably brought an awareness of a status hierarchy formed by wealth. His father had moved to town from his family's farm, becoming a bookseller, printer, paper and (at one point) ice dealer. He had personal ties to Ōhara Magosaburō, the textile magnate and founder of the Ōhara Institute for Social Research. For Uno *fils*, these connections were doubly significant: he heard from his mother, and learned for himself, about the working and living conditions of Kurashiki's women textile workers (ice was needed to treat their frequent illnesses). And he was later to marry Takano Maria, the daughter of institute director Takano Iwasaburō. Uno's fellow townsmen included the socialist leader and Rōnō-ha founder Yamakawa Hitoshi (1880–1958)—Uno's father was antipathetic to Yamakawa's Christianity. Among his closest friends from boyhood was Nishi Masao, a "splendid literary youth" and later Communist Party activist; Uno's closeness to Nishi was in part the source of what he described as his practice complex—his envy of political activism and feeling that he himself was incapable of emulating it, a complex that dissipated only with the legalization of the left in Japanese politics after 1945.

Small wonder, then, that Uno was drawn to socialism, first as something scandalous, forbidden, and "scary"—especially the anarchist socialism as embodied by Ōsugi Sakae (1885–1923). It was also a socialism resistant to vanguardism, to party centralism, and to "foreign" domination. Although Uno repeatedly, and justifiably, distinguished himself from the Rōnō-ha in a political sense, he clearly did not stray far from his early inclinations and affinities. Rather than command or be commanded, he preferred to argue. He retained, so he said, a trace of anarcho-syndicalism in his thought: an attraction to an image of workers' élan vital and heroism, and the conviction that the most an intellectual could do was to bring workers to consciousness of what they were spontaneously capable of achieving.[16] The point, however, was that that work, too, had to be done. In this sense, antiintellectualism was inexcusable.

Such considerations seem, even before the Russian Revolution, to have brought Uno to a particular concern with *Capital*. Reading the socialist journal *Shin shakai* had made him aware of the "formidable" figure of Marx. But he had come to understand that more than Marx the man, Marx the text had to be confronted. If he could not be a movement activist, a "real" Marxist or socialist, he was determined not to be a mere commentator who falsely regarded himself as Marxist. For such people Uno felt contempt.[17]

Uno first read *Capital* in German, and in Germany; his economic studies at Tokyo Imperial, from which he graduated in 1921, had been of no use in preparing him for this task. Prior to making this long journey in the fall of 1922, he had worked for a number of years at the Ōhara Institute but was frustrated at not having time to read for himself. On board ship, he read Nikolai Bukharin and Evgenii Preobrazhensky's *ABC of Communism* (1919), despite warnings from a White Russian refugee that it was "a very bad book." Newly married and financed by ten thousand yen from his father, Uno remained in Berlin for two years, reading, reading, reading: *Capital*, Lenin on imperialism and against Karl Kautsky, the socialist and communist daily press. And listening and observing, attending party rallies, sharing life and information and acquaintances with other Japanese in residence.

Uno returned to Japan via London and Marseilles with no career prospects, having resigned his position at Ōhara while still in Germany.[18] The good fortune of a post at Tōhoku Imperial, a lectureship in economic policy, soon came his way. This was a subject about which he knew little and toward which—insofar as it evoked the German Historical school and *Sozialpolitik*—he was unfavorably disposed. Uno had read the neo-Kantian philosophers Heinrich Rickert and Sōda Kiichirō sufficiently to be insulated against *Vulgärmarxismus,* but he remained cool toward Weber's work. This may have been because Uno's own emergent synthesis of developmental stages bore a close similarity to Weber's ideal-types. Uno's argument was that without the anchor of basic principles abstracted from real capitalism to provide a ground for objectivity, Weber's ideal types simply "floated" in time, prone to all sorts of subjectivism. As for Friedrich List, Uno duly recognized the influence of his ideas on the protection of infant industries and on tariffs. But he found List's stage theory, particularly his ideal of a final stage that harmonized agriculture, commerce, and industry, little more than a slavish rationalization of those policies. And because List could not explain "why the development from the agricultural to the industrial stage had proceeded through the development of capitalist commodity economy," he was "hardly worth taking seriously" as a political economist.[19]

This is not to imply that Uno disregarded historical difference or contingency. It is certainly true that over the long run, Uno spent most of his scholarly time in the domain of "pure capitalism," precisely in order to highlight its singularity and transience as a form of society. More to the point, Uno attached great importance to differences in historical development, declaring (in the *Principles of Political Economy*) that the "ultimate goal" of political economy was to carry out empirical analysis "of the actual state of capitalism, either in the world as a whole or in each different country." For Uno, the notion of stage was indispensable as a specifying medium that allowed the "pure" to be brought into relation with the "actual" and vice versa.[20]

If he considered List's version of developmental stages to be theoretically groundless, Uno was no less critical of attempts to move immediately from *Capital* to concrete analysis without any stage theory at all. In the controversy over Revisionism, Eduard Bernstein and Kautsky had argued respectively that *Capital* was either passé or that it remained unassailably valid; in doing so, Uno asserted, they had set back the task of analyzing the phenomenon of imperialism by at least ten years.[21] Even Rudolf Hilferding, whose *Finance Capital* (1910) represented a huge intellectual advance, had "tried to deduce finance-capital, the dominant form of capital in the imperialist stage of capitalist development, directly from Marx's theories of money and credit." But this was impossible. The former pertained to the history of capitalism, the latter to the logic of the commodity economy, "which can only synthesize a purely capitalist society in which use values are totally subsumed under the form of value."

No such society actually existed: this was why Lenin, who was otherwise so dependent on Hilferding (as well as on J. A. Hobson), did not attempt to "deduce the necessity of imperialism through the purely commodity-economic logic." Monopolization had to have other, contingent causes that helped to define the epoch; these had to do with the particulars of "late" development and the so-called Prussian path having emerged in a world already dominated by capitalist powers. Although he spoke of imperialism as the highest or latest stage in capitalism, Lenin was hardly successful in theorizing or explaining the causes of this phenomenon (whereas his grasp of the consequences was quite acute).[22]

But the very absence of a forced linkage in Lenin's pamphlet between *Capital* as a theory and imperialism as a phenomenon was of decisive significance for Uno. It provided him with the justification he sought for the methodological separation of the two levels of analysis, the basic principles and the stage theory. In this sense, Uno's appropriation of Lenin allowed him to be both scrupulously scientific—in a manner different from what he saw as Kautsky's peculiar orthodoxy—and politically correct.

"NO INDUSTRIALIZATION IN THE ABSTRACT": THE CAPITALISM DEBATE

The events, particularly the agricultural crisis, of the early 1930s placed extraordinary pressures on anyone, like Uno, charged with giving intellectual order to those events, let alone those seeking to draw policy prescriptions from them. Indeed, Uno more or less flatly rejected the latter possibility. Already in the preface to the first (1936) edition of *Keizai seisakuron* (On economic policies) he argued that

> the scientific study of policy must examine individual policies in detail, and in so doing bring to light their historical determinants. Needless to say, without relying on economic theory, this is impossible. . . . Accompanying the confusion that has recently beset the capitalist economy, studies—no, assertions—concerning economic policies are running rampant on a world scale, so much so that what can only be regarded as irresponsible talk is given virtually free rein. It may be thought that the mention of "economic policy" means that some new rescue plan has been discovered. But I have nothing of the sort to present. It is my view that imperialism must never be treated with such a goal in mind. . . . Without a clear specification of mercantilism and liberalism, I believe, a full understanding of imperialism too will remain beyond our grasp.[23]

Clearly, Uno was already antipathetic to policy expertise without theoretical—historicizing—moorings. It was a stricture that applied both to
Japan's *Sozialpolitiker* and Marxists, and Uno showed no hesitation in
expressing his criticisms. His attitudes toward Stalin, the Soviet Union,
and Soviet socialism, however, are never directly revealed in his writings
prior to Stalin's death in 1953. His retrospective account stresses his (and
others') ignorance of real conditions, but this is hardly satisfactory today.
It is impossible to know whether, as of the mid-1930s, Uno had any
doubt that the Stalin regime was legitimately socialist. But why should
Uno have insisted on the need to treat imperialism—perhaps the most
pressing issue in contemporary analysis—in terms of the stage theory as
separate from and mediating the basic principles? The framework of
Uno's system of political economy was in place by this point, at least for
lecture presentations. His conviction that "science has no *Träger*" is not
borne by or entrusted to a specific class, it would follow, was already
formed.[24] If no state, party, or organization, acting in the name of class,
was to be the arbiter of science, did this not imply that Marxism itself
might have to be protected against its official guardians?

Such considerations, I think, underlay Uno's intervention from the
margins in the broader debate, which he followed keenly, over the nature
of Japan's capitalism. In a powerful essay, "Shihonshugi no seiritsu to
nōson bunkai no katei" (The Process of Rural Differentiation and the
Establishment of Capitalism, 1935), Uno directly addressed the question
that had provoked that intellectual and political schism: what did the
current crisis in the Japanese countryside reveal about the nature of
Japanese capitalism? How indeed was Japan's mode of production to be
characterized?[25]

Uno begins by registering his agreement with Sakisaka Itsurō's critique
of Yamada Moritarō's recent *Nihon shihonshugi bunseki* (Analysis of
Japanese capitalism, 1934), and of the "feudalist" Kōza-ha, or Lectures
Faction, generally for emphasizing the particular or backward features of
Japanese capitalism so far as to make it incapable of development or
unrecognizable as capitalism—and without providing empirical evidence
for the "noneconomic coercion" that would have to characterize its
"semifeudal" production relations. At the same time, though implicitly,
he rejected Sakisaka's argument that rural differentiation had in fact
occurred. His concern, however, was to provide a preliminary theory
that would make it possible to assess the views of the opposing forces
rather than simply weighing in on one side or the other.[26]

The opening section of the essay reviews the process of "primitive accumulation" in England as presented in the historical chapters of *Capital*, and may be passed over here. Uno stresses the formation of a "relative surplus population" subject to social, that is, capitalistic, as much as to Malthusian laws. Growing productivity unevenly reduced the need for labor power, while expanding scale unevenly increased it, and in the process workers became vulnerable to modern, individualized poverty, both cyclical and secular. Even in England, primitive accumulation did not extirpate cottage labor or female servitude, or bring complete rural differentiation through a process taken to be economic and therefore "natural." Raw state power was needed, over centuries, to bring that result, to create that "nature."[27]

All this, however, was prologue to issues not treated or treatable by Marx.[28] "There is no way," Uno notes, "to industrialize in the abstract."[29] It would not be sufficient even to speak of "primitive accumulation" as such. Rather, what were the contours of primitive accumulation in backward societies? How did the commodification of labor power occur in a late developer—or why did it not? Did the establishment of the capitalist mode of production in fact entail the destruction of old social forms? Uno drew on German and Japanese experience to reach his conclusion that "put most plainly, even without the adoption of forcible means to bring about rural differentiation, it was possible to import the capitalist mode of production." For Uno, this was not the result of policy, particularly policy divorced from theory. German economic thinkers, making an "instinctive, practical argument for capitalism as the basis for the modern state . . . sought to realize at the policy level the primitive accumulation that was the premise and condition of English capitalism but without clarifying its basic character." They should therefore have failed: but instead, unintentionally, they succeeded. The mechanized large-scale industry that Germany imported in the mid-nineteenth century meant that capitalist commodity relations would be mediated by sectors other than the agricultural.[30] Old classes and land relations would face a piecemeal, gradual and uneven transition, and the politics of that transition could be volatile.

"Such a condition in agriculture," Uno observes, "is not simply a matter of the nondevelopment of capitalism in the industries of backward countries. Capitalism that is launched through mechanized large industry has its own peculiar laws of population." The higher organic composition of capital typical of imported advanced technology entails piecemeal proletarianization and a large surplus population, notwithstanding the great increase in domestic demand. The late developer must contain the political tensions generated by the attempt to develop capitalism while preserving a rurally based social hierarchy that neither can nor need be dissolved; sector must be played off against sector, interest against interest. "Protection" can only be carried out "capitalistically and partially"; differentiation can only be slowed or distorted, while compensation (the absorption of labor capacity) is sought, particularly in the capture of foreign markets.[31]

Domestic development, therefore, was not only a domestic matter. German and, even more so, Japanese development came under new international conditions marked by the transition from industrial to finance capital: the very form of capital had mutated in a way favorable, Uno argues, to late developers. "Catch-up" was made possible through concentration and use of the joint-stock system. At the same time, finance capital brought new forms of "nation" to the fore, the competitive colonialists of the late nineteenth century. Under these circumstances, "the unification of agriculture and industry on a national basis, which was virtually impossible economically, became absolutely indispensable politically"; hence, Uno argues, the shift to protectionism (belated in Germany) and the reach for colonies. At least in Germany, thanks to decades of rapid development, there was in fact capitalism to protect. Japan by contrast saw the temporal overlap of the establishment of capitalism with the shift to imperialism. There was no time to prepare, and thus the pressure to combine low domestic wages with competition for external markets was extraordinarily intense.[32]

Neither in Germany nor in Japan, however, did protection and imperialism turn aside differentiation entirely, or even prevent the entrenchment of capitalist reproduction, whose universalizing demands insistently remained. The issue in the transformation of policy lies in the extent to which—not whether—the reproduction process can be blocked. At that level, the "law of capitalist development," like the proletariat, knows no country; indeed the development of the former, Uno avers, guarantees the development of the latter. Yet though capitalism developed by means of the same laws "whether in England, prewar Russia, Germany, or Japan," it must by the same token work through particular histories of "distortion" or "blockage." If both did not hold, economic analysis is impossible and fruitless.[33]

One point made by Uno in passing deserves more than a passing word. "It is vital to note," Uno argues, "that in its process of capitalist reproduction, the modern national state does not necessarily strive to

establish agriculture domestically along completely capitalist lines."
Domestic agriculture may be turned to export or reduced through proletarianization, but it also may remain, as Japan's had, with its old forms
intact. For this reason, "the process [of capitalist reproduction] is set on
a firm basis only through confrontation with agricultural countries." But
does this not imply that the development of those countries is in turn to
be obstructed—a hint, perhaps, of the "development of underdevelop-
ment"? For this reason, Uno insists that the "confrontation with agricultural countries" as a component of capitalist development "provides no
basis for any theory calling for the acquisition of agricultural regions by
means of imperialism."[34] It is a statement that must have been directed at
soi-disant Marxists who used theory to justify Japanese colonialism, and
it must have pointed to the great unstated problem of that colonialism:
its relation to Japan's imperial system—the *tennōsei*—and its dynamic of
external aggression.

Why did Uno leave such a grave issue to the ability of his audience to
read between the lines? In part, no doubt, out of rhetorical savvy, learned
at the expense of the Kōza-ha. The Comintern's 1932 Theses, which
formed a keynote for Kōza-ha social analysis, had called for the overthrow of the imperial system. The official response, of course, had been
vigorous repression. But the Rōnō-ha's circumspection was more than
rhetorical, reflecting as well the political judgment that the imperial
apparatus was a vestige to be swept away in the coming socialist revolution, and not the proper focus for analysis. Uno's account, in a sense,
split the difference: social analysis was one thing, and political practice
another. As he later recalled:

> For me, it seemed no more than a matter of course that a socialist political
> party would deny the imperial system. This didn't come out of my theory;
> it was a product of how, in my vague way, I understood socialism. The
> problem we had to deal with was why villages remained as they had, and
> I thought it was up to the [socialist] parties to make the link with the issue
> of the imperial system. . . . Later on, the prosecutors used this as proof that
> I had "cheated" them; well, from a certain point of view that was unavoid-
> able. But this was what I believed, with utmost seriousness. That was why I
> held the activists in such regard, had a complex toward them; and constantly
> told myself that if I failed to understand *Capital* on some point, it was due to
> some lack on my part. Whereas the problem, after all, lay with *Capital*.[35]

In the end, Uno did far more than work up a preliminary theory for the
assessment of the capitalism debate. Neither that debate, nor even "the

special forms of Japanese capitalism" were his ultimate interest; that lay instead in "the determinations general to late developers" upon which such "special," or indeed "extreme" forms were premised. In turn, Uno saw those general determinations in terms of developmental stages: but development seen in the light of the laws or basic principles of capitalism. In 1936, Uno began lecturing on those principles, in tandem with the course on policy. The essay, in short, presented the problem of Uno's system *in nuce*, not so much the system culminating in conjunctural analysis as the one Uno actually produced, which remained largely at the level of the interplay between basic principles and stages.[36] Once *Capital* and *Imperialism* are recognized as arising, so to speak, from different dimensions, once their methodological separation is allowed, what was to be done? As Sekine remarks, "Uno is not the only one to have noticed that the theory of *Capital* often presupposes a purely capitalist society; it does not take a man of his caliber to merely realize that there are three stages to the development of capitalism. That the pure theory and the stages theory must *somehow* be distinguished can be a serendipitous discovery to any ordinary thinker."[37] The question of intellectual caliber, of originality—and of political intention and practice—is bound up with another: Not just how to systematize, but why? This was the question that "history," in the form of arrest and deprivation of academic position, had compelled Uno to ponder in isolation for almost ten years.

REWRITING "CAPITAL": UNO'S "KEIZAI GENRON"

For Uno, Japan's defeat in 1945 was a foregone conclusion. So it had been for many. It was also a confirmation of basic outlook. But in contrast to those for whom such confirmation was framed in terms of a world-historical, or providential, tragedy, Uno reacted with undisguised joy:

> At Mitsubishi we had learned quickly . . . about the Imperial Conference held on whatever day it was in August. So when we heard the [surrender] broadcast we weren't in the least surprised. At the house next door to mine they all cried and so forth, but I only thought: finally, perhaps liberation is at hand. Now I should add that at Mitsubishi, as we were rejoicing over our liberation, Inoki Masamichi, who was working in the next office, grew angry. Finally, our noisy celebration was just too much; "shut up!" he finally shouted. "Better close the door," we said, and so we did.

Along with it, however, came characteristic detachment:

The military and government officials had been lording it over the people, and suddenly, in an instant, there's a transformation of values. A man in my neighborhood association who had been much given to demonstrations of militaristic spirit immediately joined the Communist Party. To this day my wife often talks about that. With people like that joining it, she says, the party wasn't to be counted on. . . . It's not that I had such enormous hopes. Of course I was extraordinarily concerned. For the land reform, because it would change the villages, I had great expectations. . . . That the labor unions would grow larger I didn't consider as important . . . As to the *zaibatsu* breakup, I didn't put much trust in that.[38]

Immediately after the war, Uno was active, as were most economists, in a range of official projects and surveys. But he did not have the policy influence of, say, his contemporary Arisawa Hiromi. Uno published an article, "Shihonshugi no soshikika to minshushugi" (Organized capitalism and democracy, 1946), arguing that "postwar conditions" entailed an open competition with socialism that would press capitalism to allow the formation of large labor unions and bring workers into greater managerial roles. "Only to the extent that it is organized democratically," Uno wrote, "will capitalism be genuinely organized."[39] The essay thus gestures toward the notion of state monopoly capitalism, not as a matter of advocacy, but as part of a theoretical agenda that he himself was never able to follow out.

The legalization and legitimation of leftist politics after 1945 may have relieved Uno of his practice complex, but the chances of his making the leap into socialist politics were slim. One the one hand, Sakisaka had long since done so, and perhaps this provided Uno a vicarious sense of political involvement. On the other hand, while he had not made the life-long political and spiritual pilgrimage that had led Kawakami Hajime to join the party when he was nearly sixty, Uno's understanding of Marx was far more profound. For Uno, the dramatic reconfiguration of Japan's politics brought new social approbation, a settled livelihood, and a chance to work in a receptive atmosphere. The result was the completion of his major works, first *Keizai genron* and then *Keizai seisakuron*, and the formal appearance of his system as such. *Keizai genron* is a rewriting, a translation, of *Capital*. Half-facetiously, we might say that it stands in the same relation to *Capital* as Arthur Waley's "translation" (1935) does to the *Tale of Genji*. Neither resembles its original, the voices are wholly other, and yet intellectually, those originals exert a magnetic pull on their "translators" such as to shape their vision of life and society. To be sure, Waley's *Genji* would never have emerged had there been no Bloomsbury group. But more importantly, there would be no "Japan" in the West had Waley not been drawn to the *Genji*. Similarly, Uno's text would never have emerged without the impact of Historical school economics and the interwar capitalism debate. But more importantly, there would be no pure capitalism, with its all-generative structure and powerful dialectic with "impure" history, had Uno not been drawn to *Capital*.

Why did *Capital* need to be rewritten? The question is not as straightforward as it might seem. Rewritten as opposed to what? Being extended, as Hilferding was thought to have done? Attacked as internally contradictory, as Eugen von Böhm-Bawerk claimed, and subsequently abandoned? Fundamentalist exegesis was clearly out. But something had to be done with it. Uno's analysis of rural differentiation had taken note of the fact that as of the late nineteenth century, capitalism had not everywhere brought the complete dissolution of old social forms; the 1946 essay "Organized Capitalism and Democracy" had focused on its massive concentration and on state intervention. Both of these were examples of conjunctural analysis, albeit in essay form. They were treatments of history. But was *Capital* history? For Uno, the answer was no. Capital*ism* was, to be sure, a product (and producer) of history, but accidentally: Enclosure and the process of primitive accumulation were but fortuitous effects of the competition between the English and continental woolens industries, had led to capitalism only in England, and required the state to move decisively to remove possibly tenacious obstacles to the functioning of the market system—obstacles that included the state's own former policies.[40] Its relative success set a new "start-line" for future international competition; henceforth there would be pioneers and followers (among industries and industrial sectors as well as nations as a whole). The fact that England had been "first," however, was not in and of itself the point; what was pivotal was the depth, extent, and indicative power of the transformation of social relations that was bound up with the "great leap forward" in productive technology.

In its mid-nineteenth century form, capitalism had attained an unprecedented degree of approximation to pure, unfettered operation. For the first time, commodity-economic relations dominated society. Human relations were simplified and reified to the extent that "economy," or (sub)structure, could function as a self-contained, self-sufficient, self-developing, and self-perpetuating system, in short, as a subject/object unto itself.[41] As such it required a minimal legal apparatus; or perhaps more accurately, the use of state power in the stage of liberal capitalism was directed toward the maintenance of the market at home, and the creation of new ones abroad. Such indeed was the process depicted in the historical sections of *Capital*'s first volume.

So strikingly advanced was the commodification of social relations that it became possible to conceive of an abstract and objective model of capitalism that could ground a new science of political economy: for Uno, that was the achievement of *Capital*. *Capital* was a theoretical model of pure capitalism, not a historical description of its formation or development.[42] Marx, Uno said, "worked at the right time." Capitalism, a set of material relations, was also an object of cognition. As such, it had grown sufficiently "gray" that Marx could do more than "copy it as it was"; he could also copy its "method of abstraction and synthesis." He could build on the tradition of political economy, which had identified the economic as an " 'Other,' in principle susceptible of study on its own," and on the "dialectical method of total comprehension" that Hegel had applied to the self-developing world of thought. Only such a method could grasp the congruent but material phenomenon of capitalism itself. Though it arose through historical accident, and not as a reflective product of idealist dialectic, capitalism had attained, and seemed to be bent on purifying, those "powers of self-abstraction and self-synthesis" that made dialectical analysis possible.[43]

Yet Marx's massive text was also incomplete on its own terms, and even in its finished sections was adulterated with "references to historical changes, . . . ideological forecasts and prejudices, . . . and logical inconsistencies."[44] Were cyclical crises, for example, "necessary" in the same sense that Marx claimed that socialism was? The basic problem, Uno argued, was that Marx failed to discriminate sufficiently between capitalism in theory and its epochal character, either as "English" or in a world-historical sense, to say nothing of correctly predicting its developmental trajectory. The *Principles*, Colin Duncan has remarked, were

> intended to be a thought-experiment in which the very idea of capitalism was taken to its logical extreme, a realm in which class struggle and the state were to be held in abeyance because *ex hypothesi* human relations have become as reified as possible. In such a situation class struggle could not occur and therefore the state would not be necessary. Class struggle requires precisely human beings who do not accept the role of things. Uno wanted to explore what it would be like if the capitalists had it totally their way.[45]

For some critics, the abstracting, even at the theoretical level, of politics and the state is to vitiate Marxism and concede the field to neoclassical equilibration. I defer such discussion for the moment, recalling only that an essential point of the *Principles,* as of *Capital,* is that even if "the capitalists had it totally their way," crises are part of the grammar of capitalism. To put more modestly the nature of Uno's project, we can say that it explores "the economy which would have materialized if the tendencies toward purification which capitalism most clearly manifested in England in the 1860s had prevailed over the countertendencies which gave rise to the era of finance capital (or imperialism)."[46]

The structure of the *Principles* is simple, and its elaboration intricate: three "doctrines," of Circulation, Production, and Distribution recast the contents of *Capital's* three volumes. An "inner logic" works through and between each doctrine: the first traces and develops the forms of circulation from commodity through money to capital. On this basis, the second analyzes what Uno terms the "labor and production process," that is, the colonization of production by the logic of the commodity and its consequences: it is here that Uno (unlike Marx, who introduces it prematurely) argues for the labor theory of value and derives the category of surplus value. This, of course, is the heart of the matter, the "essence of *Capital,*" and of capitalism. The concluding doctrine treats the distribution of surplus value among capitalists and landowners, and it is here that Uno presents his theory of business cycles and crises. As its placement suggests, Uno rejected the underconsumptionist and disproportionality arguments that ran through the Marxian tradition; his own view was that the cyclical crises endemic to capitalism were the result of capital excess. This did not mean that crises lacked a social cause and character. The dynamic tendencies of profit rates and wage levels that determined capital excess also determined the need for labor power, the supply of which was problematic even in purely theoretical terms. Uno differed from Marx in arguing that surplus population was not a chronic condition but was rather caught up in the characteristic boom-and-bust cycles of capital. Growing labor productivity came as capital sought to innovate its way out of depression, thereby decreasing the need for labor power, while expanding scale on this new footing increased that need. But the process across economic sectors was highly uneven as profit, wage, and interest rates moved: there would always either be "too much" or "too little" labor power available. Profits and wages, of course, were merely names for the relationship of capitalists to workers, one that with each cycle would have to be redefined (with the mediation of technological innovation and rationalization): this was a delicate reference to class struggle. The law of value, therefore, had as its necessary complement the "law of population peculiar to capitalism." The commodification of labor power, Uno asserted, was "pivotal to the theory not only of accumulation (this goes without saying), but of value and of crisis"—in other words, to capitalism in both its secular and cyclical movements.[47]

Uno's "capital excess" theory of crisis is no more immune to criticism than the theories he rejected. Indeed, the *Principles* seems rather rigid on this score; Uno's approach has been modified from within the school, in part as successor principles have come to be written. In general Uno recognized that his linking of labor-power commodification to these other major domains of Marxian economic theory ran the risk of reductionism, and "at times led [him] to logical developments at odds with that of *Capital.*" (His attempted clarifications sometimes had the opposite effect.) Most consequentially, Uno saw no foundation for the Marxian tenet of immiseration; and he did not interpret the "law of the tendency for the profit rate to fall" as "in any sense [implying] that capitalism is doomed to collapse of its own accord." To the contrary, as a "manifestation of the law of relative surplus population on the surface of the capitalist market, [it] preserves capitalism from self-destruction . . . by assuring that the capitalist market can achieve an equilibrium with some positive rate of profit, however low."[48]

Because such arguments raised the stakes for organized praxis, they involved both intellectual and political risks. For Uno, risk was the very sign of scientific practice and did nothing to affect his conviction that *Capital* was the distilled essence of capitalism. Alone among Marx's works, it occupied a position as the founding text of the science of political economy; only *Capital* offered a scientific means to grasp capitalism as a distinct and transient form of society. As such, it deserved, and could certainly withstand, criticism and appropriation at the highest intellectual level.

But could *Capital* withstand history? Only if it were "translated" into a pure theory of capitalism. This was done, however, not to protect it from history, but to "liberate" the historical materials, the stuff of contingency, partiality, and the "furies of private interest," to do their actual work. In a theoretical sense, it is a question of the treatment of "use-values, the ever-present contingent elements in economic life." For though capitalism can only produce commodities, commodities can be, and in fact are, used. They make the world go 'round. There would otherwise be no value—bound in contradiction with use value—for price to measure. "In pure theory, use values are so neutral and inactive that they efface history; in reality, they are so naked and rampant that they obscure theory." His recognition of, and ultimate respect for, history's messiness led Uno to argue that "the mediation of stages theory, in which use values appear as a type, is necessary."[49]

Such mediation was necessary for another reason. "Use values" sounds positive and almost friendly, but steel and rolling stock and heavy weaponry were the use values Uno had foremost in mind. Similarly, the term "contingency," with its Baudelairean overtones, points to what was its apparent opposite but in fact its complement: the state and its role. The contingency of capitalism, that is, presumed the necessary permanence, the noncontingency, of the state. As Robert Heilbroner has put it, "Remove the regime of capital, and the state would remain, although it might change dramatically; remove the state, and the regime of capital would not last a day . . . Domination must precede exploitation."[50] The issue for Uno was the specific modes of domination and exploitation, their nexus and interaction. It was the issue of policy in the context of capitalist development.

CONCEPTUALIZING DEVELOPMENT: STAGE THEORY

Much has already been said here about Uno's early and abiding conviction that the notion of stages of development was essential to understanding the history of capitalism—or modern history itself. Closely tied to it was the question of what—if any—stage characterized the present. Had capitalism ended, and if so, when? Or if not capitalism, then had the notion of stage itself become outmoded, and if so, in favor of what?

Uno never published any work on stage theory per se. The study of economic policies was only a part of that effort, and "had to be supplemented by in-depth, stage-theoretic explanations of agriculture, industry, commerce, finance, transport, and colonies." Among these, Uno held, preeminent importance went to the area of public finance *(zaiseigaku)*. "Whether it is the mercantilism of the seventeenth and eighteenth century, the liberalism of the nineteenth, or the imperialism of the twentieth," only in combination with the "specifications provided by studies of finance" can the study of policy become "the scientific"—that is, total— "study of the state."[51]

The first edition of *Keizai seisakuron* presented Uno's lecture materials on the economic policies of mercantilism and liberalism. Though he had long lectured on imperialism, he was not to add that crucial section until the second edition of 1954; this was followed by a final version in 1971. Essentially, Uno argued that specific economic policies—charters and corn laws under mercantilism; their contested abolition under the free-trade regime; protective tariffs, dumping, capital export, and colonialism under imperialism—derived, inevitably, from the limited and sometimes conflicting perspectives of political and economic interests:

> The direction of development that an enacted policy brings about in the economic process is not determined by the goal of that policy, since the latter is arrived at through interest relations that are incapable of recognizing such direction. Rather, such policies ultimately bring about unintended results.[52]

Policies alone did not create or define stages, though they did have their own kind of causality. Rather, stages formed the medium, more or less amenable, through which the capitalist drive to commodify every possible use value worked in the world. Ultimately, the laws of motion associated with that drive would be served; or more accurately, they would always demand to be served, and the cost of both resistance and compliance could be high. Policy might distort or retard them, but they would also act upon policy, perhaps via correction through another policy. "The realm of the political in human history" was therefore a "veritable tissue of contingency"—and conflict.[53]

The contingency in question was not limited to the internal politics of economic policy. Perhaps more consequentially, it affected entire nations as historical actors:

> The policies that a late-developing country such as ours carries out in the process of primitive accumulation of capital will differ in so far as that process itself entails causes historically different from those [encountered in England]. Nevertheless, as a late developer, it will naturally imitate the measures taken by various nations elsewhere. Even so, it most certainly does not adopt them with an understanding of their historical significance. . . . Unless we make explicit the historical significance of *both* English mercantile policies *and* the subsequent stage of capitalist development, we will be unable to explain the historical course followed by the late developer.[54]

Uno located the strongest defining force for a given stage in the technology and organization of capitalist production in the succession of leading countries and leading sectors of their respective economies.[55] To schematize: "genesis" with English woolens and domestic handicraft under merchant capital during the seventeenth and eighteenth centuries; "growth" with English cotton and light mechanization under industrial capital from the mid-eighteenth century through the 1870s; "maturity" with German heavy industry, particularly steel, under finance capital (which also had important American and British variants), from the 1870s through World War I.

Uno was not attempting to write history, still less a history of "winners." Despite its dry, highly systematic presentation, the work has an epicenter in the first, devastating experience of industrial crises of the mid-nineteenth century. The purpose of such a historical typology of economic policy is as an explanation, and a warning. In its purest form under liberalism, capitalism generated, not as an exceptional phenomenon but typically, a series of decennial crises that compelled the state to seek "strengthening" policies that would keep the "capitalist commodity economy, which shouldn't have required any special policy at all," from breaking down or exploding. As we have seen, however, those policies were not self-consistent; but this merely points to their character as the externalization of capitalism's internal relations. The point is worth repeating that "pure capitalism" was about objective, specifiable "contradictions" starkly revealed. It was a starkness in which Uno sought the basis for a new political economy, and which he regarded as a vantage point from which "science" could also grasp the transhistorical norms of social provisioning that until then had been invisible. Pure capitalism, that is, was a clearing on a historical path through the branches and brambles of contingency that afforded a vista on the way taken, and the way still to be (necessarily) taken. Here was the broad significance of the fact that, as Colin Duncan puts it, "in the liberal stage, the real approached asymptotically to the model in *Capital,* and then fell away again."[56]

A concatenation of trends and countertrends, technological, political, economic, and social, yielded the typical "impurities" of "maturing" capitalism. Thus, at the theoretical level, development was impurification. The succession of types, moreover, was not fortuitous. Genesis, growth, and maturity pointed to an end, to decay or senescence. For Uno, this sequence was explainable in scientific terms as a single process only if the "law of population peculiar to capitalism" (which the basic principles disclosed) were taken into account. In the stage of imperialism, the "gigantism" of fixed capital with high organic composition had come to inhibit the mobility of capital, and tended to block the law of the equalization of profit rates. And in contrast to earlier modes, accumulation in this last phase was compelled to proceed via labor-power commodification based on a seemingly permanent surplus population. This could be countered imperialistically, and perhaps only at the price of war. As a problem in stage theory, war could not be shown to be necessary in the same sense that cyclical crises were in pure theory: as real capitalism "fell away" from its model, it was politicized, and as such did not generate war as the inherent working of any of its laws. To be sure, Uno seconded Lenin's view that the wars of the twentieth century were "a further, different expression for the policies of finance capital that had already taken the form of tariffs and possession of colonies"; or more specifically, policies of unevenly developed national units of finance capital engaged in rival imperialisms. But the point is that "finance capital" was a thoroughly political category.[57] To use Uno's terms in a way he did not, war was the "practice" *(jissen)* of states.

Let us remain briefly with Lenin's *Imperialism.* There is an interesting ambiguity about the subtitle of Lenin's pamphlet that has some bearing on this present discussion, and will also lead us to the transition from Uno himself to the Uno school. In its first published form (from September 1917), "imperialism" is described on the title page as the "latest" or "newest stage" of capitalism. But the version in the collected works gives the better known "highest stage." Who changed the subtitle and when, and what did the change mean?[58] It must have meant something: intuitively, "latest" implies "most recent" rather than "last." "Highest" implies that there is no "higher." Did this betoken greater—strategic—militancy on Lenin's part amid the revolutionary upsurge of 1917? Was it anti-Social Democratic and anti-Menshevik? In any case, the sense seems to be that once imperialism has ended, capitalism as a system will have ceased to exist. Or perhaps there was to be a new stage of capitalist development. That would have been a matter of some importance.

How did Uno, who thought *through* stages, approach this issue? In the first postwar edition of *Keizai seisakuron,* Uno specified that he was "limiting the scope of its object to the developmental stage of capitalism through World War I," leaving open the question of whether the phenomena of the interwar era merited designation as a new stage. What difference did the Russian Revolution make? The stepped-up state interventionism? Fascism? Uno's tentative answer was that this period "pertained to the world economy as conjunctural analysis," which was the "ultimate purpose" of his system. He did not think that interwar capitalism was qualitatively different from imperialism. A decade and a half later, in the revised edition, Uno removed the "limit," affirming that indeed, capitalism since World War I, and more importantly since World War II, remained an issue for "contemporary analysis." No new stage had emerged. Why? Because the emergence of the socialist bloc was not a development *of* capitalism but against it. Uno was of course cognizant of decolonization as a complication for the theory of imperialist rivalry, and of certain features of state monopoly as self-imposed curbs on capitalism for its own sake.[59] But for him the reconfiguration of the world economy into two rival camps was of preeminent importance.

APOTHEOSIS

Precisely because he regarded the theorization of stages, and particularly that of imperialism, as so important, Uno later expressed disappointment that his work in this area seemed to have had little impact compared to the *Principles*.[60] Perhaps this was because the exposition of stages as developmental types inevitably seemed mundane and commonsensical in contrast to the sustained and masterful concision of the basic principles. But there must have been more to the reaction.

Uno's complaint should be placed in context. As noted, the *Principles* in their first edition of 1950–52 sold some fifty thousand copies. The early 1950s were to be sure the heyday of Marxism in postwar Japan. But as Sekine notes,

> When Uno's doctrine emerged . . . no one really understood it. Marxists, for the first time freed from political restrictions . . . , found too many exciting things to do. To many of them political activities were as important as academic research if not more so, since Marxist doctrine emphasizes the unity of theory and practice. In 1951 the Communist Party adopted a new programme, to which the regrouped Kōza-ha responded with the publication, between 1953 and 1955, of eleven new volumes on Japanese capitalism under U.S. domination. Uno's call for a distinction of theory from ideology was untimely. It not only remained unheeded but rather sparked vitriolic reproaches.[61]

The content of those reproaches will occupy us shortly. But we observe that within a decade, the Uno school came into its own. Two major factors were at work here. The Stalinist system of state socialism that Uno (and many others) saw as competing with, and modifying, capitalism came under critique, and with it the ideological authority of the Communist Party. That same moment saw a capitalist surge—one not limited to Japan but thoroughly unexpected in its scope and temporal extent—that placed Marxism itself, as a critique of capitalism, in question. The very framework of the erstwhile capitalism debate, namely the fate of Japan's large and backward agrarian sector, began to dissolve; this was twenty-five years, roughly, from the time of Uno's early essay on rural differentiation. Writing in 1956 from a perspective different from Uno's, the political scientist Matsushita Keiichi captured the significance of this moment in a theoretical article concerned chiefly with the general process by which "the mass state, under the condition of the change in social forms during the stage of monopoly capitalism, emerges as the system transforms 'class' into 'mass.'" In his concluding paragraph, Matsushita noted: "In Japan too, incidentally, the general condition of the change in social forms in the stage of monopoly capital is advancing, albeit with peculiarities of its own. The problem, not only of 'feudal versus modern,' but even more acutely of 'the modern' itself, has to be raised."[62]

This moment of the "the modern itself" was also the moment of the Uno school in Japan, the moment when developmental stages began to give way to the as yet undefined contemporaneity of the "world economy." It is not that stage theory itself was immediately set aside in those years; the opposite seems to be true, as witness the work of Alexander Gerschenkron and Walt Rostow—with Barrington Moore pointing the way toward structure. But in the long run, Japan's "lateness" in world time could no longer be correlated with material backwardness, and lateness everywhere came increasingly to be translated into structural, spatial, or systemic terms. Under these circumstances, it was perhaps the fate of Uno's system that what he regarded as its crucial mediating element, the fulcrum that would enable and enrich conjunctural analysis, was perceived as an obstacle to just such analysis. A partial reverse of this pattern seems to be at work now, in reaction to the Hayekian neoliberalism of the 1980s and the complexities of the post–Soviet era transition. Things like "transitions" take time, not only space, and beg the question as to what continuous conditions they usher out and in. The point here is that insofar as Uno saw only three possible stages in a given sequence, the historical limits of his system would have been reached just as it attained its strongest influence in Japan.[63] The systematization that was meant to protect the integrity of Marxian ideas against politicization and abuse was also a case of the "owl of Minerva" taking flight.

But could there be *Principles* without stages, that is, only *Principles* and conjunctural analysis? Or perhaps new *Principles,* or none at all? The answers to these questions—that is, the pattern of de- and reconfiguration of Uno's system among his followers in Japan—will concern us in the chapter that follows. By way of conclusion here, I wish to take up some of the more general questions concerning the relation of political economy as science to ideology and Marxist philosophy, and that of theory to practice, as Uno himself addressed them in his final decades. These seem to have become more acute as Marxism itself, in the mid-1960s, "was placed on the laboratory table" following the defeat in 1960 of the anti-U.S.-Japan Security Treaty movement and the Sino-Soviet split.[64]

It was the conceptual disjunctions, and the formal quality of Uno's system, that always disturbed his critics, both Marxists and others. "Neo-Kantian" in epistemology, "aridly scholastic" in method, and "reactionary" in its political implications are all characterizations that were applied to Uno's three-level system. The chief objection was that the system, and the conception of science that underwrote it, seemed designed to inhibit praxis while continually raising the stakes placed on it.

On the one hand, Uno was determined to limit the scope of political economy, or more accurately the claims of dialectical logic, to the movement and laws of capital itself. He never sought a covering law for all social phenomena, let alone to unify the natural and human sciences under the aegis of materialist dialectics. For Uno, dialectic was an operation of the synthesizing mind; the dialectics of nature he regarded as an absurdity. Physical science, on which much social science sought to model itself, was a deceptive guide to knowledge.[65] It was true enough that laws of nature—high probabilities, repeatedly demonstrated—could be discerned and applied for technical purposes: hence the phenomenal growth of "productive forces" that fed the modern fetishism of natural science. Total comprehension from within, however, was an illusion; nature was dialectically unfathomable, its order always already self-created. Social science, by contrast, was the self-study of society, and society in principle was no mystery; it constructed its own subject matter as it went. The laws (or probabilities) it claimed to discover were metaphorical—powerful metaphors, as in the laws of motion of capital, but metaphors nonetheless—and could not even be applied technically in the form of policy. With the advent of capitalism, and only then, political economy could "comprehend the object of its study completely and totally," since reified human relations functioned virtually as natural objects in motion. Paradoxically, however, the "complete and total knowledge" promised by this integral social science could—or should—only lead to the graduated disavowal of necessity as conceived by historical materialism. Why so?

Uno regarded capitalist society as unique and transient. Grasping that transience, however, brought with it the methodological presumption of the self-regulating and self-perpetuating capacity of capital:

> The pure theory of capitalism must represent the capitalist commodity-economy as if it were a self-perpetuating entity in order to divulge its laws of motion. It therefore seems to me quite impossible for economic theory to demonstrate at the same time a transformation which involves the denial of these laws. . . . The laws of pure capitalism cannot possibly be exposed without envisioning an infinite duration of pure capitalism itself.[66]

Working on the assumption (if not the hope) that capitalism in some form was likely to last, Uno qualified the conditions under which one could speak of its supersession or abolition as "necessary." Cyclical crises were demonstrably inherent to capitalism at every level of purity—or impurity. Policy was meant to forestall or soften them, but could never eliminate their causal mechanism, which was the circuit of capital itself. Secular or general crises, following from immiseration and falling profit rates, were another matter. Marx, Uno felt, had overestimated the "progressive" tendencies of capital in this regard, and even more problematically had linked such breakdown, via the medium of proletarian self-knowledge gained in the teeth of alienation, to the alleged necessity of socialism. It is impossible not to be gripped by these passages in *Capital*.[67] But they were not realized. War and revolution—the imagined choice between barbarism and socialism—were, again, necessities of two different orders. War was unexplainable at the level of pure theory; empirical analysis mediated by stage theory might, with immense comparative research, show how its likelihood grew over into necessity. But could that necessity ever be analogous to that of cyclical crises? Revolution, in the sense of the conscious abolition of the law of value, was dependent on the practical activity of the working class. It would never occur of itself.[68]

Thus, more and more had to be left open to contingency; the purpose of political economy was to provide specifying "standards"—derived from stage theory—for the conceptual organization of that contingency and its transformation into knowledge: and thence to praxis. But between knowledge and praxis lay a crucial disjunction, and as it were, a leap of faith. "Social science" as a rigorously systematized knowledge of its object could offer no "economic explanation of the process of transition from capitalism to socialism. . . . The correct use of the knowledge of society," Uno insisted, "is to frustrate ill-advised actions; this is of paramount importance."[69] At the same time, historical materialism—as summarized, for example, in Marx's preface to his *Contribution to the Critique of Political Economy* (1859)—was no more than a hypothesis; it could not prove itself. The conclusion was inescapable:

> That Marxist philosophy, which links theory and practice, validates its core of dialectical materialism by means of the principles of political economy, which lie at the farthest remove from practice. This is the conclusion I have come to after many years of study in political economy.[70]

Beyond that, one moved to the domain of political judgment and the "organized practice of socialist movements." As Uno himself suggested, this was a huge leap. Could judgment be nurtured and disciplined and directed merely by scientific knowledge? It was on this point that Uno was criticized most sharply, albeit respectfully, by the Marxist philosopher Umemoto Katsumi, and by Maruyama Masao, certainly the most important liberal (or liberal-left) political thinker of the postwar era. Both represented positions that we might term nonaligned in their respective practical domains: Umemoto had left the Communist Party in 1960 after a decade of membership; Maruyama had never joined any party. While agreeing to disagree on many points, both Umemoto and Maruyama believed that Uno was far too prone to treat ideology only as an obstruction to knowledge, denying to it any positive, constructive power. For Maruyama, who attached great significance to the motivational force of "ethos" in understanding social action, this was particularly problematic as an approach to the analysis of capitalism. Umemoto rejected Uno's conflation of "ideology" with "thought," which both denigrated the latter, and promoted a notion of practical life in which all judgments were derived from science. Uno did not in fact believe in such a possibility, but Umemoto's point was well taken.[71]

Uno's system brought socialists to the brink of action, saying, "it's all up to you now," but offered no assurance that the leap would be successful. Was that his responsibility? No, he was merely being honest, and refused to make false promises of a necessary breakdown. But would Marxism last without a moral theory, a personal "principle of hope"? No, and indirectly, Uno's apparent determination to protect Marxian political economy from Stalinist degradation was proof of the need for such a principle. Uno cared about the prospects for socialism, understanding as he did that "uncommoditised labor power can still be subjected to extra-economic coercion."[72] In the name of science, he rejected both economic determinism and the vanguardism and revolutionary catastrophism that were no more than its mirror images. Precisely for this reason, Uno ought to have been less dismissive of Bernstein's "revisionism," of Weber's "idealism." The same intellectual tradition that inoculated Uno against "vulgar Marxism," that led him to systematize, might also have offered him insight into the realm of ethics—a close neighbor of the praxis on which he staked the future. In the long run, it was not better science that Marxism needed, but better ethics.

CHAPTER 5

School's Out?

The Uno School Meets Japanese Capitalism

To speak of Uno Kōzō is also to speak of the school of economics, or political economy, that developed under the impetus of his ideas. Set against the background of postwar privation, economic recovery, and the capitalist surge that the school was fated to explain, the story is one of dramatic coalescence and academic dominance, but also of deepening scholasticism, paradigm shifts, and ultimately of decomposition. In this sense, the trajectory of the Uno school is both a case study of social science history and an episode in the intellectual history of Marxism.

Uno-school political economy, according to a recent formulation by Furihata Setsuo, formed one of three dominant streams of postwar Japanese social science, alongside the political science of Maruyama Masao and Ōtsuka Hisao's economic history.[1] At first sight, the distinction between the latter two seems somewhat tenuous in comparison to the sharp differences separating them from Uno's Marxian economics. Maruyama was as much a practicing historian as a political scientist; apart from differences in subject matter, Maruyama and Ōtsuka shared a basic tendency to trace genealogies—of "modern" thought in Japan, or "really revolutionary" small-producer capitalism in Europe. Their search for a morally charged model of human subjectivity came in the wake of the massive institutional failure and irrationality that, for them, had made Japan's military defeat inevitable. Yet it could be argued that Uno's model of capitalism as a self-activating, self-sustaining subject/object of knowledge was essentially an objectivist, structural rendering of the same human subject that was the grail of so-called modernist social science. As such, Uno's capitalism was in fact broadly congruent with the tendency of that movement to seek a pure, albeit historically grounded, "type" as the lodestone of its scientific imagining of society and social change.

With this modest qualification of Furihata's formula, it seems clear that the Uno school did attain the stature claimed for it by its adepts. A survey of Marxian economics in Japan from 1962, prepared by younger members of the Uno school, situates it in interesting fashion.[2] The authors open by denouncing the moral triumphalism prevalent among Marxists in the wake of Japan's defeat:

> Amid a postwar situation in which the deepest self-examination was being urged in every field, Marxism appeared on the scene virtually as a victor. For Marxism, there was nothing to be repented; its role was to criticize, to attack, or to take revenge on others. Under these circumstances, how can we speak of "postwar" for Marxism? If there is anything resembling a "postwar" for Marxism, we may make a case for the Sixth Congress of the Japan Communist Party, or for the impact of Khrushchev's criticism of Stalin. But as far as the period immediately following the Second World War is concerned, there was nothing of this kind of "postwar" to be found in Marxism. To put it paradoxically, for Marxism, "postwar" was no postwar. And this is the peculiarity of Marxism among all the elements one finds simply lumped together under the rubric of "postwar thought."

Under these circumstances, "Marxists and Marxian economists were the darlings of journalism," leading to the unfortunate result that the "low" intellectual level of prewar—particularly Kōza-ha, or Lectures Faction—economics persisted even as its value came to be inflated.[3]

The exception to this inflationary trend, one that in the authors' estimation reached a peak of absurdity in the ten-plus volumes of the *Nihon shihonshugi kōza* (Lectures on Japanese capitalism, 1953–55), was the Uno school. Exceptional, but not because Uno Kōzō had met the advent of postwar as a historical penitent: as we saw earlier, the contrary was the case. What was important about Uno was that, in 1953, fully three years before de-Stalinization, he carefully lifted the veil of circumspection he (and others), pleading ignorance of actual conditions, had long placed over the assessment of Soviet-style socialism.

The occasion was the appearance of Stalin's *Economic Problems of Socialism in the USSR* (1952). Stalin's "ideological testament" had argued that even under socialism (in its extended opening phase), some forms of commodity production and exchange would continue; he offered a necessitarian reading of passages from Engels' *Anti-Dühring* (1878) to support his contention that the "law of value," indeed all "economic laws," must remain operative, no more susceptible of abolition than the laws of nature, but like the latter capable of conscious application.[4] Uno found "fundamental problems" running through the text, questioning Stalin's interpretation of Engels and repeatedly drawing attention to what he delicately termed the "lack of clarity" in Stalin's conception of the law of value. Stalin's treatment of these issues,

> it must be said, obscures the relation between the economic principles that are contained within and undergird the laws of commodity economy on the one hand, and their historical form on the other, rendering vague the historical significance of abolishing the commodity form.

At one point, Uno was moved to rebuke:

> When I hear [Stalin] say that "the law of value is first and foremost the law of commodity production . . . [that] it preexisted capitalist society . . . and has continued to exist even after the overthrow of capitalism," and therefore does not define "the essence of capitalist production," I feel . . . like emulating his reproach to Notkin not to fiddle with the meaning of "means of production," and saying to him: "don't fiddle with the meaning of 'commodity production' "!

On the crucial question of the broader significance of Soviet socialism, Uno found Stalin's approach deficient:

> There is a problem as to whether or not the case of the Soviet Union as is can be treated as a typical opening phase of the development of socialist society. To do that, there at least have to be basic definitions made by abstracting from concrete processes, but with Stalin, somehow or other I get the feeling that the concrete processes of the Soviet case are being juxtaposed in the raw to the abstract, general definitions taken from Engels.[5]

Thus, the exceptional status accorded Uno's system was due to his insistence that, by walling off "science" from "ideology," and assimilating Marxian economics entirely with the former, he had safeguarded it from Stalinist politicization; his treatment of Stalin's economics stood as proof. Uno had vindicated Marxism against the party intellectuals who had vilified his *Keizai genron* (Principles of political economy) and its accompanying system when it had first appeared at the beginning of the 1950s. Even if not in a strictly moral sense, therefore,

> three-level analysis can truly be termed a product of the postwar era, and . . . it is impermissible to ignore the significance of Uno theory for the development of economics in postwar Japan. And, when we consider this in conjunction with the fact that three-level analysis is not merely a

method in economics but has intervened vigorously in the broader field of social science and philosophy, we are bound to say that one cannot even speak of social science without reference to the Uno school of political economy.[6]

"Three-level analysis," it will be recalled, is a shorthand for Uno's system, which was comprised of "basic principles" *(genron)* of "pure capitalism"; a "stage theory" *(dankairon)* that posited a triple periodization of mercantilist, liberal, and imperialist stages of capitalist development; and *genjō bunseki*—"the empirical analysis of the actual state of capitalism either in the world as a whole or in each different country."[7] Uno held this last level of analysis, which would subsume the basic principles as mediated by stage-theoretic considerations, to be the "ultimate aim . . . to which political economy can apply itself." Although he produced volume after volume in the decade following 1945—*Kachiron* (1947), *Nōgyō mondai joron* (1947), *Shihonron no kenkyū* (1948), *Keizai genron* (1950–52), *Kyōkōron* (1953), and *Keizai seisakuron* (1954; 1971)—Uno left little more than scattered articles to demonstrate the intellectual (or as he would have preferred, "scientific") substance or potential of the empirical analysis he called for. His period of greatest productivity had coincided with the high point of Marxism in postwar Japanese life; that dominance, in turn, had been underwritten by the apparent tenuousness of the prospects for the recovery of Japanese capitalism from the devastation of war and defeat. By the time Uno published his major works on the theory of cyclical crises and on economic policies in relation to the stages of capitalist development, Japan's economy was moving from its long-awaited recovery into the early phase of what became a most startling run of growth. This is hardly to say that his system, or even its ascetically deferred goal of a modern society that has transcended the commodification of social relations, promptly fell out of date. Indeed, the coherence and audacity of Uno's project, albeit without a completed capstone, had won for his system literally hundreds of adepts, particularly among economists with ties to Tokyo University, where Uno had moved shortly after the war had ended: included among their number are Suzuki Kōichirō, Ōuchi Tsutomu, Ōshima Kiyoshi, Watanabe Hiroshi, Tamanoi Yoshirō, Hidaka Hiroshi, Ōuchi Hideaki, Sakurai Tsuyoshi, Iwata Hiroshi, Itō Makoto, Shibagaki Kazuo, Sekine Tomohiko, Baba Hiroji, Furihata Setsuo, and many others. These scholars in their turn trained their own students, so that over the two decades from the mid-1950s through the mid-1970s, Marxian economics in Japan came to be dominated by, or at least to assume its strongest academic "personality," in the Uno school; this was a position safeguarded by the institutionalization of required courses in Marxian economics *(marukei)* prior to the ascendance of modern economics in university departments.[8]

One final aspect of the school's impact at its height bears mentioning. This same combination of a demonstrated anti-Stalinism (Stalin being portrayed as willfully distorting Marxism) with a powerful systematizing drive that provided Uno's economics its academic bona fides may also have made it attractive to elements of the radical student movement and a left-wing fraction of the Socialist Party. As with the modernism of Maruyama and Ōtsuka, the testing ground in the move from theory to practice proved to be the 1960 Anti-Security Treaty ("Anpo") movement and its aftermath. An intriguing, but I do not think idiosyncratic, account of the role of Uno-school economics comes from the literary critic Karatani Kōjin, who had begun his academic career as a radicalized economics major at Tokyo University; in 1960, the freshman Karatani joined the Communist League (Kyōsanshugisha Dōmei), otherwise known as the Bund.

> What attracted me to the Bund was its destructiveness *[hakaisei]* and extreme activism; I could not have cared less about all the theoretical prattle. But if the Bund had a "theory," I suppose it consisted of conclusions drawn from the ideas of Uno Kōzō—conclusions at odds with what he himself intended. In other words, historical materialism is ideology, while *Capital* is science, and therefore no practical policy or goal whatever emerges from it; despite that, its logic is fulfilled, beyond any arbitrariness of our own will. . . . This meant that based on these ideas of Uno, any kind of subjectivism in practice could be "affirmed." That at least was how I regarded the significance for the Bund of Uno's theory. In actuality, even though, beginning with the makeshift notion of state monopoly capitalism cooked up by [the economist] Aoki Masahiko, matters were always discussed in terms of economics, in my view the role of Uno theory, all too ironically, was to have liberated the political movement from economics; or perhaps from its entire "theoretical grounding" as such. . . . What was truly silly was the utterly serious clerical spirit one saw, for example in the group who went over to the Revolutionary Marxists, having made their self-criticism as petty bourgeois Bundists and vowing to manifest "proletarian humanity"; or among the "theorists" who switched over from the Uno school to modern economics.

Karatani himself did not remain with economics or activism, and while (like Maruyama) professing to feel none of the sense of "failure" that had followed in the wake of Anpo, turned to writing for a living.

But supposing that I did indeed feel no concern for external events: it was
not because I denied the existence "out there" of a structural force, at work
regardless of anything I might happen to believe. It was there, perhaps, that
the Uno school's ideas remained in my mind; then again, the very fact that I
read Uno in this manner may have been due to thoughts of my own that had
nothing to do with him.[9]

Karatani's remarks are useful as a general reminder of the dynamics
by which ideas can be lifted out of a systemic context and transformed
into political or organizational doctrine. The typical Uno-school themes
are there: "Marxian" science versus "Marxist" ideology, the implacable
character of capitalism—in this case "state monopoly capitalism," to be
discussed presently—and the resolute intellectualism that in Karatani's
view differentiated the Bund, for example, from Zenkyōtō and its proclaimed "revolt of the intellect" in the closing years of the 1960s.

Interestingly, Karatani's evocation of the ethos of the Uno school overlaps with Uno's own recognition, in the last decade of his life, that his
school's acquisition of academic citizenship required it, as a practical
necessity, not just to critique but to explain in its own terms the economic
growth that was transforming the world around it, most strikingly Japan
itself. And that it would have to do so at a time when Marxism—
Marxian political economy—was in "ebb tide," challenged by three
interrelated but distinct, even in part conflicting "flood tides": the ascen-
dant trend of "growthism," which assumed, approvingly, that Japan's
industrial society was convergent with those of the West; a secondary,
reactive yet complementary orientation toward "culturalism" that saw
Japan's mode of growth, also approvingly, as divergent from those societies; and, underlying both tendencies, a combined drive toward math-
ematization of economic research and its move from the academy to
officialdom (and to corporate sponsorship). How well would Uno's system of three-level analysis and the constituent elements of this conceptual
inheritance stand up to these tendencies? What could it achieve in its
analyses of capitalism that other groups, other orientations, could not?
Conversely, how would the attempts from within the Uno school to meet
the intellectual challenges of growth and growthism transform its members and their work?

I do not propose to offer here a full survey of Unoist or Marx-Uno
political economy, as the work of the contemporary Uno school is
known. Instead, I will try first to indicate the substance of the specific, if
undeveloped, ideas that Uno himself left as resources for the analysis of
high growth, and in so doing make clear the limitations of his system;

then, at the risk of idiosyncrasy and undue reduction, I wish to outline three particularly significant and representative trajectories followed by economists who studied directly with Uno: Ōuchi Tsutomu (b. 1918) sought to *complete* Uno's unfinished system by introducing the notion of state monopoly capitalism and making it the foundation of his analysis both of the world economy and of Japanese capitalism; Baba Hiroji (b. 1933), through a reconsideration of the category of finance capital, sought to *change the paradigms* of the system while preserving its analytical structure; and Tamanoi Yoshirō (1918–1985), by reembedding Uno's system in a world of both noncommodified relations and its ultimate physical matrix, set about to *transcend* it. Each of the three was unmistakably marked by his engagement with Uno's system, and each reveals something of its rich potential. At the same time, taken together, they demonstrate how attempts to reconfigure the system instead pushed it toward decomposition.

THE CALL OF THE PRESENT

The "ultimate aim" of Uno's political economy lay in "the empirical analysis of the actual state of capitalism either in the world as a whole or in each different country." At his death—or more broadly, as a result of his systematizing tendency and sense of obligation to meet every serious criticism along the way—Uno left no more than 30 percent of this ultimate aim realized. If Uno may be said to have bequeathed to his followers a viable system and program of research, this was in two senses a productively negative legacy. Methodologically, Uno's system presented a "negative heuristic": to be a member of the school was to accept three-level analysis; to reject or go beyond it was to exit the school.[10] Debate within the school seems to have been encouraged, and could, perhaps predictably, take on an arcane quality. Especially when reading works by followers of Uno concerning the "higher" reaches of value theory, the outsider can sometimes feel like an agnostic among eucharistic theologians arguing over the mode of Christ's presence. There is no question that in its later phases, the Uno school manifested a kind of hermeticism and penchant for commentary on and exegesis of the Marx-Uno canon. Such technicalities, however, are essential to those involved. Like the religious arguments over "real presence," which had immense and sometimes violent social consequences, or other debates among Marxists in which terminological differences have turned into weapons at the factional or (under "actually existing socialism") state level, disagreements within the Uno school could extend into the area of political struggle. But the system's very character qua system—apart from generating the scholastic, hermetic tendencies noted by its critics—acted to inhibit a total "transubstantiation" from the academic to political domain. In the history of Marxism as a body of thought, the problem of scholasticism has come up less often, and with far less unhealthy consequences, than has that of the intellectual debasement and corruption that reached its apogee in Stalinism.[11]

The second "productively negative" legacy is the more intellectually substantive. For Uno, "the analysis of capitalism after World War I had to be handled at the level of 'contemporary analysis' . . . but this was not a conclusion he had come to on the basis of his own positive studies of contemporary capitalism. Rather, it is, so to speak, a negative conclusion arrived at from the vantage point of his studies of the period up until World War I, as crystallized in *Keizai seisakuron*."[12] "Contemporary" capitalism, Uno held, had not entered a new stage of self-development but rather one of counterdevelopment, or counteraction, to the emergence of socialism. Mature capitalism was in its final phase of existence; a world-historical transformation, the transition to socialism, had begun. But by rejecting the notion of a new stage of capitalist development, Uno left open—and open to confusion—the issue of how the present was to be characterized. In what relation did it stand to imperialism and finance capital, the posited stage and mode of accumulation characteristic of capitalism's maturity—and senescence? Conversely, how could capitalism have ended if it was so evidently alive and functioning? How was the call of the present to be answered?

How indeed. At this juncture we must identify and defer a problem: namely, that the "present," as Uno and those who followed him conceived it, was defined as transitional to a socialist future that history has, for the moment, rendered moot. In this post–Cold War moment, it is all too tempting to broaden the question of "the call of the present" to ask whether, in the light of the evacuation of its telos, Uno's system as such can have anything but historical interest. But we must resist, not the question, only its timing; we must first, imaginatively, step back into a world in which socialism was considered not a moot but a live issue, and seek elements of Uno's answer, as far as it went, to the call of that present.[13]

Uno's characterization in the *Principles* of "empirical analysis of contemporary conditions" *(genjō bunseki)* suggests two possible directions for attempts to grasp contemporary capitalism. First, in "the world as a

whole," or second, "in each different country." As a programmatic statement this is less than satisfying. Why is this an either/or proposition? Is
there no relationship between the two? And did the "world" signify the
capitalist world economy alone, or the bifurcated world economy composed of the two rivalrous ideological power blocs, one capitalist, the
other socialist?

Concerning the world economy, Uno left one suggestive, but tentative
and poorly developed statement, which at least conveys his sense of how
the "problem of the world economy" had come into being, what linked
it with, and differentiated it from, the national economies as such. What
is most striking now, and yet typical of Uno's perspective, is the enduring
focus on the interwar and agrarian origins of the problem:

> Capitalism, in the process of its emergence, separated and made independent
> from agriculture the industry that until then had spontaneously been united
> with it, causing industry to develop along capitalist lines. But agriculture
> itself by no means formed a base that was amenable to capitalist manage-
> ment. The confrontation of agriculture with industry presents capitalism
> with an insoluble dilemma. I even believe that the development of capitalism
> in England was carried through by transferring to foreign countries the
> responsibility for the problems of England's own agriculture. And it hardly
> bears repeating that the agricultural problem that arose together with
> the development of capitalism in Germany and other backward countries
> gives rise to the particular character of capitalism in each such country. . . .
> The agrarian problem that was imposed on world capitalism following the
> earlier great war could not, like the agrarian problems in late nineteenth-
> century Germany and the other Western countries, be a problem simply
> for each of their national economies. It had in actuality become the defining
> problem of world capitalism itself. The various nationalist policies of the
> 1930s were in one aspect an attempt to erect a bulwark against this prob-
> lem. . . . What happened was that while the capitalist industrial countries
> faced a situation in which they had to import agricultural products, out of
> consideration for their own agriculture, they were in no position to import
> such products freely; and at the same time, the condition of the late develop-
> ers, which had to export agricultural products, was such that they were not
> necessarily able to increase their imports of industrial goods. This inevitably
> meant a situation of virtually chronic excess of agricultural products world-
> wide. We can say that it became clear on a world scale that the ability to
> solve the agrarian question would entail the ability to construct a new soci-
> ety to replace capitalism, and we may regard the League of Nations as hav-
> ing been one such attempt. The solution to this problem, of course, means
> no more than the external expression of the internal contradictions of capi-
> talism, and cannot occur unless the issue of class relations is solved. In this
> sense, the failure of the League of Nations was only to be expected.

In short, for Uno, "the world economy . . . does not constitute a single economic entity. It exists only in terms of the international economy composed of individual countries. Of late, however, it is becoming increasingly less such a merely international economy"—that is, one constituted by trading relations among various national economies. Its structural character had become "particularly obvious in the case of the agricultural problem," where rival protectionisms had provoked a global depression, and with it a global political catastrophe; clearly these policies could only provide makeshift responses to the essentially insoluble problem generated by the "external contradictions" of capitalism—the inability of any capitalism to incorporate land and land-based relations entirely within a commodity economy. This he saw in contrast to the problem of unemployment, "which is based on class confrontation"— that is, the internal contradictions of capitalism—and presumably had to be overcome within each given society.[14]

Along with his considerations on the centrality of agrarian issues to the world economy, Uno left similarly suggestive but preliminary remarks on the character of capitalism in the post-1945 period. For Uno, the second global slaughter was simply inexplicable within the framework of interimperialist rivalry in the stage of finance capital that he saw as having made "necessary" the war of 1914–18. The structural problems he had identified as giving rise to the world economy, along with the bifurcation of the world's politics between capitalist and socialist blocs, represented an unprecedented development. Nazi economic policy, in Uno's view, was a first, failed attempt, made in response to socialism, at the forcible rationalization, or organization, of capital. But it was not the only one; Japan had also tried. Evoking Rudolf Hilferding's notion of "organized capitalism" along with Nikolai Bukharin's "state capitalist trust," Uno argued that in the new epoch, capital would seek to organize itself "democratically" by allowing the development of the labor union movement and promoting greater worker participation in enterprise management; only by so doing would capital for the first time be "genuinely organized" and able to meet the challenge, certain to arise, of a successful Soviet-style socialist economy. This meant, in fact, that capital would be yielding to the state some important element of control in order to sustain itself.

> The control [kanri] of capital by the state, if realized, even without the top-to-bottom organization of the economy, may be termed the highest form of the organization of capitalism. Capitalism today, in each and every one of the

world's powerful countries, is being pressed to solve this difficult issue. The form of finance capital is no longer capable of performing this duty. At the same time, imperialist policies are not compatible with domestic control of this type. Unlike investment in colonies that has been the rule hitherto, foreign investment will now have to take a form that corresponds with that of domestic investment. Capitalism has reached a momentous turning point in which, unless it is able to develop a new form of capital by means of democracy, it will be unable to assert its existence vis-à-vis Soviet socialism. . . . In the case of Japan, here again an extremely grave crisis looms for capitalism, of having to bring to fruition in a single, short span of time a process that in other capitalist countries took place over many years.[15]

The differentia specifica of contemporary capitalism, as Uno perceived them, should be clear. Capitalist national economies were now bound by structural links that had been formed as late developers came into rivalry with more advanced economies. States were increasingly led to intervene in their economies in order to counteract or forestall crises whose origins might lie outside the nation's borders but would be experienced within them; and they did so cognizant of the division of the world into capitalist and socialist blocs, not through the ineluctable workings of capitalism's laws of motion, but through the organized political struggle of the "party of the proletariat" amid utter contingency and the constant threat of failure. These were the developments that had made it necessary to conceive of "contemporary analysis" both in terms of a world economy that was no longer entirely capitalist, and as "the assemblage of analyses, so to speak, of capitalism in one country, including the concrete development of backward countries."[16] They also explained why the world economy could not be conceived or analyzed except on the basis of an elaborated theory of stages of development; for it was the coexistence of national economies at various stages of development that shaped contemporary capitalism and determined its conflicting policies, both within and between nations. For Uno, no matter how far the world economy might attain to "conceptual" reality, "it cannot be treated in a manner uniform with the capitalist economies of various capitalist countries, each of which, albeit preserving the remains of productive methods handed down from the past, in any event forms an organic whole."[17] Capitalism remained national capitalism, and the world a world of nations and national states. But what idea could link these nations to that world?

In a comment (from 1980) on Uno's discussion of organized capitalism, Wada Haruki has remarked that, in his view, Uno was not so much advocating such a policy as pointing out, at a very early moment in the postwar era, the "objective logic" of capital's next world-historical development. "In present-day terminology," he notes, "this organization of capital would be called 'state monopoly capital.'"[18] And it is with the appearance of this term and idea that we come, at length, to the real transition from Uno to the Uno school. For though he presented elements of a conception of contemporary world capitalism, Uno could provide it no specifying name. The call of the present, in the end, went unanswered.

ŌUCHI TSUTOMU ON AGRICULTURE AND STATE MONOPOLY CAPITAL IN JAPAN

"State monopoly capital": what alien and alienating words! How heavily they fall on the ear! Like "dictatorship of the proletariat," "stamocap," or "SMC," as it is sometimes known, calls up images of a discarded machine that has been superseded by a better one. But we must not forget that barely a decade ago, entire societies and political systems, not to speak of economies, were guided by the tradition that produced these words.[19]

One minimalist formulation of the notion of stamocap runs: "Following the Russian Revolution, capitalism fell into a general crisis, and could no longer tolerate mass unemployment. For this reason, it abandoned the gold standard, and by financial and monetary means sought to absorb unemployment. Such a form of capitalism is referred to as state monopoly capitalism."[20] "Financial and monetary means" refers, of course, to the so-called Keynesian mix of demand and currency management, strategic inflation, and so on, that emerged throughout the industrialized economies during and after World War I, and especially during the great depression; the practices of the Weimar Republic, the New Deal, and various Popular Front governments all contributed elements to it.

Though named by Lenin, stamocap remained conceptually inchoate; after World War II, when the prospect of a possible new "general crisis" emerged, it was revived in the Soviet Union, and then taken up—with the burden of explaining yet another protracted end for capitalism—in the East bloc and Japan. It is not a term for state ownership, control, or even planning of production; it is also difficult to quantify. For Ōuchi Tsutomu, "the primary function of the state" under SMC

> is to mediate the relation between Capital and Labor through direct intervention instead of relegating this charge to the movement of commodities itself; i.e., to the law of value, because, at this stage of development capitalism is no longer able to rely upon the natural laws of economic motion. We

consider this specific mode of action to constitute the special determining feature of SMC. The class relation between Capital and Labor is altered by state action as the government moves to regulate the markets where money and labor power are exchanged, and this function is therefore necessarily one of both economic control and class rule. This interpretation allows us to comprehend fully, and for the first time, the fundamental unity of political and economical state action.

The implication is that, with the partial decommodification of its most essential relation, capitalism yields up some of its substance to the state in the interest of its own survival. In this somewhat technical sense, capitalism will have "ended," but without any revolution. It is important that as far as stamocap is concerned, the "arrow of time" flies only forward. Once the preconditions for it had emerged—the abandonment of gold, emergence of a socialist state, and perception of possibly irretrievable breakdown—there was no way back to "classic" monopoly capital. The state was permanently "back in," now performing a preemptive role.[21]

This, roughly speaking, was the concept by means of which Ōuchi sought to respond to the call of the present, to complete and ultimately to extend the reach of Uno's system. Ōuchi, the son of the eminent economist Ōuchi Hyōe, was a wartime (1942) graduate of Tokyo Imperial's economics faculty. At age twenty-four, he was perhaps slightly older than the norm, but norms and war did not go well together; and his father's 1938 arrest in the so-called Professors' Group incident must have complicated matters. In 1947, Ōuchi joined the new Institute of Social Science as an assistant professor, coinciding with the arrival of Uno Kōzō himself. In 1960, Ōuchi moved to the economics department proper; retiring in 1979, he moved immediately to a post at Shinshū University.

Nothing in his intellectual experience was to sway Ōuchi's belief that "the empirical analysis of the actual state [of capitalism]," though it might entail the explanation of Japan's extraordinary episode of capitalist surge, could be undertaken without any significant alteration of Uno's systemic perspective. In fact, Ōuchi's prolific and rich body of writing culminates in his own "system of political economy," beginning with considerations of the Uno school's three-level analytical method, followed by an exposition of basic principles, moving through the study of imperialism (including its "prehistory" of mercantilism and liberalism). Finally, Ōuchi produced parallel studies of the world and Japanese economy set in the framework of "the success and breakdown of state monopoly capital"—the latter as a result of the puzzling phenomenon of "stagflation" in the 1970s.[22] Ōuchi, tongue firmly in cheek, writes that the idea for this massive undertaking came to him more or less by accident—"like a colt jumping out of a gourd." After participating in a joint project (with an identical structure) early in the 1960s, Ōuchi once allowed to a colleague as how he might like to produce such a system entirely on his own, and as he neared retirement, thought that rather than accumulate yet more "half-digested knowledge," he could better use his—long—remaining years by seeing how well he could "ride the colt" of his intellectual ambition, and set out his version of "economics as a whole."[23]

A crucial feature of Ōuchi's completion of Uno's system, and the strongest indication of Ōuchi's faithfulness to its original and animating problematic, was his sustained effort to link stage-theoretic considerations to the issue of the mode of incorporation of agriculture into the broader system of commodity production, particularly at the national level. For Uno, whose intellectual formation bridged the Second and Third Internationals in their German inflections, *die Agrarfrage* remained the question of questions. It was a perspective to which Ōuchi succeeded, and one to which, for a decade following Japan's surrender, he gave his concerted attention. His account of state monopoly capitalism in Japan, within whose generalizing framework he was to place Japanese agriculture, came only in the early 1960s, after years of preoccupation with the structural dynamics and "special character" of that agriculture.

In the context of the late 1940s, when Ōuchi began to publish, such a preoccupation was to be expected.[24] Japan's prospects were bleak, and a clean sweep of what seemed a failed society the only rational step. It was the great mandate of social science to identify such steps in each domain of politics, economy, society, and culture. Combining statistical analyses with a critique of treatments spurred by the prewar "capitalism debate," Ōuchi was faithful to that mandate. In setting out his analysis of Japanese society's most backward sector, he relied, not yet on Uno's perspective of a "late development" effect, but on a combined—or synthetic—view that incorporated both the Kōza-ha emphasis on structural causality versus the Rōnō-ha's conjunctural dynamics, and the latter's insight that eight decades after the Meiji Restoration it no longer made much sense to continue to invoke "feudalism" as an explanation for the backwardness of Japanese agriculture. In other words, all those features that had bedeviled the development of capitalism in the countryside—the minuscule holdings, low wages and producer prices, high rents, limited village markets, and so on—"did not originate from within Japanese agriculture but had been determined by Japanese capitalism" itself.[25] It was the structure of Japanese capitalism, not the procrustean bed of semifeudal social relations among the peasantry, that prevented the rural differentiation, or proletarianization, without which capitalism could not reach its maturity. By preserving village society intact at the price of perpetuating ultra-parcelized cultivation, state policy had long since erected a petty-bourgeois bulwark against the proletariat—and, so to speak, against history. And while the elimination of tenancy under the occupation was unquestionably progressive, to the extent that the same reforms ramified the category of the *kashōnō,* the "excessively smallholder," Ōuchi argued, they were also complicit in shoring up a uniquely "distorted" mode of exploitation.

The impact of Uno's perspective became evident with Ōuchi's explicit embrace, in the early 1950s, of a late-developing capitalist framework that treated Japanese agriculture as fundamentally of a piece with that of continental Europe. The excessively smallholder was assimilated into the larger category of "smallholder" *(shōnō)* typical of the late developer. Differentiation among this large population was sluggish; accelerated sharply by periods of economic crisis, it stopped during the intervals of stability or prosperity. But the historical trend, for Ōuchi, was clear: From late Meiji until the eve of the Pacific War, middle and largeholders had declined, and excessively smallholders increased in number; some of these, in turn, had even expanded their operations.[26] Insofar as rural society was subject to capitalist exploitation, it "tended to differentiate deformedly, toward its lower stratum." Differentiation overwhelmingly meant proletarianization, the "fall" of the peasant, not the rise of the independent producer.[27]

As with Uno himself, though more quickly and more thoroughly, the issue of "early versus late" development was subsumed in Ōuchi's thinking within a framework of imperialism and monopoly capitalism. The mutual antagonism and rivalry of unequally developed capitalisms mattered because it gave rise to imperialism; imperialism, in turn, assumed political and economic agency such as to "deform" the latecomer's developmental process through chronically depressed agricultural prices; in Japan's case, this meant a scarcely diminished pool of surplus population in the countryside as a condition for the existence of capitalism, and as a consequence a problem of rural poverty that would go unsolved as long as capitalism continued. Facing the prospect of proletarianized poverty rather than self-management, and "educated and trained" by crisis, Japan's peasants must organize themselves "for joint union management" *(kyōdō kumiai keiei)* of their holdings. "They will learn through ever more powerful experience that their liberation can never come without the liberation of humankind from capitalism."[28]

Such was Ōuchi's vision of the countryside on the verge of high economic growth. Leaving aside the appeal to socialism, one might ask if it was essentially mistaken. As a historical interpretation of Japanese capitalism through 1945—or 1955—it was not. Ōuchi was hardly alone in arguing for a link between the developmental structure of Japanese capitalism as a whole and the perpetuation of rural poverty, in calling for collective action by small producers, or in worrying that even with the elimination of tenancy, the parcelized character of farm holdings would inhibit the emergence of viable capitalist farming.[29] These apprehensions in no way prevented Ōuchi from recognizing the striking turnabout in the rural economy by the end of the 1950s: the shift to favorable producer prices, increased consumption levels, the remarkable development in agricultural technology, and the spread of discretionary by-employment. Yet positive indices were no more than that: overpopulation remained rife, incomes from by-employment indispensable. The *shōnō*, if understood as a household unit living on income derived from labor on its own lands, had no future. The strongest indication was the deepening dependence of rural society on state policies—massive public works, price supports and various other subsidies, and so on. Without it, Ōuchi suggested, the smallholder was doomed to disappear.[30]

"Bringing the state back in" always causes complications, conceptually and politically. On the one hand, as with the land reforms, the application of the state's juridical power rectified a longstanding injustice that had at best been partially remedied before 1945. So too with the "payback" that transformed rural Japan after the mid-1950s, but particularly during the 1960s. But what of the accompanying rural tutelage to state and party that was inseparable from it? In Russia half a century earlier, certain of the "legal Marxists" and "legal Populists" had found themselves arguing for state-led industrialization as preferable to what they imagined would be a more predatory, class-driven version, called capitalism. But was the state in fact an autonomous agent, a "third term," independent of capital and capable of realizing the historical interest of the "nation," or of the largest segment of the nation? Could the "forces and relations of production" really be socialized through the state? Conversely, if the state were autonomous, would its ministrations over society necessarily be freer of coercion and their outcome one of greater fairness?

By criticizing the structural dependence of agriculture on state sufferance, Ōuchi seemed to be arguing that Japan's postwar agricultural policies represented an ersatz socialization that would ultimately prove counterproductive, and that it was up to enlightened critics to represent a rational, and national, standpoint before all comers. In order to do so, he moved a large step closer to the notion of state monopoly capital. But to articulate it fully, he first had to discover America.

In the late 1950s, Ōuchi spent fourteen months at Stanford University. While professing "no interest in or concern for American agriculture," Ōuchi discovered at Stanford not only that what was widely regarded as the "particularism of Japanese agriculture" could be found in the United States as well, but that the very "laws of agricultural development under state monopoly capitalism" now stood revealed. With profitable farm prices and a favorable agricultural economy—"conditions that in fact are only to be expected during a period of state monopoly capitalism"— the population of tiny holdings was flowing out of agriculture, while vacated lands were being combined into large farms.[31] Here was a type case of the rural "polarization" (ryōkyoku bunkai) posited in Lenin's Development of Capitalism in Russia (1899). But now, as Japan entered a phase of high growth, "the current state of American agriculture was imagined to represent the direction of change in that of Japan, and the outlook for the modernization of Japanese agriculture became certain."[32]

With this prospect in view, Ōuchi did not shrink from policy conclusions that are reminiscent, mutatis mutandis, of Pyotr Stolypin's 1908 "wager on the sturdy and the strong" as against the peasant communes of late Tsarist Russia: "The government has placed its wager . . . on the sturdy individual proprietor who is called upon to play a part in the reconstruction of our Tsardom on strong monarchical foundations." Ōuchi too, having participated as a consulting specialist in government deliberations over the new Basic Agricultural Law of 1961, called for policies that would promote either the withdrawal of ultrasmallholding cultivators from farming, or the concentration of their tiny holdings to form farms of a scale sufficient to bring income on a par with an urban worker. Ōuchi's commitment to modernization also led him to be critical of rice price supports and other direct economic assistance, and to call instead for an expansion of land improvement policies, even though he was cognizant of financial limitations on such projects. In so doing, he had placed himself at odds with his allies in the Socialist Party and the agricultural cooperative movement, but just as much with small business and conservative interests who feared that villages would cease to be a source of low-wage labor power. Ōuchi was not sanguine about the political chances for "rationalization" over "protectionism," but he had made his own choice clear.[33]

Analytically, the yield of Ōuchi's work during these years constellates around a number of linked claims. State monopoly capital, first of all, had proven capable of averting the deepening of agricultural crises; state authority could intervene to counter the tendency toward surplus production to a certain extent. The inevitable fluctuations of the business cycle would become incremental and piecemeal, as it were a disguise for the "chronic slump" characteristic of agriculture under monopoly. The jagged downturn of the interwar years, Ōuchi felt, need not recur. Here was a sentiment and claim that must have struck home forcefully for those who had experienced that debacle, but was also politically problematic insofar as it suggested the permanence of a supposedly senescent capitalism.

Of greater interest is Ōuchi's attempt to link the advent of state monopoly to a widely remarked phenomenon of rural society: an "upward shift in the axis of rural differentiation" *(bunkai kijiku no jōshō)*. "With no essential change in the problem of the ceiling imposed by the pressure of monopoly capital," Kase Kazutoshi observes,

> profit does not materialize, nor, as a consequence, does capitalist management. But thanks to intensified policy support, it does gain stability and is therefore enabled to reach the upward limit of manageability on the basis of family labor power; as such, at the opposite pole of the large number of part-time farmers, a minority of large-scale farmers are thriving.

Ōuchi's term for such farmers was "*ōgata shōnō.*" But in what sense did the *ōgata shōnō* exemplify the definitive emergence of state monopoly capital in Japan? No longer in the classic sense that villages provided a source of cheap labor power. As of the early 1960s, that quintessential prewar role had passed from them—to the cities, which played their own increasing part in sustaining the "dual structure" within Japanese industry. Instead, with stable employment opportunities outside agriculture as yet insufficient to absorb the numbers of rural migrants, it was the concern of state policy to prevent unemployment through rice price supports, as well as to maintain villages as collective consumers in the domestic market.[34]

As links in the chain of the full employment mechanism, these policies succeeded. But Ōuchi's concern with the *ōgata shōnō* was more broadly historical as well. The pattern *(kata)* of "upward shift" in rural differentiation, Ōuchi claimed, had been underway (with only a temporary wartime interruption) since the 1930s. The 1930s and the 1950s, in other words, belonged to the same era, one defined by the decline of the landlord elite relative to the preceding period, and by the precipitous drop in "full-time" farming households by the late 1960s.[35] This argument for transwar continuity in the workings of a new pattern of rural differentiation was highly suggestive, with implications for the understanding of what had been regarded and experienced as a series of historically discrete episodes: depression, war, occupation, and "take-off" into high growth. Prefiguring much current discussion, Ōuchi "read backward" from the early heights of growth through the institutional history of Japan's stamocap, identifying when and where structures had formed or changed: for reasons of their own, occupation authorities had undertaken to eliminate tenancy, tried to break up the *zaibatsu* (shoring up the ongoing separation of capital from management) and promote a degree of democratization in the labor-capital relation. In so doing, for Ōuchi, MacArthur's New Dealers acted as "unwitting agents" in the rationalization of state monopoly capital. His was in no sense a brief for the economic—let alone political—"winners," or an argument for inevitability. After all, according to Ōuchi's original conception, stamocap should at best have "dispersed the energy of crises gradually in the form of recessions appearing over short periods"; it should not have produced sustained high growth.[36] Yet not only in Japan, but elsewhere among the former Axis countries as well as France, just such growth had occurred. Why did it happen?

Ōuchi's now familiar argument for Japan is that the interventionist practices of the state under the received regime of monopoly capital combined in a new way with what he termed "postwar characteristics"—the need to recover from war damage, the sense of historical break or vacuum—and the technological and institutional dualism, or backwardness, inherited from the prewar past. The result was the generation of growth that, so to speak, should not have occurred, and which Ōuchi and many other distinguished analysts thought would soon run aground, perhaps by the mid-1960s.[37] Growth remained exceptional or peculiar, and Ōuchi was never to transcend that mental horizon. Yet the phenomenon of stagflation in the early 1970s that brought such growth to an end was not to be interpreted as the extension of stamocap, but as its breakdown. This was due, Ōuchi argued, not to "capital excess," or a quantitative "labor power deficit" per se, which was the Uno school's default interpretation of crisis. It pointed rather to a qualitative failure under such conditions of stamocap's political and social interventions to "contain labor power" as had hitherto been the case. Workers' "power to organize and to negotiate" had indeed strengthened since the 1960s, but this now had to be used in struggles against entrenched and co-opted union leaderships who had joined with corporate capital to restrain wage growth and dampen inflation; actions such as prolonged unauthorized strikes and sabotage bespoke a form of worker "desocialization," a lack of the internal discipline that had earlier underwritten the success of state monopoly capital. Ōuchi, certain leftist critics argued, positively disapproved of this indiscipline rather than attempting to see in it a possible prefiguration of "class struggle" or resistance to commodification under an emerging post-stamocap regime. Though he continued to write in favor of a "new image of socialism" based on worker autonomy, Ōuchi maintained a strongly productivist and disciplinarian stance. The desocialization he deplored was an unwanted, imported "disease of civilization" from which "the nation" could legitimately seek protection. In this sense, Ogura Toshimaru asserts, Ōuchi's socialism was also a form of "Japanism."[38]

"Japanist" as well was the perspective that would ultimately inform Ōuchi's writings on agriculture. As of the early 1960s, Ōuchi retained his apprehensions about unemployment and rural poverty. From the perspective of recent decades (until the early 1990s), of combined "ultrafull employment" and the vast reduction of labor requirements in agriculture through technological inputs, these worries may seem quaint. But such a perception merely underscores the dramatic transformation of Japanese society over the course of the 1960s. Ōuchi recognized this, noting, on the one hand, that agricultural issues no longer posed a "social question" as that term had been understood through most of the century. To be sure, "excess population" remained, no longer of young male heads of households but of their aging parents—and wives. But agriculture was now (as in the United States) a "minor sector" of the contemporary economy, whose surplus production could easily be dissolved through compensatory payments. This success, as Kase observes, led Ōuchi to a deepening pessimism. With his expectations for socialist transformation through rural collective management diminished by the end of the 1950s, Ōuchi saw a countryside thoroughly dependent on the state and hardly likely to survive external pressures for market liberalization, which were growing increasingly insistent. Certainly agriculture would remain as a political problem; but the classic *Agrarfrage* had been "solved."[39]

There is a plaintive quality—unsurprising given the decades of intellectual, perhaps even emotional, investment he made in the study of agriculture—in Ōuchi's most recent work. This was not just a matter of introducing ecological and resource concerns in the 1970s, or more recently of anxious observations about Japan's lack of self-sufficiency in food. We see instead a reassessment, from a number of specific angles, of the entire category of the *shōnō* and the role of agriculture in an advanced state-monopoly capitalist economy. From his portrayal of a "negative entity that, since it was unable to secure a profit, stopped its scale of operations within the limits of the complete combustion of family labor power," Ōuchi shifted to an understanding that "by its nature, agriculture is an industry suited to family operation," one better able than employed labor-power to cope flexibly with the complexities of decision-making under ever-changing natural conditions. Just those households able to sustain operations were able to participate in a market economy: contrasting "agriculture as occupation" to "agriculture as enterprise"— that is, "an operation striving to realize a profit (albeit low) that goes beyond the labor-wage portion [of income]"—Ōuchi outlined a future for the *ōgata shōnō* as the crucial "bearer" of Japanese agriculture.[40]

Along with this belated acceptance of an argument that had been circulating for a decade among agricultural economists, we also find a series of justifications for policies that, as Ōuchi himself admitted, amounted to an act of repentance for his long-held modernism. Agriculture, he urged, has to be considered as a public good, with values in various non-economic domains that justify its inefficiencies in cost. Instead of "cutting loose" marginal cultivators and marginal lands, Ōuchi now proposed that such districts ought to be the target of concentrated public support. People should be encouraged to remain, or settle, in mountain and forestlands; to "let the land be" is not to assure a more abundant nature, but mere irresponsibility in a Japan whose villages are emptying out.[41]

It is fitting, metaphorically speaking, that in Ōuchi Tsutomu, Pyotr Stolypin and Wendell Berry—one the maker of the "wager on the sturdy and the strong," and the other the defender of farm communities in disintegration—should finally meet, and under the aegis of Uno Kōzō's system of political economy. As indicated, Ōuchi had inherited the agricultural preoccupations of Uno's analysis of capitalism's developmental stages; as he remarked, each one of those stages had its characteristic form of *nōhonshugi*, or "agrocentrism."[42] By the same token, he could not simply treat agriculture and its problems as self-contained, but as elements of a dynamic political economy: hence his antipathy, shared by

Uno's school with the Rōnō-ha, for appeals to unique semifeudal social relations that had somehow escaped from, and yet supported, those of capitalism.

The "Stolypin-meets-Berry" element enters the picture when we consider a salient difference, notwithstanding all that was intellectually common to them, between Ōuchi and Uno. Both scholars worked in a Japan that was not just in need of, but receptive to, economists who could combine systematic training with a commitment to social transformation. The desperate conditions of the early postwar years were enough, perhaps, to demand that. But the nub of the matter lies in the fact that, rather than liberal or neoclassical approaches, it was the historically minded (or historicist) economics of Marxian "stage theory" (itself a critical response to that of List) that had survived the war and appeared amid the rubble as the only coherent system going. Equally important, the upholders of that coherent system found themselves for the first time in a tolerant political atmosphere in which the circulation, rather than choice, between academic and official positions was a possibility.

The vectoring effect of national service was indeed crucial. Uno Kōzō had pledged his intellect to the struggle for a Marxian economic science free of Stalinism, but he was constitutionally uncomfortable making policy recommendations. Ōuchi, like Arisawa Hiromi, did so energetically, putting Marxism at the service of the national economy. True to the intent of Uno's system, Ōuchi sought to complete it by mobilizing the notion of state monopoly capital for the task of contemporary analysis, and to foreground the question of agriculture in carrying it out. This commitment pressed him to engage with a rapidly changing economic reality, in terms both of its recent past and its likely future: Ōuchi argued fervently for capitalist modernization, believing that socialism could appear only by transcending capitalism. To that extent, he would have to bear responsibility, politically and intellectually, for the results.[43] Uno's system afforded no still, transcendent point for contemplation. It is perhaps the mark of Ōuchi's integrity that, while struggling to maintain the coherence of the system that had formed him, he would end by arguing with himself.

EXCESS AFFLUENCE AND CULTURAL DISORIENTATION: BABA HIROJI

In a poignant eulogy for Uno Kōzō, Ōuchi Tsutomu writes of accompanying the body of his mentor to the crematorium, and gathering his ashes. "He had been magnificent in appearance, but now all of him, even his head, so filled with true learning, had been transformed into fragments of whitened bone. It was then that I felt, keenly, how great a loss this was." Ōuchi's role bespeaks a relationship of deep intimacy and trust extending beyond intellectual matters. It is a role rarely played, one would imagine, by anyone other than immediate family members. Elsewhere in his remarks, Ōuchi notes ruefully that Uno seems to have seen his own scholarly views "projected, in a distorted and enlarged form," onto those of his student, and that "perhaps regretting" this influence, Uno may have taken the occasion to reconsider certain points in his own teaching.[44]

If Ōuchi's views, so close to his own, nevertheless caused Uno to "reflect" on certain of his own positions, one wonders how he would have reacted to the self-described "paradigm change in Japanese Marxian economics" carried out over the course of the 1980s by another former student, Baba Hiroji. The salient fact of capitalism in the advanced economies, Baba contends, is not the progressive immiseration of the working class, but the "spread of affluence" *(fuyūka)* through the instrumentality of massive corporations, and its sociocultural effects. A new paradigm, based on "mass affluence," is necessary for Marxism to survive as a system of political economy. Baba does not (any more than Marx himself, at least) merely celebrate the productive capacity of capitalism. He recognizes it, emphasizes it, tries—whether convincingly or not—to explain it, and to assess its impact on advanced societies directly, and on the (former) East and (current) South as well. He means the related notions of "mass affluence," "mass enrichment," and particularly "excess affluence" to be tools of social analysis—and criticism.

Baba is the gadfly of the Uno school, and like any gadfly must have credentials that demand to be taken seriously: a 1957 graduate in economics from Tokyo University, Baba left off his graduate work to teach at Kanagawa University, then returned to his alma mater to join the Institute of Social Science. He retired from that position in 1997, assuming a post at Daitō Bunka University. Like Ōuchi, his direct mentor, Baba has written on American agriculture and has grappled—more directly than Uno was able to—with the emergence of American economic hegemony in the post–World War I era. Other works treat "core and periphery in the world economy," and—as will be discussed presently—seek to address the problems involved in accounting theoretically for sustained economic growth by reconsidering the category of finance capital. As a whole Baba's writings are distinctly less systematic than either Uno's or

Ōuchi's oeuvre.[45] The style is breezier, on occasion pugnacious, and the
rhetoric more tart: on socialism, Baba asserts, Uno's "few direct remarks
are incomprehensible . . ."; Japan's Ministry of Education, which he
believes should be abolished, oversees the education of "desocialized"
children to be no more than "plastic robots with tape recorders installed
inside"; in the face of the exhaustion of natural resources and the
inevitability of mass reactions against the just as inevitable decline in living standards, utopian calls for "regional economic communities produced by wannabe critics come a dime-a-dozen, and amount to nothing
more than well-intentioned foolishness."[46]

In one of his first publications, Baba set out a critique of Uno's—
admittedly cursory—treatment of the notion of the world economy.
Uno, it will be recalled, had argued that ultimately, "national" economies
were truly "organic entities," in contrast to which the world economy
remained as yet a largely conceptual "reality." Baba challenged this view,
arguing that, from the standpoint of international trade, labor, and capital flows—that is, of individual capitals in motion—"there was from the
outset no qualitative distinction between the national economy that
formed an 'organic whole,' and the world economy that did not." To
make such a distinction, Baba held, was to adopt "the standpoint of the
bourgeois state, which, while taking capital as its material foundation,
enjoys relative autonomy of power; but it is not the standpoint of capital. . . . It is the world system of prices itself, with all of the local distortions it contains, that constitutes the world economy." Furthermore, the
ideology of the national economy to which Uno himself was significantly
attached was not even the creation of the "bourgeois-citizen states" of
capitalism's liberal stage, but rather of latecomers like Germany and
Japan, seeking their "rightful" shares as nations in the world market.[47]

Baba's argument "may have been the first to have thoroughly broken
the spell of the 'national economy' in Japanese economics." There certainly is a "world system" or "core versus periphery" strain in the collective corpus of Uno school's writings, some of which, particularly by
Iwata Hiroshi, antedate that of Immanuel Wallerstein, and were significant in the formation of Baba's ideas.[48] Unlike Iwata, however, and like
Ōuchi, for Baba the capstone of "contemporary analysis" was formed by
capitalism both in Japan and of it. Baba's early critique of Uno's own
conceptual bias toward the "nation" was important, but (while he professed no specialist knowledge of Japan) his more significant contribution to the Marx-Uno school was to have brought it squarely face to face
with Japanese high growth. Even that growth demanded attention not

because of any sui generis quality, but because of what Baba termed its "pan-capitalist" character; only on this basis could it be used to argue for something as fundamental as a paradigm change. Although they may have played an initial role as the anomalies that provoke new discovery within the framework of Marxism, neither Japanese economic growth, nor growth in general, was to be seen as finally anomalous but rather as paradigmatic of the stage of finance capital.

Japanese Marxians, Baba argued, long held to three paradigms that had now been "nullified by reality": "that the pauperization of the working class is an inevitable concomitant of capitalist development"; that "socialist economies are unquestionably superior to capitalist ones"; and that Japan is to be regarded as a "backward country." As to the first two, perhaps little comment is needed.[49] Concerning Japan's backwardness, however, enough has been said here to indicate that in one form or another, whether as backward or peculiar or distorted, the perspective of Japan's difference from a putative model has certainly not been transcended. What Uno and his followers have sought to do is to explain that difference in terms of some larger framework, whether that of late development (in the case of Uno himself), imperialism (Ōuchi), or finance capital (Baba) so that Japan becomes at most an "extreme" case of something larger than itself. The cardinal point would be that nothing outside capitalism was to be adduced a priori to explain capitalism; but it was also important that capitalism was marked by unevenness, not only along a scale-measure of development, but in the simultaneity of real-world processes.

But why the focus on finance capital? Like Ōuchi, Baba also works by reasoning "backward." Marked by the experience of depression and war, and perhaps for this reason confirmed in his orthodoxy, Ōuchi formulated his theory of state monopoly in order to explain the postwar stabilization, rather than the expected dissolution, of capitalism. For him, growth was anomalous and by implication unrepeatable. The true trajectory of state monopoly—insofar as it was "monopoly" capital, and despite the deep insinuation of the state into the labor-capital relation—was to stagnation and breakdown; such indeed was the frame within which Ōuchi viewed the crisis of welfare state capitalism in the 1970s and the advent of neoliberalism in the decade that followed.[50] With Baba, looking back from the economic heights of the 1980s, the perspective is inverted, and the temporal frame stretched further into the past. Finance capital, Baba argues, "can generate prosperity on a larger scale and for a longer span of time than industrial capital." This is not just a matter of speculative booms—Uno himself had recognized that these could be greater under finance capital as the dominant mode of accumulation in the stage of imperialism. Baba's position is more sweeping. Both in terms of its "relation with labor power" and of "the amount of capital money at its disposal," finance capital seems virtually predisposed to generate growth.

> Finance capital, which takes the form of gigantic stock companies, undertakes growth on a scrap-and-build basis . . . [T]ranslated into the terminology of business-cycle theory, scrap-and-build growth means simultaneously vertical deepening (i.e., accumulation accompanied by increased productivity) and horizontal expansion (i.e., expansion through absorption of additional labor power, keeping preexisting technology intact) . . . Moreover, given the fact that [finance capital] can step up productivity even in the absence of an economic crisis, the expansion of the economy can last for a considerably long period.

The same "gigantic stock companies" also make it possible to amass "a sizeable quantity of social money through stock issues," while the ever more intimate relationship (as Hilferding also saw it), between bank and industrial capital made available "vast loans" and facilitated mergers and rationalization.[51]

This much is about potential. But Baba is making an argument about actuality, about history. "Mass enrichment" through sustained growth had occurred only in certain societies, as part of what Baba calls a "two-stage deformation of capitalism." In the imperialist stage, with the predominance of finance capital, Baba holds, the bifurcation of society into two great classes was "arrested," and their relations made more complex. Firms developed internal labor markets of considerable size, though a still larger residuum remained "outside." Parallel to these trends was the increasing intervention of the state in the economy; the combined effect was to alter the form of the business cycle. At a wider remove, but asserting their own causality, were "movements demanding the restoration of . . . 'social principles,' " of which the Russian Revolution was the most dramatic in its consequences; this was the second-stage deformation of capitalism. Here, of course, Baba follows his teachers in arguing that the necessity to confront socialism, both as an internal movement and as an external power, brought a partial transubstantiation of capitalism: official recognition of "people's right to a livelihood," "a more equitable redistribution of income," and "equalization of rights for both capital and labor." In a direct sense, the premise for this partial "socialization" of capitalism was the dismantling of the gold standard, which ensured that the periodicity and regularity of crises would be subject to national policies, ranging from the New Deal to the Nazi New Order; it meant as well that the free play of those policies, given the literally gigantic stakes involved, could and would involve an unprecedented degree of political violence within and across national boundaries.[52]

It is well to keep this last point, perhaps more typical of Ōuchi Tsutomu's perspective, in mind; for in Baba's treatment it is sometimes occluded. In what is admittedly one of his more schematic formulations, he describes the outcome of the "two-stage deformation of capitalism" as follows:

> The process of capitalist deformation, in terms of the social relations of production, corresponds to the process of mass democratization. The process of capital accumulation under finance capital, which facilitates deployment of an increasingly larger amount of social productive power, corresponds to the process of mass enrichment. It should be kept in mind . . . that these two sets of phenomena are closely interrelated.[53]

At first sight, Baba seems to be saying that for the advanced economies of the West, the yield of its sanguinary conflicts and former imperialism since the turn of the century has, on balance, been positive. That is, in fact, only part of his intentions, as we shall see when his analysis of the ultimate costs of "excessive affluence" is taken into account. But there is first the issue of Japan's growth—of Japanese finance capital—to be considered.

In an argument modeled on Uno's *Keizai seisakuron*, Baba has sought to redefine the developmental series—mercantilist, liberal, imperialist—in favor of a new sequence of overlapping, wavelike stages. The new first stage, in brief, was the era of the Industrial Revolution in Britain, which had its outer boundary zones in the United States and Western Europe; the second, marked by "adaptation or amplification" of the major features of the first, began with the shift from German-American cohegemony to that of the United States alone. (Here again, in its devaluation of Germany in favor of the United States, Baba's thinking reflects more of Ōuchi than Uno.) This second stage lasted from the so-called second industrial revolution through to the mid-twentieth century: this was the world of giant corporations, the Taylor system, and consumer-goods production undergirded by the heavy and chemical industries. Japan, for Baba, was the quintessential latecomer, the lone occupant of the capitalist boundary zone in the era of American hegemony after World War I. In subsequent decades the initial wave of capitalist industrialization was to spread further; but for Baba the more significant development was the new, second wave—the spread of affluence, spurred by finance capital. Originating in Germany, it hit "home" in the United States, beginning in the 1920s, but above all in the "Fordist linkage between mass production and high wages" following World War II.[54]

From this point of view, Japan's "shift to affluence" was again late, coming in the 1960s and 1970s, many decades after the initial wave of capitalist industrialization had washed over the country. Baba accepted with qualifications the explanation, associated with Ōuchi Tsutomu (and with a number of "modern" economists such as Shinohara Miyohei and Ohkawa Kazushi) that inherited dualism was, as it were, a built-in "macro" factor conducing to high growth. That may have been true for some time after 1945; but why, he asked, did the Italian "miracle" fade compared to that of the Japanese? And how could backwardness explain the sustained high growth rates of Japanese capitalism following the oil crises? It could not. Instead, Baba argued, the answer was to be sought in the distinctive "micro" aspects of the forms of capital at work in each setting.

In Baba's writings from the early 1980s onward, those crucial "micro" factors are captured in the term "companyism." The second industrial revolution had been driven by steel and heavy industry under a regime of finance capital centered in the joint-stock system. In the process of its transfer from Germany to the United States, this regime had metamorphosed to one of enterprises based on "managerial capital," and (along with defense industries) devoted to automobile and other mass consumer durables. Latecoming Japan, for its part, had been at the receiving end of transfers from the United States—and from Europe as well—of technologies and organizational modes that drove the process of automated production. The initial harvest of that transfer in Japan was the extraordinary growth of "second industrial revolution" sectors such as steel and autos, but also—and for Baba more significantly—the development of electronics industries that would signal a "third industrial revolution." It was a harvest reaped, Baba argues, under two particular circumstances: it reflected the imperative to recover quickly from the stagflation that sapped the energy of the advanced economies in the early to mid-1970s; and was owed directly to the workings of the "micro" or "software" domains, the organizational habitus or culture, of the firms that dominated Japan's industrial economy. Japan's extraordinary spate of growth, it would appear, bridged two phases in techno-organizational development, emerging in between the second and third industrial revolutions. It never dominated the former; but would it dominate the latter?

Baba himself is unsure, at times referring to Japanese capitalism as a "second-and-a-half" stage of development, at others linking it explicitly to a third stage more or less coterminous with the dominance of microelectronic production. But he is in no doubt that technological and macroeconomic factors alone are insufficient, and attention to companyism necessary, to explain how Japanese capitalism, through a concerted restraint on energy consumption and enhancement of productivity, recovered from the twin "shocks" of the early 1970s, eventually winning recognition as a possible new type or model to be studied and emulated.[55]

"Companyism"—*kaishashugi*—is a term of Baba's own devising.[56] It makes no pretense at elegance, lacking even the semblance of gravitas that attaches to "state monopoly capital." Companyism seeks both to describe the dominant institution in Japanese capitalism and to meet the Uno school's critical, universalizing mandate of seeking links among the three levels of analysis. At the level of the institutional infrastructure of accumulation, Baba argues, "the governing ideology of Japan . . . may be called "companyism.'" The elements are familiar: the "trinity" of lifetime employment, seniority wages, and enterprise unionism forms the backbone of labor-capital relations in an industrial economy dominated—and in Uno's sense "represented"—by massive firms with extensive internal labor markets. In recent presentations, Baba has taken increasing note of the interaction of wartime and early postwar trends in later creating the mix of practices that make up companyism: "the transformation of workers into 'company employees' advanced" during wartime, "when labor unions were not allowed." In the postwar period, "the drive to homogeneity among employees at every level of the same enterprise" may have been "politically retrogressive" at a time when the sharpening of class differences was taken as a sign of political maturation. But it emerged, at the end of a long period of struggle, as a lasting compromise that formed the pattern of unionized labor-capital relations.[57]

As the Japanese term suggests, *kaishashugi* is clearly meant to pun on its resemblance to *shakaishugi*, the word for "socialism." Characterized by vast and highly developed internal labor markets, under companyism, "an enormous pool of workers' services is available free of charge" to firms, so much so that Baba has come to doubt "that Japanese workers are really selling just their labor power as a commodity." "Frankly," he says, "I also doubt whether Japanese capitalism really merits the name of capitalism. My impression is that the Japanese system is capitalist at the macroscopic level but socialist at the microscopic level."[58] Companyism is indeed an "ism," an ideology of worker self-motivation and enterprise membership:

> The company is nothing other than capital; as a means toward its primary goal of pursuing profit, productive efficiency is pursued. For the sake of this latter, subsidiary goal, solidarity and competition prevail at every level of organization, from small groups at the work site on up. Individual workers, oriented toward the particular goal of the group to which they belong, perform their roles, and in so doing—including mutual competition—contribute to the group. Through this arrangement, solidarity and self-realization, the two great ends of labor, are simultaneously achieved. Here, the alienation of labor that everywhere accompanies capitalism is either dissolved, mitigated, or concealed, as the subjective autonomy [shutaisei] of the worker concentrates on raising productivity. The goal of capital is realized via the medium of the employee's own expression of subjectivity. And because capital is in control, productivity rises with unsurpassable speed. Has there ever before been a system so favorable to this purpose? I am not saying that it's the best of all social systems—Heaven forbid. But of the organizations formed by capital [shihon ni yoru soshiki keitai], it is the best conceivable, and that is because the direct domination of private property ownership has withdrawn to the greatest possible extent.[59]

Companyism, then, "is the product, concretely speaking, of the peculiar circumstances of Japan's high economic growth," and indeed, it had appeared for the first time in Japan. Still it was not, Baba argues, a uniquely Japanese phenomenon, but also possessed "a pan-capitalist universality. For among the various forms of enterprise generated by the history of capitalism, it is likely the most advanced framework for the development of productive forces [saikō no seisanryoku hatten kikō]."[60]

Clearly, Baba's work prefigured and overlaps with other recent attempts to theorize the competitive capitalisms of the post–Cold War era. His notion of companyism is similar, for example, to that of "Toyotism" or "Ōnoism," which is often discussed as a Japanese counterpart to American "neo-Fordism" and Swedish (or German) "Volvoism." The first is a model of work by incentive, the second of work by command and the third a model of work by negotiation (leading either to reduced hours or expanded social welfare).[61] But it does seem that Baba's main animus lies in contrasting the companyist future with the unhappy fate of the United States, should it cease to be a manufacturing society. In such a case—discussed more in the late 1980s than now, a decade later—America would become nothing more than a parasitical economy, dominated by speculators and rife with a "lumpen" population of service workers. For industrializing Asia, companyism provides an alternative to such an "inhumane" social polarization; "just because companyism happens to be thoroughly developed does not mean that it can save human society, but it may mean that the social collapse that comes with polarization can be avoided." A tense contest between the two alternatives, Baba asserts, is underway.[62]

One may not be persuaded by such a bald and journalistic formulation. There does seem to be a fairly consistent streak of such sentiment in Baba's writing, with its frequent invectives against rampant desocialization, collapse of family ties, juvenile delinquency and drug use, worker absenteeism, "confusion over sex roles and morality," and so on. All this can give his commentary a markedly conservative tinge. In this respect, he shares with certain strands of the Marxist left, both in Japan and elsewhere, a horror of commodification and a high valuation of social order. The issue, though, is how that order is achieved and maintained. In any event, it does pose the question as to the nature of the social criticism Baba clearly intends to offer on the basis of his "paradigm shift." That is, as a result of having performed this intellectual move, can he present critical analyses that would otherwise not be made?

Let us consider first Baba's relationship to the Marxian tradition as the immanent critique of capitalism. As noted, *"kaishashugi"* is a deliberate play on words, depending on the still positive connotations of *"shakaishugi"* for its claim to attention. Thus more than word play is involved. Baba's version of the paradigm shift to mass enrichment is one of a long series of such developments within Marxism, which to be sure vary widely in their accompanying political conclusions. Eduard Bernstein had dared to raise this possibility against the "immiserationist" orthodoxy of the German Social Democratic Party; his views were officially rejected in 1903 but found an "objective correlative" in the party's policies under Weimar. In his writings on "organized capitalism," published in the decade after 1915, Rudolf Hilferding argued that "in conjunction with the dominance of large corporations and banks, the increasing involvement of the state in the regulation of the economy had brought an important element of planning into economic life and prepared the way for socialist planning."[63] A generation later, similar sentiments were imputed to Paul Sweezy and Paul Baran, on the basis of their assessment of postwar Keynesianism. For his part, Baba retained a concern, as Ōuchi had, with the capacity of workers for autonomous self-organization and explicitly warns against the temptation to substitute a "cultural" for a "political" movement. But on the whole, whatever his aspirations, by the mid-1980s Baba held out no hope for a specifically "socialist" transformation. Why so? Because, insofar as the conceivable models of socialism continued to fetishize the "productive forces," they would be liable to present, in a cruder, more politically inimical form, the same sort of dilemmas that now beset those capitalist countries that had achieved such growth.

Notwithstanding his distaste for American-style capitalism, it is not the homogenizing drives of "McWorld" that Baba finds most problematic. In one sense, it is the opposite. To be sure, the various social pathologies Baba laments are tied to the "excessive dissolution of human relationships into relationships among commodities." But this phenomenon, in turn, is itself the product of the loosening, since the late 1920s, of capitalism's "autonomous control mechanism." The "law of value, i.e., the regular repetition of cyclical fluctuations, or even the gold standard" that underlay social order, may have collapsed. With the weakening of regularities (as in the periodicity of crises), "the process of accumulation has become increasingly ungovernable."[64]

Yet we must attend to his sense of the meaning of "ungovernability." With no real coordinating mechanism, international trade and economic conflicts sharpen, and problems of distribution and adjustment within societies and between regions come to be accompanied by "the rampant self-assertion of cultural particularities." Some of this "rampant self-assertion," originating in the third world or among marginalized peoples within the advanced core countries, might in an earlier era have been "silenced . . . by force . . . , but under contemporary capitalism, the unlimited use of force has become virtually impossible."[65] This would seem all to the good. What is troubling to Baba, rather, is not cultural self-assertion per se (which he engages in without hesitation), but its rampancy. The absence of coordination from capitalism is paralleled in his view by the growing inability of culture to police itself, and more importantly to police capitalism. For Baba, it is wrong-headed to search culture for the sources of sustained and rapid economic growth. Such a phenomenon bespeaks not the operation of culture, but its weakening or absence: "a proper culture" *(matomo na bunka)* such as that of China or India, with millennia of civilization as their achievement —"acts to restrain economic development."[66] This may not be meant to sound reactionary, or to cast a bleak sentence of poverty on countries outside the capitalist core. It is typical of Baba's bluntness, and unfortunately

occludes the important corollary question as to the distribution of surplus product. But one does not have to be reactionary to ask whether
growth is the solution to every problem.[67]

In short, the specter that haunts Baba is indeed growth, unchecked
and self-justifying; along with it he attacks the penchant of affluent societies, in their different ways, to gear their institutions—and the domain
of social and cultural reproduction generally—to its pursuit. This situation, for Baba, has brought capitalism to the verge of a "general crisis."
And it is only in this context that Baba is able, at length, to venture his
critique of Japan and Japanese companyism.

Prolonged high growth, for Japan, had massively disorienting effects.
As with the discussion of the "micro" factors leading to that growth,
here too the symptoms are familiar. Writing in the mid-1980s, Baba
spoke of "the great likelihood that the Japanese system may collapse."
This "devastating fate," Baba argued, would come not because of severe
competition in the international market—this was to be expected—but
through an irretrievable internal collapse of "society." On the one hand,
generations had become strangers to one another; children were deprived
of contact with nature and of a range of human experiences: of facing life
and death, of labor, of companionship. And with the disappearance of
the "original, disciplined"—and "male-dominated"—form of the capitalist system, women's work had become a visible, commodified necessity. To what end? Baba's target is not women's work, but the basic structure of social reproduction itself. Japan, he argues, has "injected all the
energy of its society and culture into private firms."[68] Though it employs
only a third of Japanese workers, the "modal" sectors exert—to use a
phrase he employs in a different context—an "irresistibly strong demonstration effect" on the entire workforce. The production of that working
population, of course, is the chief task of the educational system, which
suffers from a basic imbalance between the "incompleteness of the postwar reforms" and an unassimilably high rate of economic growth. The
Ministry of Education, for its part, has no better idea than to "take the
educational system back to prewar days," and should be eliminated.
Thanks to its ministrations, Japan had become culturally bankrupt, its
children little more than "plastic robots with tape recorders installed
inside." The country had in some respects become a fool's paradise.
Whatever the achievements of companyism, they came at a high price
indeed. The conundrum of companyism, however, is not that workers
only seem to have autonomy within the firm, but in fact do not. To
the contrary, it is that "while they actually control these companies

autonomously to a significant extent," they do so at the cost of effacing all meaning from their private lives. Yet the task of recovering personal meaning can only be undertaken socially, in solidarity with others. Japan's workers and "ordinary people" must mount a political, not only cultural, movement for the recovery of meaning—in other words, out of a corporate world seek to create a "civil society."[69]

In *Shin shihonshugiron* (A new treatise on capitalism, 1997) Baba holds out the ultimate prospect that the very mechanisms of growth that advanced capitalism has developed may lead to a kind of negative transcendence—a final, irretrievable ecological crisis. Imagine a world in which the gross domestic product rates of advanced countries were miraculously matched by Third World societies whose per capita consumption is one-twentieth that of the West. Without some means of lowering the standard of consumption—not just reducing the capital stock—in the wealthiest countries, and of anticipating and facing politically the inevitable popular backlash at that prospect, there is no hope for the continuation of world society. Could a resource-saving regime of companyism, Baba ventures, perhaps contribute to a solution by offering an alternative to capitalist industrialization in the Third World? Without denying similar depredations committed by others there and elsewhere, the suggestion, one must say, seems less than serious. Japan's corporate record as a consumer of timber and other resources in Southeast Asia points in quite another direction. Would the training of local cadres in "Japanese" management techniques make an appreciable difference? By the same token, Baba also neglects to mention Japan's own heavy reliance since the 1970s on nuclear power. This can hardly be said to reflect a reduced demand for energy, and brings with it risks of which the "inadvertent criticality" at the Tōkaimura nuclear power plant in the fall of 1999 provides a stark reminder.[70]

But even these objections may not change the larger picture. In a real sense, capitalism is as Baba describes it: "a Pandora's box crammed to the gills with freedom, desire, self-regard, self-interest, calculation, haggling, and avarice."[71] In the United States since the early 1980s, the trend has been toward an increasing compensation gap between top-level executives and salaried employees: from an estimated forty times the annual earnings of a factory worker in 1980, the gap between CEO and worker salaries grew to eighty-five times by 1990, and as the decade ended is reported to have grown to four hundred and nineteen times. Not only that: this hypertrophied "compensation" is being used to reward "turn-around experts" with capacious "golden parachutes," *after,* in some cases, their slash-and-burn restructuring has not only failed to increase shareholder value, but even driven their firms toward bankruptcy.[72] Such capitalism may not be all about the anarchic destruction-through-production of the classic Marxian vision. But it is socially destructive, and whatever the animus that drives him, Baba surely speaks for a broad constituency in judging it according to the standards of the "corporatized" egalitarianism that represented the social compact of Japan's postwar era. By those standards, the unquestioned sway exerted by the demand for shareholder profits in American capitalism is a kind of ideopathology, a social Darwinist retrogression from the movement for the "restoration of social principles" that forced state monopoly capitalism to yield some of its substance to the state. As Nitta Shigeru remarks, "What the philosophers of neoliberalism consistently ignore is the fact that the capitalist market economy is tougher than the flesh-and-blood human beings whose lives are crushed by it."[73]

On the other hand, companyism seems a remarkably weak instrument of resistance, if it is one at all, to such a force. Baba's own characterization of it is highly conflicted, almost schizophrenic. Insofar as it provides the "most advanced framework for the development of productive forces," companyism is thoroughly complicit in raising the consumption levels that threaten to bring negative transcendence to the globe. In terms of the "relations of production," he lauds it as the fairest, because it is the least capitalist, of capitalism's contemporary forms. But suppose that the companyist system, in which "the goal of capital is realized via the medium of the employee's own expression of subjectivity," is also one that literally works those subjects to death? If the "alienation . . . that everywhere accompanies capitalism is either dissolved, mitigated, or concealed" under companyism, what judgment on this system is rendered by the phenomenon of "death by overwork," or *karōshi*? Baba argues that Japanese employees "actually control [their] companies autonomously to a significant extent," but at the cost of personal meaning in their own lives. Yet "autonomy" evacuated of personal meaning would seem to be a contradiction in terms.[74] In any case, which is worse—grossly excessive CEO "compensation" and systemic employee insecurity, or self-extinction on behalf of an entity that is "nothing other than capital" itself?

Baba verges on a recognition of this problem; to that extent he echoes the concerns of an earlier generation of analysts, particularly Uchida Yoshihiko, who saw a direct link between the "weakness" of Japanese civil society and the success of corporate capital in building fictive communities within its constituent enterprises. One cannot escape the feeling, however, that Baba's turn to the issue of global survival is at some level a displacement. In the early to mid-1980s, Baba wrote with forebodings of a social collapse caused by the hegemony of companyism. In *Shin shihonshugiron,* these fears disappear, and companyism is presented as an alternative, more humane form of capital that may even help to avert disaster by restraining the consumption of resources in an excessively affluent society. The shift in perspective is unexplained, merely left to readers of earlier texts to note. It is as if the problems flowing from the hegemony of companyism, which Baba had once considered as possibly "devastating," had turned out to be paper tigers. Was his awareness of the problems of the global disparity of resource consumption so sudden and overwhelming as to have this effect? This seems doubtful. It may be that with the collapse of the bubble and the prolonged and dispiriting malaise that have defined the Heisei era, Baba lost the intellectual will to face his own conclusions—that companyism is not really a viable alternative to the predatory capitalism he despises.

IN SEARCH OF TRANSCENDENCE: TAMANOI YOSHIRŌ AND THE ECONOMICS OF THE LIVING SYSTEM

The third and final filiation of Uno-school political economy to be treated here is that formed by the work of Tamanoi Yoshirō (1918–1985).[75] As we have seen, both Ōuchi Tsutomu's completion of Uno's system, and Baba Hiroji's attempt to shift its paradigms gravitated toward, and then worked outward from, considerations of "stage theory"—the middle, and mediating term, of that system. Though they spoke about growth, as it were, in different keys, the melodic—narrative—structure of their work is essentially the same, with the middle element of the "system" continuing to be conceived in terms of a determining and determinant historical stage. Tamanoi Yoshirō, by contrast, dealt only implicitly with *dankairon* as such. To be sure, he retained a concern with "middleness," or mediation. But he came over time to approach these matters in terms of synchrony and space, placing particular emphasis on "communities" and "regions" as means of transcending commodification. While Ōuchi and Baba adhered to historicism, Tamanoi turned decisively toward a structural, and anthropological, perspective. For him, history was more a matter of place than of destination.

   Born in Yamaguchi, Tamanoi was a student at Tōhoku Imperial during Uno's final prewar years there. Following graduation, he continued on as a lecturer and shortly thereafter was appointed as assistant professor in the history of economics; his first publication appeared in 1944. Tamanoi moved to Tokyo University in 1951, remaining at the newly opened Komaba campus for nearly three decades. His final teaching years were spent in Okinawa, a move to the periphery undertaken, he said, so that the center of authority and its structures of control would become more clearly visible.[76] Tamanoi was of course deeply conversant with Uno's system but was also steeped in the broader history of economic thought, both Western and Japanese. Here, his teacher was Kuruma Samezō (1893–1983), a historian of economics, onetime director of the Ōhara Institute and a noted Marxian theorist in his own right. In an image that was typically appealing and appealingly typical, Tamanoi likened his intellectual life to a "long trip on a slow-moving local train, made up of chance encounters, some short, some extended, with no particular destination."[77] At the same time, the journey into and beyond what he called "political economy in the narrow sense" did have its points of no return. Ultimately, Tamanoi was led to formulate a critique (to be discussed presently) of Uno's system at the level of its basic principles. Breaking the confines of three-level analysis, Tamanoi sought under the primary inspiration of Karl Polanyi to resituate the study of economics in a broader field that contained noncommodified labor and production; to see whether it would be possible conceptually to reembed the economy in society. In search of this "political economy in the broad sense," Tamanoi went further, extending his own field of vision to the physical matrix of social production and reproduction, that is, to the "living system" (seimeikei) itself. Here was a web of dependencies far transcending the "economic" or the market system, but which the market seeks at all costs to colonize.

The issue for Tamanoi, as for Baba, was that of the outcome of the contest between commodifying forces and those resistant or alien to them: Would the "externals" of the market system be subsumed according to the principles of that system, or would they be internalized in such a way as to transform it? In Baba's dystopia, transcendence was realized negatively with the collapse of "excessively affluent," hypercommodified contemporary societies due to the fatal exhaustion of their resources. Tamanoi by contrast imagined transcendence positively, even redemptively, working through restored regions and communities that were located both below and above the level of the nation-state. By eliminating the commodification of labor power and land, and compelling economic development to be consonant with ecological continuity, restored communities would save the world.[78]

If Tamanoi was self-consciously "off-center" in his intellectual trajectory, he was or became so under the impetus of specific and strong intellectual currents that themselves were redefining the "center" of academic political economy in Japan. An overview of those currents reveals a complex and interesting pattern, to which Tamanoi stands in a complex and interesting relation. Tōhoku Imperial, Tamanoi's alma mater, was distant from the hub of academic authority in Tokyo, authority that itself derived from the university's proximity to the country's bureaucratic center. As with Uno, so with Tamanoi: A sense of critical detachment remained even after both had taken up their respective positions in the "center." At the same time, the Uno school to which Tamanoi came to adhere had an antagonistic relationship to established groupings within Japanese Marxism then at the height of their postwar influence (recall the vitriolic criticism aimed at Uno's *Keizai genron*).

The Uno school's own success came precisely as a school, that is, as an academic formation, and at the moment of the "modern," when the framework of the *Agrarfrage* was losing salience in Japan. (One criticism of Ōuchi Tsutomu, in turn, was that he clung for too long to this framework.) The advent of the modern was also marked by the political drama of de-Stalinization, to which Marxists of all factions and varieties of thought, were obliged to respond. Here, Uno-school economists fared better than the more orthodox—Uno's very system was a gingerly repudiation of Stalinism. Success, in other words, would have to mean that the school had something cogent to say about capitalism as such, and not just about Japan's backwardness or failure to attain "normality." This is precisely what Uno's principles had provided, against initial resistance, for Japanese Marxism.

That success was quickly challenged by so-called modern economics, particularly in its presentation of an alternative economic science that positively encouraged political pragmatism over party fealty; hence its notable strength among government economists. In this respect, Uno's disciples were more vulnerable than other Marxists, since if science was all and had no *Träger*, there was no reason not to embrace a "better," more persuasive economics of whatever class or party provenance; the alternative was to turn toward hermetic exegesis of a putative Marx-Uno canon. But better at what? Better at explaining the long postwar boom in capitalism, culminating in the startling success of the Japanese variant in generating unprecedented rates of growth. Ultimately, the social and political bill for that growth came due, followed by the collapse of both Marxian and modernist dogmas—the former for their sluggishness in recognizing growth as a significant phenomenon, the latter for having ignored or apologized for the social damage that growth brought in train.

As an adept of Uno's principles, Tamanoi Yoshirō had established his reputation with two studies of the development of classical economics, the first tracing the well-marked, if dialectical, terrain leading from Ricardo to Marx, from a world of value-creating labor to one in which exploited labor power yielded surplus value; the second surveyed the broader legacy of political economy from the seventeenth century but similarly culminated in Marx's *Capital* as the fulfillment and negation of that legacy.[79] While we may pass over much of Tamanoi's argument here, it is striking that in reissuing his textbook on "legacies" in 1980, Tamanoi explicitly called attention to Uno's complete systematization of "pure capitalism," not in relation to *Capital,* but to Joseph Schumpeter's posthumous *History of Economic Analysis* (1954). Tamanoi had long argued that Marx's work marked the end of the history of "political economy in the narrow sense"; a new era had begun, in reality and in thought. Tamanoi was dissatisfied (as Uno had been) with Schumpeter's claim that "economic phenomena" could be identified in an unbroken continuity from antiquity, that there was such a thing as Greco-Roman economics. To the contrary, economics or political economy pertained to capitalism, which was a distinct and self-contained form of society: it had a beginning and an end, and could therefore be grasped via a final and complete theory. It made little sense on the one hand for Schumpeter to suppress the "fragments of cultural sociology" that he thought had adulterated his earlier work in the interest of "dry economic theory" if, on the other, he purported to present history as a succession of one idea after another, an endless forward movement in saecula saeculorum. For surely the point was to elucidate the structure of determinate reality that had generated the very notion of "the economic" itself. Without such a limit or disjunction, Schumpeter could at best offer a "common-sense view of history."[80]

We are reminded, again, of Uno's epiphany that "the economic" as a real and knowable phenomenon had emerged only with the colonization of the process of production by the logic of the commodity, when labor became labor power, and wealth became value. Lacking this objective grounding, Uno held, even Weber had fallen into the subjectivism of transhistorical ideal-types. For Tamanoi in turn, Uno's dialectical "realism" had been a revelation of the first order. As he wrote in his eulogy-cum-critique of his teacher: "For me at least, the fact that Uno theory ceased to posit the unknowable thing-in-itself as a conceivable hypothesis, and instead steadily deepened its thinking by considering the question as to what actually existed—*das eigentliche Reale*—exerted the utmost intellectual appeal."[81]

Yet what was this supposedly "real," actually existing entity that formed the object of study in political economy? In an almost Buddhist apprehension, the real turns out to be the tangible commodity "form," rather than an imputed but inaccessible substance assumed by value in the process of exchange under the regime of capital. And that form, moreover, had multiplied and mutated: from the commodity to money to capital. Uno's great originality as a theorist of Marxian economics, Tamanoi argued, lay in his vivid and penetrating insight that the determinate *form* of value was the reality that mattered. And he traced this insight to Uno's initial doubts about Hilferding's attempt to derive "the necessity of money" from a consideration of exchange in a commodity-producing society—a society whose production can be grasped via the labor theory of value. In Hilferding's account, Uno wrote, "money is not developed out of the commodity form itself, but rather from a perspective in which, in the absence of money, commodity-producing society completely loses any standard for [the regulation of] social production." While correct in arguing that money had emerged out of a social need, Hilferding nevertheless failed in a theoretical sense to establish the specific developments in the process by which money arose out of the exchange of things. Had he followed Marx more closely in keeping in view the dual (and contradictory) nature of the commodity, Hilferding would not have been led to slight the issue of the form itself.[82]

Part of this was Marx's own fault, however. As observed earlier, in Uno's view Marx had introduced the labor theory of value prematurely into his analysis of the commodity; and it was this that presumably led Hilferding astray. That theory properly belonged not to the domain of circulation—the movement of "forms"—but of production, which Uno called the labor-production process. Here precisely was the germinal idea for his rewriting of *Capital*: that "Marx's original theories of forms of value . . . can be reformulated as theories of forms of circulation without referring to the substance of value as labor."[83] Yet if Uno had resolved one of the theoretical problems of Marxian economics by unifying its logic as that of the self-sustaining movement of "forms of value," Tamanoi came eventually to believe that he had opened up another: the origin or history of those forms. Capitalist society was not just one in which value took the form of the commodity, or commodities themselves took a growing, even unstoppable multiplicity of "dead" physical forms. It was uniquely a type of society that subsisted on the exploitative consumption of commodified labor power; one in which commodities were indeed produced by commodities, but by commodities that could not be produced directly by capital. Drawing on the terms of value theory, Tamanoi puts the issue as follows: "While the 'form' appeared in the 'space' between community and community, 'substance' is located within the community. If so, we are bound to think that capitalist society comes into being at the very moment when 'form' and 'substance' are joined into a single whole."[84]

But how, Tamanoi asked, was one to draw the connection between the elaboration of commodity forms—from the commodity to money to capital—and the commodification of labor power that formed the "essence" of capitalism? Hilferding might have failed in his attempt to ground what he imagined to be a logically necessary, or inevitable, movement. But in the end, had Uno not fallen into a similar dilemma? Was there after all any logical "necessity" that transformed labor power into a commodity? There was not:

> In his exposition of the basic principles, the "upward journey," beginning
> with the commodity, followed by money and then capital, one concept
> positing the next, proceeds very much as if the concept develops in and
> of itself. In this regard it is enough to remind ourselves of Hegel's logic,
> but the crucial point that must not be overlooked is that the "commodifica-
> tion of labor power" which is at issue here is not in fact logically posited.

As Tamanoi notes, Uno was quite aware that this was a problem. In a dialogue with the philosopher Umemoto Katsumi, Uno recalls the wry metaphor offered by a friend, as it happens also a philosopher, of the commodification of labor power as being "thrown into the 'system'" from without, in the manner of someone "slipping into a game of jump-rope." Here, then, where logic passed insuperably over into history, "capitalism" emerged as an epochal form of society that "entrusts its destiny to things." This was why, for Uno and for Tamanoi, a historically minded political economy was both central to social science and yet delimited in its claims to authority. It was central because the commodification of human relations and the accompanying phenomenon of alienation were so widely advanced, and the "world picture" so intractably inverted; and limited because these processes in fact bespoke a beginning and an end, but also because, for the Uno school at least, political economy could not dare to vouchsafe the success of any given program of praxis.[85]

For Tamanoi, the fact that Uno's system depended organically on a process of labor-power commodification that just "happened" was of deep significance, and, it turned out, irremediably problematic. It implied the necessary existence outside capitalism of a world not yet commodified—a world, to speak in the idiom of *Capital*, made up of communities that might still be, or could again be put, right side up. For commodified labor-power was not a normal commodity. It was living but alienated human essence, and lay beyond the capacity of capital to produce at will. And another commodity was like it: land itself, which constituted, so to speak, the alienated natural essence of society in its physical aspect. As commodities, these two were "unnatural" *(muri)* but at the same time they formed a "historical and institutional given for capitalism qua modern society."[86]

Uno had recognized all this, to a point. The problem lay with his dialectical presumption that capitalism, in order to be understood, first had to be studied in its perfection; with his conviction that it was necessary to "let capital tell what . . . capitalism is all about." Granting to capitalism the status of referent society—"standardization," or *kijunka*—was supposed to be followed by its relativization—*sōtaika*. After all, capitalism was supposed to be the anomaly or inversion that revealed the norm. In Uno's terms, its "laws" *(hōsoku)* were the fetishistic projections that in some sense hid, and in some sense revealed, the truly universal "norms" *(gensoku)* of social provisioning. If not Uno himself, Tamanoi came to feel, practitioners of Uno's system had lost sight of that dialectic. It was as if they remembered only Marx's dictum that the anatomy of the human being clearly reveals that of the ape; as a consequence, they had ceased to think historically, and to that extent became poorer observers of the contemporary world. Even if on the surface they rejected the arrowless time of neoclassical equilibrium, they had buried themselves so deeply in the "logic of the commodity" that they were unable to find their way out.[87]

In the face of such dissatisfactions, Tamanoi came to regard the world outside capitalism as having the greater claim on his attention, and to search for a method to approach it. From one point of view, this seems to have led him to a kind of interdisciplinary vagabondage; indeed Tamanoi himself extolled the virtues of scholarly "drifting." But in fact, however far he moved, via whatever route, Tamanoi was driven by the perduring

antipathy of the Marxian tradition for the phenomenon and consequences of commodification. He continued to embrace what we may call
the "community romance" of that tradition: the belief that "community"
referred to a social substance antithetical to the commodity form—as a
world of real and direct human contact, the community made no distinction between labor and labor-power. The issue was whether (assuming that one believed in this "lost" world), community could ever be
restored, by what means, and at what sociohistorical location. Tamanoi,
as one interpreter remarks, made a number of intellectual turns *(tenkan)*
but never fell into apostasy *(tenkō)* against the tradition that first formed
him.[88]

In 1958–60, at the same time that Ōuchi Tsutomu was at Stanford
University, Tamanoi was a Rockefeller Fellow at Harvard; he would later
spend 1969 and 1973–74 in Europe, mainly Germany. These periods
abroad signaled, if they did not bring about, the intellectual turns just
mentioned. The earlier stay had deepened Tamanoi's knowledge of modern economics, to say nothing of the world's only aboriginally modern
economy (while at Harvard, Tamanoi conducted research on the 1929
crash, and later wrote a book on the intersection of Marxian and neoclassical approaches). It also afforded him a distant vista on the initial
phase of high-speed economic growth in Japan—the so-called Jinmu
Boom—which seemed to vindicate much of the "modern" gospel. Yet
even after returning to Japan, Tamanoi maintained that distance. There
was perhaps no question of a simple reaffirmation of Marxism: his logical difficulties over commodification remained, and he also came to
question whether the Marxist concern for the "development of productive forces" had not degenerated into a mere ideology of industrialization.[89] To be sure, structural reformism was making its energetic emergence in Marxist circles worldwide. One might have expected that the
latter, with its concern to revitalize Marxism along humanistic lines,
would have been attractive to Tamanoi. But there was, Kabayama Kōichi
remarks, an "unbridgeable gulf" between the two. Tamanoi's perspective
had already grown too global to be confined within the former's essentially partisan, albeit revisionist, framework.[90]

Over the course of the 1960s, Tamanoi focused his energies on the
comparative—and largely collaborative—inquiry into macroscale economic systems. In part a legacy of his exposure to recent neoclassical and
Keynesian approaches as well as to the literature on system convergence,
this was meant as a transideological critique of industrial societies, in
which the conventional polarities of capitalist versus socialist would be

rigorously downplayed. The famous debate between Friedrich von Hayek and Oskar Lange over the problems of pricing and allocation in socialist economic planning had early on caught Tamanoi's attention; he read and corresponded with contemporary East-bloc economists such as János Kornai and Ota Šik, who did so much to theorize the—impossible?—project of market socialism; he grew interested as well in the path of industrialization in China.

But the critical opening for Tamanoi came in the mid-1960s, when he was introduced to the work of Polanyi.[91] He had already encountered—and was attracted by—Schumpeter's treatment of the vast variety of economic ideas. But there was something theoretically indiscriminate about this catholicity that, as we have seen, made Tamanoi wary. With Polanyi, by contrast, Tamanoi found both abundant empirical evidence and a compelling argument for the exceptional character of "market society" and its extraordinarily utopian claims to self-regulation; the universality of the scarcity principle ("the more nonsatiation the better") and drive for gain turned out to be powerful myths. Not only that: in *The Great Transformation* (1957) Polanyi showed the extent to which these myths of human propensities depended on the prior and forcible creation of the autonomous market through the application of state power to society. As the enabler of the market and the commodity fiction, in other words, the state was thoroughly complicit in the destruction of community or society. Thus far, Polanyi and Uno could be said to have been in almost perfect sync: they agreed on the "fictitious" character of the major inputs of industrial capitalism—commodified labor power, money, and land, including all that is extracted from it. They agreed as well that these commodity fictions were in deep contradiction with the "substance of society."

But where to go from there? Uno's choice was to sever form from substance—commodity from use value—and to work toward the perfection of his system of political economy. The achievement (and risk) that came with that choice was to have created a virtually transparent medium through which capital could express itself. The price of theoretical perfection, Tamanoi ultimately decided, had been too high; too much of "life" and the "living system" *(seikatsu, seimeikei)* had been peremptorily excised so that Uno's basic principles could be articulated. Was it not possible to conceive of basic principles on a new, broader footing?

For Tamanoi himself, who was not a systematizer, this was impossible. But in Polanyi, Tamanoi found his guide to a "political economy in the broad sense"—one that could account for all those "externals" to the system of commodity exchange and its premise that everything that is made is made in order to be sold. In fact, Polanyi insisted, "reciprocity" within communities was not only a feature of primitive economies, but remained salient in the present. It was one thing, of course, to recognize the existence "out there" of societies whose productive and distributive arrangements did not rely on market mechanisms, or to portray market economies as islands surrounded by a sea of nonmarket economies, with riches brought to the former from the latter. But even within capitalist society, the market was not uniformly developed, and the economies of the contemporary Third World (as it was only beginning to be called) simply could not be explained by a market model.

Ultimately, history and anthropology were not Polanyi's chief concern; they rather served as empirical means to prefigure a redeemed future. The difficulty of attaining that redemption, however, was patently clear to Polanyi. *The Great Transformation,* after all, was written during World War II and refers to a double phenomenon: both the rise of market society *and its end.* And this had brought not redemption but Soviet communism—and fascism. The goal nevertheless remained. "In my view," Tamanoi wrote, "the keynote in Polanyi's case is the call for a 'return to community.' But for that very reason, the image of a community reborn at a horizon beyond that of Descartes' modern world must be given greater theoretical definition."[92]

"The image of a community reborn" might not be found in Uno's system, since he had explicitly disavowed any attempt to touch the "substance" of society.[93] But in a sense, community retained a kind of palimpsest existence, or absent presence, in Uno's thought and in that of his school. Recall that Uno, and Tamanoi following him, embraced Marx's argument that commodity exchange has its origins external to the community; community is what is lost to commodification. Marx had also argued that capitalism, although it might subordinate agriculture to industry, was incapable of resolving the "external contradiction" between the two. For the ideologically committed, that was the task of socialism, which meant abolishing commodification itself, of labor power as well as of land.

But what if socialism failed? Tamanoi's embrace of Polanyi and his categories of space and synchrony reflects just this sense of failure; or more precisely, it reflects the inversion of once optimistic theories that saw societies converging for the better to the extent that they industrialized. Instead, industrialization was seen to promote convergence for the worse by preserving mutually hostile but increasingly similar political regimes. From the late 1960s onward, and deepening throughout the 1970s, Tamanoi pursued his transideological "political economy in the broad sense," defining "broad" first in social and regional, then (moving beyond Polanyi) in ecological terms; the regional was paired with the ecological for the rest of Tamanoi's life. His quest was at the conceptual level to overcome the "industrial" view of production along with the "mining mentality" in agriculture; to reembed industry in agriculture, and economy in society.[94] The issue was how to tie such conceptual aspirations to the analysis of real situations in the past and present.

It is well to recall here the *political* aspect of Tamanoi's political economy. For he was never unaware of the composition or structure of the state and how it used its power in relation to economy or society. Indeed it was the state that interposed itself between both regional communities themselves (seen as comprising local socioeconomic networks) and between such communities and the physical matrix of their activity; but what determined the contours of that state, and how was the regional community in turn affected? Typical of his considerations was an essay, "Kokka to keizai" (State and economy, 1973), which in its subtitle— "Chiiki bunken o motomete," or "A call for regional decentralization"— clearly signaled Tamanoi's basic stance. It was typical in another respect, namely, that as the decade progressed he gave increasing attention to the situation of Japan's political economy. Although the perspective is unfailingly comparative, transideological, and avowedly hypothetical, the concern is ultimately directed toward Japan. Invoking J. S. Mill's dictum that "power must be decentralized, knowledge might be centralized," Tamanoi takes up the issue of how centralization and its ills can be overcome. His explicit, even roseate ideal, is that of the "compound states" of Western Europe, which, he claims, are able to integrate their markets more effectively precisely because they have preserved medieval traditions of regional government and ways of life. In this mix was included both the remains of aristocratic landholding and a still salient culture of petty craft production, both of which had been destroyed in much of Eastern Europe in the mania for nationalization and forced collectivization. For capitalism and its accompanying politics to be healthy, such dispersal is necessary. An excess of centralization, regardless of system, creates massive economic distortions, stagnation, and political rigidity (or despotism); it suffocates civil society and promotes atomization.[95]

Writing as Japan's postwar growth faced its first real crisis, Tamanoi held that the country had systematically deprived itself of sustenance by concentrating all of its resources and capacities in the center. Japan had "the provinces," or *chihō:* beggared in local autonomy, the victims of highly unequal distribution of economic stock, and lacking in community identity. To this situation Tamanoi contrasts the vitality of the hundreds of communes—*Gemeinde*—that comprised the states *(Länder)* of the West German federation, and the consequent political autonomy of those states themselves. Japanese, Tamanoi observes, had a mistaken view of Europe, particularly of Germany, and this for two reasons. One was recent: that as a legacy of defeat, postwar Japan regarded Europe through an American lens. All it could see was "old" Europe whose day was over and springs of vitality hidden; at best it was a continent made up, as in the Wilsonian vision, of self-determining national states. Over the longer run, owing to the experience of Meiji, Prussia had hegemonized Japan's image of Germany. The real story of the Reich, Tamanoi contends, was that of the preservation of the states and the apparent administrative weakness of the empire that was in fact a strength. "Weakness" permitted the continued life of regional Germany; though Hitler had (for a time) subordinated the *Länder* in a most un-German fashion, postwar West Germany had fortunately restored this valuable medieval legacy. The true paragon of centralized power in Europe was France; and the more important point, for Tamanoi, was that if anything it was Japan and France, not Japan and Germany (as opposed to Prussia) that, from the point of view of centralization, made the better pair.[96]

Hence the real issue: Where did the drive to centralize authority in Japan originate? Why did it continue to hold such sway? In an argument drawn from Uno and more broadly from Rōnō-ha scholarship, Tamanoi pointed to the Tokugawa-era separation of samurai from the land as the distant cause for the desuetude of what might have been an aristocratic backbone for regional—not just provincial—life. More proximately, this original severance enabled the Meiji-era liquidation of samurai claims on national income, and the ability of the new state to erect a tax structure that thoroughly subordinated the prefectures. In this sense modern Japan was aboriginally centralized. Compared to the slow and piecemeal unification of the German Reich, Japan underwent a rapid and truly dramatic—but ultimately also harmful—experience of total concentration of power in the center. What Japan ought to have learned from Germany, Tamanoi wrote, was decentralization, devolution, and respect for regional difference.[97]

Tamanoi's considerations of decentralization and the "restoration of community" almost unfailingly include references to another case—that of China after 1949 but prior to the reforms of Deng Xiaoping. The stakes, again, are clear: that in contrast to Japan with its "center and provinces," China, which he visited in 1977, had created a "layered state" of districts *(xian)* each of which constituted its own regional center but also built upward toward a national apex. The "basic social unit" in each regional center, "corresponding to the *Gemeinde* and communes of Europe, [was] the people's commune . . . For these, " 'country' *[kuni]* meant district, or at most province." North Korea, Tamanoi noted, was similar; Japan again was the great exception in Asia.[98]

Tamanoi's interest in China went beyond identifying its administrative layering as an "object lesson" for Japan. By the late 1970s, a concern for the sustainability of development, regardless of ideological framework, was becoming increasingly prominent in Tamanoi's analyses. In their own differently imperfect ways, Tamanoi argued, both Adam Smith and Marx had understood that if the physical or natural matrix of society is destroyed, production and consumption, industry and trade, cannot remain viable. Smith had kept nonmarket production via "living" nature as an important element of *The Wealth of Nations* (1776); Marx, for his part, had spoken of labor as a "process by which man . . . controls the metabolism between himself and nature." Undeservedly forgotten thinkers, such as the German Social Democratic theorist Eduard David, had even more of value to say. Bound up with the question of reconstituting community was that of eco-economy. From this point of view, Tamanoi saw in Chinese socialism a fundamental challenge both to the Soviet and to capitalist modes of industrial development. The revolution of 1949 had liberated all (not only agricultural) land from landlords, bureaucracy, and colonial powers, delivering it to the peasantry. The road to commodification of land was closed off. At the same time, however, a Soviet model of industrialization was applied, only to be abandoned for having (as Mao put it) "drained the pond to catch a fish." After 1958, Tamanoi wrote, "it is evident that China began, on the basis not of a market but of a nonmarket society, to construct an authentically continental pattern of agriculture-led development in its economy and culture." This, he stressed, was an integral agriculture in which foodstuffs, forestry, and fisheries were included; on this basis, the people's communes, with their vast store of noncommodified labor power, rather than the cities or central authorities, would be depended upon to generate demand for industrial products.[99]

Needless to say, the turnabout in Chinese socialism Tamanoi described was known as the Great Leap Forward. By design, perhaps, the account focuses on the core of rational policies that are to be found in the leap, while its more horrific consequences are not so much as noted. It is doubtful, though, how far politics and policy can be separated in the analysis of Mao's struggles. Yet in its curiously bloodless fashion, Tamanoi's account captures the central, utopian ideal of the Great Leap: to advance without ceasing from socialism to realized communism, to attain for China almost overnight the development of productive forces equal to those of the West, and to do so on the basis of a gigantic mobilization of labor power that worked its way up from the commune through the several intermediate levels of administration to the national center.[100]

Most important, Tamanoi stresses, this was to be a mode of development marked by the populist delinking of urbanization from industrialization and modernization. Mao's pithy critique of Soviet-style industrialization was brilliantly farsighted. But in the wake of the Great Leap, the link was reestablished, and despite the interval of the Cultural Revolution, from the early 1970s onward China had embraced a policy of introducing by state fiat the sort of large-scale technologies that lay far beyond the demand-creating (to say nothing of productive) power of the communes. Indeed, Tamanoi had barely set down his thoughts when decollectivization began to remake the Chinese countryside.

Tamanoi's assessment of Chinese socialism would seem in short order to have become irrelevant, at least at the level of policy prediction. Writing in 1975, Tamanoi posed the question of the future for Chinese socialism as a choice between the reintroduction, with no further criticism, of the Soviet model, or the maintenance of regional decentralization. While we may refrain from upbraiding him for not foreseeing the decollectivization of Chinese socialism, Tamanoi did seem to write as if the problem of poverty in China's villages had been solved. At another level, Tamanoi's judgment was borne out. The top-down introduction of massive technological inputs had generated industrial pollution on a matching scale. To what extent, Tamanoi asked, could the "base units" of society act to counter the destruction of the country's environment? Did not the authorities' subversion of the principle of decentralization make a serious problem virtually insoluble? As he wrote:

> In China, the "Three Wastes" was promoted as a mass movement. This referred to the recovery and reuse of waste fluids, waste gas, and solid waste; the idea was that waste was to be transformed into goods [zai] . . . "From the standpoint of dialectical materialism," it was said, "there was no more than a relative difference between waste and what was not." But between the small-scale industry at the people's commune level and the latest massive

plants introduced at the "national" level, there is an unbridgeable technological gap; and the complex waste products and the repercussions of their
influence are such that they cannot be dealt with by the "Three Wastes"
movement or the doctrine of dialectical materialism.[101]

It was such considerations—the combined issue of community and eco-
economic viability—that preoccupied Tamanoi in his final years; here he
found kindred spirits in E. F. Schumacher and Ivan Illich. He grew pessimistic about China's capacity to face this problem, as he had of Japan's,
where centralizing tendencies seemed bent on the integral destruction of
society's communal and natural matrices; Europe appeared to him to
provide more promise as a model for Japan. It seemed to Tamanoi that
with the "living system" at stake, much of the received literature of economics, certainly "in the narrow sense" but perhaps even the somewhat
broader version represented by Polanyi, had reached the limits of its usefulness. The former had been driven by a "centripetal" quest for the ever
deeper understanding of the movement of commodities, a quest that had
finally issued in the Marxian critique. What was needed now was a "centrifugal," or embedded, political economy that would de-center commodity production and exchange rather than merely expand the area of
"life" subject to market-measuring criteria.[102]

The empirical problem was that the latter domain, particularly with
the virtualizing revolution in full sway over the advanced economies,
continued with great speed to generate new forms of production and
commodification based on "soft" information technologies; and these
were subsuming the economies of many societies outside the capitalist
core. Tamanoi, however, was increasingly drawn to what he regarded as
the "real" world of nonmarket relations of production and exchange—
as he put it, the "life-size" world. Alarmed by the postmodern reconcili-
ation with high technology capital, Tamanoi risked marginalization as an
anti-(post)modernist; his concerns for regional spaces and historical
diversity in economic forms appeared to some critics as retrogressive and
hermetic.[103]

Did he choose wrongly? The question is unfair. Given his interest in
how social relations external to the market shaped its contours, Tamanoi
could easily have followed a long line of analysts (from Yanagita and
Ariga Kizaemon to Nakane Chie to Murakami Yasusuke) and turned to
the intensive examination of the "Japanese system of political economy";
his student Kumon Shunpei did just that, stressing just those factors of
nonmarketized familistic and communitarian relations as its distinguish-

ing and determining features. But Tamanoi demurred. To be sure, he wrote of regions (Western Europe was full of them; Okinawa had been and was potentially one again) as economic zones in which an extensive web of "basic relations" not within the ambit of the market continued to operate in the sphere of production and exchange. For Tamanoi these relations, including parent-child, sibling, and spousal ties (gender, one interpreter remarks, "was not his strong suit"), though themselves in flux, remained significant enough in local economies that these resembled more the workings of a family than either a perfect market or system of planned labor allocation: the work of those with limited "productive capacity" due to age or disability could still be valued in local life. At the same time, the family (or quasi family) was clearly incapable of functioning as a basic unit of modern production. Not even the simplest regional economy could pretend to self-sufficiency, nor could it survive without high degrees of affiliative action.[104]

What Tamanoi did not argue—indeed could not have argued—was that Japan was uniquely oriented to a familistic mode. National cultures as a whole could not be families, or even familistic; regions might, but even at that level the analogy was partial at best. Thus, although Tamanoi took Japan as his "zone of engagement," he remained largely aloof from a nationalist perspective. I think there are two reasons: the continuing hold of the Uno school's conviction, embodied in stage theory, that the "nation" does not explain but rather must be explained, and second, what one may term the "ecological universalism" that is sometimes encountered among economists of the left who have migrated from "red" to "green" in their commitments.[105]

After the mid-1970s, Tamanoi delved into systems theory—he was interested in its accounts of different modes of self-sustenance, from "objective" homeostasis to "subjective" autonomy. Beyond that he was especially attracted to the growing literature on entropy, a concept taken from thermodynamics that, under the impetus of ecological concerns, was beginning to be applied to industrial processes. What, Tamanoi wondered, would political economy look like if rendered from the perspective of the living system? "Behind the 'making' of things," he observed, "lies the 'breaking' of some sort of order. Is not the stern human—and in its turn, social—responsibility involved in 'making' bound up with this basic understanding?" The problem was first perceived in societies that had achieved high growth, since in essence modern economies were "wide-open systems for producing waste."[106] The "dirtier" the system, the higher the entropy, and the longer "real" or "irreversible" time required for the damaged environment to be healed. These "negative production processes" had to be theorized as such; pollution, from this point of view, was unassimilable waste. An economics that took no notice of it was scientifically short-circuited, even ethically problematic. Working with the physical chemist Tsuchida Atsushi and his fellow economist Murota Takeshi, Tamanoi sought to develop a combined theoretical approach to the "human life-cycle, the socioeconomic production and consumption cycle, the ecocycle, and the global water cycle" as "linked together by the processes of low entropy inflow and high entropy outflow"; this was a "structure of entropy flows" whose continuance was synonymous with life itself. Interestingly, one historical case of such a "living" system was the metropolis of Edo, with its "highly systematized practice of barter exchange between vegetables and human excreta." "The ecocycle of Edo," Tamanoi and his colleagues noted, "maintained its fertility without generating any pollution, in the presence of a dense human population, and without the need of international trade."[107]

Yet there could be no more Edos; and for a similar reason, Tamanoi was critical of Kenneth Boulding's notion of "spaceship earth," which gave the false impression of a closed, albeit highly complex, mechanical system, whose waste could be recycled ad infinitum. Boulding was to be praised for placing the earth in "heliocentric" perspective, revealing it to be limited in resources and in need of protection. But, Tamanoi urged, "the space that is proper for life on earth is the geocentric world where the sun rises in the east each morning, and in the evening sets in the west." To sustain life in this living system, economies would have to shrink; their infinite growth would be lethal. Tamanoi dreamed of a world of "open regions" with linked economies; it was a dream still intact when he died in 1985. "The theoretical world image of an 'economics in the broad sense' grounded in the 'counter-principle' [taikō genri] of the living system should, perhaps, be a system that reconforms the geocentric world within the heliocentric one. This is the way toward creating an open economics of the 'community.'"[108]

·   ·   ·

As even his most sympathetic commentators note, no one rode what one student called "the Tamanoi local" all the way. Different reasons are adduced, but the three most cogent point, first, to a lack of focus in the later work and a perhaps understandable impatience among economists to remain, as Tamanoi did, wandering "the side roads that run alongside the major arteries" of their profession. A second holds that, despite his critical perspective on received economics, including that of Uno himself, Tamanoi's approach rested on a "fateful separation" between theory (or "science") and historically conditioned thought (or "ideology"). Without a grounding in intellectual history, Yagi Kiichirō argues, Tamanoi in the end "could do no more than produce a myriad of captivating fragments." A third flaw is related to the second: that Tamanoi, for all his attraction to the world of the real and irritation with mere simulation and virtuality, was himself trading in the beautiful fiction of community. Yet he was significant, for Yagi, because his work encouraged others to explore new intellectual worlds after the dogmas of postwar social science, Marxian and modernizationist alike, had collapsed. For Yoshitomi Masaru, Tamanoi's importance lay in his prescience in seeing beyond the polarization of capitalist versus socialist systems, and subjecting both to a critical comparative gaze: How, Tamanoi asked, were the price mechanisms in these systems related to the communication of information needed for production and management? Similarly, Tamanoi's early attention to the differing ways in which, and extent to which, labor power was commodified in differing societies presaged the intercapitalist rivalries of the post-1989 era, no small element of which lay in the variations in modes of worker "subjectivity." Not least, finally, Tamanoi raised the issue of the relationship between environmental pollution and technological innovation in a profession (and in a country) strongly disposed to regard productivity gains as sacrosanct.[109] In one sense, Tamanoi can be seen as exploding the hermeneutic of the Uno school even while he preserved some of its most essential elements. But it was no longer a system.

CONCLUSION

Japan barely figures in Marx's *Capital;* but *Capital* has figured importantly in the intellectual world of Japan.[110] Indeed of all the texts introduced to that world from the outside since the mid-nineteenth century, *Capital* seems the single most consequential in its traces. And among those traces, in turn, Uno Kōzō's daring and original act of appropriation stands in a class by itself. *Capital* had been left incomplete at Marx's death, and at Engels' as well; Uno may be said to have completed it properly, that is, with the necessarily rigorous exclusions that followed from his basic apprehension of the self-contained, self-sustaining, and self-perpetuating character of "pure capitalism." The system of political economy he developed—"nowhere echoed in Western Marxism," as Colin Duncan observed—was both intellectually rich and politically controversial. Its radical severance of science from ideology was anti-Stalinist from its very inception, a point that emerges with the necessary clarity only when Uno's own biography is taken into account. Uno raised the stakes for praxis very high, bequeathing to the intellectual world of the Japanese left not a faith but an analytic. For Uno, only workers, not Marxism, could change the world.

The response to Uno's system from certain party and activist quarters was, and remains, harsh: It offered nothing more than arid scholasticism (for some people scholasticism can only be arid) and was guilty of a scandalous avoidance of the political issues facing "progressive forces." The world of Uno's system, particularly the basic principles, they say, bears no trace of class or class struggle, knows nothing of gender or racial inequality and stratification, and even abstracts the state (or "power") from its considerations. Uno himself may not have been an apologist for capital, but at least one critic, responding to Baba Hiroji's new "paradigm," finds little else in the Uno school but such an apologetic.[111] As far as Baba is concerned, such assertions come unavoidably with his role as highly self-conscious gadfly of the Uno school. When one considers the work of other figures—Ōuchi Tsutomu, his student Shibagaki Kazuo, or the brilliant dialectician Sekine Tomohiko—ideological critique seems superficial and misplaced. The inattention to gender is, however, systemic. And the problems of Uno's system go beyond ideology.[112]

Supposing that one wished to pursue a three-level analysis of contemporary capitalism, the issue now is: Have we not passed into a historical period in which the salience of the self-possessed original type has vanished? Is it not necessary and possible to arrive at a new set of basic principles derived from the historical tendencies common to all three stages of capitalism—mercantilist, liberal, and imperialist? By doing so, one might forcefully theorize the contingency and political conflict—the "history of class struggle"—that Uno had displaced to his unfinished theory of stages and contemporary analysis.[113] Yet what would be gained by doing so? Uno would insist that such an attempt would be futile and incoherent. Only the capitalism abstracted from the liberal stage

> can have a theory . . . largely because only under pure capitalism could the economic achieve sufficient independence from the political to be anywhere near making a successful bid to run society in its own self-image. . . . While it is true that in order to understand capitalism fully in its concrete aspect,

one must grasp both its theory and its history, it hardly follows that the two must be physically contained within the same volume.[114]

On the other hand, rather than looking at the first two levels of the system as booster rockets to be jettisoned in diachronic "methodological time" so that the ultimate goal can be reached, surely a "globalized" economy does require a synchronic approach in which the three levels can be turned "sideways" and be seen to operate simultaneously. It reflects both a recognition that contemporary modes of commodification may have surpassed the theorizing capacity of any diachronically oriented system, and that antagonism or resistance to those modes also remain inevitable.

Resolving the issue of new basic principles is a compelling task for social science. But it is not one that can be resolved by the Uno school or its system. To be sure, the school made a striking contribution to the understanding of Japanese capitalism, precisely because it insisted on seeing it in the context of mediating stages rather than as mere deviation from an actual norm or manifestation of perennial culture. In its "third generation," however, the school has decomposed across the board. It possesses no critical mass, with the necessary social resonance, from which one may expect a synthetic breakthrough. Naturally, it will be said: Marxism itself has been discredited, and may it rest in peace. But that is not my meaning here. The future of Marxism as a "core" set of ideas will have to be worked out via a process of negotiation with other intellectual tendencies. Uno himself was probably right in refusing to try to theorize the contingent; the entire cast of his mind militated against this.[115] But the school's ascetic deferral of the problem of praxis (apart from academic or professional commitment) finally left it without political imagination or resources. In another domain, its characterization of social scientific knowledge, especially in relation to nature, was already being called into question by Tamanoi Yoshirō. The dichotomy of social subject as self-knowing versus natural object as ultimately unknowable, he realized, was endangering the literal life chances of human communities; some sort of intersubjectivity was desperately needed. Uno's system had its task: to attack the strong current of politically enforced determinism, of antihistorical historicism, within Marxian political economy. This it accomplished, brilliantly so. The role of reconstruction and synthesis lay beyond its intellectual powers to perform.

CHAPTER 6

Social Science and Ethics

Civil Society Marxism

In surveying the achievements and problematic legacy of Uno Kōzō in chapter 4, I concluded with the idea that "what Marxism needed was not better science, but better ethics." Taking up this theme, this chapter explores the attempts by Japanese Marxists, including the critical legatees of Marxism, to develop a viable ethics for the postwar Japan that constituted their "zone of engagement." The argument, in essence, is that among the notions around which they sought to construct such an ethics, "civil society" was of particular importance. This was not something easily predicted: the term "civil society" had had little direct presence in the broader current of social thought in modern Japan, while orthodox Marxists, who were more attuned to European conceptions of civil society, regarded the notion with disdain. But it proved, nevertheless, to be a sort of "bridge idea" that drew together thinkers who shared the aspiration for radical but uncoerced social transformation.

Following a "prehistory" that culminated in attempts by social scientists to promote the "rationalization" of what they saw as the atavistic elements of Japan's wartime regime, the explicit discussion, and advocacy, of civil society as such began early in the postwar years. Conceptually, civil society was a product of the attempt by public intellectuals to look critically at the imperial system and its failure through the frame of Marxism. For reasons explored here, these discussions reached critical mass only in the 1960s, leaving a considerable "afterlife" as well. The seemingly intractable malaise that has marked the post–

Cold War era in its turn has prompted a reconsideration of that earlier episode. But before we can address the legacy of that long-ago efflorescence to those now witnessing the apparent decay of Japan's postwar order, we must account for that efflorescence itself.

PREHISTORY: PROMISE AND PROBLEM

The redoubtable dictionary *Kōjien* defines civil society *(shimin shakai)* as a "modern society composed of free and equal individuals, having abolished all privileges, control by status or relations of subordination. Advocated in the seventeenth and eighteenth centuries by Locke and Rousseau."[1] So the notion of civil society was European in origin and had to be translated, indigenized. Did that happen? Did the translated term itself come to evoke, for a broad generality of Japanese, something identifiable in their own experience and political *Weltanschauung?* In other words, did the "prehistory" of civil society ever become "history"?

To sketch an answer: The "revolutionary Restoration" of 1868, the narrative would begin, had done nothing if not create the political and legal framework, the formal preconditions, for such a society. One would then call attention to the early Meiji discourse of natural rights, to Protestant social criticism and activism, and especially to Fukuzawa Yukichi's attempt to pry loose the consciousness of his fellow Japanese from the "feudalistic" habit of turning to authority, or the state, for moral validation. All of these were currents of thought and action in which the central role was taken by former samurai, many of them political "losers" whose values and livelihood seemed to have been cast onto history's trash heap along with the Tokugawa regime. Fukuzawa argued that he and his fellow "scholars of Western learning" could serve as Japan's "middle class," albeit a virtual one, since its sociological requisites were still lacking. The point is that for Fukuzawa, and not only Fukuzawa, the middle class was the maker of history in the modern world. One could point out, further, the Spencerian arguments of Tokutomi Sohō, who in effect proposed that, indeed, the middle class was the maker of history, but that Fukuzawa's version of it belonged to the "old men of Tenpō"— the samurai reformers of the generation before Meiji. Samurai values, Tokutomi held, availed nothing; former warriors had no claim to the part of history-maker. Japan's "commoners," the *heimin,* could and would assume the honor. Thus Tokutomi in 1887.[2]

And yet, amid the profusion of neologisms that sought to stem the categorical flux of Meiji society, "citizen" does not stand out. "Nation," which is rendered as both *kokumin* and *minzoku;* "people," rendered as *jinmin* or *shomin;* and "middle class"—all of these had their champions in the Age of Civilization and Enlightenment. But citizen? It may be only a slight exaggeration to say that citizen was at best the conceptual and moral stepchild of Japan's modernization. Instead, the official bearer of the tasks of development, and in this sense of making history, was the imperial subject, *shinmin,* clad in a neotraditionalist mantle of loyalty, filial piety, and self-sacrifice on behalf of the national community. Installed in hegemony over these other designations for modern Japanese, it nevertheless failed to displace them. Collective identities vis-à-vis that of imperial subject were to be negotiated from positions of unequal strength, their descriptors reflecting greater or lesser consciousness of difference from official subjecthood, with difference extending by degrees toward more radical estrangements.

Legally speaking, not every subject was as free an individual as every other: the household, or *ie,* system enshrined a patriarchy that remained in force until 1945. In any case, rights were not inherent in nature but were granted by the state, which had been elevated to an object of worship. Kawakami Hajime would later put this in binary terms: "In the democratic lands of Europe, human rights are granted by heaven, and the state's rights by the people. . . . In Japan, the state's rights are granted by heaven, and human rights by the state."[3] By the 1890s, "society" *(shakai)* emerged on the scene, but as a problem, the seedbed of conflict and strife and division among the emperor's subjects. With urbanization and industrialization, gifts in some sense of Japan's successful imperialism, society came all too soon to be captured by that most polarizing notion of "class," especially ominous when it bore the adjective *"musan"*—"propertyless."

A propertyless class, of course, implies a propertied one. A considerable distance was traveled from the age of Fukuzawa's "virtual" middle class to the unmistakable reality of concentrated, industrially based wealth in the bourgeoisie of the 1920s. Indeed, at first sight, the former would have found the latter unrecognizable. Fukuzawa's vision was of a morally independent, nationally minded class of individuals who subsisted on their modern skills. Although notoriously divided over the nature of Japan's capitalism and over revolutionary strategy, Japan's Marxists were united in the perception that the Japanese bourgeoisie was a signally sycophantic class. It depended on state favor for its position, and it remained so weak politically that the coming revolution—one that would usher in socialism—would nevertheless require the working class and its party to carry out first the "bourgeois democratic tasks" left unfinished after 1868. Capitalism may have developed in Japan, but never a fighting bourgeoisie, and perforce no "bourgeois" or "civil" society. The tasks of civil society were delegated, as before, to a virtual class—this time of reformist officials, incipient "free" professionals, intellectuals (especially university-educated and -based), journalists, and social activists. Particularly after World War I, their achievements were real. Japanese civil society, even without the hegemony of the "citizen" in political and social discourse, was not the "primordial and gelatinous" morass that Antonio Gramsci perceived in Russia.[4]

Even so, this civil society did not enjoy broad moral or conceptual legitimacy until the massive failure of the imperial system associated with military defeat had significantly eroded the moral stature of the state and the attendant category of imperial subjecthood. And to the extent that "one cannot understand prewar Japan without looking at the villages," it must also be said that as long as the landlord-tenant relation remained the crux of rural society, "citizen" would have to wait in the ideological shadows.[5] Notwithstanding this compelling prehistory, the moment for the articulation of citizenship as a positive ideal did not come in Japan until 1945; it would take still longer for it to assume the status of an "objective" category for social analysis. From either point of view, the history of civil society in Japan—that is, a "self-conscious" or "self-aware" history—belongs to the postwar era.

I turn now to the work of three thinkers who gave voice to that moment. Two of these, Uchida Yoshihiko (1913–1989) and Hirata Kiyoaki (1922–1995), were economists and historians of economic thought who, while profoundly influenced by Marxism, were little constrained by considerations of dogma. Known as "civil society Marxists," they advanced a conception of civil society that combined moral, political, and critical perspectives. Each of these, they thought, had to be brought to bear in concert with the others in order to intervene effectually in contemporary social debate. The third thinker, Maruyama Masao (1914–1996), was a historian of East Asian, especially Japanese, political thought and a working political scientist. Far better known outside Japan than Uchida or Hirata, Maruyama was personally close to Uchida, and he shared with both men a strong conviction that the task facing socially conscious intellectuals was to contribute to the fullest possible realization of Japan's "modernity," which they felt had been left tragically incomplete at war's end.

In this respect, all three were critical legatees of the "particularist"

Marxism of the Lectures Faction, or Kōza-ha, whose influence over Japanese social science and social thought extended well into the postwar era. In the famous "debate over Japanese capitalism," this group of Marxist social scientists had argued that the Meiji Restoration ushered in an "absolutist" imperial regime whose social foundation was a "semi-feudal" peasantry. In dissent, the so-called Worker-Farmer Faction, or Rōnō-ha, contended that, however pusillanimous, Japan's bourgeoisie had in fact triumphed in 1868, and that the Meiji regime rested on a properly capitalist, albeit backward, foundation. From this perspective, it might be said that for the Kōza-ha, Japan was a nation of subjects, while for the Rōnō-ha, it was already, if incipiently, a society of citizens.

Maruyama differed from Uchida and Hirata in one striking respect: He largely avoided the use of the term civil society, which Uchida and Hirata invested with serious moral and intellectual capital. As should become clear, the fact that he avoided it is significant for the understanding of both Maruyama and postwar Japanese conceptions of civil society, as it was, is, and ought to be.

THE CRUCIBLE OF WARTIME THOUGHT

Uchida Yoshihiko was, in the words of his intimate colleague Hirata Kiyoaki, "first and foremost an economist"; and, in its turn, economics was first and foremost a "moral science." For Uchida, the ethical and social element preceded but did not displace the analytical. What produced the economic phenomena that form the object of analysis in a particular society? Uchida's sophisticated intellectual culture and wide range of involvements, along with his close attention to form and the high literary quality of his expositions, were all directed toward situating economic analysis in the dual context of history and of his self-examination as a "producer" of economic knowledge. In this regard, Uchida's work evokes that of Kawakami Hajime, the founder of Marxian economics in Japan, but more importantly, a founder determined to impart to Marxism that very ethical perspective he found lacking in its official, party-authorized formulations. It was Uchida in fact who first gave proper scholarly attention to Kawakami's work.[6]

Uchida's critical, ethical, and national perspective was in place early on. As a graduate student in economics at Tokyo Imperial he would have been especially sensitive to the demands of status. Indeed, Uchida left off his studies to take a position as a researcher at the Tō-A Kenkyūjo (East Asia Institute) from 1940 to 1942; there he conducted surveys of rice production and the "monoculturalization" of the Malay economy under British rule. As Sugiyama Mitsunobu observes, Uchida's work, like that of the Kōza-ha theorist Yamada Moritarō on Chinese paddy agriculture, drew on Marxist critiques of Western imperialism, and to that extent it co-opted Marxism into the functional support of Japan's own imperial project.[7] From January 1943 to August 1945, Uchida was affiliated with the Sekai Keizai Kenkyūshitsu (World Economy Institute) at Tokyo Imperial. Such was his contribution to "contributionism," the peculiar compulsion felt by social scientists, in their capacity as public intellectuals, to offer their services to the state and the national community in a time of crisis. But his work was interrupted, first by a brief period of conscripted service in the navy, then by four months' imprisonment while under suspicion of having violated the Peace Preservation Law.

Sugiyama also points to the dramatic difference between the efforts of Uchida and Yamada on the one hand, and the "true-believing" embrace of Japan-centered pan-Asianism by Hirano Yoshitarō, the influential author of *Nihon shihonshugi shakai no kikō* (The system of Japanese capitalist society, 1934), on the other.[8] That work, together with Yamada's *Nihon shihonshugi bunseki* (Analysis of Japanese capitalism) of the same year, had virtually laid the foundation for the Kōza-ha Marxist analysis of contemporary Japanese society and political economy, one centered on the notion that the modern imperial system was an absolutist regime along the lines of the post-1905 Russian tsardom. The rural "community" as the cell form of a persistent semifeudalism was matched at the elite level by the dominance of absolutist elements in the state and the corresponding fragility and sycophancy of the bourgeoisie. From the Kōza-ha perspective, Japan had no citizens, no autonomous individuals, and perforce no civil society—or only the barest beginnings of each—but it had developed a species of capitalism. Capitalism, in other words, was not the same thing as civil society.

Under the circumstances of political repression and wartime mobilization, Kōza-ha Marxism was bound to be taken in unwonted directions. In his path breaking analysis of 1934, Yamada Moritarō had left open the possibility that skilled workers in *zaibatsu*-run firms could "use the judgment and discipline they developed on the job to good advantage in a revolutionary movement," that even with the legal left and the union movement suppressed, wartime industrial rationalization might produce "dissident elements"—dissident, that is, by virtue of their modernity itself.[9] Following his embrace of Greater East Asianism, Hirano Yoshitarō, by contrast, argued that Western economic forms had to be prevented from penetrating any further into the region, lest they undermine small-holder communitarianism by bourgeois individualism.[10] The typical Kōza-ha insistence on the need for Japan to complete its bourgeois revolution now became an assertion that revolution was no longer necessary, or that Japan itself was the necessary revolutionary force.

As if to split the difference between these two views, the labor economist Ōkōchi Kazuo (1905–1984) advanced the notion that wartime labor policy, by bringing about a vast increase in the number of highly skilled and "self-activating" workers, might effectively transcend the spuriously paternalistic "social policy" of the "Prussian type" capitalism typical of prewar—absolutist—Japan. Through this enhancement of the "productive forces"—labor power being recognized as a crucial element of those forces—the social relations of production would be altered, and the "profit motive" and "blind greed" of individual capitalists would be overcome. The "total social capital" could be directed to a rationalized end as a by-product of war mobilization itself: the active agency *(shutai-sei)* of workers and managers alike would be dedicated to the greater national good. In place of its earlier, backward form of capitalism and the impossible burden of realizing socialism, the Japan of what Ōkōchi termed the "third way" could become, he hoped, a "productive-forces-rational" society.[11]

That did not happen; could not happen. The economic distortions and distensions associated with breakneck wartime production and catastrophic destruction made sure of it. But the vision of Japan as a productive-forces-rational society did not evaporate with defeat; quite the contrary. Virtually as soon as the war ended, Uchida assumed the role of sympathetic critic and legatee of the Kōza-ha, and from that position he followed a research trajectory that refined his perspective, adjusting it to radically changing circumstances of failed total war, fitful recovery, and rapid growth. In an article of 1948, he assessed, even championed, Ōkōchi's productive-forces theory as a form of antifascist contributionism-cum-resistance, a position greeted with widespread skepticism. Beyond that, he argued, the "contradictory development" *(mujunteki tenkai)* of Japan's economic structure had indeed pushed the country's Prussian type capitalism into its last phase, that of an unwinnable war. In some sense, Japan had defeated itself.[12] And finally, with that defeat, with the powers of reaction in abeyance, it was possible to contemplate the creation of a new society.

REDEEMING HOMO ECONOMICUS

A new society: civil society. In one of those "slighter gestures of dissent" that loom so large in historical reconstructions of wartime experience, Uchida had apparently been reading deeply in Adam Smith. And following the surrender, in the face of a dramatically renascent Marxism, Uchida, like Kawakami Hajime in an earlier era, tried forcefully to link his affirmation of structural transformation with a concern for the form of subjectivity needed to make it effectual. For his orthodox contemporaries, civil society was a term of opprobrium, a rationalization of bourgeois egotism and acquisitiveness, a theodicy of exploitation. Developmentally, civil society was at best a pre-stage to or an instrument for ushering in socialism, and it would not continue in any substantial way once socialism was achieved. But for Uchida, freed from the distorting—and demoralizing—effects of wartime coercion and violence, civil society was the very essence of positive social transformation.

From his reading of Smith, Uchida drew the idea that real *Homo economicus* was not just a cold calculator but the individual constituent of civil society, in which market relations and the social division of labor itself must be, and in fact are, underlain by a basic human sympathy between equals who recognize the "sanctity" of each others' good faith efforts, their labor. Uchida invested great moral significance in the notion of one commodity, one price *(ichibutsu ikka)*—of equality in the market. Here, for Uchida, was a vital "moral sentiment," without which social life clearly becomes intolerable, and which must be restored to consciousness. Even as he came to immerse himself in the early Marx and the *Grundrisse* (texts that had become available anywhere only after the 1930s), Uchida held fast to a reading of Smith's civil society that was strongly oriented to a kind of national productivism, one far more positive than the laissez-faire individualism of the stereotype.[13]

As an inheritor of the Kōza-ha perspective on Japanese capitalism, Uchida understood that while Smith may have "used the term 'civil society' to refer in a positive sense to the society in which he lived," in France and even more so in Germany, civil society meant more than what Smith had imagined: in those countries it functioned critically in relation to "actually existing" capitalism. And beyond such relatively advanced "late starters," in Russia and Japan, where capitalism retained its semi-feudal agrarian base and Prussian characteristics, civil society was something still to be achieved.[14] Indeed, in an early postwar essay Uchida writes of the Russian populists, or *narodniki*—those opponents of capitalist industrialization who had done so much to educate Marx himself on conditions in Russia—as the very bearers of Russian civil society thinking. Why? Because insofar as they envisioned a liberated peasantry now possessed of land and following the lead of local large owners toward upward mobility—what Lenin called the "American path"—"the *narodniki* were advocating capitalism in the name of anticapitalism."[15] Such considerations were intensely topical: just as Uchida, along with many others, was turning his scholarly attention to the history of Russia's peasantry, Japanese villages were on the verge of being transformed in a strikingly similar direction.

And here lay the key to Uchida's ideas on civil society, and the key to their appeal—in their orientation to the future. Civil society in Japan could not possibly be the mere ideological reflex of bourgeois hegemony, because that hegemony had never formed. No, the problem with Japan's bourgeoisie was its continued failure to internalize the principle of "one commodity, one price" and its premise of equality in the market, and, indeed, in society more generally. If anything, Uchida pointed out, "bourgeois thought," particularly literary thought, from the Meiji period onward was antieconomistic. Its criticism of the "economic world" was not so much a recoil from the cold calculation of a (misunderstood) *Homo economicus* as it was an attack on advancement through worldly success *(risshin shusse)*. Uchida uses the example of Ozaki Kōyō's serialized novel *Konjiki yasha* (The golden she devil, 1897–1902) and its portrayal of those who advance through making use of personalistic connections *(kane wa kone nari)* to arraign Japanese capitalism for its lack of a healthy, modern ethos.[16]

So, too, for the domain of labor. In the early postwar years, Uchida's views seemed fully corroborated by works such as John Bennett and Iwao Ishino's study of "boss-protégé" *(oyabun-kobun)* relations in industry, which was based on research done during the occupation, and legal sociologist Kawashima Takeyoshi's influential study of the "family-like structure" of Japanese society.[17] For Uchida, the problem with capitalist society in Japan was that although (as in feudal society) the sanctity of ownership was recognized, the sanctity of labor was not. In a system based on status or personalistic difference, the best workers could hope for was status-appropriate "fairness," never equality. And under those circumstances, institutional (that is, state or corporate) interest, clad in the mantle of service to the "community," could be used to justify unending demands for labor. In other words, the principle of one commodity, one price did not apply to labor power either.

With the mediation of the principle of "one price per commodity," i.e., of the law of value, capitalist acquisition [of property] comes into being. However, even if the law of value is not fully realized, capitalist acquisition does in fact materialize. Japanese capitalism may be capitalism in this latter sense, but it does not constitute civil society in the first sense. The inclination toward civil society . . . contains within it an inclination toward pure *capitalism*. But at the same time, pure capitalism is a society in which, via the mediation of the law of value, property acquired through labor is definitively converted into *capitalist acquisition,* and as that occurs, demands for *earnings proportional to ability* are suppressed. In this sense, the question inevitably arises as to whether capitalist society can be called a society of citizens. To the extent that the issue of acquisition *not through status or connections, but according to ability* is forced out, civil society takes on an abstract character and drops away from *pure capitalism*.[18]

In Uchida's thinking, civil society was a future-oriented but immanent critique of Japan's capitalism and, more broadly, of the complex of institutions at all levels of society that perpetuated the hold of premodern values over social life and relations. In the economic realm, the "objective correlative" of this premodernity was the much discussed "dual structure" of the industrial economy. In the face of such circumstances, Uchida became a "pure capitalist" in the domain of thought, but only provisionally. All social relations have to become commodified first— under the aegis of a large and active labor movement—such that the "one commodity, one price" principle can be made to reward labor "according to ability." Thus would capitalist society in Japan also become civil society. Yet, insofar as Uchida was a Marxist as well as a devout Smithian, the development of civil society relations would necessarily generate contradictions in the form of antagonistic relations between capital and labor. The supersession of the purely capitalist values of civil society is implicit in their own development. Such is the Marxian logic of his position.

Two questions arise at this juncture. First, to what extent was Uchida's position Marxist? That is, to what extent did he look to the intensification of contradictions leading to socialist revolution as the medium of development? Second, to what extent did the actual trajectory of Japanese capitalism accord with his expectations for the realization of civil society? Or, to be less coy about it, how did Uchida respond to the remarkable spurt of growth in the Japanese economy, and did that growth affect his basic stance as a "moral economist"?

In a sense, the two questions resolve into one. Uchida had never lost the concern for the "subjective," or moral, dimension of production relations: It will be recalled that he had begun to ponder the issue of civil society, in the context of economic mobilization for total war, as in part a covert act of protest against his own contribution under duress of professional knowledge to that misbegotten process. Yet he had never championed egotism or self-interest as such, either during the war or in its aftermath. Like Kawakami, Uchida was uncomfortable with the "self," and he regarded civil society as a space, or place, for genuine—that is, autonomous and uncoerced—self-transcendence.

Whether from this elevated perspective or from one that was more affirmative of the masses' attempts to defend their everyday lives and hard-won comforts, civil society was clearly operative in the heated ideological struggles of the 1950s. In striving to settle accounts with the "old order" represented by Prime Minister Kishi Nobusuke and blunt his drive to "discipline" Japanese society as part of a program to restore the country's role as a military power, the movements leading up to and including the demonstrations against the U.S.-Japan Security Treaty (Anzen Hoshō Jōyaku, or Anpo) of 1960 represented for Uchida the collective action of a self-aware citizenry. Its like had not been seen before. The galvanized and convergent energies of a range of quite disparate social groups, the huge scale and variety of protests, the sense that individual commitment and engagement need not come at the price of ideological subordination to any party—all of this was new. This was civil society.

CIVIL SOCIETY IN THE WAKE OF ANPO

The outcome of these struggles is well known. The so-called 1960 Anpo led to an epochal political defeat for the left that fixed the category of citizen in a variety of modes of protest. In this sense, 1960 Anpo was the ne plus ultra of Japanese civil society. It also prompted a shift toward a full-court press of government policies designed to maximize the economic growth that was already underway, accelerating the rate of urbanization and the state-dependent "embourgeoisement" of the countryside. As Uchida clearly understood, the success of the government's income-doubling measures could not be ignored, but neither was it merely to be celebrated. It had to be explained and anatomized—defetishized. But how?

In this context, a gap opened between the realities of the new "affluence"—including popular attraction to it despite the steady accumulation of social and environmental costs—and the capacities of received "progressive" thought and old left institutions to offer a credible critique. Would those who criticized the "old left" do better? This was the moment in which civil society discourse attained critical mass in the Japanese intellectual world. Why so? One can see the 1960 Anpo in quasi-geological terms: almost as if two tectonic plates, after having been closely aligned, slowly begin to pull apart. In one sense, discussions and arguments about "organizing the spontaneous" (in Takabatake Michitoshi's memorable phrase) or the activities of the antiwar movement Beheiren (Peace for Vietnam Citizens' Alliance) point toward the emergence of the so-called new social movements, in which class and status, and indeed the notion of productive labor, recede in favor of a neocommunitarian ideal of residency as the basis for shared identity and collective action. "Community" here, however, has nothing in common with local chauvinism but as in Beheiren could support a counternetwork of local, autonomous nodes in a national, or even international, movement. Along with this came critiques (by Kitazawa Masakuni, for example) of "managed" or "administered" society. Rather typically, Takabatake betrayed strong fears that the infinitesimally fine net of "administration" would all too soon insinuate itself into every movement, even as he understood that "spontaneity" could only subsist through organization.[19]

On the other hand, for early postwar proponents of civil society such as Uchida, the 1960 Anpo was an end, and the role they played was increasingly that of Minerva's owl. Indeed, Uchida's own interests shifted away from labor unions and their struggles to passionate involvement in the salon of intellectuals that formed around Yamamoto Yasue, an actress of the (prewar) Tsukiji Little Theatre and a patroness of the oppositionist elite.[20] Yet, because the cleavage between Uchida's vision of civil society and that of the not-yet-articulated new social movements was still relatively slight, Uchida's writings found, if anything, even larger audiences as the 1960s wore on.[21] Furthermore, the critical tasks of the post-Anpo years accorded well with Uchida's long-standing approach, one that had already separated him from Marxist orthodoxy. This was another point in his favor. Not for the first time, he would question the moral worthiness of the collective, on behalf of which the efforts of labor were being claimed, and whether those efforts were receiving just recompense. In a classic essay from 1967, "*Shihonron* to gendai" (Japan today and *Das Kapital*), Uchida summed up his thinking, using the coincidence of the centenaries of the Meiji Restoration and of Marx's great work to allow the one to illuminate the other.

The fact was, he recognized, that "'*Das Kapital*—100 Years' sheds a wan light in comparison with the luster (bluster) of '100 Years of Meiji.'" Japan had advanced far beyond the "developing countries" that might see socialism as a goal to be attained: "If Europe is headed from the modern to the 'supermodern,'" Uchida remarks, "then Japan is running still further ahead . . . toward the 'super-super modern' [chō-chōkindai]." What constitutes this super-super modernity of Japan, however, appears to be its greatest debility:

> A kind of old patriotism is being dredged up, not as a cultural or sentimental thing but as a politically useful andiron in forging Japan's super-modernization. The central themes are production and development. Both democracy as a humanizing factor in industrialization and European modernity as something to be admired are being played down by the super-modernizers who are trying instead to counterbalance the "excesses of democracy" in postwar Japan by mass producing the antidote—patriotism. We are paying a big price in the loss of democratic freedoms in order to build our super-modern machine.[22]

Underlying this political criticism lay a series of linked historical claims concerning modern Japan, read against and through the threefold schema of social development as outlined in Marx's *Grundrisse*.[23] Since the Meiji period, local autonomy in Japan had been drastically sacrificed to centralization, and a virulent statism—conflated with emperorism—subordinated both local autonomy and individual (or human or natural) rights to the "needs of the state, *for the development* of the state." Finally, Uchida asserts, in the absence of "natural law thinking and the labor theory of value," a species of "pseudo-Darwinism" was mobilized to insure that "the right to live" was given only to those able to survive. As a corollary, "sanctity of ownership as a widely held concept was never broken by a belief in the sanctity of labor."[24]

In this "sanctity of ownership" Uchida saw a fundamental continuity with Japan's feudal "premodernity"—the "irrational" perpetuation of personalism in spheres where it did not truly belong, such as in the exercise of public or corporate authority—but as combined with a more than requisite share of "impersonal" values. This could take the form, for example, of the hyperidealization, or fetishism, of material indices of performance. The result, on the one hand, was that "premodernity assumed a kind of viscous tenacity in common thinking that has never entirely disappeared." On the other hand, under unprecedented postwar conditions this modernized premodernity had clearly fostered in the industrial workforce, both blue and white collar, an extraordinary ethos of "service to enterprise." As he puts it:

> If you look beneath the surface of our social and economic life, there is a degree of premodernity in both social relations and thinking patterns. It is precisely this premodernity that has made our startling leaps in production possible, while at the same time, this same factor has rendered it extremely difficult to understand the basic nature of the problems confronting our society . . . Among the reasons it has been possible to supermodernize so super-quickly is, I think, that Japan has not eradicated her premodernity but has sustained it in her institutions and in her thinking. Far from impeding modernization, this left-over premodernity has *helped create* what I call supermodernity at an unprecedented rate of speed.[25]

In short, to recall a paradox noted earlier, "in Japan, capitalism has developed thanks to the weakness of Civil Society."[26]

Civil society, then, was the vital "medium" (literally, between state and enterprise) that enabled resistance to the overdetermined forces of supermodernity. These were forces that should be resisted because, at least as of the apex of Japan's high growth, they threatened to strip Japanese workers of any genuine autonomy, society of its incipient democracy, and the physical environment of its elemental livability. In putting matters this way, Uchida had both inherited and transcended the Kōza-ha perspective. The problem now was not simply that of "overcoming community," but of overcoming its co-opted modern forms. The officialized discourse, whether at the state or corporate level, that sought to diminish the sphere of individual rights, of equality, of justice—all in the name of community—ignored the basis in real human sympathy that in fact sustained any viable market, or any society modeled on the market. Yet Uchida was no mere proponent of enlightened self-interest. To this extent, one can say that his notion of the market, civil society, and "civil society capitalism" is reminiscent of the "anticapitalist capitalism" of the Russian populists. Just as the appeal of the *narodniki* to an anachronistic notion of the village community led Lenin to see them as "petty bourgeois democrats," so too Uchida, mutatis mutandis, appears to rest his arguments on an idealized, and similarly anachronistic, mode of preindustrial, or at least premonopoly capitalism. In this respect, it is slightly *amattarui*—ever so sweet at the core. At the same time, he does not flee into cultural exceptionalism, and he resolutely rejects any attempt to "relativize" the issue of the rights of persons under the guise of resisting Western imperialism. No synonym for contemporary bourgeois society, let alone capitalism, civil society is also not fated to disappear with the advent of socialism. For Uchida, civil society possesses a virtually transhistorical status. More abstract and with a longer history than just that of the "modern West," civil society is a slowly and painfully built-up "society composed of self-aware individuals" that must—as its historical condition of possibility—be "educed" out of resistance to the process by which "civil society is incessantly converted into capitalist society."[27]

CIVIL SOCIETY AND SOCIALISM/SOCIALISM
WITHOUT CIVIL SOCIETY

As noted, Japanese discussions of civil society peaked in intensity in the 1960s—in part as an effort among progressive social scientists to catch up with a Japan for which their conceptual legacy had not really prepared them, and in part as an effort to revitalize that legacy. In this context, the work of Hirata Kiyoaki is of central importance—fully complementary to Uchida's in that, for both writers, Japan's "late"-developing capitalism had in fundamental ways warped its civil society, and in that both regarded the task of social science as helping to push the ne plus ultra of that civil society beyond its current point. For both, civil society was a reality and a "category" for its critique: To act on that critique was to enact civil society.

But to what political end? As of the late 1960s, to inquire into capitalism (including the issue of its relationship to civil society) was to inquire into the prospects for socialism. As was indicated earlier, for the orthodox, civil society was, if not a term of abuse, then no more than history's unworthy instrument in the transition from capitalism to socialism. Uchida had sought to detach civil society from this allegedly inevitable transition, focusing his efforts on the internal dialectics of the capitalism–civil society relation, rather than on its putative resolution. For his part, Hirata took up the task of critically examining "actually existing socialism" not only from the point of view of Marx's own texts, but also in terms of an affirmation that socialism in crucial ways meant the continuation and full realization of civil society. Such a reconsideration had been long delayed in Marxist circles. But with the Sino-Soviet split and the Russian invasion of Czechoslovakia, the contradictions of state socialism had grown too obvious and too dangerous to ignore.

In an influential 1968 essay, "Shimin shakai to shakaishugi" (Civil society and socialism), Hirata worked through exegeses of a number of key passages to restore to Marx his proper status as a critical legatee of the notion of civil society, rather than its implacable antagonist. The work is notable for its sometimes brusque manner, and for its embattled and personal tone: "Speaking as one who has in his own way pursued economic research for all he is worth, the thought of the situation facing us today brings pain to my heart." Hirata wrote in full awareness of the gap that separated him from his opponents.[28]

Marxism today, Hirata begins, is facing an "internal collapse of values," and it is by no means clear that its adherents are capable of responding with the necessary depth and sincerity to the crisis that has come upon them: "Descartes' *cogito* must be revived *now.*" The "basic categories" of *Capital,* Hirata argues, have been "lost." Property, commerce *(Verkehr; kōtsū),* and civil society have all fallen victim to the pernicious influence of "'Marxist-Leninist' cant." Yet, in fact, they constitute a system that must be restored as such. Property has its origins in productive labor (the making of things) and in the acquisition by others of that product. The "intercourse" of ordinary people in civil society as they exchange what they make actualizes both "property as production" and "property as property," introducing the dialectical moment in which the fateful alienation of work from property occurs and is perpetually reproduced. Civil society is the place where this exchange takes place; it is the act itself: "'Citizens' refers to ordinary, concrete human beings in their quotidian, economic life; they are the real foundation of the free and equal subjects of law."[29] Capitalism developed, and ceaselessly continues to develop, from civil society, as its partial negation. "Individual private property . . . founded on the labor of its proprietor," Marx had said, is transformed into capitalist private property.[30] For Hirata, here lay the basis of the "private exclusiveness and mutual indifference" that "soiled" the quotidian sensibilities of bourgeois society.[31] But through its own mode of (re)production, that society would generate its own self-negation.

This "negation of the negation" does indeed reestablish "individual property on the basis of the achievements of the capitalist era: namely, cooperation and the possession in common . . . of the means of production produced by labor itself."[32] This foundational Marxian tenet, Hirata insisted, had been misunderstood for a variety of reasons as meaning the final elimination of civil society. But for Hirata, this was an unwarranted reading. The legacy of capitalist civil society to what followed, he argued, consisted of "cooperative labor" in mechanized industry, in contradiction with "dispersed"—privatized—production. The resolution of that contradiction was a synonym for socialism. But insofar as it was premised on the restitution of individual ownership to workers of their product, and the continuation of legal rights to protect individual property and life, socialism was also a synonym for the fulfillment of civil society. "Only those who can positively value the freedom and equality of civil society—only they may criticize them. That which substantiates such criticism is civil society itself."[33]

By this measure, the system of contemporary state socialism was "socialism without civil society" and therefore not genuinely socialist. It was a system incapable of resolving long-term problems, such as the continued limits on the absolute volume of wealth that would lead to inequality and conflict, or the continued functionality of the division of labor and how it is to be prevented from "ossifying," as in capitalist society. Socialist society will continue to require some "internal" measure of work (such as labor time) to determine reward and aid in the planning of production, but it need not perpetuate the money fetish. The promise of socialism was that social relations would become direct, with "private" property yielding to individual possession and fully restored communality replacing universal commodification. But instead, a socialist Leviathan had emerged that combined, in a perverted form, the "suppressive compulsion of the state under the dictatorship of the proletariat" with the "external regulative standards of the civil state." Less abstractly, Hirata was speaking here of the use of "socialist legality" as a weapon in bureaucratic oppression and terror.[34]

Hirata concludes with a discussion of the "theocratic tendencies" of socialist systems that have arisen in backward societies, where solidarity among individuals—premised upon a requisite development of productive forces—is lacking. Here, both the individuality and communality of the human being are "alienated" in the deification of the Leader. The ultimate cause, Hirata argues, lies in the "backwardness" at society's base, the fatal weakness of those checking mechanisms that civil society alone can provide a people in the course of their political development. Such a pathological alienation, Hirata suggests, can only end with the "overcoming" *(Aufhebung; yōki)* both of the vestiges of old community relations and of the immaturity of new, individually based communal forms.

When one considers Hirata's conclusions, it is no wonder that his essay met with bitter criticism by those vested in the belief that "actually existing socialism" was already genuine. But it can hardly have been more comforting for those who believed that it might yet be made so.

CONTEMPORARY CIVIL SOCIETY

In a remark I quoted earlier, an observer suggested that one cannot understand prewar Japan without looking at its villages. The observer in question was Yamada Toshio, an economist and student of Uchida, and a devotee of the French *régulation* approach and its neo-Marxist analysis of capitalism.[35] Yamada continues: "And one cannot understand postwar Japan without looking at the corporations."[36] I would like to modify that statement to read: "And one cannot understand civil society in Japan without looking at the corporations." As noted, following his period of greatest influence in the 1960s, Uchida turned increasingly toward the intellectual life of the salon. In wondering how Uchida might have reacted to the apparently epochal shifts in Japan's political economy since 1989, however, an examination of Yamada's work, along with that of Hirata in his own last years may be instructive. An important indicator is *Gendai shimin shakai to kigyō kokka* (Contemporary civil society and the enterprise state, 1994), with a keynote essay by Hirata and contributions by five scholars, including Yamada.[37]

Hirata identifies the "enterprise state" *(kigyō kokka)* as a hegemonic formation distinctive of postwar Japan. Its contours are familiar: strong bureaucratic guidance over economic decision-making, the presence of networks of massive firms with highly elaborated internal labor markets dominating a deeply segmented workforce, and so on. The notion of mutually imbricated state organs and corporations seeks to bring together the "micro" and "macro" aspects of political-economic analysis that other treatments have tended to leave in isolation. I cannot assess their arguments here except to note that both Hirata and Yamada express some skepticism that Japan can be usefully described as "post-Fordist," since, they feel, it had never been "Fordist." Yet it was only under the "Fordist compromise" of the decades after 1945 that "sustained economic growth based on high productivity was realized through the fair distribution of productivity." The lesson of Fordism was, "without fairness, no efficiency." Under the enterprise state (or "Toyotist" regime), it was "no fairness, yet efficient" leading to "unfair, therefore efficient."[38] Here was a theodicy of exploitation of a different stripe.

This point bears on the issue of civil society, "a world," as Hirata puts it, "of value, law, and sign."[39] How does one capture the quality of civil society under the regime of the enterprise state? By pointing out that neither individual nor community life is accorded any innate significance, only instrumental value for the corporations that employ "labor" but do not, as Uchida put it, recognize the labor theory of value. Instead, tremendous "cultural" work goes on within firms to shape the subjectivity of employees such that no demand for labor can be refused (as opposed to being subverted) since its performance is perceived as a direct expression of that subjectivity. At its most effective, this system produces "workers vested with the soul of capital (of self-expanding value)."[40] At its extreme, worker "subjectivity" under this regime takes the form of "death by overwork" *(karōshi)* brought about by excessive, and unremunerated, overtime. The link to civil society is cruelly empirical. When workers lack free (or "leisure") time, they lack an essential requisite of civic or associational life. The measurement of free time, correlated with patterns in the instances of *karōshi,* speaks volumes about the condition of civil society in Japan; such is the argument of the contribution to *Gendai shimin shakai to kigyō kokka* by the sociologist Katō Tetsurō.[41]

To be sure, the enterprise state has been challenged since the late 1960s by local residents', women's, citizens', and other so-called new social movements. The range of these movements has expanded dramatically, forcefully placing the continuing operation of discriminatory structures under scrutiny. In so doing, they have certainly relativized the "location" of the large minority that makes up the "corporate employee" segment of the national population within the space of "actually existing" civil society in Japan. The historian and political scientist Maruyama Masao once noted that "unless the army is revolutionized, the revolution will not succeed. And the army is the last element to be revolutionized."[42] If an analogy may be permitted, it is one thing to have even strong social movements active outside the corporate "core," but unless the "army" of workers within it is revolutionized, no revolution will succeed.

In modern times, Japan had gone from semifeudal to supermodern through the agency of war, reconstruction, and growth, but without the full realization of civil society. Would Uchida have found in the decadence of the postwar "system" a chance for a fundamental redefinition of Japan's civil society? Or would he have thought that in the name of global normalization, civil society was again being sacrificed to the gods of capital? On the one hand, while severe competition eroded profits, technological innovation also created new possibilities for their realization by reducing "socially necessary labor time." In this situation, some workers could find themselves with less (or shared) work but increased "time sovereignty" and the chance for enhanced participation in civic life, as the collective narcissism of the enterprise gave way to a more mature and diversified perspective. On the other hand, in a society that has tended to equate the status of "human being" *(ningen)* with enterprise membership, greater unemployment would surely bring pervasive anomie or worse, while those who retain their identity as corporate employees might find themselves subject to still greater demands for unrewarded labor.[43] As far as civil society is concerned, Uchida would say, capitalism promises nothing that it cannot also take away.

As an active category in Japanese social thought, civil society belongs to the postwar era; only then did it generate the analytical and moral force necessary to make it meaningful as more than a translated term. And yet this new discursive status did not constitute a new hegemony. That honor, if such it was, went to the "enterprise community." As Takashima Zen'ya wrote in 1950, social science must be more than the "science of civil society"; it must also serve as its critique. But that is because civil society itself, in Japan as elsewhere, has a dual character. It *is* by virtue of what ought to be; it is affirmed and valued to the extent that it is self-critical. As Hirata argued, once the historical process was completed through which civil society was "articulated" by *(bunsetsu sareta)* and separated from the state, that same civil society was destined to act as a counterweight to the state. The task for contemporary analysis, however, lies in grasping the many and complex ways in which the two are being reconnected, particularly through economic institutions. In his final work, Hirata observed that in Japan the state—in the form of the enterprise state—despite the "hollowing out" of its substance by the capitalist economy from the 1960s onward, "remains in full force."[44] Is the category of civil society empirically rich, analytically acute, and morally centered enough to be brought to bear on the contemporary reality of Japan? Uchida and Hirata thought that it was.

MARUYAMA MASAO AND CIVIL SOCIETY: A POSTSCRIPT

Critics though they were of received versions of Marxism in Japan and elsewhere, Uchida and Hirata belong to that tradition as they did to no other. At the same time, their "faithful departures" from orthodoxy in the conception of civil society were attractive to thinkers more clearly outside, if not antagonistic, to Marxism. As critics from within of Marxist notions of civil society, they gained prestige both from the imprimatur of that system and from the fact that they sought to challenge it. Such was the intellectual context, the peculiar symbiosis, through which Japanese civil society thought, which had achieved its first serious and self-conscious articulation only in the postwar era, was mediated to the non-Marxist intellectual world.

Among the luminaries of that world, none shone brighter, perhaps, than Maruyama Masao. An intimate of Uchida, Maruyama was also a political thinker in a way Uchida was not; this seems to have been a difference of some consequence. Tellingly, Maruyama, apart from a scattering of instances in his early writings and later notes, appears to have deliberately avoided the term "civil society," but not because he and Uchida did not share similar concerns. One has only to consider his role in the 1960 Anpo, his lifelong immersion in the work of Fukuzawa, his remorseless examination of what he saw as the moral pathology of an "ultranationalist" state that arrogated to itself the authority to define its subjects' values, his declaration of 1946 that "it is precisely the 'petit bourgeois character' that has formed the core of all that is most precious in the spiritual legacy of the West," or two decades later, that he "would never lower the flag of liberalism."[45] Why then not speak of the Japan he envisioned as one in which civil society had "matured" and become able to support the "permanent revolution" of democracy? One reason appears to be Maruyama's sense that in the twentieth-century West, civil society had become a "mass society" capable of producing fascism (an argument that is suggestive of Maruyama's own engagement with Marxism). Even the United States had seen McCarthyism—"fascism in the name of democracy." Given these historical—and contemporary—realities, civil society smacked too much of an idealized West (and was too lacking in social and national specificity) to be accorded the position of jewel in his political lexicon. For Maruyama, civil society could not be the answer to mass society—including its postwar Japanese avatar. The road to overcoming the contradictions of mass society—social atomization, hyper- or total politicization—lay rather in the self-conscious combination of "radical democracy with radical spiritual aristocratism." This was what had enabled a politically awakened Thomas Mann to turn in the depths of his being against the Germany that had produced Nazism.[46]

To be sure, Maruyama never ceased to affirm a modern, democratic, and open society as his critical ideal. But in the end, he was most concerned with its "spirit," or "gut feelings," speaking of a "sense of the 'Other'" *(tasha kankaku)* as essential to the kind of society that Uchida, looking through idealizing lenses at a purified market relation, would call "civil." Yet as Ishida Takeshi and Kang Sangjung have remarked, Maruyama's sense of the "Other" was compromised by his quest to uncover the "deep substrata"—with ethical, historical, and political dimensions—of a single national consciousness. It was as if Maruyama, while rejecting civil society for its economic assumption of homogeneity among its constituent members, then assumed just such a political homogeneity for Japan. But as Ishida goes on to say—and as is sometimes forgotten—Maruyama's final major work was a profound, even loving, exposition of Fukuzawa's *Bunmeiron no gairyaku* (Outline of a theory of civilization, 1875). In turn, Hiraishi Naoaki has proposed that Maruyama also absorbed through Fukuzawa a positive notion of civil society, one traceable to the French constitutional monarchist and historian Guizot (1787–1874). Here, Hiraishi argues, was a version that could act as a check on the (apparently) stronger, Hegelian current that Maruyama found badly wanting.[47] If any figure deserves to be called the *fons et origo* of civil society thought in Japan, it is surely Fukuzawa, whose thought so effectively bridged the categories of the economic and the political. Even with Maruyama, then, the dilemma of civil society remains: in the modern world, to be both different from, and the same as, the Others among whom we live, and who we ourselves are.

CHAPTER 7

Imagining Democracy in Postwar Japan

Maruyama Masao as a Political Thinker

"We are all democrats today," John Dunn has observed. "We" in the West, however, were not always democrats. Still less was it to be taken for granted that "they"—the rest of the world—would, should, or could be. Yet if any western idea has extended its reach beyond its own parochial core, democracy is that idea. To be sure, democracy, along with many other notions, such as nationalism, accompanied the "consolidation of the world market . . . and the invasive thrust of western imperialism." But it has also outlasted the conditions under which it was first introduced. Even now, with the passing of post-1989 euphoria and the emergence of the seemingly endless series of civil conflicts that have accompanied so-called globalization, democracy retains its unique value as both a mode of governance and a moral-political ideal. In fact, as Dunn notes, "we have two really distinct and developed democratic theories loose in the world today—one dismally ideological and the other fairly blatantly Utopian."[1] Clearly, if democracy has developed along both of these lines, some sort of dialectic must be at work that relates one to the other. Ideology cannot exist without utopia, and vice versa. Ultimately, democracy in either aspect depends upon the development of a broader political and social discourse within which its constitutive elements can contend, a development in which the social sciences necessarily play an active, though hardly a hegemonic, role. To discuss the democratization of a society is to discuss the specific historical process by which this broader public discourse is formed.

This chapter and the next explore just such a process. I focus on the discourse of democracy in postwar Japan, as mediated by a single, and singular, thinker: Maruyama Masao. Maruyama, I argue, was the preeminent imaginer of democracy in postwar Japan. This was a role he professed not to desire, but one that his class, status, and intellectual formation made it impossible to evade. In attempting to understand the genesis, appeal, and limitations of Maruyama's utopian notion of democracy, substantial attention goes to the broader intellectual milieu of Maruyama's early maturity—the world of Japanese social science from the 1920s through the early postwar period. It was through personal struggle with the imperial system in its last crisis-ridden decade that Maruyama formed the notion of democracy to be discussed below. Using methods of social science forged in crisis, Maruyama sought to inculcate democratic ideas and sensibilities among his fellow Japanese at a time when catastrophic defeat and national humiliation had cast doubt over all received values and institutions. In short, Maruyama, by publicizing a "scientifically imagined" notion of democracy in postwar Japan, attempted to create a mass citizenry. The purpose here is to examine this attempt and to trace its fate amid the institutional and ideological transformations of the years since 1945. In doing so I hope to make clear the dialectical relation of ideological to utopian elements in the discourse of Japanese democracy.

MARUYAMA THE MODERNIST

As has long been recognized in Japan, an element of genius, or at least of idiosyncratic brilliance, confronts any reader of Maruyama's work.[2] More importantly, his particular mode of practicing social science links him to an identifiable transwar generation, a determinate social stratum, and to a network of individuals with a shared, though differently inflected, set of ideas and ideals. Taken together, these ideas have since the late 1940s been associated with "modernism" *(kindaishugi)*, and their proponents—such as Maruyama himself, the economic historian Ōtsuka Hisao, the legal sociologist Kawashima Takeyoshi, and others— known as "modernists."[3] What were these ideas? Specifically, what was the imagined relation between modernity and democracy?

Typically, modernists, both literary and scientific, called for the "establishment of the autonomous self," or a "modern human type," in Japan. In doing so, they echoed—and intensified—a call made by Japanese intellectuals as early as the Taishō period (1912–26). Both then and after Japan's defeat in 1945, the "autonomous self" was recognized as the indispensable basis for any true democratization. Indeed, democracy was no more or less than modernity in its political aspect. Significantly, postwar modernists, like their Taishō forebears, conceived of politics less in terms of institutional processes than of spiritual and intellectual transformation. But the historical conditions of the years after 1945 were radically different than those of Taishō. Earlier thinkers such as Yoshino Sakuzō (1878–1933) and Minobe Tatsukichi (1873–1948) believed that imperial Japan had already acquired the political "infrastructure" necessary for democracy; they professed a qualified optimism about the possibilities for broader political representation under the existing constitutional system. Revolution, they felt, was historically unnecessary for Japan. Yoshino died in 1933 and was thus spared the catastrophic failure of the system he served. Minobe, however, survived into the postwar period long enough to become an anachronism. By continuing to defend the Meiji constitution as essentially compatible with liberal democracy, he betrayed his failure to appreciate the sense of crisis with which a later generation approached the task of reconstruction. For postwar modernists such as Maruyama, the entire process leading up to Japan's launching of a total war had already proved the bankruptcy of the "emperor system" *(tennōsei)*; defeat simply put an end to a demonstrably irrational political and social arrangement. It would be the first—and indispensable—task of intellectuals to subject past institutions and values to scrutiny, destroying those that appeared to be obstacles to democracy. Modernism, in other words, would put the vanquished emperor system on trial.

Of what was the *tennōsei* guilty? From the modernist point of view, it had rendered the Japanese populace "vegetative," intellectually inert and dependent on patriarchal authority in all spheres of life. They had been imperial subjects, but they lacked "subjectivity" *(shutaisei)*, without which democratic citizenship was inconceivable. The inculcation of subjectivity thus required an enlightened stratum to translate to this populace the body of ostensibly universal ideas and ideals that would liberate them from their historical inertia. These "enlighteners" would "open the window" to Western thought, art, and technology once again. More than literature, which in the early postwar years was marked by nihilist and existentialist tendencies, the great vehicle for this work of popular enlightenment was to be a renascent social science. Social science was to guide the democratization of knowledge in postwar Japan.

Yet unlike the enlighteners of early Meiji, Maruyama and his fellow modernists should not be seen as mere Westernizers. The object of their concern was no longer an "Asiatic" or "feudal" society wholly removed from the world.[4] Japan was rather a significantly, albeit partially, modernized society whose modernization, to follow the idiom of Kōza-ha, or Lectures Faction Marxism, had been "distorted." Those distortions had produced a powerful state that relied on an increasingly strained traditionalism in effecting social discipline; this state, in turn, created a colonial empire that both reflected and exacerbated those distortions. The ultimate price of imperial expansion was total military defeat and the apparent total collapse of the values of empire: defeat and foreign occupation were the defining conditions of modernism.[5] And although modernists welcomed the advent of these conditions for the historical possibilities they presented, they themselves had done little to bring them about. Indeed, if that meant acting consciously to make the situation facing their country even more desperate, they could not possibly have done so. A sense of guilt mingled with one of victimization, therefore, is inseparable from the purely intellectual content of modernism.[6] It was in this sense a quintessentially postwar project, one whose transitional nature should become clear in due course. Well-known critics such as Etō Jun and Shimizu Ikutarō (himself an ex-Marxist and ex-modernist) saw modernism, along with "postwar," or occupation democracy, as little more than an illusion or sham.[7] But in the tense, thrilling, and highly anomalous atmosphere of Japan's defeat, the modernist vision was more than mere fantasy. And in certain respects, it has retained its cogency.

MODERNISM, NEOTRADITIONALISM, AND MARXISM

Postwar modernism, including Maruyama's notion of a scientifically imagined democracy, has a prehistory; in its substance, it is the product of transwar intellectual struggle. But struggle against what? With what weapons, and to what end? Modernism is best understood as a reaction, via Marxism, to the "neotraditionalist" discourse of community (kyō-dōtai) and ethnos (minzoku), which had a powerful impact on prewar social science, Marxism included. Let us consider briefly how this was so, in general terms and in terms of Maruyama's intellectual biography.

In the course of its development, modern Japanese social science revealed certain tensions between institutional duty and commitment to perceived scientific truth among its practitioners.[8] To the extent that self-identified sociologists, economists, historians, political scientists, and legal scholars became professionally committed to the "quest for a science of society" in Japan, they could be implicated in the uncovering, questioning, and relativizing of the "deep things" of the social and mental structures of Japanese existence.[9] Social scientists thus exposed themselves and their enterprise to immediate and dangerous political forces—those operating in self-appointed defense of particularity.[10] In Japan, this "particularity" meant above all the imperial institution and its modern political apparatus; in short, the "national polity" *(kokutai)*.

By and large, the history of institutional, or insider, social science was not made by individuals of radical temper, and in Japan as elsewhere it is far from being a history of resistance to intellectual or political coercion.[11] It is rather one of adjustment and co-optation, one that has left an ambiguous pattern of accommodation leavened by coded gestures of doubt and criticism. Even in this form, however, social science proved to be politically vulnerable. As industrialization progressed, it became the task of social science to confront the inevitable problems of displacement, discontent and radicalization; to search for, and if possible discover, a "Japanese" solution to what was called the "social problem."

No small element of the social problem was intellectual. Powerful officials such as Yamagata Aritomo understood that the social problem became all the more intractable as it was refracted and defined in the domain of thought, and they vigorously attacked philosophies of "social destructionism." It was feared that study of the social problem would lead to identification with "society": sociology would lead to (a still pre-Marxian) socialism. And indeed, the earliest organizations of professional sociology in Japan—those active around the turn of the twentieth century—did not always make this distinction rigorously. Under concerted political and legal pressure, however, they learned to do just that. Eventually, advocacy of the dangerous, radical, and "foreign" discourse of socialism gave way to political accommodation or silence—and to an avowedly "safe" sociology.[12] Infrequently, but with significant consequences for later public discourse, genuine heresies also arose, among both outsiders and favored insiders. Though not the only one, the longest-lasting and most fruitful form of heresy in late imperial Japan was Marxism.[13]

But for its debt to and confrontation with Marxism, modernist social science would not have taken shape at all. Indeed, in the years after World War I, the term "social science" came to be synonymous in Japan with Marxian class analysis. More than a mode of analysis, social science became a "movement" unto itself.[14] This is probably testimony to its systematic and heavily textual, even scriptural, character, more than to the work of a revolutionary party. The two cannot, however, be wholly disassociated.

As Maruyama noted, this Marxism was no crude economic determinism. Rather,

> Marxist philosophy and interpretation of history held not only that...economy, law and politics were ineluctably linked, but that even the fields of literature and art had to be seen not in isolation but as linked mutually with them. By pointing out the common foundation from which the various aspects of the "superstructure" arise, Marxism may fairly be deemed the first *Weltanschauung* in modern Japan which compelled one intellectually to explicate the transformation of social systems in a total and coherent fashion.

It was indeed a "grand theory of modern idealism, *which bore the name materialism.*" As such its "methodology presented a startling freshness of vision as an integrating, systematic science" to Japanese mired in a precociously overspecialized academism.[15] To be a social scientist, then, was to be a "totalist" in this sense. And, when this totalism was joined with a serious commitment to Marxism as a doctrine of revolution, to be a "social scientist" was also to reject the imperial institution in its totality. Marxism in action, therefore, was an officially defined and most obnoxious heresy from the political and social mainstream of Japan before 1945, and as such a fit object of repression.

"THE TYRANNY OF GERMANY OVER JAPAN"

It would be a distortion to claim that only repression was available to the state in dealing with the ideological effects of social change. There were properly intellectual resources within Japanese tradition that could be mobilized to counteract the burgeoning and multiform critique of Japanese modernization. The challenge of socialism in general, and Marxism in particular, lay in its attack on class rule. In responding to this attack, defenders of the social order drew upon an ideal of "community" *(kyōdōtai)*. This had both local (rural), and national (imperial) resonances. With its ties to the presumed cultural specificity of the family-state, community provided an apposite ideological construct with which to counter the unhealthy intellectual effects of late capitalist development.[16] These effects took the form of theories of class or social conflict but went beyond them to include all seriously comparative theories of social change that were not dependent on a simple binarism of Japan versus a single or collective Other. Such binarism rested on the premise of noncomparability. The national polity, after all, was peerless *(muhi)*. And it was the rural community that provided the normative unit of that polity. Thus for national and local elites, the discourse of community was a cultural prophylactic that essentially sought to protect the system of private property at all social levels. By the late 1920s, it had challenged and begun to undercut the Marxist hold over social science. Community became the paradigm of Japanese society in mainstream analyses. Takata Yasuma, for example, was one of many sociologists who rejected his own former class-based approach in favor of the *gemeinschaftlich* values of rural society. From the village to the family state itself, Japan was presented as a concentric series of *kyōdōtai*. To advocate community, therefore, was in part to silence the question of class conflict.[17] Although it was impossible to achieve total silence, the discourse of *kyōdōtai* nevertheless rendered domestic social antagonisms morally and conceptually illegitimate. They were either deprived of any historical meaning, or, as will be discussed, projected outward onto the regional and international plane along ethnic/national lines. Political dissent easily became social and cultural deviance. As Ishida Takeshi puts it, community was a "common measure that frequently became an Achilles' heel" for social scientists in prewar Japan.[18]

It is highly symbolic that the term *kyōdōtai,* whatever its traditionalist resonances, was a neologism based on the German *Gemeinschaft.* Both the orthodoxy and heresies of prewar Japanese social science could claim a common heritage—namely the mediating role played by German thought, across fields ranging from philosophy to natural science, in imperial public discourse.

To be sure, the road to the eventual triumph of conservative and/or radical *volkisch* ideology over those heresies differed widely in Germany and Japan. There is obviously no Japanese equivalent to the vast dispersal and liquidation of the Central European intelligentsia after 1933. There are, nevertheless, a number of enduring and specific parallels in the eventual triumph of *volkisch* thought that are worth pursuing. Most fundamental is the shared reaction against the relativization of cultural values that lies at the heart of modern social science. Now that is not to suggest that Germany and Japan were alone in this reaction. The form of its expression, however, seems to separate them from other cases. First, the penchant for "historicism, holism, idealism, voluntarism, and social Darwinism" clearly worked "to the detriment of methodological individualism, historical materialism, structuralism, and analyses of social change"—these were indispensable elements of the critique of Japanese modernization mentioned above. In both national settings, as an alarmed Karl Mannheim put it in 1932, "a conception of the essential uniqueness of the historical" had been made "into a myth, thereby closing . . . off all those fruitful insights that comparison and generalization would be capable of bringing out." This myth was in both cases that of the *Volksgemeinschaft/kokumin kyōdōtai*—the national community. Theorists of this community, in brief, posited a *volkisch (minzokuteki)* "subjectivity," whose "mythical 'totality' . . . escaped"—or at least hampered—"sociological analysis."[19]

Social science in prewar Japan, therefore, was marked by the idealizing, abstraction, and ultimately the conflation of the *Volk* and the state: Japan became a perfect political community, a modern polis, precisely because its members were preternaturally disposed toward harmony-in-hierarchy. To be sure, individualism—meaning corporate selfishness, or factional behavior—marred the community. But the key assumption was that conflicts of interest should not exist; thus politics should not be necessary. This exemption from social science analysis of what had been its central problem had numbing effects on scholarship. Maruyama Masao was far from alone in complaining of tendencies to make a fetish of methodology and to translate empirical concerns into textual concerns.[20] Following Eliza Marian Butler, who wrote of the *Tyranny of Greece over Germany,* we may perhaps term this "the tyranny of Germany over Japan."[21]

Within this "tyranny," however, we can also discern a striking dissonance, one rooted in a fundamental dissimilarity between modern German and Japanese historical experience up to 1945. In Germany, modernity had paved the way to the catastrophic and sanguinary total war of 1914–18, humiliating defeat, collapse of the monarchy, abortive revolution, and a democratic republic under Weimar that traditional elites, much of the mandarinate included, declined to support. For Friedrich Meinecke and other theorists of *Kultur, Bildung,* and *Volksstaat,* history threatened to destroy values, and it evoked an obsessive search for "cultural synthesis." This effort was to be guided by an elite, and it aimed at restoring to the national community the binding ties of sentiment, spirit, and values in the face of the onrush of machine-dominated *Zivilisation.*[22] Ultimately, no synthesis was in the cards. The final contest was between end-stage adherents of value-autonomy, mainly neo-Kantians, and an array of thinkers best designated as postrationalist. The outcome is well known. In discourse, history did destroy values, as in the real world; National Socialism made horrific nonsense of the national community and the public sphere as well.

In Japan, by contrast, a "unique" modern history confirmed the core values of the harmonious nation-as-community. There were no massively destructive wars fought on Japanese soil. The imperial institution was insulated by both constitution and custom from all political responsibility; and hence from any immediate revolutionary threat. In their late imperial forms, myth and history were thoroughly intertwined, and inseparably conflated with value. Public discourse on society, social science included, succumbed to a fallacy of misplaced concretization.

Despite all the genuine parallels that can be drawn with Germany, and despite the continued appropriation by Japanese thinkers of German concepts from *Kultur* to the Heideggerian *Angst* (anxiety), the underlying tone of Japanese public discourse was not pessimistic, but optimistic.[23] German pessimism flowed from a Lutheran and Kantian current that despaired of the possibility that reality and value, *Sein* (is) and *Sollen* (ought), could ever be synthesized. Hope came up against hope. In Japan, a powerful optimism flowed from what Maruyama called a "continuative mode of thought," in which reality and value, nature and norm, were seen in terms of mutual confirmation.[24] To the extent that there was a pessimistic or agonistic strain in Japanese political and social thought, it came from the doubt that reality and value could ever be separated. So it was with Maruyama. It may be that Japan and Germany represent different, culturally specific forms of *volkisch* myopia. There is no question that the conditions sustaining historical optimism in Japan ultimately contributed to the catastrophe of war and defeat. But this process was broadly similar, not so much to the triumph of technological nihilism in Nazi Germany as to the mobilization of the "Ideas of 1914" and to the launching of World War I.[25] Such was the demonstrative power of Japan's unchallenged imperial system over public discourse that serious social thinkers were hard put to resist co-optation into the "national community," or later into the "world-historical" tasks Japan claimed to be carrying out. As the émigré German authors of *Japan in Transition* remarked in 1938, "Because of the close interrelationship between religion, myth, and history, and because of the transcendental elevation of the dynasty, . . . a spiritual revolution of staggering proportions" was required for Japanese to separate themselves from the national community.[26]

Despite—and, for a tiny minority, because of—the power of this exceptionalism, the language of interwar Japanese social thought was that of crisis. As a whole, public discourse in Japan continued to be strongly informed by European, particularly German, impulses. And it will not do to minimize the precipitous economic downturn and political instability that hit Japan in the late 1920s. Naturally, where there is smoke, there must be (or must have been) some fire. Owing to the basic conditions of Japan's modern history, however, a combined sense of desperate crisis and deep disillusionment did not really take hold until very late in the Pacific War.[27] Only then could anyone begin to contemplate the imminent dissolution of the "mythical totality" of fact conflated with value. The questions were: how to contemplate this dissolution, and more importantly, how to remake Japanese society under these unprecedented conditions.

MARXISM IN EXTREMIS

Marxism, as we have seen, had already gone some way toward providing "scientific" answers to such questions. Social scientists of Maruyama's generation owed to Marxism more than a general conceptual debt. Every one of them was marked by the fact that their engagement with Marxism, whether they ultimately rejected it or not, coincided with their experience of the final crisis of the imperial regime. Their very definition of that crisis—which they saw as beginning with Japan's agricultural depression, later joined to the worldwide crisis of capital—was systemic. All sought comprehensive—in some cases, revolutionary—solutions. Marxism alone, many felt, could enunciate such a comprehensive understanding and provide guidance for political practice. But by the early 1930s, political practice had been drastically redefined. The years since 1928 had seen mass arrests and the full elaboration of the legal procedures for bringing about *tenkō* (ideological recantation, especially by leftists). As with Western Marxists of the same period, Japanese party members and their sympathizers increasingly came to regard theoretical and historical work as a form of practice in itself.

The crisis of Japanese capitalism that began in 1929 soon dovetailed into a crisis of polity, and therefore of the nation. Social scientists of this generation found themselves being pulled in two directions. Few had any commitment to Japanese capitalism per se, and the necessity to critique its mode of development and consequences was taken to be self-evident. On the other hand, many believed in historical progress and had Hegelian visions of ultimate harmony as the resolution of a social dialectic. They were prepared, in other words, to argue that conflict was a historically creative force. But could they explicitly declare the national crisis to be due to late capitalist/imperialist antagonisms, in which Japan was implicated, at the risk of thorough alienation from the national community? Or would they try to incorporate a systemic understanding of these dual crises somehow within the pale of orthodoxy—for instance, by claiming that Japan was not an imperialist but was in fact a victim of imperialism?

In the event, a tiny, terribly harassed minority chose the former path, which led either to long years in prison or to Asian exile. The vestigial few who remained faithful to Marxist internationalism, however, were subject organizationally to a mythical totality of their own in the party itself; open repression meanwhile deprived them of any chance for public expression of their "faith." The majority, including many Marxists, moved in the latter direction, albeit across a broad and intricate spectrum. A number of activists, such as the sociologist Shinmei Masamichi (1898–1984) and the philosopher Miki Kiyoshi (1897–1945), rewrote the Hegelian-Marxist dialectic to substitute ethnos for class. According to this theory of the world-historical New Order, Japan's was a struggle to supersede the Anglo-Saxon West both temporally and spatially. Modernity itself, with its assumptions of temporal linearity, progress, and individual rationality, was revealed to be an ideology: Its universalism was no more than the parochialism of the colonializing West. Whatever there was of value in it was now to be sublated into a higher form. According to the "philosophers of world history" associated with the so-called Kyoto school, Japan as the embodiment of "absolute negativity" would deny and synthesize all prior historical forms.[28] The "theory," as Takeuchi Yoshimi notes, was inherently opportunistic and full of hubris.[29] For some who sought to "overcome modernity" in this fashion, conscience and consciousness alike suffered the strain of accommodation. The "anthropological Marxist" Miki Kiyoshi, it will be recalled, broke with the New Order in 1942 and rejoined his former colleagues on the left. Arrested in March 1945 for harboring a suspected Communist, Miki died in prison at the end of September. In a sense Miki represents prewar Marxism, and prewar social science, in extremis.

Prewar Japanese social science, then, suffered from a vitiating historical optimism. And from this tendency to conflate fact and value, there followed a corollary tendency to invest certain "amuletic" words—kokutai, kyōdōtai, minzoku, and so on—with overwhelming suasive power.[30] On a far smaller scale, but of central intellectual importance, was an analogous conflation that took place among the Marxist remnant. Here too there were dual conflations. The first was a "substantial-ist view of concepts": Marxist analyses, particularly those of the Kōza-ha, fostered a visceral sense that *tennōsei* was indeed a real and fearsome thing.[31] They did so, paradoxically enough, not through the vividness or stylistic daring of their writings, but through formalism and obsession with terminological precision. The reality of *tennōsei* was brought home through the triumph of the literal over the metaphorical. The second con-flation was that of Marxism with social science as a whole. It should be clear, however, that for Japan the conflations associated with national polity orthodoxy were far more tragic and debilitating than those associ-ated with Marxism.

MARUYAMA: THE ESSENTIAL TENSION

It is in this context that the work of Maruyama Masao is best under-stood. By both engaging and challenging Marxism, Maruyama made a serious and successful, but necessarily provisional, attempt to rupture the presumptive unity of fact and value that marked Japanese social science. He began to do so even as that unity was forced upon thinkers with ter-rible intensity.

What was the "something" that enabled Maruyama to engage seri-ously with Marxism yet hold back from commitment to it as a system? More importantly, what was the "something" that alienated him intel-lectually, and protected him emotionally, from the undertow of *kokutai* ideology?

Maruyama's bare biography is suggestive. He was born in Osaka in 1914. His paternal forebears were "lower class" retainers of the domain of Matsushiro—a *tozama,* or "outside lord's," domain. Maruyama's father, Maruyama Kanji, had "run away to Yokohama" as a young man and was disinherited by his family.[32] He went on to become a prominent journalist with the Osaka *Asahi* and the *Mainichi,* an admirer at first hand of British institutions, a firm empiricist, and, significantly, a sharp critic of both the political domination by the "Satsuma-Chōshū clique" and abuse by the military of its constitutional position. The household was frequented by journalistic associates like Hasegawa Nyozekan, whose critiques of the "metaphysical view of the state" were widely read. On his mother's side, Maruyama's family included figures such as Inoue Kiroku, a journalist associated with the Seikyōsha, whose nationalist views ran well to the right within that group's distinctive Japanist line. Maruyama's formative years, therefore, were spent in the Anglophile atmosphere of his immediate family and among other relatives and associates whose outlook was both journalistic and solidly nationalist.[33] "Taishō democracy" was an element of personal and family experience.

This experience, moreover, was translated into institutional terms. Like many future modernists, Maruyama received his higher education and made his career at the apex of the imperial system: at the First Higher School (abbreviated Ichikō; 1931–34), then as an undergraduate in the law faculty of Tokyo Imperial (abbreviated Tōdai; 1934–37), and finally as a graduate assistant *(joshu;* 1937–40), assistant professor (1940–50), and professor (1950–71) in that faculty. In general, graduates and young faculty members of the imperial university were guaranteed high social status, relative physical safety, and protection, though not immunity, from ideological persecution. They enjoyed presumptive social approbation and assumed the right, if they desired, to fill positions of national intellectual leadership. As public men, they were to be the teachers of the nation.

High public status by itself, however, can only establish a frame for a more specific intellectual biography. A brief comparison of Maruyama to another major modernist, the economic historian Ōtsuka Hisao (born in 1907, Ōtsuka graduated from the economics faculty of Tokyo Imperial in 1930) may help to highlight both what is true to type, and what is distinctive, in Maruyama's intellectual experience. Both Maruyama and Ōtsuka, prior to their engagement with Marxism, had sustained contact with some combination of Kantian or neo-Kantian thought, Protestantism, and empiricist rationalism. For the Protestant Ōtsuka, membership in Uchimura Kanzō's "Non-Church" (Mukyōkai) was of the greatest moment, along with his immersion in the work of Max Weber. This combination engendered in Ōtsuka a sense of the irreducible difference between fact and value and a concern for understanding the "non-rational" wellsprings of human action, which he identified with the realm of faith. Thus, although Ōtsuka drew heavily upon Kōza-ha scholarship in his own work on comparative economic history, he retained an overriding concern with the historical sources—in the Reformation and "spirit of capitalism" itself—of individual human autonomy. Indeed, Ōtsuka's essentially religious zeal to foster a new human type, the "modern personality," in Japan came to form a leitmotiv in his professional work. He tended to see Japan as a society that had industrialized on the basis of a still-premodern, rural social base and consciousness, that of the "community." Japan, that is, had industrialized but not yet modernized. Here lay its tragedy and its hope: the process could now be "completed."

For Ōtsuka, the community was an outstanding problem to be solved; the modern human type could not otherwise be formed. Ōtsuka's solution was Weberian and twofold: a rigorous separation of scholarly analysis, almost exclusively of European history, from apologetics, but a deep and frequently expressed belief nevertheless in the need of Japanese society for a Christian-inspired ethic suffused with local—national— concerns. For Ōtsuka, a modern society was ruled in the last analysis by the consciences of its members, who also recognized their duties to the whole.[34]

Maruyama too is known for his concern with "interiority" (*naimensei*; Maruyama favored this Hegelian term) and his ambition to inculcate subjectivity. As a student of Nanbara Shigeru (1889–1974), Maruyama spent his university years partly at the fringes of Uchimura Kanzō's Mukyōkai movement; thus Protestantism was not an intellectual milieu foreign to him.[35] Indeed, Maruyama's unmistakable concern for the inviolability of conscience and physical personhood almost seems a transmutation of Mukyōkai concerns. Maruyama's distinctiveness, however, lies elsewhere. First, unlike Ōtsuka, he took up the task of confronting the "national community" with texts drawn from its own tradition.[36] Second, he defined that tradition in the light of methodological concerns that stemmed from his early engagement with German idealism and with the sociology of knowledge as elaborated by Karl Mannheim.

Maruyama emerged as a historical thinker in the period ending with his appointment in 1940 as assistant professor in the Tōdai law faculty. A combination of methodological self-consciousness and documentary expertise in Japanese political thought marked Maruyama's passage to intellectual maturity. Its key feature, at least in Maruyama's later reconstruction, was its countercyclical quality. For example, rather than taking the "road most traveled" into Marxism, Maruyama held back. While still at Ichikō, he had begun to read the German neo-Kantians, who had by then yielded their place in intellectual circles to phenomenologists and neo-Hegelians. Although unsystematic, his reading of Heinrich Rickert and Wilhelm Windelband left Maruyama unable to accept in toto any social science founded upon a reflectionist epistemology: the idea, in other words, that knowledge of the world comes about through the process of accumulating more or less accurate representations or "pictures" of a "reality" whose independent existence is assumed. Rickert's *Der Gegenstand der Erkenntnis* (The object of knowledge, 1928), he tells us, "swept all such accumulated detritus out of my head." Similarly, Windelband's exposition of the difference between "critical" and "genetic" method proved to be an intellectual tonic. By refusing, with Windelband, to "deduce" the meaning of historical phenomena from their genesis or function within an assumed developmental sequence, Maruyama was led to doubt the logical validity of a naive positivism in historical explanation—the view of history as an accumulation of "facts." Not that Marxism was a naive positivism; it should be remembered that for Maruyama, Marxism could be justly proud of its Hegelian, that is, dialectical, legacy. Nevertheless, he felt that Marxist historians were insufficiently conscious of their own dependence on "axioms," that is, "critical" principles that underlay the standards by which they distinguished historical tendencies. In their actual expositions they frequently dissolved such critical judgments—as to "progress," "reaction," "stasis," etc.—into the events themselves. The result was methodological confusion. Maruyama, as a believer in these very tendencies, was not immune from the temptation to reify. In general, however, whatever criticisms one may make of Maruyama's work, "methodological confusion" is not one of them.[37]

The significance of neo-Kantianism for Maruyama, in short, was "negative" in the sense that this philosophy taught him little about the positive content, or meaning, of history. Rather, it bred a concern for the defense of values against too close an identification with historical particularities; it bred discrimination, and skepticism, of vast teleological claims. At the same time, Maruyama had become a historian. He believed that history had a discernible direction, even had stages of development. More importantly, he believed in its "cunning," its lack of transparency. The meaning of history, including that of his own society, had to be wrested from events through methodologically informed intellectual struggle. The key point was Maruyama's assumption that neither Japanese tradition nor its Marxist antagonist could independently provide a satisfactory method of analysis.

Maruyama's struggle "for history" was made possible by his reading of Karl Mannheim. Mannheim's *Ideology and Utopia* (1936) presented Maruyama with the idea of a conditioned "mode of thought," within which one could comprehend the various works of any given thinker; this freed him from narrowly biographical or genealogical approaches to intellectual history. Along with it came the idea of "frames of reference," through which social groups apprehended and gave meaning to reality: the concept of the "Five Relations" of Confucianism was a cardinal example.[38] As with Marxists, Mannheim held that, in concert with shifts in the social base, these frames of reference also shift. But he stressed that, in some sense, change was not "real" until it had been apprehended via a frame of reference; that is, not only the "base," but also the totality of social life and thought, made up reality. Mannheim's approach made it possible, Maruyama notes, not simply to distinguish fact from meaning, but also to link them in historical narrative. "Linking," in turn, did not denote the radical devaluation of meaning in favor of function, as in a vulgar theory of ideology. Rather, the intent was to trace a dialectic of fact and meaning mediated by modes of thought whose individual articulations demanded close and nuanced reading.

Of particular importance to Maruyama was Mannheim's insight into intellectual movements of "return." Here, a group of intellectuals who have begun to be "cast up by the social process" of emerging modernity "takes refuge in the past and attempts to find there an epoch or society in which an extinct form of reality-transcendence dominated the world, and through this romantic reconstruction . . . seeks to spiritualize the present."[39] Maruyama was able to see that Tokugawa-era movements of return, such as Motoori Norinaga's "nativism" (kokugaku), depended upon categories and modes of thought "that had ostensibly been 'overcome' "—in this case, the "Sinophile" Ancient Learning of the Confucian philosopher Ogyū Sorai.[40] It also became clear that the significance of such movements lay not so much in their recovery of "eternal" truth as in their social and ideological character. They provided a vital insight into how social groups "thought through" (to use a key term of Mannheim's) the great transition from feudalism, via absolutism, to modern society. For these reasons, Mannheim's method and approach were "decisively important" for Maruyama; indeed, he "could not have written" his early studies of Tokugawa thought without the stimulus and guidance that Mannheim provided.[41] Underlying this strong response was a value position Maruyama shared with Mannheim. To "think through" the transition from feudalism to modernity, explicitly for Mannheim, was to wrestle with the process of the "democratization" of society and thought.[42] And although democratization does not appear as the explicit concern of Maruyama's work until after 1945, it is hard to read even his early writings except in such terms.

By the early 1940s, Maruyama, as a historian of Japanese political thought, had defined his position and persona in terms of a conscious affirmation of modernity (kindaisei) in the face of powerful tendencies bent either on rejecting or "overcoming" it. What then did Maruyama's modern stance consist of? How did it infuse his important wartime work? And how was it translated following Japan's defeat?

For Maruyama, modernity denoted a mode of thought, a leitmotiv, a set of presuppositions about consciousness marked by a powerful sense of the irreducible difference between what is and what ought to be. It was this consciousness of difference, and of necessary tension, that gave Maruyama a critical stance flexible enough to survive the "nonsensification" of the late imperial public sphere, and to engage Marxism as a system of thought.[43] Precisely this consciousness, this "interiority" or self-possession, formed the normative core of Maruyama's notion of subjectivity (shutaisei). To be modern was, in short, to exercise a transcendent, universal critical faculty in a particular social/national totality. A modern, or "open," society, in turn, was one where the free and untrammeled association of individuals sets the norm, where politics was the creative space in which conflict was confronted and resolved in an ongoing history of "progress [in] the consciousness of freedom." (Maruyama took the phrase from Hegel's *Reason in History*, 1830.) It was a history made by human beings for human purposes not always—indeed seldom—understood or intuited with lasting clarity. Human society and institutions, therefore, were neither "natural" nor metaphysically guaranteed. Rather, they were vital fictions worked out by actors with some degree of such self-consciousness: this Maruyama took as a key indicator of modernity. The modern consciousness did not contrast fiction to reality or truth, but rather negated any "natural," metaphysically guaranteed order that comprehended both the cosmic and human spheres.

Here we recognize the argument of Maruyama's *Nihon seiji shisōshi kenkyū* (Studies in the intellectual history of Tokugawa Japan)—written and published separately in the *Kokka Gakkai zasshi* between 1940 and 1944, they first appeared as a book in 1952. Maruyama had provided for Tokugawa intellectual history a narrative of the breakup of Zhu Xi orthodoxy under the external pressure of social and economic contradictions and the internal dissolution of the continuative mode of thought. The negation of orthodoxy came in the form of Ogyū Sorai's paradoxical "logic of invention." Sorai as a Machiavelli-Hobbes manqué had called upon the shogun Yoshimune to "reinvent" along pristine feudal lines a rapidly commercializing social order; thus seeking to "produce nature" by the absolutist logic of invention. "In order to solve the crisis of feudal society, Sorai set out to destroy the theory of natural order but instead brought forth a demon whose actions he was unable to control."[44]

The "demon" of this logic was destined to be frustrated. Indeed, for Maruyama, Japanese history appeared as a succession of thwarted breakthroughs to universality. Japan could have become a fully modern, democratic nation-state, but it did not. In a wartime review of Asō Yoshiteru's *Kinsei Nihon tetsugaku shi* (1942), for example, Maruyama wrote that "the degree to which the European [*Yōroppateki naru mono*] makes its way into the realm of the spirit provides a barometer for gauging the total phenomenon of Japanese modernization." By this measure, Japan after the Restoration had assimilated the material techniques of the West, but it had yet to undergo a spiritual revolution. Politically, this meant that the potentially liberating logic of invention had been short-circuited after 1868 into a ruthlessly pragmatic raison d'état; trapped, so to speak, in institutions of state closed to public and popular scrutiny. In society as a whole, the senses had been liberated, but the nation had yet to confront the "European spirit" and instead persisted in treating European thought as a fetish. The intellectual world in modern Japan had therefore developed—Maruyama quotes the emigré philosopher Karl Löwith—into a "two-story house" with no staircase to connect the floors.[45] As yet, Maruyama wrote, at the first sign of absorption, all the trappings of Western thought and culture could simply be shaken off. But he believed this to be a deeply embedded fallacy, one that had led "spiritual" Japan to embark on a self-mutilating attempt to purge itself and Asia of "materialism." Far from claiming that Japan was called to "overcome" modernity, Maruyama believed that modernity—as a conscious participation by individuals in the struggle, on the social plane, of ought with is—constituted a "not yet" to be struggled for.[46] The goal, as well as the emergent form of this struggle, was democracy itself.

An obvious criticism of Maruyama's work up to 1945 would hold that he was idealizing the West and denigrating Japan for its historical failures and "lack" of a true Western consciousness. Indeed, this is a criticism that followed him for most of his professional life. At one level, it is a just one. As Maruyama himself remarked some years later:

> If I am told, "You're idealizing the European past and treating it as universal," I can only answer: That is exactly the case. This isn't because there are no universal elements in other cultures, of course. But I acknowledge that in my thinking I rely on abstractions from European culture. I consider it to be a universal legacy to humankind [*jinrui fuhen no isan*]. I firmly believe this. And I want more and more to learn from it.[47]

Precisely because the charge of Eurocentrism was accepted by Maruyama himself, I have considered it important to lay out the context and the development of that Eurocentrism, among elite social scientists in imperial Japan and in Maruyama's own thinking. We may now turn to its theoretical and practical consequences; to inquire, in other words, into the bearing of Eurocentrism on Maruyama's conception of democracy and his assessment of the obstacles to, and possibilities for, its realization that had emerged from Japan's modern history.

Before doing so, a word is in order about the relation of Eurocentrism to nationalism in Japan. It cannot be shown that European categories are ipso facto inapplicable (or applicable) to Japan. To attack them on the grounds of their origin alone, as if legitimate concepts, narratives, and tropes could be drawn only from some purely "Japanese" construction of experience, is no more than self-delusion. And a particularly problematic one at that, since "Europe" and the "West" have been indispensable both as positive models for, and as effective and affective Others to, the construction of modern Japanese identity, tradition, and social forms. Maruyama's strong affirmation of the universality within European culture as relevant to Japan came precisely at a time when an already myopic and defensive exceptionalism had taken its most brutal form; clearly, his confrontation with this exceptionalism marked his life in profound ways. Moreover, one cannot read Maruyama in context without sensing the presence of a powerful intellect marked by an overriding critical and national concern. His work, like that of the modernists as a whole, was nationalist in intent. But this was meant to be a relative, not solipsistic, nationalism; nationalism as an instrument of universalization.[48]

The problem with Maruyama's early works, therefore, is not Eurocentrism per se. It is rather that Maruyama tended to reify entire categories such as feudalism, capitalism, and modernity itself. As pathbreaking as the studies of Tokugawa Confucianism are, they posit the existence (and collapse) of an orthodoxy that seems never to have taken the form Maruyama claimed. He subsequently admitted his dependence on a rigid dialectical schema of historical evolution. Maruyama had been enchanted by the "Hegelianische Zauber," the magic of Hegel.[49] As Robert Bellah has pointed out, however, it is the break with the "continuative" and optimistic Zhu Xi mode of thought—whether articulated as a self-consistent orthodoxy or not—that matters. The "discovery" via dialectical method of such a mode of thought, along with the claim that it dissolved and gave way to the incipiently modern logic of invention, remains the key to Maruyama's analysis.[50] It is a view that has been challenged and supplemented, but not overturned. The point here, however, is not to evaluate Maruyama's *Studies in the Intellectual History of Tokugawa Japan*, but to establish his frame of mind and basic intellectual orientation as Japan faced defeat. Maruyama emerged from the war a "protestant": he had written in protest of an unfree present, and he continued thereafter to be concerned with overcoming obstacles to freedom and modernity in Japan. It is the typical claim, and the central problem, of his protestantism that such obstacles lay most thickly on the ground of Japanese tradition itself.

RHETORIC AND ACTION
IN THE IMAGINATION OF DEMOCRACY

Maruyama's commitment to a normative modernity had transwar origins. If during this period Maruyama struggled to keep in public, though circumspect, view the need to separate fact from value and to rupture their conflation under the *tennōsei*, his postwar activity called for quite a different effort. This was, in brief, to renew public discourse along democratic lines. Under strikingly new conditions brought about by the ambivalent liberation that came with defeat, Maruyama would try to place the language of conscious, engaged, mass democratic action at the center of discourse. The vehicle of translation, of democratization, was to be a revived social science itself, for which the audience was to grow enormously.[51] In this effort, the institutional, intellectual, rhetorical, and psychological dimensions of Maruyama's public work could be, and were, related—as they were for anyone active at the time—with unprecedented dynamism.

The first task, clearly, was that of negation: to destroy the *tennōsei* in the domain of thought and ideology. At no other time in his career could Maruyama have felt so vindicated as by this opportunity for public expression: As a student at Ichikō he had been arrested, jailed, beaten, deprived of personal papers, and placed under surveillance for attending a legal gathering of the Yuibutsuron Kenkyūkai (Society for the Study of Materialism). The Peace Preservation Law, which he had run afoul of, symbolized for him the legal paranoia of the family state, and now the entire apparatus was being exposed to public scrutiny.

Thus it is not surprising that in these early postwar essays Maruyama explicitly presents himself as a pathologist of his society. In context, the negation—the decoding—of the *tennōsei*, meant an attack on the "tenacious familial *[dōzokudanteki]* social structure and its ideology, which is the hothouse of the old nationalism."[52] It was self-evident that defeat and occupation alone could not accomplish this negation.

Nor, despite its prodigious legacy of historical interpretation and vision of a liberated Japan, could Marxism do so. Political exigency and conceptual limitation had combined to prevent Marxists from understanding how the *tennōsei* could have "taken hold of the Japanese people's modes of behavior, way of life, and *forms of thinking.*"[53] As we have observed, prewar analyses of *tennōsei* took it as a real object formed by a determinate set of economic, social, and political relations. As a corollary to this basic perspective—one extremely productive in its fashion—*tennōsei* as ideology appeared at the mass level in the form of false, even irrational chauvinistic consciousness, or as merely derivative of "real" material causes. In Maruyama's view, this approach concealed the very problem it should have raised: that of the mobilization, or rationalization, of the "irrational" primary attachment to family in the service of the state.

With the publication in the new opinion journal *Sekai* of "Chōkokka shugi no ronri to shinri" (Logic and psychology of ultranationalism, May 1946), Maruyama appeared—"like a comet," as the formula had it—to illuminate the devastated intellectual landscape. His attempt in this essay to decode the *tennōsei* as ideology was enormously influential. Indeed, it seems to have had a virtually physical impact on readers.[54] To begin with, Maruyama's description of "power dwarfing" (or better, "the dwarfing of authority" *[kenryoku no waishōka]*) captured a salient aspect of the public posture of key civilian and military elites: they had at times sought to minimize their personal responsibility while emphasizing their lofty position of proximity to the source of ultimate value. In effect, this closeness to the emperor granted them the privilege of being dwarfed. Also penetrating were the observations concerning the "transfer of oppression," which recalled the common experience of many Japanese who found themselves projecting outward and downward the recurring sense of anger and violation that was inseparable from the regimentation and constant subordination of imperial Japanese society.

Most important was Maruyama's jarring insight into the "exteriorization of morality" and its consequences. These were the "pathological" identification of the petty self with expansive state power, and along with it the severely compromised capacity to resist authority, or to live according to a moral standard internal to the personality. It was in this feature of the imperial state, the fact that it "trampled with shod feet on the mind *[seishin]* of every single person," that Maruyama saw the core of "ultra" nationalism. Here he was writing of truly public matters, of the common experience of his countrymen. Everyone "knew" what he was saying; he was trying to provide not just description but concepts for the analysis of this experience. In this sense, this first major postwar article of Maruyama's opened a new phase in public and social science discourse.

Yet questions have been raised about the empirical foundations for Maruyama's claims about the moral pathologies attendant upon ultranationalism. In his idiosyncratic fashion, the critic Yoshimoto Takaaki argued that Maruyama's remoteness from the actual masses of soldiers led him to portray the rank and file as mere "puppets," acting out an abstract notion of *kokutai*. Rather than "ideology," Yoshimoto claimed, some sort of "ethnic current that determined the form in which *tennōsei* itself existed" ran through common soldiers. This "current" was such that, under the conditions characteristic of war, it issued in atrocious violence. Only someone in the position to "transfer oppression to another," such as Maruyama himself, could have seen these atrocities in terms of ideology—as, in effect, a mirror image of the official, loyal imperial subject at war.[55]

Yoshimoto's views are both illuminating and problematic. He overargued his point, creating false dichotomies, such as that between ideology and ethnic current. But Yoshimoto was correct in stressing that Maruyama's work depended upon his alienation from, even "antipathy toward," the masses. The imperial public sphere itself was constituted by just such institutionalized distance. Thus there is no small truth in Yoshimoto's argument that Maruyama's writing reflected the "poverty of his life history" *(seikatsushi)* and that his definition of the "task for the masses" did not come from the masses.[56] Yoshimoto charged that Maruyama, on the combined basis of status and his own anecdotal observations, made unwarranted generalizations that passed as scholarship. Yoshimoto could not sustain his charge empirically: he did not interview and survey the perpetrators of atrocity. His response to Maruyama's first essayistic foray into contemporary issues, however, did raise the significant issue of class, or status, bias. He questioned whether Maruyama's concept of ultranationalism and its components met the criteria for what Alfred Schutz would call "adequacy" as a term in a "scientific model of human action."[57] Without at all making his own standpoint clear, Yoshimoto held that Maruyama, lacking "ethnic" sympathy and writing as a "typical" intellectual suspended between complicity and resistance, should be found wanting.

Yoshimoto's point is brought home all the more when we consider Maruyama's analyses of "Japanese fascism," which appeared shortly after the first *Sekai* essay. There Maruyama made the still-controversial claim that the "middle stratum," in the grip of an enduring traditionalistic social consciousness, provided the strongest support for fascism in Japan. This was a variation on the "transfer of oppression" theme, and it remains valid as far as it goes. Virtually all contemporary analyses of fascism, Maruyama's included, followed the Comintern's positions of the 1920s and early 1930s in identifying nonelite strata as the chief support of fascism.[58] Maruyama's analyses were frankly defective, however, on two counts: First, they ignored the role of technocrats and of the "intelligentsia" as a whole in an empire dependent on academic pedigree in awarding preferment. More specifically, in what must have been a frustrating search for expressions of resistance by the "true" intelligentsia, Maruyama failed to analyze the "reactionary modernism" that was far more typical of his fellow elites. Such an analysis would have given his insights into "fascism from above" an intellectual content they largely lack.[59]

In retrospect, then, Maruyama's analysis of fascism excludes any consideration of the social and political role played by the mobilized intelligentsia in late imperial Japan. To this extent, it may be deemed both systematically flawed and insufficiently self-critical. At the same time, Maruyama's project of rooting out the pathologies of the *tennōsei* deserves to be viewed in its context; to recognize his contribution is to see it as possible both because of—and to a degree despite—his status and basic intellectual orientation.

The descriptive and analytical tools Maruyama was using were forged in a highly charged, polemical atmosphere. This was a period of intense and radical rejection of empire, and of judgments based in part on the language of the Potsdam Declaration, new constitution and occupation directives, and the Tokyo trials.[60] It was also a penitent phase, in which the authorizer of discourse had declared the past open to scrutiny, albeit on the basis of a still partial and veiled historical record.[61] The "guilty conscience" could only be assuaged through confrontation with the national past, but that confrontation had been made possible only by defeat. Both historically and rhetorically, the situation was fraught with irony: not the language of the eternal *kokutai*, nor that of revolutionary triumph, nor that of the conqueror could do it justice. Elements of each would have to be mobilized to capture the experience, and it was precisely the stratum of young and disaffected public men like Maruyama who possessed the ability to mobilize language in this manner. Only those, in other words, who had been "in" the imperial system but not "of" it could conceptualize and verbalize the new dispensation.

Maruyama's self-appointed task was to serve as postwar Japan's public ironist. His texts relied heavily on an irony that sought "to split their audience into insiders and outsiders (and split each member of it)."[62] Thus, on the one hand, a certain arrogance is unmistakable:

> We have all met men in barbers' shops, bath houses, and railway carriages who treat those around them to their lofty opinions on inflation or the American-Soviet question. These men are what I call the pseudo-intelligentsia, and on asking them their occupation, we find that they mostly belong to . . . the middle stratum.[63]

The harsh tone—the lack of sympathy—is regrettable. Clearly Maruyama was using irony and sarcasm as weapons, as if trying to excise what he saw as a credulous and petty mentality by laughing it to scorn. One senses little fellow feeling for the objects of this irony.

On the other hand, Maruyama directs a fiercer irony, even ridicule, at the wartime leadership and other elites. This subjection of the formerly powerful to shame has the effect of drawing together speaker and audience as "elect." Maruyama's portrayals of figures like Tōjō Hideki, Kido Kōichi, and Konoe Fumimaro provide examples of this rhetorical strategy; they and many other imperial officials appear as "pitiful," "fatuous," "slippery as eels, hazy as the mist," even "asinine."[64] Maruyama found these characteristics to be common to the ethos of the "ruling class" rather than mere personal weaknesses; it will be recalled that he generalized these observations into his celebrated description of Japanese fascism as "dwarfish." By this means, Maruyama may have sought to awaken in his audience a latent capacity for historical judgment. He felt he had the right to assume such a role by virtue of his status. He was saying: Let us not fear these people. But also: Join in the irony or be subject to it.

Irony, then, was Maruyama's chosen rhetorical vehicle for negating the mentality of imperial subjecthood. Yet he was no nihilist, and as Leszek Kolakowski has pointed out, "Negation is not the opposite of construction—it is only the opposite of affirming existing conditions."[65] To what end did Maruyama methodologize this ironic stance—the standpoint of negation? What did he seek thereby to construct, to affirm?

The answer could now be stated openly: democracy. But what democracy? Whose democracy? Democracy in what spheres? Despite the powerful presence of "Amerika" as occupier and as a model state and society, it was self-evident that democracy could neither be imposed satisfactorily from without nor exhumed from some ostensibly "liberal" status quo predating 1931. It would have to be imagined and affirmed in the context of new and fluid actualities. Writing in the bitter aftermath of MacArthur's banning of the 1947 general strike, Maruyama defined the task as follows:

> It has now been made our task to accomplish what the Meiji restoration was unable to carry through: that of completing the democratic revolution. We are being pressed to confront the problem of human freedom itself. The situation facing Japan, of course, is not such that it can be resolved simply by rejoining the orthodox lineage of modern freedom. The bearer of "freedom" is no longer the "citizen" as conceived by liberals since the time of Locke; but must rather be the broad working masses with workers and farmers at the core. Even then the issue is not merely the sensual liberation of the masses, but rather how and how thoroughly the masses are to acquire a new normative consciousness.[66]

For Maruyama, then, democracy would entail the awakening in the masses of political subjectivity. In his view this could not arise except pari passu with a "new normative consciousness." This, in turn, would require a strong commitment from scholarship, broadly conceived: the democratization of politics required the democratization of scholarship. In this effort, the role of the social sciences, again broadly conceived, was to be crucial.

Clearly, Maruyama was a self-conscious heir of the European, and Meiji, Enlightenment. For the most part, he addressed his educated audience through media of limited reach—university and public lectures, appearances before community and educational organizations, publication in opinion journals, rather than mass-circulation dailies, etc. Although he was involved in projects such as Kibe Tatsuji's Shomin Daigaku (People's University), Maruyama's professional identity remained closely tied to Tokyo University, where he held the chair in East Asian political thought until his retirement in 1971.

Maruyama's organizational commitments, meanwhile, were also small-scale. After 1945 he joined a number of groups, among them the Seinen Bunka Kaigi (Youth Culture Conference), Nijusseiki Kenkyūjo (Twentieth-Century Research Institute), Shisō no Kagaku Kenkyūkai (Study Group for the Science of Thought), Kenpō Mondai Chōsakai (Constitutional Problems Survey Group), Heiwa Mondai Danwakai (Peace Problems Discussion Group), and so on. Some of these memberships lapsed quickly; others were kept up. Maruyama never became a party ideologue of any kind on a national level, remaining instead an independent member of the left.[67]

Maruyama, in short, relied implicitly on the diffusion and "translation" of his ideas into the workaday world via a greatly expanding student and white-collar stratum. Indeed, he had come to recognize that enlightenment by and for the academically pedigreed could only go so far in rooting democracy. This was above all to be an age of the masses, of organized capital and labor—including mental labor. As was the case for the entire Japanese left throughout the 1950s, for Maruyama too the relation of democracy to socialism became a pressing issue. Political independence could not equal apathy.

Underlying the question of any political commitment, however, was the intellectual problem of "attitude determination." Maruyama could not embrace the notion of "class subjectivity" championed in the late 1940s by Marxists such as Umemoto Katsumi. This threatened to degenerate into formalism: the "party of the proletariat" could not presume to define a new normative consciousness. Ill at ease with such formalism, and contemptuous of wartime "apostates" who had now returned to the leftist fold, Maruyama initially refused direct political engagement. Although he clearly rejected as elitist and politically reactionary the "old" Japanese liberalism, which had been uncomfortable with any notion of mass politics, class—or social—conflict, Maruyama's political commitments after 1945 were "diagonal" at best.[68]

The incarnation of the Cold War in Japan, however, forced Maruyama to clarify and make public his position. In 1950, self-proclaimed "realists," such as the Tokyo University historian Hayashi Kentarō, called for Japanese intellectuals to choose sides in the ideological struggle against communism and in support of a bilateral rather than a comprehensive peace treaty. Maruyama demurred. He did so for a number of philosophical and practical reasons, which he expressed in his "Aru jiyūshugisha e no tegami" (Letter to a certain liberal, 1950).[69]

First, it ran against the grain of Maruyama's self-described pragmatism to be compelled by external forces to subscribe to the rigid metaphysics of Cold War theology. By doing so, one precluded in principle the formation of political positions that would respond to, and help define, the objective demands of a given situation. Order, Maruyama argued, must not be elevated to a value in its own right. In practice he refused the "liberal's" demand that he forswear any support to the Communist Party, newly chastened by Cominform's criticism and reeling from the so-called Red Purge. We need, he said, to recognize the "paradox that the establishment of the autonomous human person moves forward via the energy provided by *groups* that, in comparison with Western societies, *stand relatively speaking on the left.*[70] Maruyama would give his support to those tendencies that fostered what he termed the "modernization" of Japanese society, and would oppose those that did not.

It is easily forgotten that the 1950s in Japan were a decade of serious and consequential conflict over the politics of modernization. Along with Shimizu Ikutarō, Maruyama was recognized as an intellectual godfather of the anti–Security Treaty (Anpo) movement that ushered in the end of that decade. In it he saw an engaged public—students, white collar workers, and urban housewives, particularly—embodying the ideals of democratic subjectivity he had sought to translate to the Japanese body politic. It does appear that in this case, Maruyama and his audience were on a strikingly similar political wavelength. The new normative consciousness he had called for in 1947 had taken hold:

> How do we conceive of politics? Not as work carried out in unimaginably remote circles beyond the reach of normal folk, by some special breed apart; nor as if it involved abandoning our common everyday life and plunging into some totally separate world. Rather, it's a matter of habit, of seeing politics as activity that, even if it makes up only a small part of what we do, day in and day out, still occupies that place *consistently,* as part of carrying out the commonest of our social obligations. More so than any other ideology, however magnificent, or any system, however formally equipped it may be, democracy depends on this kind of thinking. This is its true foundation. Here in Japan we may have lacked the tradition of direct democracy practiced in the Greek city-states. But instead we have as our intellectual heritage the splendid concept of "homespun [lay] Buddhism." Put in contemporary terms, this means the political activity of non-professional politicians. You don't have to "take the political tonsure" in order to get involved in politics. When politics is left to politicians and Dietmen—people whose purpose is politics per se, or to groups such as parties who approach it in the same way—from that moment democracy begins to die.[71]

However, while the movement brought down the government of the archtechnocrat and inveterate anticommunist Kishi Nobusuke, it failed in its chief aim. Together with the defeat of union-led strikes at the Miike mines, the Anpo struggles paved the way for an "economistic" settlement under Ikeda Hayato that in effect redefined Japanese democracy. The institutional framework laid out in 1947 and 1955 remained, along with the democratic rhetoric of that period. But its normative core would no longer be formed by social mobilization and broad political criticism. Instead, it entailed consumer participation in an expanding gross national product driven by "large-scale mergers and the development of designated contracting systems."[72] The anti-Treaty demonstrations looked to be an exceptional, albeit vital episode, while the meaning of the postwar enlightenment grew clouded.

Thus for Maruyama the 1950s ended and the 1960s began with disillusion. His key text in this regard, unquestionably, is *Nihon no shisō* (1961).[73] Its argument is complex and typical in its ambiguities, on the one hand giving full vent to the agonistic strain that ran so deeply in Maruyama's thought, while on the other revealing nuances not present in his writings of a decade earlier.

For Maruyama, the essence of Japanese thought is to have no essence. Japanese tradition has no "axis" analogous to Christianity in the West or Confucianism in China. It is a "tradition without structure," in which "history" (Maruyama paraphrases Kobayashi Hideo) becomes the nostalgic "welling up" of national "memory," something "akin to the attachment felt by a mother toward a child she has lost." The intellectual landscape is far from empty, of course. Japanese thinkers have accumulated an extraordinary "stock" of discrete ideas to draw on for their own purposes. What is lacking is an "absolute being or a 'Way' that logically and normatively orders the world in its own characteristic manner." In its absence, Maruyama argued, "Japanese thought" formed a tenacious pattern by which "faith in felt reality" *(jikkan shinkō)* and "faith in theory" *(riron shinkō)* operated as functional equivalents, cutting off the dialectic of mutual negation, testing, or correction that Maruyama, from his transcendent position, took as essential to the "normal" operations of the socialized intellect.[74]

Maruyama was not principally concerned with accounting for the origins of Japan's non-axiality. He begins in medias res, looking back across the great but not far-distant rupture of 1945. His argument has to be understood in terms of the political function and consequences of tradition as Maruyama experienced and perceived them. How did "tradition," as mobilized under the modern emperor system, actually function? As of the late 1940s, Maruyama would have answered that it functioned in a uniformly oppressive manner, for reasons that need no repetition here. By the time of *Nihon no shisō*, he has softened considerably his attitude toward tradition, which he discusses in terms of an ethic of "being" as opposed to "doing." Maruyama does not call, as he once seemed to, for the elimination of the ethic of being, but for its incorporation in a synthesis of traditional and modern styles of life and thought. Echoing Max Weber, Maruyama finds that being is functional in the sphere of art and culture: Indeed, it stands in immediate need of protection from an obsessive "modern" concern with producing results. (As he observed elsewhere, "*The Tale of Genji, Hamlet,* and *Faust* cannot be shot off as rockets.") At the same time, he finds Japanese society lacking in a political ethic of doing, where results—the rationalization of means according to publicly determined ends—do indeed matter. By applying criteria of instrumental rationality where they did not belong, Japan had become hypermodern in one sphere and insufficiently modern in another.[75]

But how does this relate to Japanese thought? The answer lies in the totality of elements—premodern, modern, and hypermodern—and in their particular distribution, or valences, within the social system; it is in the whole, rather than in any of its parts, that the Japanese mode of thought operates. And as Maruyama shows, there are definable historical patterns to this operation, which now can, and must, be challenged. The ideology of *kokutai*—the unbroken line of imperial rule over Japan—had legitimated rapid institutional modernization in the name of the monarch. At the same time, it claimed that the monarchy was the supreme embodiment and validator of the entire system of patriarchal, factional, and personalistic human relationships that characterize village society.[76] The *tennō* became the unassailable sign of a system of social/national givenness and of a certain style of bureaucratically mandated change; the *tennōsei* was

> purely pragmatic and opportunistic in that it avoided the attempt to establish itself on the basis of a fixed dogma such as is found in Christianity or Confucianism. At the same time, it took as its highest purpose the preservation of the system of authority with the emperor at the apex; and on this basis made it a taboo to question the legitimacy of its authority.[77]

The *tennōsei* in this sense was the most powerful and consequential "invented" tradition of modern Japan. It provided the institutional and linguistic frame through which all other "inventions" received their official imprimatur. The task now was to differentiate, to overcome the deep-seated "need" for the all-encompassing legitimating frame that was at once so comforting and suffocating. Could Japanese people (as Irokawa Daikichi asked) "comprehend their fate"—and create their present and future—without recourse to a mental metaphor of *tennōsei*? Could they overcome Japanese thought?[78]

Surveying the contemporary scene, Maruyama seems uncertain. In an enduring metaphor, he noted the tendency of organizations of all kinds in Japan to form themselves into "octopus pots" *(takotsubo),* in which the group's activities, ideas, and values become largely self-referential, the authority of the group self-justifying, and socially isolating. This includes "modern" organizations—political, business, and technical as well. Parallel to this is the increasing sophistication, centralization, and uniformity of the mass media. The result of their interaction is a society in which lateral ties between groups of all kinds are weak; groups form images of themselves and the "world" that go unchallenged and "walk on their own." In the absence of such ties and of genuine feedback throughout society, critical and democratic consciousness is fragmented and blunted. It is precisely in this mix of hypermodernity in one sector with premodernity in another that Maruyama sees functional continuity with *tennōsei*, albeit sans *tennō* in the prewar mode.

Counterposed to the octopus pot is the *sasara*, a bamboo whisk with a shared base that is finely separated toward the tip. The finely separated tip connotes articulation, differentiation, specialization, and pluralism as a value. But how is the shared base of the *sasara* to be understood? Does it refer to a single nation or ethnicity with an intuited cultural code? It would seem not. Speaking of the development of the European social sciences, Maruyama refers almost enviously to a "long common tradition" linking "Greece, the middle ages, and the Renaissance" with the modern emergence of highly specialized disciplines; the comprehensive systems (or at least catholic concerns) of "Hegel, Stein, and Marx, or Bentham and Comte" that were typical of the early nineteenth century give way by its end to the specialized sciences familiar today. It was these latter—the finely separated tips of the *sasara*—that had been cut off from their roots and transplanted to Japan. The shared root, in other words, was a history of dialectic, argument, contestation. Without this history, the disciplines of social science in Japan were fated to be "academic" from the beginning, and even more susceptible than in Europe to self-enclosure. More consequentially, the "academy" itself was presumed to exist for the service of a state-defined public good.[79]

Nihon no shisō, Maruyama asserts, is also his own "self-criticism" from the point of view of "radical intellectual aristocratism [*kizokushugi*] linked interiorly with a radical democracy": he looks forward to a *sasara*-type society, one in which the image of "Karl Marx reading Hölderlin" would capture the intellectual life of its people.[80] Although it seems to set out an uncompromising task of mental revolution, and therefore remain true to modernism, *Nihon no shisō* is good-natured and surprisingly upbeat in tone. "We (or you?) can do this!" is its chief message, and in this sense it is rather far removed from Maruyama's writings of the early postwar years. It points to a modernism in process of differentiation, one making its peace via the categories of aesthetics—including linguistic play—with nationality. Would modernism be drawn from that point into a discourse that valorized its moment as one of modernity achieved, pressing forward to the presentation of Japan as a new model of development? Would modernism retain the capacity for "utopian" resistance to the status quo, even at the risk of marginalization? Under what conditions, with what social allies? What, in short, would be the intellectual consequences for Japan's democracy of coming to terms with nationality?

Maruyama nowhere specified how social groups are to function in a Japanese democracy. His concern remained less with social solidarity at the peripheries than with personal subjectivity and political integration at the national level. By the early 1960s, to be sure, Maruyama could write that "any system that lacks feedback of counter communication from the periphery will corrupt."[81] Even here, however, Maruyama showed relatively little concern with the identity of the "periphery" or with the content or social character of the feedback it generated. What mattered to him was that it function in a normative manner. Maruyama's democratic imagination tended to be limited to the translation of democracy to the periphery. At most it points up a role for intellectual migrants to the periphery as producers of "counter communication" whose content remains vague indeed.

The reason for this vagueness is not far to seek: Maruyama's image of the periphery was one of traditionalism and irrational attachments. Although he had argued that democracy had to become "irrationalized"— or deintellectualized—this still left unanswered the question of how the center is to be "reintellectualized" from below. And because a backward and traditionalistic periphery was, in effect, a structural requirement of his thinking, Maruyama could never answer such a question.[82]

Insofar as democracy at any level is an intellectual and spiritual concern, however, Maruyama's strictures against "complacency" or "blind faith" in ideology or institutions were well taken.[83] Maruyama remained a protestant. For him, democracy was indeed a priesthood of all believers; it calls for faith in carrying through what he called a "permanent revolution," in which "institutions are no sooner made than they are destroyed, and no sooner destroyed than made anew."[84] For ultimately, democracy inhabits all institutions only provisionally; it is a vital "fiction." The question of democracy is not how to fix it within institutions, but how to expand the scope of participation in its making and inevitable remaking. No value, that of freedom (or democracy) included, can be made "real" simply by being divested of utopian elements. "Realism" as the ideological affirmation of the status quo, and the identification of the established order with democracy as such, in effect kills democracy in its own name. Thus Maruyama answered a nationalist critic of postwar Japan's occupation or "sham," democracy: "As for my own choice in the matter: Rather than opt for the 'reality' of the empire of Japan, I'll put my money on the 'sham' of postwar democracy."[85]

DEMOCRACY AND DESIRE IN THE PRACTICE OF SOCIAL SCIENCE

At the heart of Maruyama's democratic imagination, then, was an abhorrence of stasis and corruption, and a desire for movement. Yet movement must be directed. It must be productive—that is, based on systematic knowledge and "pregnant with a further growth in the human capacity."[86] The final section of this chapter explores the methodological connection between democracy and desire in Maruyama's vision.

Maruyama frequently made use of corporeal and sexual metaphors in describing and analyzing the Japanese polity. The likening of a nation, society, or community to a body is hardly uncommon. It may seem all the more "natural" given the intensely corporate political culture of Japan. But how did Maruyama employ such metaphors? What sort of body is being imagined?

First, the democratic body is one whose members possess "normal" desires for power. Yet Japan was not always normal, and had to be made so. Second, those who analyze the operations of this body—social scientists—also possess such desires, but they must restrain their "erotic" desire for power in the interest of truth and knowledge. The fact of political desire comes head-to-head with the value set upon truth. In other words, Maruyama follows Max Weber in arguing that social science, as science, is essentially an ascetic discipline. He further argues that such asceticism is vital to the health of the whole national body, drawing from modern Japan's history evidence of the dangers flowing from its absence. In the light of more recent studies, particularly by members of the People's History (minshūshi) school, it must be admitted that in some respects Maruyama's version reads like a poor caricature of popular experience. The concern here, however, is not with his treatment of this or that episode so much as with his general interpretive and narrative strategy.

For Maruyama, Japan had "lost its virginity" in the Sino-Japanese

War, and it went on to present to the world a monstrous spectacle of "oversexed" nationalism.[87] Japan's precocious imperialism was abnormal, and under these conditions, the life of the domestic political body, including its intellectual life, was disordered. As the Tokugawa regime showed signs of collapse, peoples' "senses" were liberated from their bondage under the status system and Confucian morality. These trends continued after 1868. But though a revolution of the senses had occurred, it had not transformed—or been allowed to transform—the political sphere. Maruyama points to the fragmentation and eventual failure of the Freedom and Popular Rights movement as the crucial episode. This was a failure, he suggests, not only of politics but of intellect. He quotes (admittedly in polemical context) the autobiography of Kōno Hironaka:

> I was riding on horseback when I first read [John Stuart Mill's *On Liberty*]. In a flash my entire way of thinking was revolutionized. Until then I had been under the influence of the Chinese Confucianists and of the Japanese classical scholars . . . Now all these earlier thoughts of mine, *excepting those concerned with loyalty and filial piety,* were smashed to smithereens. At the same moment I knew that it was human freedom and human rights that I must henceforth cherish above all else.[88]

Given such a leadership, Maruyama argues, one looks in vain for a history of popular revolt: Instead one finds a history in which "people complained in private . . . but in the end had to cry themselves to sleep"— *nakineiri shita rekishi.*[89]

Among the masses, the realm of immediate, sensual life remained "vegetative" and subject to familistic morality of the state. With August 15, 1945 came a sudden release from the long repression of genuine subjectivity; this repression was inherent in the conflation of public and private under the full-fledged imperial regime. History appeared to repeat itself. As Maruyama wrote in "Kaikoku" (1959), the evidence was all around for the liberation of long-repressed sensuality. A kind of fleshly existentialism reigned amid a riot of pornography and sexual license: all reminiscent of Japanese society immediately after the opening of the country a century earlier.[90]

Maruyama's point was not to condemn carnality per se, though there are hints of a Confucian and Kantian rigorism in his comments. But he does seem to say that the persistent identification of self with sensation was symptomatic of the pathology of the Japanese public sphere, now laid bare with defeat. Analogous to this short-circuiting sensuality, as we shall see, Maruyama identified a complex dual fetishism of organization and theoretical purity by the left, which had its own harmful effects on the growth of political autonomy and full subjectivity among the masses.

As a historian and analyst of political theory, Maruyama sought to "normalize" this condition, to outline the proper relation of politics to science in a democracy. In a classic essay, "Politics as a Science in Japan" (Kagaku toshite no seijigaku, 1947), Maruyama clearly articulates an ascetic vision of the polis, or public sphere.

"Since 15 August 1945," he observes, "the complicated process of forming the national will, which was formerly carried out in obscurity, has been opened to the public." It was now possible to "criticize rationally the very hub of State power"—that place formerly darkened by the pseudo-public glare of *kokutai* ideology.[91] The opening of political processes to the public was not, of course, the result of the direct assertion by the Japanese people of political subjectivity; this "guilty" knowledge hurt. Indeed Maruyama later described postwar intellectuals—those who despite, or because of, their public status and expertise had been unable to prevent the nonsensification of discourse or the concrete decisions that led to total war—as a "community of contrition."[92] In Maruyama's view, the former intelligentsia was guilty of passivity and impotence, lesser sins of omission in contrast to the sins of commission originating in the military and ruling elites.[93] Only a tiny minority, he recognized, had stood resolutely and unambiguously opposed to the "trend of the times." But the problem of impotence in scholarship, he intimates, was deeper; indeed it was written into the institutional structures of knowledge production under the imperial system. The paradox of a political and social science constitutionally prohibited from studying the "hub of State power" is a clear illustration. It was bound to produce deformations—sterile methodological debate and textual empiricism masquerading as the interpretation of positive law. At the other extreme was the fatal conflation of power—the "reality" of imperial Japan—with value:

> During the national crisis that developed after the China Incident, a number of political scientists were unable to endure the excessive gap between their scholarship and its real object. They left their studies and plunged into the vortex of raw politics. In the end they established personal relations with specific politicians and military men, and they tried feverishly to use such private relations to move political events in the direction they thought desirable. Seeing all this I could only think it the tragic fate of political science in Japan.[94]

Maruyama refers obliquely here to certain of his senior colleagues—Yabe Teiji, Rōyama Masamichi, and others—some of whom he was shortly to be involved in evaluating during the purge of "rightists" in the university. He does not name names and in any case is trying to make the larger point that both intellectual sterility and yielding to the desire for power did harm.

What is to be done? For the social scientist, the task is twofold: to protect one's work from "direct subordination to political forces," and the "far more difficult" task of "bracketing," that is, of "preventing subjective value judgments from insinuating themselves into the cognition of political phenomena." There is no permanent solution to this dilemma, since temptation is constant and the struggle against it, as it was for Weber, may be extremely bitter. Nevertheless, only an awareness of subjective values as such and the consequent will to "subordinate all . . . political aspirations, hopes, likes and dislikes . . . to the requirements of the cognitive process" can produce scientific analysis worthy of the name. The point is not to extinguish desire—the "erotic" quest to link theory with practice, or knowledge with power. As Maruyama notes, "abstinence is meaningful only when desire is present. . . . If a person has lacked desire from the very beginning, then he is physiologically deformed." Indeed, for this reason " 'strict neutrality' is also a political position," and in constructing a "theory of a political situation, the scholar is ipso facto committing himself to a specific political course of action." To pretend otherwise is harmful self-deception. There is no such creature as a "mere spectator in the all-out political struggle among various types of *Weltanschauungen.*"[95]

Maruyama was writing in 1946, a time when recriminations against the military, old elites, and the "theorists" of the New Order were powerful political weapons. Similarly, it was a time when the left, including many intellectuals, and a newly emancipated labor movement were engaged in an unprecedented struggle with capital for control of the production process. Thus Maruyama's call for a "spirit of abstinence" was very much to the point. The possibilities for self-deception, toadyism, and cynical manipulation of popular aspirations were legion.

The problem of guilty knowledge took specific forms on the left. In the postwar atmosphere of convulsive change and uncertain political currents, knowledge of failure had come to be mixed with a powerful need among intellectuals to be "forgiven" by history and/or the masses. Only thus could they be healed of their impotence and work productively for the unity of theory and practice—concretely, for the democratization of Japan. In the course of his discussion of the community of contrition, Maruyama touches on the excesses of *inaori*—aggressive repentance— among fallen members of the Communist Party and among newly minted intellectual fellow travelers. Their past sins, either of falling away from the revolutionary cause or of positively embracing the New Order, were failures of abstinence. Now, after the defeat, in their anxiousness to be healed, whole, and productive (and sometimes to conceal or avoid confrontation with their own pasts), these public men were again succumbing to the fallacy of misplaced concretization by giving "total" allegiance to a dogmatic Marxism or a party line. In short, as Watanabe Yoshimichi put it, party membership and activity were used as a cloak for their unwillingness or inability to face the past.[96] The result was given arresting expression by Fujita Shōzō, a talented and close disciple of Maruyama. The context is an analysis of the transformation of the Association of Democratic Scientists (Minshushugi Kagakusha Kyōkai, or Minka) from a vigorous and multifaceted operation of intellectuals on the left into a Communist Party front. Unfolding between 1946 and 1951, the process is an apt symbol of the whole problem under discussion here. For Fujita, Minka as an organization, and many of the individuals within it, had come to exemplify what he calls "castrated thinking" *(danshuteki hassō)*. Here the transformative impulse of the theory/practice relation is somehow blocked by dogmatism, blind obedience to the organization and leadership, and a destructive tendency to eliminate through public castigation and purge those whose ideas are deemed unacceptable in a given situation. Once so branded, the heretic is then shown to have been corrupt from the outset, and his theoretical and political nullification a heroic act. Here Fujita calls explicitly to mind Maruyama's critique of de-Stalinization, in which he discussed the "disease of orthodoxy" as this afflicted both Soviet and Japanese public life.[97] What is interesting is the implication that in Japan, the worst, most pathological facets of Stalinism and *tennōsei* orthodoxy were combined, as if to mock the hopes of the left to lead the struggle for the democratization of Japan. It is also meant to point up the moral consequences of deformed subjectivity.

The foregoing examples have highlighted the rhetorical and psychological link between Maruyama's intellectual style and the environment of postwar thought. I have focused on problems of leftist thought because it was to the left that Maruyama and many of his contemporaries looked for the realization of a democratic Japan. And in a world in which Kishi Nobusuke is depurged, ostensibly in order to protect

Japanese democracy, their judgment had some merit. This is not to min-imize the mistakes and fallacies that bedeviled the left in Japan; these deserve a full evaluation that cannot be attempted here. I will close instead by reflecting briefly on the present-day significance of Maru-yama's position and mode of expression.

BEYOND MODERNISM?

Over nearly five decades of public life, Maruyama Masao involved him-self intellectually and politically in the struggle to define and realize Japanese modernity and democracy. Indeed, for him, the two were insep-arable parts of a world-historical, moral whole and were by no means the exclusive possession of the West. In the process of working out a "pragmatic" position and role in changing circumstances, he enormously enriched the language of social science and historiography in Japan. In the years following Japan's defeat in 1945, Maruyama provided lan-guage for the articulation of thoughts and feelings hitherto restricted to ideological or illicit expression, and in this sense he made history.

Reflecting upon—and rejecting—much of what he regarded as the dead end of prewar Japanese scholarship, Maruyama also asserted the possibility of an "objective" political and social science. The "trial of the emperor system" had created this possibility for the first time by promis-ing that the bourgeois democratic revolution in Japan could now be brought to completion on the basis of what he termed a "new normative consciousness." This formulation recalls both Maruyama's profound and self-acknowledged debt to Marxism, and his departure from it. Despite his strong sympathy for the cause of the political left, Maruyama, as a "scientific imaginer" of democracy, called for the transcendence of Marxism in both political theory and practice. In the former regard, Maruyama had long rejected class analysis as a sufficient synonym for social science. Modern political systems and phenomena from Stalinist parties to right-wing nationalist sects, he argued, could be "passed through" certain interrelated ideal-typical constructs that serve as objec-tive media. "Political power," "political technique," and "political jus-tice," Maruyama suggested, were necessary constructs in any analysis. They were to phenomena as developing fluid is to a photograph; by their proper use, one could reveal both the essential and distinctive features of these systems and phenomena.[98] As for political practice, we have already seen that Maruyama evinced strong concerns over the policies and mentality of Japan's Communist Party. He distrusted the claim that the party could speak unerringly for the proletariat; more fundamentally, he did not believe that class politics was sufficient politics.

Japan did not become a democracy in the sense that Maruyama imagined it. Yet this failure was not inevitable, and there is no doubt that the bipolar "realism" of the late 1940s, along with the nationalist economism of subsequent decades, was deeply disillusioning for him. From the mid-1960s, though with some earlier foreshadowing, Maruyama's explicit concerns tended to be more purely historical than contemporary. He focused on the history of "cultural change and cultural contact" between Japan and the outside world. "The introduction to intellectual history of this perspective . . . which includes the problem of 'translating' words, necessarily involves the rejection of universalistic theories of stages of development."[99] In line with this shift, Maruyama came to explore what he called the "ancient substrata" *(kosō)*—and later termed basso ostinato—of Japanese political, historical, and ethical consciousness. These, he found, were thoroughly resistant to schematization in terms of a narrative of inevitable, if dialectical, progress through stages.[100] Maruyama seems to have grown ever more pessimistic about the potential of Japanese consciousness to overcome its inclination to celebrate the "eternal now" and finally break through into "universality." He continued to lament the identification of the "universal" with what is "external" to Japan: Japan is by definition, and irremediably, "particular."[101] It is therefore appropriate to view Maruyama's late return to the "deep things" of Japanese historical consciousness as a moment in his disenchantment.

This must not, however, be taken to imply the slightest valorization of a neoconservative revisionism. Maruyama did not renounce his conviction that the concept and norm he chose to call "subjectivity" remained valid for Japan, not only in political but in scientific terms as well. Maruyama remained a "modernist" in the sense that he could not imagine democracy apart from individual autonomy. Nor did he abandon his nonholistic, "bracketing" approach to social science, which he regarded as the only, albeit provisional, means of approaching objectivity in analysis. Indeed, for Maruyama, one facet of subjectivity consists of the ability to "separate for a moment the knowing subject *[ninshiki shutai]* from reality as directly given," and, "standing in acute tension with this reality," to "reconstruct the world logically."[102] It follows, therefore, that in social science, objectivity requires subjectivity, and vice versa. So too in politics. For Maruyama, as we have seen, democracy was in a crucial sense a spirit that "blows where it wills." How then could one hope to foster democracy as long as the political and social status quo is regarded as a reality "directly given" and not the product of human striving—or perhaps of inertia, the failure to strive? Without a critical, that is, "subjective," outlook, no clear understanding of reality, or of the "spirit," is possible, and nothing can be changed.

To be sure, Maruyama's position met with criticism, for example by Umemoto Katsumi and other Marxists. Maruyama, Umemoto wrote, recognized that with the postwar collapse of the equivalence between Marxism and social science, nothing remained to link the various fields. He saw that it was necessary somehow to transcend this absence, but he consciously refrained from rendering a judgment as to what the underlying principle should be. Here, Umemoto observed, lay the reason for Maruyama's continuing affinity with Mannheim and Weber. Here also was the link between Maruyama the historian and Maruyama the social scientist. The question of whether modern political science, indeed modern politics, is possible in Japan is one for intellectual history to answer; but this answer can never be an "ought," only an "is."[103]

If Marxists were impatient with such a position, and in general with Maruyama's "democratic fiction," so too were others. Two critical views of Maruyama's modernism, quite different in ideological orientation, will concern us as we conclude these reflections. The first is that of Takeuchi Yoshimi (1910–1977), an influential interpreter of Lu Xun and commentator on postwar literature and politics, who used the term "modernism" to describe—and reject—both the Communist Party's definition of itself, including its claims concerning Marxism-Leninism as a "science," and modernism à la Maruyama. For Takeuchi, insofar as both orientations were essentially Western-derived, they represented no more than a language of intellectual "slavery," and in following them, Japan would merely be occupying the role of "top student"; in Gramscian terms, modernism fixed Japan's status as subaltern to the great powers.

It was not that modernism was to be condemned in its entirety. Its significance, Takeuchi argued, was transitional. In the wake of defeat, it helped Japanese intellectuals to "forget the nightmare of a blood-soaked ethnic nationalism" by conceiving of ethnos *(minzoku)* in abstract terms. Now, however, modernism was holding back real modernization, which could only proceed in the spirit of Chinese revolutionary nationalism. For Japan, this required a reconnection with, and development of, the critical literary lineage formed by Futabatei Shimei, Kitamura Tōkoku, Ishikawa Takuboku, and later the Japan Romantic school of the 1930s. "There can be no revolution," Takeuchi declared, "that is not rooted in national tradition." By focusing only on "self" or "class," and preventing the return of the "thrown away" ethnos to literature—to public life—modernism blocked the people's capacity for self-transformation, perpetuating a pre-modern consciousness among them.[104]

Maruyama accepted such criticism insofar as it pertained to his earlier views of China.[105] But it does not seem to have shaken his fundamental position about Japan itself. His doubts about the revolutionary potential of Japan's masses were profound. Takeuchi's position that Japan ought to emulate China in spirit, on the other hand, seems cruelly farcical—though it is to be remembered that such a dismissal assumes a conservative recuperation of Japanese tradition that was still very far off when Takeuchi wrote in 1951.

But it did raise the issue of positive nationalism; nationalism of content and not, as in Maruyama's case, of intent. And in the long run, the reality of successful Japanese exceptionalism, not the fantasy of revolutionary Japanese nationalism, seems to have put Maruyama in the shade. As Yoshida Masatoshi has observed:

> The true "limits" of modernism, which were all too inherent in its historical setting, have as a matter of course been made clear by historical developments themselves. The true value of modernism, whose significance lies in the unique conditions of defeat and occupation under which it emerged, has come into question. For with the revival and reconsolidation of Japanese capitalism, "modern society," fictitious [giseiteki] in form though it may be, has at length emerged in Japan.[106]

Let us flesh out some of these assertions, taking the example of the late Murakami Yasusuke's "Japanese model of political economy" both as a description of successful Japanese-style modernity and as an example of post-"modernist" social science.[107] According to Murakami, the modus operandi not only of Japanese enterprise but also that of the polity derives from a combination of traditional household (ie) and village (mura) principles. These principles, combined with what Murakami usefully terms "late-developer conservatism," have served until recently as the basis for postwar Japan's remarkable consensus for growth. They have further seen to it that Japanese politics has evolved (he quotes Inoguchi Takashi) into a "bureaucracy-led mass-inclusionary pluralism." And, although presided over by a single party, "the postwar Japanese political system [is] one of the more satisfactorily working parliamentary democracies. In respect to freedom of expression and association, it compares favorably to any society and is better than most."[108]

Although much of Murakami's "Japanese model of political economy" is beyond the scope of this discussion, it is noteworthy that, according to Murakami, explicit nationalism (i.e., militarism) was not a driving force in Japan's postwar social settlement. Instead, he argues, a diffuse and unorganized "traditionalism" has served the Liberal Democratic Party well in winning it a critical mass of electoral support (albeit one whose size has declined since the mid-1960s), while the ideological antitraditionalism of "opposition-in-principle" parties has guaranteed that they could never come to power. Murakami is unclear as to the content of tradition, although he suggests that cultural homogeneity and "the organizational heritage from the prewar years" may be its most important functional components. In any case, he notes, "pessimistic" academics such as Maruyama have failed to see the virtues of Japan's distinctive form of polity and economy, insisting instead on pointing out "barriers" to modernization.[109]

The current situation (Murakami was writing in the mid-1980s) poses special problems for Japan's postwar conservatism. On the one hand, the national consensus for "catch-up" growth, with its largely "instrumental" values, has begun to give way to the "consummatory" values of Japan's "middle mass"—class having become a noncategory in the discussion of Japanese society.[110] On the other hand, the so-called Pax Americana seems to be a thing of the past. The United States—and the style of capitalism that has undergirded it—has begun to manifest clear signs of economic and political decline. It is in this context, moreover, that Japan has vastly increased its trade with southeast Asia, and having displaced the United States in this sphere, Japan generally seems to sense that its future once more lies in Asia. Murakami hints that meeting this ideological challenge—of satisfying or co-opting material domestic demand and enunciating an "active foreign policy"—will severely test the skills of Japan's leadership. It is fair to speculate that widespread frustration over failure to meet this dual challenge might make aggressive nationalism an attractive expedient.

Whatever the outcome, Murakami's point was that Japan, having succeeded in modernizing on the basis of its exceptionalism, had now entered its own form of middle mass postmodernity. And so we are brought back, via Murakami, to an ironic confirmation of Takeuchi's argument. Modernism may have presided over the demise of a "blood-soaked ethnic nationalism," but it also ushered in a form of postmodern traditionalism. As such, it was a necessary moment in the dialectic of national self-definition. In terms of the broader concern here with the theory and practice of social science in Japan, a few points should be clear. First, although the national "self" now being defined can no longer be a simple rehash of " predemocratic" emperorism, it is taking the form of a "national community" that consciously and energetically affirms the values of "traditional" social organization. The binarism of Japan versus Other(s) has for the moment regained conceptual pride of place. Rather than the national past, Japan's relations with the outside world constitute the main problem. Second, the epistemological and political assumptions of Maruyama's modernist social science seem to have been rejected or co-opted. His universalist model of subjectivity, with its Weberian asceticism, has faded, and its critical edge has most certainly been blunted. Third, if Murakami's position can be taken as typical of the "conservative" mainstream, democracy is no longer a problem, but rather a given, for Japanese social science. Japan, in this view, has become a democratic national community, both in a formal and a substantial sense. Indeed, the democratic status quo, to recall Dunn's observation, may not be so much dismally ideological as dismally *non*-ideological. In any event, for analysts like Murakami, the modernist project has been completed, and its utopian criticism is no longer functional.

Yet some caution would seem to be in order. The postwar recrudescence of Japanese exceptionalism is a fact; indeed, it is an industry in itself. That it is not a simple reflex of rising national confidence, but something more complex and unstable, is beyond question. Certainly Maruyama's perduring pessimism and congenital elitism remain irritating to conservatives and to the neopopulist left. His concerns for informed, normative democratic agency do seem countercyclical. Recent events, however, have revealed the coercion and violence that lie barely concealed beneath Japan's national community. In December 1988, as Emperor Shōwa lay dying, Mayor Motojima Hitoshi of Nagasaki voiced his opinion that the soon-to-be-late monarch was indeed "responsible" for Japanese aggression and his own people's suffering. Shortly after delivering himself of these remarks, Motojima was ousted from his position as head of the local Liberal Democratic Party, stripped of his post as consultant to the national party, and publicly upbraided by party secretary Abe Shintarō. In the interim, Motojima refused to back away from his statements. Finally, on January 18, 1990, Motojima was shot and seriously wounded by a member of the Sane Thinkers' school (Seiki juku), a group who found the mayor's expressed opinion beyond tolerance. To be sure, the shooting was condemned by the Liberal Democratic Party and government spokesmen. Given the salient fact of Motojima's political ostracism, however, these protestations rang somewhat hollow. When seen in the light of the Motojima affair, Maruyama's negative valuation of the national community appears less puzzling and less deserving of marginalization. In the end, Maruyama may best be seen as a utopian pessimist: utopian in spirit, but pessimistic about the capacity for self-transformation in the "deep things" of Japanese social structure. His importance may lie less in what he "taught" than in the chill that followed his departure from center stage.

Conclusion

"A small country out in the sticks" *(henpi no shōhō)*, "a piece of the larger world" *(sekai no ikkan)*—these phrases were used to describe Japan, the first in the thirteenth century by the great Zen master Dōgen, and the second by Tosaka Jun, a Marxist philosopher of the twentieth.[1] For Dōgen, the comparison of Japan to India and China was unflattering. His country seemed to him a peripheral land of the willfully ignorant, and lacking in wisdom. Yet the Buddhist law, despite or because of this deficiency, had made its way east, and Japan had now been brought to share in the religious destiny of the civilized world. For Tosaka, matters may have seemed the same. Capitalist development and the revolutionary response it engendered had sent a historical tide from west to east, from England and France to Russia, and perhaps now to Japan and China. Vividly aware of the delusory ideology of Japan's national uniqueness, which he took as one of his targets, Tosaka sought to clear the path for Japan's own transformation. For both of these thinkers, the "real" world was not the unprepossessing land of their birth, but rather the globe, or that part of it caught up in the universal movements of their time.

The theme of the mediation of the universal to the particular (or of the "great" to the "small") encapsulates the history of Japanese social science well enough; to "think the world" of modernity and Japan's ostensibly late incorporation into it has been its consistent and inherent concern. But this is only part of the story. For along with it has come a countermovement, an inversion, a transvaluation. Could not Japan itself be "great"? Could not the historical tide, whether of Buddhism or modernity, reach its completion in Japan? Was it not the particular that in fact had to be mediated to the universal so that the universal itself could be realized? Was not Japan the uniquely necessary particular that troubled every claim to universality—in religion, in social development, in political forms?

I have tried in these studies to capture the broader significance of the universal-particular relation in Japanese social science through the notion of "developmental alienation." Here, I proposed, was a condition shared by three late developing empires—Germany, Japan, and Russia—each of which had retained control of its polity and politics, yet whose "lateness" or "backwardness" substantially conditioned its historical and cultural self-image vis-à-vis the "Atlantic Rim." The alienation was developmental because the Atlantic Rim included prime models of development already attained and thus to be striven for by others; development was alienated, because each "model country" was also a threat and a constant reminder of material difference, and lack, of existence as an object of condescension, contempt, or reciprocal fear. It was as a response to this condition that the strategy of neotraditional rationalization was elaborated over the decades from the early 1880s to the 1910s.[2] The formative years of Japanese social science—of academic social thought more generally—were stamped with the hegemony of the family state. This entity became the prohibitively favored reference point for any and all attempts to think systematically about Japan's emergent modernity. To serve it was by definition to serve the cause of national progress. The vector of national service was very powerful; thinkers who were internally alienated could often be restored to the national community by being convinced that their personal and private estrangement would exacerbate the nation's own collective alienation from the "advanced" world. Simply put, an objectively alienated Japan could not afford the presence within itself of subjectively alienated individuals. Social solidarities that were not aligned with the nation were dangerous to the nation.

LEGACIES OF THE KŌZA-HA

When reified, neither the position of one-way universalization nor of perennial particularity has much to offer. And that reification has happened persistently because each position has been tied to one or another ideological parti pris, and to deeply vested claims of group identity

within the constellation of active political forces. Yet these two categories need not be simply mirror images of one another, mutually
dependent and mutually defining. The case of Japanese Marxism, to
which I have given pride of place in the preceding pages, bears eloquent
testimony to this. At its most extreme, Kōza-ha, or Lectures Faction
Marxism was both universalist and particularist in precisely the same
degree. Japanese capitalism was classified as inherently, structurally
deviant, and only the deus ex machina of an external shock could alter it.
Mechanistic rather than dialectical in its apprehension of change, Kōza-
ha Marxism tended to reproduce conceptually that to which it was
morally and politically most opposed: the world of the "national polity"
(kokutai) and the real conditions of exploitation that underlay the imperial regime.

This was a limitation, a kind of intellectual equilibrium trap. But it did
not (as shown in chapter 3) prevent the work of Yamada Moritarō from
acquiring a protean character. The difference between the "national poli-
tarians" and Yamada was not just that the one's rendering was positive
and the other negative; it was that the former conceived of the *kokutai*
ontologically, while for Yamada capitalism was to be apprehended
methodologically. As long as this was borne in mind, there was a way out
of the trap. Yamada's analysis of Japan's capitalism, its "semifeudal"
base *and* superstructure, shaped the understanding of a generation and
more of social scientists as they confronted the issue of what made
Japanese capitalism both Japanese and capitalist. By the same token, my
discussion of thinkers broadly in the Kōza-ha line—Uchida Yoshihiko,
Hirata Kiyoaki, and above all Maruyama Masao—has, I hope, demonstrated both the difficulty of transcending the Kōza-ha perspective, and
the intellectual possibilities that open up upon so doing. The notion of
"civil society" developed by Uchida and Hirata could only have emerged
under particularist impetus, and only in a world in which the imperial
state claimed to function as the ontological locus of moral values. With
the implosion of that structure after 1945, civil society itself no longer
required the protective mantle of a mechanistic economism, and was
freed to assume the ethico-political character it had always covertly possessed. Maruyama, as noted, was uncomfortable with the notion of civil
society, but there is no room for doubt that he invested that of modernity
with as potent an intellectual and moral charge as he could muster: and
that modernity, though it necessarily arose amid historical particularity,
for Maruyama also transcended any particularity. "To understand others
as others" *(in ihrem Anderssein)* was not merely a prelude to their assim-

ilation into self. It was by definition to experience individual and collective self-transcendence, to become "Other" in and as oneself.[3]

The particularist perspective of the Kōza-ha, to repeat, was itself a negative replication of the hegemonic vision of "national community" or "family state" that conditioned the entire development of social science in Japan. It was perhaps necessary that an attempted frontal challenge to the imperial system take such a form, that it issue from a place as close to the heart of matter as possible. The problem was that the Kōza-ha disavowed the task of thinking in explicitly cultural or ideological terms—precisely the currency in which the officialized public sphere traded. Moreover, its closest antagonist within the Marxian tradition, the Rōnō-ha, or Worker-Farmer Faction, presented a theoretically more consistent view of capitalist development. There was something sensible (and empirically justified) in its claim that the extent of commercialization even in the Tokugawa, let alone Meiji, economy made it difficult, if not incoherent, to speak of Japanese capitalism as undergirded by a "feudal" base. "Feudalism," in other words, was "always already" a cultural and political—rather than strictly economic—problem, and could not be solved except in those spheres. In his own way, and in his own terms, Yanagita Kunio had also understood this well: a comprehensive village-based ethnography was necessary as an attempt at the *cultural* reconstruction of a long-lost, "real" community.

The Kōza-ha as such—that is, those who adhered to the Comintern or Communist Party position—was ill-equipped to grasp this point. But because the Rōnō-ha itself shared the assumption that political transformation had to be economically driven, its superior comprehension could guarantee it no more than the position of a critical supplement. It was not enough merely to demonstrate that rural class polarization had taken place to this or that extent. The issue was why, despite that, what even the Rōnō-ha acknowledged to be feudal vestiges seemed so hardy, and why, as Uno Kōzō remarked, "the villages remained as they had been."[4]

UNO AND MARUYAMA: STRUCTURE AND SUBJECT

Of the three Marxian approaches analyzed in this work, it was that of Uno Kōzō and the so-called Marx-Uno school of political economy that did the most to articulate a perspective on Japanese capitalism as a single dynamic structure embedded in "world time," rather than as an "either-or" in a game of categorical ping-pong. Through the frame of his three-level analytical method, Uno saw "backward" capitalism as nonetheless genuine—that is, it was as subject as any other capitalism to the demiurgic forces of the "pure" type. At the same time, since in a late developer capitalist relations were mediated by industry rather than agriculture, the problem of backwardness remained to shape "policy" in accordance with the conjunctural dynamics that attended developmental "lateness" in a given stage. To be sure, Uno's scientism and studied disavowal of necessitarian arguments (which he saw as the epochal illusion of the Second International) left him and his school open to accusations from the left of reactionary quietism. Uno preferred this—and I think justifiably—to the corruptions of Stalinism. This does not mean that he solved the problem of practice, despite his worries over the relation of science to ideology. He was true to this neo-Kantian facet of his intellectual formation (a link to the liberal social science of the 1920s), insisting first on making the logical discriminations essential to the construction of a method, at the cost of (not) specifying the practical implications of the understanding gained through its application.

But what then did the subsequent development of the school mean? What bearing did it have on the broader issue of practice within the social sciences in Japan? And might the answer to these questions in turn suggest something of the current standing and "fate" of their originary condition, that of developmental alienation?

The Uno school was unique to its period. In no other capitalist country were university students trained so systematically in Marxian economics, and among the approaches taken, that of the Uno school was dominant. All the more interesting, therefore, is the process of its decomposition: in its second generation, the "vectoring effect of national service" overcame the asceticism of the founder; and it seems to have been inevitable that the system's own culminating demand for "analysis of current conditions" would prompt numbers of its adherents both to search out new venues for practice and adopt better (more "scientific") methods. In the economically uncertain and ideologically fluid years following 1945, this could credibly lead to an academic life with significant state and opposition-party involvement, as in the case of Ōuchi Tsutomu. But the long-run consequence (which the career of the left-Keynesian Tsuru Shigeto also revealed) was that a commitment to social equity contributed more directly to the formulation of policies of growth above all, or in the third generation to Baba Hiroji's schizophrenic vindication of Japanese enterprise. To address, let alone redress, the costs of that growth in turn, Uno's system as such availed little. Tamanoi Yoshirō found that its basic principles worked as a conceptual straightjacket, and respectfully set them aside; students on the radical left used (or abused) its scientistic portrayal of an implacable capitalist metasubject as a license for self-justifying violence against the putative agents of that capitalism.

One is tempted to see in this result the makings of a supreme irony. If Uno-school Marxism was appropriated by elements of the radical left as a weapon in the critique of Japanese monopoly capital and its educational apparatus, it was also the case that among the chief targets of its protests was none other than Maruyama Masao.[5] Uno had set out to construct a scientific political economy from which all self-seeking ideology had been excised; this was in order to safeguard the domain of practice from false promises of guaranteed political success. In contrast to Uno's "objectivism," Maruyama's "subjectivist" grail was democratic mass citizenship grounded in a viable ethos of personal responsibility. The result of their convergence should have been a politically mature, morally vibrant, independent left—not to speak of a discerning and critical social science capable of grappling with postwar conditions. Instead, it is as if these two great shapers of Japan's postwar social science had been forced into combat in a distorting mirror, the image and intentions of each thinker rendered virtually unrecognizable.

This is not a call to rest in nostalgia for the age of great men, nor simply to arraign the radical student left for its antiintellectualism or generational rebellion. A mirror, however flawed, is after all a mirror—of something. In this case, the targets were badly and unfairly chosen, but the question of who was responsible for Japan's not-so-distant past, and therefore the present, was legitimate. The point, rather, is to suggest that in the collisions of the late 1960s, the way may have been cleared for a more consequential co-optation of both lines of social science thought. This co-optation took shape in a series of overdetermined alignments and equivalences: universal, scientific, and objective on the one hand, with particular, ideological, and subjective on the other. In contrast to the *image* it projected of a capitalist demiurge, Uno's *method*, for its critics on the left, offered no more than an elaborate description, and was at best reformist. It could easily dovetail with and promote the advent of an ultrascientific economics, such as econometrics, and as such exemplify what Maruyama had castigated as "faith in theory."[6] This sort of "freedom from thought" was the polar opposite of what Maruyama imagined social science to be. In place of critical engagement came affirmation of the status quo; in place of Weberian agony—the human drama of trying to practice science and live as a political being at the same time—came an ideology called "the end of ideology." Science became a rationalization of the given, the universal a cover for the particular, objectivity a guise of subjectivity.

Nor, on his side, was Maruyama's own thought spared. He had made his famous "bet on the sham of postwar democracy" in 1960, and lost. Unwilling to accept "income doubling" as a substitute or compensation, Maruyama was deferentially written off by those who had engineered that policy and supported it academically. As this was occurring, the first critique of Maruyama from the post-Anpo left was produced by Yoshimoto Takaaki (see chapter 7). At the end of the decade, Yamamoto Yoshitaka, a major figure in Zenkyōtō, followed up in *Chisei no hanran* (1969). In this polemic, the ethic of "doing" over "being" advanced in *Nihon no shisō* was turned against Maruyama, who stood accused of "retreating" into procedural formalism for refusing to accede to student demands for self-criticism. By clinging to the "being" of forms and structures, the argument ran, Maruyama had proven that his advocacy of revolutionary personal autonomy *(shutaisei)* and praxis was disingenuous.[7] The imputation of bad faith is, I think, ludicrous; but the "charge" that Maruyama attached greatest importance to argument (even knock-down-drag-out argument) following accepted rules, and simply refused any demand based on coercion, is perfectly true. The physical effects on Maruyama of his treatment by *enragé* students, as is well known, were quite damaging and hastened his retirement. This episode may also—though there is no direct textual evidence—have deepened his pessimism about the capacity for the conscious, revolutionary self-transformation of Japanese society.

At some level, for Maruyama the convulsions in the university system must have been inexplicable. His contempt for the "Nazi-like" behavior of those who attacked him was on the record; for him, there could be no stronger expression of disdain than that. It must have been a bitter thing to see his ideal of democracy as permanent revolution thus reduced. But the experience did not drive him into a defense of the status quo; his politics remained what they had been, that is, independent and left-internationalist (rather than loftily cosmopolitan). Instead, from that point and well into the 1980s, Maruyama's work was preoccupied with the "deep things" of Japan's history, in particular with what he successively termed the "prototype," "ancient substrate" *(kosō)*, and finally the basso ostinato, that operated in various dimensions of archaic Japanese consciousness.[8] Its effect was not to prevent change but to pattern it. "Change" was apprehended in terms of an élan of succession without end *(tsugi-*

tsugi to nariyuku ikioi) that seemed to work against a progressive, teleo-logical view of history. However, he remarked,

> The concept of a linear and continuous succession of generations [as of bloodline] or events, as symbolized in the phrase *tsugitsugi,* did not neces-sarily mean that the meaning of history is invested uniformly in each and every moment, and therefore did not necessarily exclude the recognition that there are stages or turning points in history. . . . The ancient substrate did not connote progress, but rather bears an uncanny resemblance to the notion, modeled on biological science, of evolution as a process of infinite adaptation. . . . What constitutes the core of the image of history in the "ancient substrate" is neither the past nor the future, but is nothing other than the "now."[9]

In the sphere of politics, Maruyama discerned a view of government *(matsurigoto)* conceived as service to a superior, that is, in terms of the "subjecthood" of the subject as such. Basing himself on Motoori Nori-naga's philological commentaries, Maruyama rejected Hirata Atsutane's influential notion that *matsurigoto* originated in the emperor's worship of the *kami,* stressing its originally human and political character: later constructions under the modern imperial system that prescinded from Hirata's view were in fact a perversion. The larger point, however, re-mains: that government is carried out on behalf of, not by, a monarch (or presumably a sovereign people) in whom legitimacy resides. The subject's relation to the state is conceived as a form of "contributionism." And because the source of legitimacy of the system is separated (as it was not in imperial Russia or China) from the actual possessor of power, Maru-yama argued that "revolution of the system is most unlikely to occur."[10]

In these explorations, Maruyama pushed the sources of "Japanese thought" further and further back in time, much as Yanagita Kunio pur-sued the "original Japanese" ever outward to the archipelagic periphery. "A century after Nietzsche babbled about the death of God," Maruyama observed, in its absolutization of the "now," Western historicism had in fact drawn strikingly close to Japanese sentiments *(jōkei).* "It may be," he wrote, "that the 'continuity in change' that distinguishes our historical consciousness has, in *that aspect* as well, been a factor in placing Japan at the forefront of the world's most advanced countries. Should we regard this paradox as yet another instance of 'the cunning of reason,' or as a comedy that is rapidly approaching its conclusion?"[11]

For posing this question, Maruyama was regarded by some inter-preters (including disappointed friends) as having made a virtual "return to Japan," including the shift toward valorization of the particular-as-natural that the term "return" implies. Such a view, I believe, obscures the central modalities of historical change in Maruyama's thinking. My sense is that until the end he retained, and if anything deepened, his intellectual commitment to the notion of necessary revolution. His answer to the question he posed was: Let us by all legitimate means hasten the "comedy's" end. The forms of political, historical, and ethical consciousness that Maruyama came to discuss in terms of sudden "welling up" from the historical (not social) depths, or of a submerged musical line breaking through as the dominant "theme," are no more than the reverse of the forms of political subjectivity that he hoped would emerge from, and promote, the process of democratic revolution in postwar Japan. Indeed, it was Maruyama's ongoing concern with democratic revolution as a world-historical process, his attempt to foster the development of a self-aware and self-activating mass citizenry in Japan, and his sense of the fearsome obstacles to that development, that determined his turn to the ancient and "deep things" of consciousness. The subterranean continuities that Maruyama drew from the traces of Japanese historical, ethical, and political discourse were meaningful not so much in themselves but in terms of their implications for the possibility, or otherwise, of revolutionary transformation. It was the "universal" that gave meaning to the "particular," movement to stasis, and utopia to "reality."

It will not satisfy every critic to be told that the later Maruyama was increasingly pessimistic, that he wrote of the "ancient substrate" out of desperately disappointed hopes. The sympathetic (or optimistic) will note that Maruyama's final major work, his exposition of Fukuzawa's *Outline of a Theory of Civilization* (1986), is in the manner of a *ressourcement*.[12] But though the intellectual struggle might continue, the world had changed. Compared to the 1960 Anpo, the end-of-decade protests and violence were premised on acceptance of the argument that Japan's postwar democracy was not just a sham, but one not worth even the paradoxical defense—"it is real because it is a fiction"—that Maruyama had mounted. Or, worse, as the decades of growth wore on, it was taken as a given, unproblematic reality.

One line of conservative post-Maruyama commentators—let us call them the "*ie* society faction"—would simply say that his pessimism was an elitist luxury, that Maruyama ought to have appreciated the "good things" in Japanese tradition and evaluated Japan's modernity more highly. For them, Maruyama was a Eurocentric modernist who should have been another Watsuji Tetsurō or Tanabe Hajime or Kōsaka Masaaki. For such writers, Maruyama could be forgiven his dwelling in the shadows; even if in a minor key, he recognized Japan's ontological particularity after all.

A more radical line of critics is represented by Yamanouchi Yasushi, who seeks to replace a "stage" (and class) paradigm of historical analysis with one based on "systems"; the process of mobilization for total war, in Yamanouchi's view, was all-important in accelerating the transition from class to system society in Japan. Yamanouchi argues that beginning with Maruyama's wartime writings (particularly the final chapter of his *Studies in the Intellectual History of Tokugawa Japan*), Maruyama essentially pursued a rationalization of nationalism, a project held to be continuous across the divide of 1945. And in a sense it was: as Maruyama wrote in "Nationalism in Japan" (1951), "nationalism must be rationalized in the same degree that democracy is irrationalized." If we hold only to the first clause, we do encounter a Maruyama "complicit" in the formation of the postwar order. Indeed Yamanouchi has described Maruyama (among others) as a "thinker of the 1955 system."[13] But what about the "irrationalization of democracy"? It seems to me ill-advised to sever the two themes when discussing Maruyama, and that there is no warrant for ascribing greater weight to the former over the latter in assessing his thought or the character of postwar modernism. This is especially important because of the crucial role played by resistance to illegitimate authority in Maruyama's conception of citizenship. This is doubtless a matter for debate, but my belief is that a moment of resistance to such authority was never absent from Maruyama's thought. The operation of political judgment for Maruyama, as with conscience for Ōtsuka Hisao, did not, could not, lead only to spontaneous or autonomous obedience. Otherwise the very notion of subjective autonomy was truly a sham.

Clearly, however, Maruyama *was* a thinker of the nation: it was the modal form of political existence in the world he experienced, studied, and imagined. To be sure, he regarded "Japaneseness" as an ethnic identity, overwhelmingly dominant, within the political territory called Japan. But it should go without saying that he was viscerally suspicious of any appeals to "blood" or other primordial ties as the unmediated basis for unity or collective action. And he was for that reason a thinker of the state, which he believed had become the general condition for social continuity in the contemporary world.[14] (It is also true that the citizen-subject of the state as Maruyama imagined it was male, albeit ascetically so.) Finally, Maruyama was—or became—a thinker of culture, and especially of cultures in contact. "The West" and "Japan" were real to him, if contradictory within themselves, but in any case not simply nominalist phantasms. For Maruyama, Japan's modern intellectual history was defined by the cultural rupture of Westernization; this was itself the first act in the drama of universalization.[15] Whatever and however many the shared predicaments of modernity may be, the cultural cleavage experienced by Japan and other nations outside the West decisively differentiated their histories from those of Euro-America. The legacies of that rupture—and of the asymmetries of power that engendered it— were ineradicable. And there was, enduringly in Maruyama's thought, the despairing sense that the patterned recurrence of a historical consciousness that recognized only "the eternal now" might never be "overcome." It may not be wrong to see in this despair a highly sophisticated and refined expression of that same stubborn particularism that both defined and bemused the main line of Japanese Marxists. But Maruyama was enough of a neo-Kantian to believe that even in such a situation, a space could be opened between power and culture (or between politics and identity) in which a genuinely universal social science—a systematic knowledge "of the Other as Other"—could be sought and found.

DEVELOPMENTAL ALIENATION RECONSIDERED

Was Japan—Meiji Japan, modern Japan—developmentally alienated? As the subject/object of social science produced by Japanese thinkers and writers, was Japan alienated from the model states and model societies that constituted the already developed world? I hope I have shown that this was the case. But perhaps the question itself is badly posed. To look to "model states" or "model countries" as totalities, to be driven by a collective consciousness of "catching up," is already to be developmentally alienated. The model country is more than a falsely concretized utopia. As the internalization of an imputed external standard of judgment or "gaze," it bespeaks and enacts a sense of compromised agency, a sense that the nation's fate is not entirely in the nation's hands. And this condition has by no means been unique to Japan.

In concluding the historical overview of Japanese social science presented in chapter 2, I characterized it as a plurality, rather than a pluralism, of uncertain significance: neither a "Japan-West" nor "Japan-Asia" framework seems to account for the contemporary orientations of social science practice. The most powerful currents of social science thought, first the Marxist and then the modernist, lost cohesion. Captured by great visions of modern transformation, their exponents ended as

Minerva's owls. That is a title to be worn with honor, in my opinion. And in any case, in their most active periods both Maruyama Masao and Uno Kōzō were nothing if not hotly engaged with the present.

But when did the owl fly? Consider the following remark by Maruyama, from 1962: "It is undeniable that through the atrophy of the overwhelming model states [the United States and the Soviet Union], the history of longing for and disillusionment with foreign nations in Japan's quest to bring herself up to the level of other states has completed its own circle. What will come of this experience belongs to the realm of prophecy."[16] The evidence accumulates that the closing of the circle occurred over the decade of the 1960s. The disappearance, more or less, of the peasantry as a category removed the salience of much of received social theory; the huge boom in industrial production and transformation of urban society set the national life on a new axis, disclosing new sorts of social friction and conflict. Both intellectually and in terms of political allegiance, the "sons" of the left turned against its "fathers," a fragmentation that opened the way for a reconsolidation of conservative nationalism. And with it—aided in part by a perfectly legitimate rethinking of the Tokugawa era and its legacies—came the ideological rehabilitation of the past as a preparation for successful modern nationhood. In the years after 1945, the "history of longing for and disillusionment with foreign nations" of which Maruyama speaks was bound to be foreshortened.

It should be obvious that I do not regard recent "Japanist" or "culturalist" perspectives as a viable alternative to either Marxism or modernism, that is, as a "solution" to the condition of developmental alienation, or as the realization of what Maruyama had left to the realm of prophecy. To be sure, Nakane Chie and Murakami Yasusuke addressed issues and explored domains far beyond what Yanagita Kunio defined as the ambit of nativist ethnology. But the main problem is that such perspectives are essentially overdetermined and selective mobilizations of social data filtered through a single phase of postwar political economy; they are symptoms rather than analyses of the phenomena they treat. The social history of Japan must, as far as it bears on the near past or present, explain not only "success," but "failure," presuming that some consensus on the substance of these notions can be arrived at. Certainly "failure" sets the tone of contemporary discussion, but one cannot escape the feeling of déjà vu.

Once the broader charge of trying to form a more integral understanding is taken up, the contours of Japan's version of developmental alienation, and a few hints of its future, emerge rather clearly. And those contours are tantalizing. Something of what they suggest is conveyed in a recent observation by the historian W. G. Beasley. Distilling decades of reflection on the "Japanese experience," Beasley writes:

> So great a transformation as that which occurred after 1868 has inevitably carried with it many unintended results. In matters that might be called "consumer choice," they have left Japan more "western" now than it ever was Chinese. One difference, indeed, between the ancient and modern is that what was alien in the distant past was for the few, what is alien in the present is almost universal. Only feudalism, which dominates the centuries in between, seems in retrospect—not in all respects justifiably—to be thoroughly Japanese. Perhaps that is why its influence lingers.[17]

Beasley's remarks are of interest not only because he applies the designation "feudal" to the Tokugawa era. If feudalism was what seemed "in retrospect . . . to be thoroughly Japanese," its lingering influence would also, one surmises, account for Japan's response to developmental alienation: neotraditionalism à la Itō Hirobumi and its critical mirror, Kōza-ha Marxism. These, as we have seen, were expressions of particularism, the sense of a persistent "something" that gave such a distinctive shape to Japan's capitalism and its modern industrial and political regime. That is how Beasley seems to see the matter; hence his intriguing comment that in contrast with feudalism, which is indisputably indigenous, "what is alien in the present is almost universal." One wonders, naturally, how long the "almost universal" alien will remain so, or if it really is so alien even now. Can origins never be "forgotten"?

As to feudalism too, there is a further point to consider. From the time of Marx onward—including observations by Marc Bloch and Perry Anderson, and Umesao Tadao as well—Japan has been taken to constitute (in Anderson's words) the one and only "historical site of an authentic feudalism" outside that of Europe.[18] And that was important, needless to say, because however one felt about the particular versions of stage theory advanced within the Marxian tradition, there was little doubt that in some manner, feudalism had *produced* capitalism. It was the author, via a series of complex mediations and fortuities, of modernity itself. Now, Anderson goes on to qualify his argument with a set of remarks on the historical limitations of Japanese feudalism, stressing that "the fundamental impetus for [Japan's] tempestuous transition to the capitalist mode of production in the late nineteenth and early twentieth century was *exogenous*. It was the impact of Western imperialism on Japanese feudalism that suddenly galvanized internal forces into a total transformation of the traditional order. The depth of these changes was in no way already within reach of the Tokugawa realm."[19] The issue is not, and has never been, how Japan (to speak anachronistically) went from the Third World to the first. It is, as Thomas C. Smith put it, to explain how "traditional" Japan became wealthy enough to industrialize in the capitalist mode, in the sense of translating "gains in output . . . into gains in per capita income"; and to grasp the particular conditions created by the combination of competencies, opportunities, and terrific pressures associated with the opening of the country.[20]

This irruption of the exogenous into *Japanese* history led to an immense and rapid transformation that continues to reverberate in the contemporary world. The significance of feudalism to this transformation was not (only) that it provided "preconditions" that would disappear once their work was done. Instead, feudalism was reproduced as a condition and strategy of alienated development. We may call this an "invented" tradition, so long as we are not led to slight the importance of received, actual social and economic structures that were not dismantled, but revalued. The larger point would seem to be that if Japan's development into capitalism was alienated, that alienation was due to what had made Japan similar to its most advanced developmental models long before 1868. The result, on both sides of the Japan-West framework, was a tendency to magnify, even absolutize, observed differences-within-likeness. And this is no less true of the politically tenuous Japan-Asia framework of more recent vintage, in which Japan has assumed the position of model state. In either case, this more or less willing misrecognition, in turn, and again on both sides, has generated a seemingly bottomless narcissism.

ENVOY

Narcissism, yes: but only that? After all, narcissism is only a hairbreadth's distance from self-knowledge. It is not a stage but a recurrent pattern—dare one say, an "ancient substrate" or basso obstinato—in the history of the interaction of peoples. If the formation of social science has any significance, it must surely lie in its knowing, methodical challenge to the collective narcissism that is the lifeblood of the modern national state, perhaps of all modern identities. "Complicity" in the production of self-vindicating knowledge, that is, narcissism, is the risk of any institutionalized intellectual enterprise. That risk rises with proximity to power, along with the corresponding degree of responsibility to acknowledge its consequences. The capacity of mobilized social science to "arrange" the lives of masses of people in accordance with a set of categories is, to be sure, not infinite, but it is great enough to have troubled the minds of Lavrov and Weber. Even with the best of wills and the maximum effort at rigor, the results can never be known in advance; human society is simply too refractory for that. Perhaps the only "law" that can be invoked would be that when the categories are corrupt, purely political, or nonnegotiable by those affected, disaster will follow.

This book began with a Russian parable, Tolstoy's story of Sergei Koznyshev, a social scientist who embraces the nation as a compensation for the failure of his own work to achieve a "revolution in science." One might be led by this story to think that the main problem for social science has been ineffectuality, that its methods and results have little or no bearing on the contemporary world. Tolstoy may have thought so. And to some degree it is true, at least at the level of the many individual practitioners who are the Koznyshevs of our institutions. But surely the more serious issue is to sort out the extremely complex causal links between "thought" (or "people thinking") and action. For this we need individuals, and they are, fortunately, always with us. Every important thinker (or social scientist) presents to the world a certain set of powerfully articulated ideas. Every such set is in fact a metonym, a concentrated expression of more generalized attitudes, beliefs, and dispositions, that in turn reacts upon them to create the possibility of new thought, new action. Such, for example, is the relation of *Capital* to the *Communist Manifesto*, and more broadly of the socialist and labor movement to capital itself on the one hand, and to socialism in power on the other. "Marx" becomes metonymic, "a beacon on the reefs" that says, "come this way" or "steer clear."[21]

However complex the mediations by which its effects are felt, social science is never innocuous. In a world dependent upon institutionalized expertise, the legislator can never yield entirely to the interpreter; to put it another way, as an expert, the interpreter can never not also legislate. Koznyshev was Tolstoy's straw man. And more than that, he was a false clue, a dodge. This or that social scientist may seem irrelevant, but in fact, collectively, the enterprise is responsible for a great deal. To say that after all, "we" social scientists—whether as intellectuals or functionaries—are powerless before history is merely to relieve ourselves of the fear that we may have done harm. The "good" that social science may do lies in enlarging collective self-understanding, by addressing "the other as Other" and by making an "Other" of self. Such work depends on category and method; it cannot take an irreducible, ontological group identity as its starting and ending point. Presenting such work to the public may or may not conduce to its unity. It may or may not sharpen its conflicts. For this reason, it is certainly unrealistic to suppose that there should be a Hippocratic oath for social scientists. But we must always ask whether our work has contributed to the dangerous tendency of modern institutions of all kinds to reify or essentialize identity. Our only "salvation"—let us not laugh at this—lies in having a transparent, communicable method. This is our only means to help society unlock its capacity for self-transformation and renewal.

Notes

1. L. N. Tolstoy, *Anna Karenin*, trans. Rosemary Edmonds (Harmondsworth, U.K.: Penguin, 1978), pt. 1, section 7 (p. 37).

2. Ibid., pt. 3, section 1 (pp. 257ff).

3. Ibid., pt. 3, section 26 (pp. 350–51).

4. Ibid., pt. 8, section 1 (pp. 803–6).

5. Ibid., p. 804.

6. Ibid., p. 805. Koznyshev's turn to the nation will be recognizable as a prototype of what in Japanese is termed *"tenkō"*: the renunciation of the left, or at least of universalistic commitments (generally under duress but with a voluntary moment as well), followed by an emotional and spiritual reunion with the "national community."

7. Edward Wasiolek, *Tolstoy's Major Fiction* (Chicago: University of Chicago Press, 1978), ch. 6; and Isaiah Berlin, *The Hedgehog and the Fox* (1953) (New York: Touchstone Books ed., n.d.).

8. "Social science . . . is an enterprise of the modern world . . . [whose] roots lie in the attempt, full-blown since the sixteenth century, and part and parcel of the construction of our modern world, to develop systematic, secular knowledge about reality that is somehow validated empirically." Immanuel Wallerstein et al., *Open the Social Sciences* (Stanford: Stanford University Press, 1996), p. 2.

9. Heinrich Heine, *Religion and Philosophy in Germany*, trans. J. Snodgrass (1833–52; reprint, Boston: Beacon Press, 1959), pp. 106–9.

10. Ibid.

11. See Immanuel Wallerstein, *Unthinking Social Science: The Limits of Nineteenth-Century Paradigms* (London: Polity Press, 1991), pp. 18–20.

12. "The Puritan wanted to work in a calling; we are forced to do so." Max

Weber, *The Protestant Ethic and the Spirit of Capitalism* (1921; reprint, New York: Scribner's, 1974), p. 181.

13. Gapon is quoted in Marshall Berman, *All That Is Solid Melts into Air: The Experience of Modernity* (New York: Penguin, 1988), p. 250.

14. Ota Šik, *The Third Way: Marxist Leninist Theory and Modern Industrial Society*, trans. Marian Sling (London: Wildwood House, 1976), p. 15.

15. As articulated, for example, by the Japanese economist Masamura Kimihiro:

> 'Social science' has, to date, influenced people's understanding of society, determined the shape of the social movement, and changed the social system itself. The ideology of 'faith in science' and the 'necessitarian view of history' has exercised great power of social mobilization, distorting the developmental tendencies of history, and engendering needless sacrifices on a scale that beggars the imagination. This fact must number among the grandest paradoxes of the twentieth century. The very 'social efficacy' of the 'necessitarian view of history' is now laying bare the fatal error of that view.

Masamura Kimihiro, "Shakaiteki kōka kara mita Nihon no shakai kagaku," in *Shakai kagaku no genba*, vol. 4 of *Iwanami kōza: Shakai kagaku no hōhō*, ed. Yamanouchi Yasushi et al. (Tokyo: Iwanami Shoten, 1993), p. 68.

16. For example, see Philippe Ariès, *Centuries of Childhood: A Social History of Family Life* (New York: Vintage, 1962), p. 415: "The concept of family, the concept of class, and perhaps elsewhere the concept of race, appear as manifestations of the same intolerance toward variety, the same insistence on uniformity."

17. Robert Heilbroner, *The Nature and Logic of Capitalism* (New York: W. W. Norton, 1985), p. 24.

18. "No previous historical system has ever been based on a theory of progress, indeed a theory of inevitable progress." Immanuel Wallerstein, "Culture as the Ideological Battleground of the Modern World System," *Hitotsubashi Journal of Social Studies*, no. 21 (1989): 9. On normality of change, see Wallerstein, *Unthinking Social Science*, pp. 15–17.

19. For this reason, the argument over what might be called "natural categories" remains a furious one. Thinkers who were prepared to see society or polity as a collectively produced, vital fiction might well exempt other identities and relations from such consideration. The Japanese Confucian philosopher Ogyū Sorai's exemption of the father-son relation *(fushi no gi)* from his category of "invention" is a prime example. See Maruyama Masao, *Studies in the Intellectual History of Tokugawa Japan* (Princeton: Princeton University Press; Tokyo: Tokyo University Press, 1974), p. 213.

20. Karl Marx, *Grundrisse: Foundations of the Critique of Political Economy* (rough draft) trans. Martin Nicolaus (Harmondsworth, U.K.: Penguin, 1973), p. 164.

21. See Berman, *All That Is Solid*, p. 111.

22. "The forces of the market act on each individual capital as a law, i.e., as compulsion from without. Unlike the laws of nature, however, this law is formed by the activity of men themselves who work under the command of each individual capital. Thus men are governed by a law that they themselves create." Uno Kōzō, *Principles of Political Economy*, trans. Thomas T. Sekine (London and Atlantic Highlands, N.J.: Harvester/Humanities Press, 1977), p. 27.

23. Derek Sayer, *Capitalism and Modernity: An Excursus on Marx and Weber* (London: Routledge, 1991), p. 155.

24. Ibid., p. 106.

25. "Change is not progress. That sounds very trivial and self-evident. To express this triviality openly, however, is perhaps to put one's finger in an open wound of our time." Wilhelm Windelband, "Kritische oder genetische Methode?" in id., *Präludien*, 3rd ed. (Tübingen: J. C. B. Mohr [Paul Siebeck], 1907), p. 338.

26. P. L. (Pyotr Lavrovich) Lavrov, *Historical Letters* (1869), trans. J. P. Scanlan (Berkeley and Los Angeles: University of California Press, 1967), pp. 135, 139.

27. "The last great movement of intellectuals which, though not sustained by a uniform faith, shared enough basic elements to approximate a religion was the Russian revolutionary intelligentsia, in which patrician, academic and aristocratic intellectuals stood next to plebeian ones." Max Weber, *Economy and Society: Outline of Interpretive Sociology*, trans. Guenther Roth and Claus Wittich (Berkeley and Los Angeles: University of California Press, 1978), pp. 515–16.

28. I owe this formulation to Hashimoto Mitsuru (Sociology Dept., Kōnan Women's University), personal communication.

29. Alexander Herzen wrote: "It is possible that for correctness in judging affairs which are outside the competence of either a police court or arithmetical verification, *partiality* is more necessary than justice. Passion may not only blind, but may also penetrate more deeply into the object, embrace it in its own fire and be blind to everything else." Alexander Herzen, *My Past and Thoughts: The Memoirs of Alexander Herzen* (Berkeley and Los Angeles: University of California Press, 1982), pp. 492–93; emphasis in original.

30. Dwight Macdonald, "Appendix: Marx vs. Herzen," in *My Past and Thoughts: The Memoirs of Alexander Herzen* (Berkeley and Los Angeles: University of California Press, 1982), p. 678.

31. Perry Anderson, preface to *Marxism, Wars, and Revolutions: Essays from Four Decades,* by Isaac Deutscher (London: Verso, 1984), p. xx.

32. On the leaps in productivity brought about through the deepening of the division of labor under succeeding technological regimes, see Heilbroner, *Nature and Logic of Capitalism,* esp. pp. 154–56, 160, 164, 170, 174.

33. John Maynard Keynes, *The General Theory of Employment, Interest, and Money* (1936; reprint, London: Macmillan and Co., 1961), pp. 383–84.

34. Max Weber, "'Objectivity' in Social Science and Social Policy" (1904), in id., *The Methodology of the Social Sciences*, trans. Edward Shils and H. H. Finch (New York: The Free Press, 1949), esp. pp. 72–81. Emphasis in original.

35. Jeffrey Bergner, *The Origin of Formalism in Social Science* (Chicago: University of Chicago Press, 1981), p. 89.

36. Alain Touraine, *Return of the Actor: Social Theory in Postindustrial Society* (Minneapolis: University of Minnesota Press, 1988), p. 68; on the definition of industrial versus postindustrial society, see pp. 104ff.

37. Touraine, *Return,* p. 40. Note that Touraine contrasts "history" as meaning "metasocial" and "teleological" to "historicity," which refers to the stakes of conflict within society.

38. Clifford Geertz, *Local Knowledge: Further Essays in Interpretive Anthropology* (New York: Basic Books, 1983), pp. 19, 23.

39. Zygmunt Bauman, *Legislators and Interpreters: On Modernity, Post-Modernity, and Intellectuals* (Ithaca: Cornell University Press, 1987). Page references are given in the text.

40. See Sayer, *Capitalism and Modernity*, pp. 46–49; Sidney Pollard, *Peaceful Conquest: The Industrialization of Europe, 1760–1970* (Oxford: Oxford University Press, 1992), pp. 45, 122, 131, 184–90, 207–15.

41. This is the position of "diffusionism." And we note that diffusion may not be all one way, from core to periphery. Consider the phenomenon, limited to be sure, of Maoism among revolutionary Western intellectuals such as Sartre.

42. Sayer, *Capitalism and Modernity*, pp. 114, 155.

43. See Weber, *Economy and Society*, pp. 24–26, 85–86, 483. I am grateful to Robert Bellah for his assistance as I composed this and the following paragraph.

44. On substantive rationality, see also Ralf Dahrendorf, *Life Chances: Approaches to Social and Political Theory* (Chicago: University of Chicago Press, 1979), pp. 62–74. "Warring gods" comes from Max Weber, "Science as a Vocation" (1918); longer quote from id., "Politics as a Vocation" (1918), both in *From Max Weber: Essays in Sociology*, ed. Hans Gerth and C. Wright Mills (New York: Oxford University Press, 1958), pp. 153 and 128, respectively. See also Wladyslaw Bienkowski, *Theory and Reality* (London: Busby and Allen, 1982), ch. 6, for a critique of Weber, stressing the distinction between economic and bureaucratic organizations.

45. Karl Marx, *Capital*, vol. 1 (Harmondsworth, U.K.: Penguin, 1990), p. 926; Barrington Moore, *Social Origins of Dictatorship and Democracy: Lord and Peasant in the Making of the Modern World* (Boston: Beacon Press, 1966), p. 29. Note, however, Sayer's comment: "Whatever his growing doubts, Marx remained a modernist to the end, impatient with those 'prophets facing backwards' who sought the salvation of 'civilization with all its evils' in 'digging up again from the rubbish' of the pre-capitalist past." *Capitalism and Modernity*, p. 22, quoting Marx in 1855. See also Uno, *Principles*, p. xxi.

46. Derek Sayer's expression. See *Capitalism and Modernity*, p. 110.

47. Weber, *Protestant Ethic*, p. 17.

48. Alexander Gerschenkron, *Economic Backwardness in Historical Perspective* (Cambridge, Mass.: Harvard University Press, 1962), pp. 24–25. See also Madhavan K. Palat, "What is Left of Marxism in Russian History," in *Was bleibt von marxistischen Perspektiven in der Geschichtsforschung?* ed. Alf Lüdtke (Göttingen: Wallstein Verlag, 1997), esp. pp. 76, 79–80, 85–86, 89–90.

49. Gerschenkron, *Economic Backwardness in Historical Perspective*, pp. 25–26.

50. Pollard, *Peaceful Conquest*, pp. vii, 31, 45, 130–31, 184–90, 207–15, 213.

51. Alexander Gerschenkron, *Europe in the Russian Mirror* (Cambridge: Cambridge University Press, 1970), p. 73.

52. Maurice Meisner observes: "However one wishes to interpret Mao's view of the 'sprouts' *(meng-ya)* of an indigenous capitalism in traditional China that proved abortive, he quite clearly viewed modern capitalist relationships intro-

duced by imperialism, if not as an unnatural phenomenon, then certainly as an alien one—and in no sense the historical prerequisite for socialism." Meisner, *Marxism, Maoism, and Utopianism* (Madison: University of Wisconsin Press, 1982), pp. 57–58.

53. This has not been the case with Marxist social scientists only—witness the long career of the American-educated sociologist Fei Hsiao-t'ung (Fei Xiaotong). Social research, he said in 1937, provides "a practical means for controlling social change . . . not by 'isms' but [by] factual knowledge." Quoted in David Arkush, *Fei Xiaotong and Sociology in Revolutionary China* (Cambridge, Mass.: Council on East Asian Studies, Harvard University, 1981), pp. 55–56. These notes courtesy Mark Metzler.

54. I owe thanks to Harry Harootunian for this formulation.

55. See Thomas R. H. Havens, *Valley of Darkness: The Japanese People and World War Two* (New York: W. W. Norton, 1978), for such a treatment.

56. The following discussion focuses more on the early phases of Japan's imperial modernity than on the later issue of continuity vs. discontinuity in the shaping of the post-1945 order. The two questions are obviously related, and the relation is treated at considerable length in subsequent chapters.

57. Phrase from English-language editorial in *Asahi shinbun* (Osaka), 26 Aug. 1918.

58. These problems were especially important in view of the heavily racial element in the evolutionary views of social development prevalent at the time of Japan's exposure to the West. See Kenneth Pyle, *The New Generation in Meiji Japan* (Stanford: Stanford University Press, 1969); Akira Nagazumi, "The Diffusion of the Idea of Social Darwinism in East and Southeast Asia," *Historia Scientiarum* 24 (1983).

59. Wada Haruki, "Nihonjin no Roshia-kan: Sensei, teki; tomo ni kurushimu mono," in *Roshia to Nihon: Nisso rekishigaku shinpojiumu*, ed. Fujiwara Akira (Tokyo: Sairyūsha, 1985), pp. 11–32.

60. Martin Jay, *Marxism and Totality: The Adventures of a Concept from Lukács to Habermas* (Berkeley and Los Angeles: University of California Press, 1984), p. 86.

61. See the articles by Kurt Lenk and M. Rainer Lepsius in *Modern German Sociology*, ed. Volker Meja, Dieter Misgeld, and Nico Stehr (New York: Columbia University Press, 1987); also the (mildly) dissenting view of Harry Liebersohn, *Fate and Utopia in German Sociology, 1870–1923* (Cambridge, Mass.: MIT Press, 1988).

62. Andrzej Walicki, *A History of Russian Thought: From the Enlightenment to Marxism* (Stanford: Stanford University Press, 1979), pp. 92–114, 290–308; see also id., *The Slavophile Controversy* (South Bend, Ind.: University of Notre Dame Press, 1989); Alexander Vucinich, *Social Thought in Tsarist Russia: The Quest for a General Science of Society, 1861–1917* (Chicago: University of Chicago Press, 1976), pp. 96–106. These were thinkers, Walicki remarks, "to whom the term 'reactionary' can be applied without any additional explanations or reservations, thinkers who were reactionary both objectively and subjectively, from the point of view of the function as well as the content of their ideas." *A History of Russian Thought*, p. 291.

63. Tolstoy saw the Russian and Japanese governments in much the same light while striving to identify the Russian people with the Chinese. In a letter to a Chinese correspondent written during the Russo-Japanese War he refers to the "madness and cruelty of both the Russian and Japanese governments . . . revealed in their true, revolting light. . . . God save China from going the way of Japan." In *Tolstoy's Letters*, ed. R. F. Christian, vol. 2 (New York: Scribner's, 1978), pp. 653–54.

64. See Akamatsu Katsumaro, "The Russian Impact on the Early Japanese Social Movement," in *The Russian Impact on Japan: Literature and Social Thought*, ed. and trans. Peter Berton, Paul Langer, and George O. Totten (Los Angeles: University of Southern California Press, 1981).

65. See Kojima Shūichi, *Roshia nōgyō shisōshi no kenkyū* (Kyoto: Mineruva Shobō, 1987), pp. 10, 15, 185; quote is from review of Kojima by Hinada Shizuma, in *Acta Slavica Iaponica*, Tomus VI (1988): 110. See also Isobe Toshihiko, "Chayanovu riron to Nihon ni okeru shōnō keizai kenkyū no kiseki," *Nōgyō keizai kenkyū* 62, no. 3 (1990): 153–65. This reference courtesy Kojima Shūichi.

66. Itō Hirobumi, "Some Reminiscences of the Grant of the New Constitution," in *Fifty Years of New Japan*, ed. Okuma Shigenobu, vol. 1 (New York: Dutton, 1909), pp. 122–32.

67. See Christopher Read, *From Tsar to Soviets: The Russian People and Their Revolution* (Oxford: Oxford University Press, 1996).

68. See V. I. Lenin, "The Fall of Port Arthur" (Jan. 1905), in id., *Collected Works*, vol. 8 (London: Lawrence and Wishart, 1962), pp. 47–55. See also in this connection the concluding comments of N. A. Levitskii, *Russko-Yaponskaya voina* (Moscow: Gosudarstvennoe Voennoe Izdatel'stvo, 1935). Extending Lenin's perspective, Levitskii saw the historical positions of Japan and the Soviet Union as reversed. Tsarism, backward and stagnant, had enabled a historically "progressive" Japan; following 1917 and particularly the economic crisis of the late 1920s, a strong and revolutionary Soviet Union would if necessary challenge a weakened Japan, whose domestic conditions "have much in common with those of Russia prior to the Russo-Japanese conflict." The Japanese should know, Levitskii concluded, that this coming war would bring the "Tsushima of the feudal-capitalist regime of their country" (pp. 303–7).

CHAPTER 2. THE SOCIAL SCIENCES IN MODERN JAPAN

1. The classic statement is Fukuzawa Yukichi's "Datsu-A ron" (Mar. 1885); *Fukuzawa Yukichi zenshū*, vol. 10 (Tokyo: Iwanami Shoten, 1960), pp. 238–40.

2. See Ishida Takeshi, *Nihon no shakai kagaku* (Tokyo: Tokyo Daigaku Shuppankai, 1984), ch. 1; Maruyama Masao and Katō Shūichi, *Honyaku to Nihon no kindai* (Tokyo: Iwanami Shinsho, 1998).

3. Alexander Gerschenkron, *Economic Backwardness in Historical Perspective* (Cambridge, Mass.: Harvard University Press, 1962), pp. 24–25.

4. Ronald P. Dore, *Shinohata: Portrait of a Japanese Village* (New York: Pantheon, 1978), p. 228.

5. Quotes from Hozumi Nobushige, *Ancestor Worship and Japanese Law* (Tokyo: Z. P. Maruya, 1901), p. 9 (emphasis added); Maruyama Masao, "Nationalism in Japan: Its Theoretical Background and Prospects" (1951), in id., *Thought*

and Behavior in Modern Japanese Politics (New York: Oxford University Press, 1969), p. 145.

6. Ishida, *Nihon no shakai kagaku*, p. 40.

7. Ōshima Sadamasu, *Jōseiron* (1896), in *Meiji bunka zenshū*, ed. Yoshino Sakuzō, vol. 9 (Tokyo: Nihon Hyōronsha, 1929), pp. 462, 464.

8. Kenneth Pyle, "The Advantages of Followership: German Economics and Japanese Bureaucrats, 1890–1925," *Journal of Japanese Studies* 1, no. 1 (fall 1974): 127–64; Ishida, *Nihon no shakai kagaku*, pp. 51–71.

9. See Kawamura Nozomu, *Sociology and Society of Japan* (London: Kegan Paul International, 1994), pp. 46–50; Ishida, *Nihon no shakai kagaku*, pp. 45–50.

10. See Kawamura Nozomu, *Nihon shakaigakushi kenkyū*, vol. 2 (Tokyo: Ningen no Kagakusha, 1975), pp. 6–11.

11. Yanagita Kunio, *Jidai to nōsei* (1910), in *Teihon Yanagita Kunio shū*, vol. 16 (Tokyo: Chikuma Shobō, 1964), p. 39.

12. On Yanagita's opposition to shrine mergers, as well as his hesitancy to take direct political action against them, see his frequently contentious correspondence with the ethnographer and botanist Minakata Kumagusu (1867–1941) in Iikura Shōhei, ed., *Yanagita Kunio/Minakata Kumagusu ōfuku shokanshū*, 2 vols. (Tokyo: Heibonsha, 1994).

13. See Tominaga Ken'ichi, "Sengo Nihon no shakai kagaku ni okeru paradaimu no sōkoku to sono shūen," in *Yuragi no naka no shakai kagaku*, vol. 1 of *Iwanami kōza: Shakai kagaku no hōhō*, ed. Yamanouchi Yasushi et al. (Tokyo: Iwanami Shoten, 1993), esp. pp. 332, 363–64. Yanagita's empirical methods were also emulated by Kon Wajirō (1888–1973), who literally walked the country from end to end, making detailed drawings and sketches of rural houses. The nostalgia provoked by Kon's *Nihon no minka* (1922) was palpable. Yanagita seems to have been dissatisfied, however, with Kon's focus on the mere "vessels"—*utsuwa*—of popular life. More consequentially, the Kantō earthquake forcibly drew Kon's attention to Tokyo and its reconstruction, decisively turning him to what he called "modernology" *(kōgengaku)* and leading to his final "expulsion" from the ranks of Yanagita's followers.

14. See Yanagita Kunio, *Kyōdo seikatsu no kenkyūhō* (1935) and *Minkan denshō ron* (1934), in *Teihon Yanagita Kunio shū*, vol. 25 (Tokyo: Chikuma Shobō, 1964). See also Stephen Vlastos, ed., *Mirror of Modernity: Invented Traditions of Modern Japan* (Berkeley and Los Angeles: University of California Press, 1998), esp. the essays by Hashimoto Mitsuru and Harry Harootunian.

15. The critical literature on Yanagita is an industry in itself. Two important recent summations include Kawada Minoru, *Yanagita Kunio no shisōshiteki kenkyū* (Tokyo: Miraisha, 1985); and Kajiki Gō, *Yanagita Kunio no shisō* (Tokyo: Keisō Shobō, 1990).

16. See P. L. Lavrov, *Iz istorii sotsial'nykh uchenii* (From the history of social doctrines) (Petrograd: Kolos', 1919), p. 51, quoted in Alexander Vucinich, *Social Thought in Tsarist Russia: The Quest for a General Science of Society, 1861–1917* (Chicago: University of Chicago Press, 1976), p. 27:

> Real sociology is socialism. The theoretical study of social questions shows invariably the need for activities aimed at the transformation of society. It is impossible to understand the facts of social life without trying to give the course of that life a particular

direction. He who limits himself to a mere understanding of facts shows by that very fact that he does not understand them. Social facts are in essence the sum total of individual contributions to the transformation of the structure of society from what it is to what it ought to be.

17. See Itō Hirobumi, "Some Reminiscences of the Grant of the New Constitution," in *Fifty Years of New Japan,* ed. Ōkuma Shigenobu, vol. 1 (New York: Dutton, 1909), p. 130: "The opinions prevailing in the country [after 1868] were extremely heterogeneous, and often diametrically opposed to each other . . . [but] at that time we had not yet arrived at the stage of distinguishing clearly between political opposition on the one hand and treason to the established order on the other."

18. Onozuka was also one of the "Seven Doctors" *(Shichi hakase),* hawks led by Tomizu Hiroto who broke precedent in 1903 with a public call for a "hard" policy against tsarist Russia. The government's attempt to punish the group and enforce conformity among its civil servants led to the first concerted defense of academic autonomy at the university.

19. See Minobe Tatsukichi, *Kenpō kōwa* (1912; reprint, Tokyo: Yūhikaku, 1918); id., *Nihon kenpō* (Tokyo: Yūhikaku, 1921); and id., *Kenpō satsuyō* (Tokyo: Yūhikaku, 1922); and Yoshino Sakuzō, *Yoshino Sakuzō hyōronshū,* ed. Oka Yoshitake (Tokyo: Iwanami Bunko, 1975); Iida Taizō, *Hihan seishin no kōseki* (Tokyo: Chikuma Shobō, 1997), esp. ch. 7.

20. Rōyama Masamichi, *Nihon ni okeru kindai seijigaku no hattatsu* (1949; reprint, Tokyo: Shinsensha, 1971), pp. 82–92, 142–43.

21. Sōda Kiichirō, "Bunkashugi no ronri," in id., *Bunka kachi to kyokugen gainen* (1922; reprint, Tokyo: Iwanami Shoten, 1972), pp. 58, 61; Ishida, *Nihon no shakai kagaku,* p. 99; Rōyama, *Hattatsu,* pp. 141–42. The Marxian economist Uno Kōzō, whose work is treated in chapters 4 and 5, below, recalls a speech given by Sōda to the Social Policy Association. "Socialism, I heard him say, was seeking to lower culture to the level of the culture of the working class. This man is completely hopeless, I thought." Uno Kōzō, *Shihonron gojūnen* (Tokyo: Hōsei Daigaku Shuppankyoku, 1981), p. 114.

22. Ishida, *Nihon no shakai kagaku,* pp. 100, 290–91. Uno Kōzō remarks that if anything, in the long run Sōda's essays in *Keizai tetsugaku no shomondai* (1922) helped him "graduate from neo-Kantianism." *Shihonron gojūnen,* pp. 113, 128.

23. For a masterly presentation of the post–World War I trends in Japanese social thought and research, focusing on the experience of Japanese "modern [modan] life," see Harry Harootunian, *Overcome by Modernity: History, Culture, and Community in Interwar Japan* (Princeton: Princeton University Press, 2000). See also the brief presentation in Kawamura, *Sociology and Society,* pp. 54–57, and (on Simmel) Jeffrey Bergner, *The Origin of Formalism in Social Science* (Chicago: University of Chicago Press, 1981), pp. 95–98.

24. See Kagawa Toyohiko, *Hinmin shinri no kenkyū* (1915) and *Ningenku to ningen kenchiku* (1920), in *Kagawa Toyohiko zenshū,* vols. 8 and 9, respectively (Tokyo: Kirisuto Shinbunsha, 1973). Some recent treatments of Kagawa have argued that in describing the outcaste population—beginning with his use of the term *"eta,"* attribution of a foreign racial origin to outcaste villagers and extending to his use elsewhere of unreflective and judgmental terminology—Kagawa

worked "from the standpoint of discrimination." The documentation on this issue is itself extensive: see Kirisuto Shinbunsha, ed., *Shiryōshū—Kagawa Toyohiko zenshū to buraku sabetsu* (Tokyo: Kirisuto Shinbunsha, 1991). A sympathetic and informed study of Kagawa is Sumiya Mikio, *Kagawa Toyohiko* (Tokyo: Iwanami Dōjidai Raiburarī, 1995).

25. See the critique of Kagawa in Takahashi Sadaki, *Hisabetsu buraku issennenshi* (1924; reprint, Tokyo: Iwanami Bunko ed., 1996), pp. 226, 323; this was published when the author was nineteen. See also the compelling theological reflections on the relationship between sin and poverty in Kagawa's thought in Kuribayashi Teruo, *Keikan no shingaku* (Tokyo: Shinkyō Shuppansha, 1993), esp. pp. 454–76.

26. See Rōyama, *Hattatsu;* Maruyama, "Politics as a Science in Japan" (1947), in *Thought and Behavior*, p. 226.

27. Katō Shūichi, "Taishō Democracy as the Pre-Stage for Japanese Militarism," in *Japan in Crisis: Essays on Taishō Democracy,* ed. Bernard Silberman and H. D. Harootunian (Princeton: Princeton University Press, 1974), p. 224.

28. Fukuda Tokuzō, *Shakai seisaku to kaikyū tōsō* (Tokyo: Ōkura Shoten, 1922), p. 3.

29. On theories of crisis and conflict during these years, see Peter Duus, "Liberal Intellectuals and Social Conflict in Taishō Japan," in *Conflict in Modern Japanese History,* ed. J. Victor Koschmann and Tetsuo Najita (Princeton: Princeton University Press, 1982). See also Kawamura Nozomu, "Interwar Sociology and Socialism," in *Culture and Identity: Japanese Intellectuals in the Interwar Years,* ed. J. Thomas Rimer (Princeton: Princeton University Press, 1990). Kawamura, however, seems to me to understate badly the development of conflict theories during the interwar period. A good corrective is the essay by Eugene Soviak, "Tsuchida Kyōson and the Sociology of the Masses," which follows Kawamura's in *Culture and Identity*. On the Ōhara Institute, see the biography of Takano Iwasaburō, its first and most famous director: Ōshima Kiyoshi, *Takano Iwasaburō den* (Tokyo: Iwanami Shoten, 1968). For an account of day-to-day work at Ōhara, see Uno Kōzō, *Shihonron gojūnen,* ch. 3.

30. Maruyama Masao, "Kindai Nihon no chishikijin," in id., *Kōei no ichi kara* (Tokyo: Miraisha, 1982), pp. 107–8.

31. Ishida, *Nihon no shakai kagaku,* pp. 119–24. Ishida even captures his point in a pun: *fuhensei* (universality) equals *fuhensei* (immobility).

32. The key texts of the Kōza-ha scholars appear in Noro Eitarō, ed., *Nihon shihonshugi hattatsushi kōza,* 7 vols. (1932; Tokyo: Iwanami Shoten, 1982).

33. See Uno Kōzō, "Shihonshugi no seiritsu to nōson bunkai no katei" (1935), in *Senjika no teikō to jiritsu: Sōzōteki sengo e no taidō,* ed. Furihata Setsuo (Tokyo: Shakai Hyōronsha, 1989), pp. 151–74.

34. Ōshima Mario, "A Distant View of the Debate on Japanese Capitalism," *Osaka City University Economic Review* 26, no. 2 (July 1991): 23–34; quotes from pp. 30, 31. See also Ōshima Mario, "Kakuritsuki Nihon shihonshugi no kōzō," in *Kindai Nihon keizaishi—Kokka to keizai,* ed. Yamamoto Yoshihiko (Kyoto: Mineruva Shobō, 1992), pp. 29–64.

35. See particular passages on semiserf condition of industrial labor (factories

as "Jammerhöhlen" etc.), sub-Indian wages, patriarchy, paucity of original Japanese patents, "unparalleled . . . double cruelty" of semi-serflike relations of production in Japanese industry and agriculture, "miserably backward" condition of peasantry, cash land rent as modern mask over a feudal form, and so on: Yamada, *Nihon shihonshugi bunseki* (1934), in *Yamada Moritarō chosakushū*, vol. 2 (Tokyo: Iwanami Shoten, 1984), pp. 35ff, 51, 61–62, 112, 150–51, 175–76, 182.

36. For Miki on social science, see his *Shakai kagaku no yobi gainen* (1929) and *Shakai kagaku gairon* (1932), in id., *Miki Kiyoshi zenshū* (Tokyo: Iwanami Shoten, 1967), vols. 3 and 6; see also Miki, Nagata Kiyoshi, and Nakayama Ichirō, eds., *Shakai kagaku shinjiten* (Tokyo: Kawade Shobō, 1941).

37. Quote on "chauvinism" from Gino Piovesana, *Contemporary Japanese Philosophical Thought* (New York: St. John's University Press, 1969), p. 186; longer quotes from Miki's *Shin Nihon no shisō genri* (1939), in *Miki Kiyoshi zenshū*, vol. 17, pp. 510, 514, 533. Until 1967, editions of Miki's works did not include *Shin Nihon no shisō genri* at all. In that edition it appears under the heading "Materials" *(Shiryō)*, in a sense distancing it from its author.

38. Note in this connection the short essay published in the *Asahi shinbun* by the philosopher Hiromatsu Wataru shortly before his death: "Tōhoku Ajia ga rekishi no shuyaku ni; Ōbei chūshin no sekaikan wa hōkai e" (Mar. 16, 1994). A representative passage: "[Build] a New System in East Asia along a Japan-China Axis!" he exhorted. "Let it become the premise for a New World Order! We have entered a period in which, provided it includes a radical reexamination of Japanese capitalism itself, this could very well serve as the slogan of the anti-establishment left." I am grateful to Yōsuke Nirei for drawing my attention to this article.

39. Arisawa is the subject of two fine articles: Bai Gao, "Arisawa Hiromi and His Theory for a Managed Economy," *Journal of Japanese Studies* 20, no. 1 (winter 1994): 115–53; and Laura Hein, "In Search of Peace and Democracy: Postwar Japanese Economic Thought in Political Context," *Journal of Asian Studies* 53, no. 3 (Aug. 1994): 752–78.

40. Particularly influential was Yanaihara's *Teikokushugika no Taiwan* (1929), which was translated into Russian among other languages. Yanaihara's writings on colonialism are collected in *Yanaihara Tadao zenshū* (Tokyo: Iwanami Shoten, 1963), vols. 1–5 and 18. See also the brief overview in Mark Peattie, "Japanese Attitudes Toward Colonialism, 1895–1945," in *The Japanese Colonial Empire, 1895–1945,* ed. Ramon Myers and Mark Peattie (Princeton: Princeton University Press, 1984), pp. 114–19.

41. On Yanaihara's wartime activities see Nanbara Shigeru et al., eds., *Yanaihara Tadao: Shinkō, gakumon, shōgai* (Tokyo: Iwanami Shoten, 1969); Yanaihara Tadao, *Watakushi no ayunde kita michi* (Tokyo: Tokyo Daigaku Shuppankai, 1975); and Yanaihara Tadao, *Kokka no risō: Senji hyōronshū* (Tokyo: Iwanami Shoten, 1982); see also the revealing diary of his eldest son, Yanaihara Isaku, *Wakaki hi no nikki* (Tokyo: Gendai Hyōronsha, 1974); and Hashikawa Bunzō, "The 'Civil Society' Ideal and Wartime Resistance," in *Authority and the Individual in Japan,* ed. J. Victor Koschmann (Tokyo: Tokyo University Press, 1978), pp. 128–42; on Yanaihara's return to the university and his early postwar work see the critical assessment in Wada Haruki, "Sengo Nihon ni okeru Shakai Kagaku Kenkyūjo no shuppatsu," *Shakai kagaku kenkyū* 32, no. 2 (Aug. 1980):

216–32. Yanaihara Isaku also wrote a superb biography of his father—*Yanaihara Tadao den* (Tokyo: Misuzu Shobō, 1998)—covering the years up through the early 1930s. Isaku himself died in 1989.

42. Yanaihara Tadao, "Kanrika no Nihon: Shūsengo mansannen no zuisō" (Oct. 1948), in *Yanaihara Tadao zenshū*, vol. 19 (Tokyo: Iwanami Shoten, 1964), p. 408.

43. Ibid., p. 410.

44. Peattie, "Japanese Attitudes," p. 118; see also Wada, "Sengo Nihon," pp. 228–29. It is interesting to note that the Peattie and Myers collection is dedicated to Yanaihara.

45. Note in this connection the revival of archaeology and physical anthropology—disciplines that experienced particular difficulties because their findings did not accord with the official mythology of the ancient Yamato state. See Walter Edwards, "Buried Discourse: The Toro Archaeological Site and Japanese National Identity in the Early Postwar Period," in *Journal of Japanese Studies* 17, no. 1 (winter 1991): 1–23.

46. The theme of the "limits" of Japanese social science was suggested to me by David Keightley. There are many such diagnoses. One example in Fukutake Tadashi, *Chūgoku nōson shakai no kōzō*, rev. ed. (Tokyo: Yūhikaku, 1951; orig. preface dated October 1945): "If correct scientific knowledge had formed the basis of Japan's politics, our foolish conflict with China would never have occurred, nor would it have followed its course of reckless expansion into the Pacific War" (p. 1).

47. See Aoki Tamotsu, *"Nihon bunkaron" no hen'yō* (Tokyo: Chūō Kōronsha, 1990).

48. For detailed discussion of the "democratic enlightenment," particularly the role of the Science of Thought (Shisō no Kagaku) group that formed around Tsurumi Shunsuke, see Andrew E. Barshay, "Postwar Social and Political Thought, 1945–90," in *Modern Japanese Thought,* ed. Bob Tadashi Wakabayashi (Cambridge: Cambridge University Press, 1998), esp. pp. 301–7.

49. See, for example, Ōkita Saburō et al., *Postwar Reconstruction of the Japanese Economy* (Ministry of Foreign Affairs, September 1946) (Tokyo: University of Tokyo Press, 1992).

50. See Takeuchi Kei, "Nihon shakai kagaku no chiteki kankyō," in *Shakai kagaku no genba*, vol. 4 of *Iwanami kōza: Shakai kagaku no hōhō,* ed. Yamanouchi Yasushi et al. (Tokyo: Iwanami Shoten, 1993), p. 43.

51. Maruyama, "Kindai Nihon no chishikijin."

52. As mentioned earlier, the postwar development of political science in Japan owed much to the provocation of Maruyama's essay on what he saw as a legacy of failure received from earlier generations. The Japan Political Science Association was formed in 1948, with Nanbara Shigeru as president. At Tokyo University, Maruyama himself lectured on political science only once, by significant coincidence in 1960. For treatments of the postwar history of the discipline, see Ishida, *Nihon no shakai kagaku,* pp. 181–87, and more recently, fully, and argumentatively, Taguchi Fukuji, *Sengo Nihon seijigaku shi* (Tokyo: Tokyo Daigaku Shuppankai, 2000). I am grateful to Mao Guirong (Meiji Gakuin University) for this latter reference.

53. Maruyama Masao, "Nihon ni okeru jiyū ishiki no keisei to tokushitsu"

(Aug. 1947), in id., *Senchū to sengo no aida* (Tokyo: Misuzu Shobō, 1976), p. 305.

54. See Yamanouchi Yasushi, "Sengo hanseiki no shakai kagaku to rekishi ninshiki," *Rekishigaku kenkyū*, no. 689 (Oct. 1996): 32–43; Yamanouchi, *Nihon shakai kagaku to Wēbā taiken* (Tokyo: Chikuma Shobō, 1999).

55. See Ishida, *Nihon no shakai kagaku*, pp. 207–9.

56. Kyōgoku Jun'ichi, *Nihonjin to seiji* (Tokyo: Tokyo Daigaku Shuppankai, 1986) quoted in Nakamura Takafusa, *Shōwa shi* (Tokyo: Tōyō Keizai Shinpōsha, 1993), p. 513.

57. Kawashima Takeyoshi, "'Kindaika' no imi," *Shisō*, no. 473 (Nov. 1963): 8.

58. See Ishida Takeshi, *Shakai kagaku saikō* (Tokyo: Tokyo Daigaku Shuppankai, 1995), pp. 28–34, 100–110; and Wada Haruki, "Kindaikaron," in *Nihonshi ronsō*, vol. 9 of *Kōza Nihonshi*, ed. Rekishigaku Kenkyūkai and Nihonshi Kenkyūkai (Tokyo: Tokyo Daigaku Shuppankai, 1971), pp. 255–82.

59. This paragraph draws from Andrew E. Barshay, "Postwar Social and Political Thought," p. 339; the Marxist thinkers and works discussed in this section are treated in detail in chapters 5 and 6.

60. Yamada Toshio, "Les Tendances du marxisme japonais contemporain," in *Actuel Marx*, no. 2, special issue: *Le Marxisme au Japon* (1987): 40. In the passage cited Yamada is summarizing the argument of Uchida's *Nihon shihonshugi no shisōzō* (Tokyo: Iwanami Shoten, 1967).

61. Marx, *Capital*, vol. 1 (Harmondsworth: Penguin, 1990), p. 929.

62. Hirata Kiyoaki, "Shakaishugi to shimin shakai" (1968), in his *Shimin shakai to shakaishugi* (Tokyo: Iwanami Shoten, 1969), pp. 73–125; see also Hirata, "La Société civile japonaise contemporaine," in *Actuel Marx*, no. 2, special issue: *Le Marxisme au Japon* (1987): 65–71; and Yamada, "Les Tendances de la marxisme contemporaine," pp. 38–41.

63. See Furihata Setsuo's annotations to Uno Kōzō, "Shihonshugi no seiritsu to nōson bunkai no katei" (1935), in *Senjika no teikō to jiritsu.*

64. See Murakami's final work, *An Anticlassical Political-Economic Analysis: A Vision for the Next Century,* trans. Kozo Yamamura (Stanford: Stanford University Press, 1996).

65. See Tsuru Shigeto, *Japan's Capitalism: Creative Defeat and Beyond* (Cambridge: Cambridge University Press, 1993; Uzawa Hirofumi, *Uzawa Hirofumi chosakushū* (Tokyo: Iwanami Shoten, 1994), vols. 1, 6–8, 10–12.

66. See Yamanouchi Yasushi, *Shisutemu shakai no gendaiteki isō* (Tokyo: Iwanami Shoten, 1996); and the twelve-volume collection edited by Yamanouchi, *Iwanami kōza: Shakai kagaku no hōhō* (Tokyo: Iwanami Shoten, 1993).

CHAPTER 3. DOUBLY CRUEL

An earlier version of this chapter appeared as "'Doubly Cruel': Marxism and the Presence of the Past in Japanese Capitalism," in *Mirror of Modernity: Invented Traditions of Modern Japan*, ed. Stephen Vlastos (Berkeley and Los Angeles: University of California Press, 1998). Used here with permission.

1. Robert Heilbroner, *The Nature and Logic of Capitalism* (New York: W. W. Norton, 1985), p. 17.

2. See Thomas C. Smith, *Native Sources of Japanese Industrialization* (Berkeley and Los Angeles: University of California Press, 1988); and Tetsuo Najita, *Visions of Virtue: The Kaitokudō Merchant Academy in Tokugawa Japan* (Chicago: University of Chicago Press, 1987).

3. Yamada Toshio, "Les Tendances du marxisme japonais contemporain," *Actuel Marx*, no. 2, special issue: *Le Marxisme au Japon* (1987): 40.

4. That is, while the ideologues of "original" capitalism denied that it was exploitative, Japanese thinkers admitted that it was, but denied that Japan was "really" capitalist. The quotation comes from a statement in graduate seminar by a Tokyo University graduate and Ph.D. student (at Berkeley) in Central European history.

5. I owe these formulations to William Johnston, history department, Wesleyan University.

6. Itō Hirobumi, "Some Reminiscences of the Grant of the New Constitution," in *Fifty Years of New Japan*, ed. Ōkuma Shigenobu, vol. 1 (New York: Dutton, 1909), pp. 128–29, emphasis added.

7. Michio Morishima, *Why Has Japan "Succeeded"?* (Cambridge: Cambridge University Press, 1982), pp. 199–200.

8. Thomas C. Smith, *Political Change and Industrial Development in Japan: Government Enterprise, 1868–1880* (Stanford: Stanford University Press, 1965), p. 85.

9. Some recent scholarship (by Richard Smethurst and Penelope Francks) has stressed the internal differentiation of the tenant population, and the economic benefits of tenancy in certain circumstances. But the issue of tenancy remains controversial, as witnessed by the extended critique of Smethurst by Nishida Yoshiaki (and Smethurst's countercritique) in *Journal of Japanese Studies* 15, no. 2 (summer 1989): 389–437.

10. See Akira Nagazumi, "The Diffusion of the Idea of Social Darwinism in East and Southeast Asia," *Historia Scientiarum*, no. 24 (1983); and Unoura Hiroshi, "Kindai Nihon ni okeru shakai dāwinizumu no juyō to tenkai," in *Kōza: Shinka*, vol. 2 of *Shinka shisō to shakai*, ed. Shibatani Atsuhiro et al. (Tokyo: Tokyo Daigaku Shuppankai, 1991), pp. 119–52.

11. Yamada Moritarō, *Nihon shihonshugi bunseki* (hereafter *Bunseki*) (1934), in *Yamada Moritarō chosakushū* (hereafter *YMCS*), vol. 2 (Tokyo: Iwanami Shoten, 1984) p. 150. Internal quotes from Marx, *Capital*, vol. 1 (Harmondsworth, U.K.: Penguin, 1990), p. 345.

12. See Yamazaki Ryūzō, "*Nihon shihonshugi bunseki* no hōhō to sono hihanshi" (hereafter "Hihanshi"), in id., *Kindai Nihon keizaishi no kihon mondai* (Kyoto: Mineruva Shobō, 1989), pp. 172–240, esp. pp. 173, 225ff.

13. Quote is from Heilbroner, *Nature and Logic*, p. 117.

14. Nakamura Takafusa, "Nihon shihonshugi ronsō ni tsuite," *Shisō*, no. 624 (June 1976): 185–97, esp. pp. 187–90.

15. On the various Theses issued between 1927 and 1932, see George Beckmann and Genji Okubo, *The Japanese Communist Party, 1922–1945* (Stanford: Stanford University Press, 1969); and Germaine Hoston, *Marxism and the Crisis of Development in Prewar Japan* (Princeton: Princeton University Press, 1986).

16. The words "*tennō*" (emperor) and "*tennōsei zettaishugi*" (imperial absolutism) appear nowhere in his text.

17. Yamada's characterization of Japanese factory wages as "sub-Indian" was based on a misreading of statistics, which "concerned not wages but the wage cost per unit of output." See Yasukichi Yasuba, "Anatomy of the Debate on Japanese Capitalism," *Journal of Japanese Studies* 2, no. 1 (fall 1975): 64–65 and note. Yasuba is citing Sakisaka Itsurō's 1935 critique of Yamada as reprinted in Sakisaka Itsurō, *Nihon shihonshugi no shomondai* (Tokyo: Shiseidō, 1958), ch. 1.

18. Yamada Moritarō, *Bunseki*, preface (pp. 3–5).

19. Ibid., pp. 4, 20, 70, 71.

20. Yamada Moritarō, "Nihon nōgyō no tokushusei" (Nov. 1945), in *YMCS*, vol. 3, pp. 169–74; quote from p. 172.

21. Yamada's handling of ideological issues in the *Analysis* is indirect and implicit: "The force that decimated the armies of China, whose Asiatic despotism had already entered in its final decay, that smashed the armies of Imperial Russia and liquidated those of Korea was not spiritual but nothing other than weaponry itself." *Bunseki*, p. 88.

22. For Maruyama, see his statements in Maruyama Masao, Umemoto Katsumi, and Satō Noboru, *Sengo Nihon no kakushin shisō* (Tokyo: Gendai no Rironsha, 1983), esp. pp. 48–49.

23. Marx provides a strong warrant for this position:

> Industrial capital is the only mode of existence of capital in which not only the appropriation of surplus value or surplus product, but also its creation, is a function of capital. It thus requires production to be capitalist in character; its existence includes that of the class antagonisms between capitalists and wage-laborers. To the degree that it takes hold of production, the technique and social organization of the labor process are revolutionized, and the economic-historical type of society along with this. The other varieties of capital which appeared previously, within past or declining conditions of social production, are not only subordinated to it and correspondingly altered in the mechanism of their functioning, but they now move only on its basis, thus live and die, stand and fall together with this basis. (Karl Marx, *Capital*, vol. 2 [Harmondsworth, U.K.: Penguin, 1992], pp. 135–36.)

24. Yamada Moritarō, *Bunseki*, pp. 19–20.

25. Ibid., pp. 13–60 passim.

26. Ibid., pp. 65–156 passim.

27. Ibid., pp. 175–76; Marx quoted from letter to Kugelmann, Apr. 4, 1868, in Marx, *The First International and After*, vol. 3 of *Political Writings* (Harmondsworth, U.K.: Penguin, 1992), p. 162; emphasis in original.

28. Yamada Moritarō, *Bunseki*, pp. 170–72.

29. Yamada's treatment *(Bunseki*, pp. 179–82) is drawn explicitly from Marx's *Eighteenth Brumaire* and its (in)famous characterization of the French peasantry as a "sackful of potatoes." See in *The Marx-Engels Reader*, ed. Robert Tucker (New York: W. W. Norton, 1978), p. 608.

30. Yamada Moritarō, *Bunseki*, p. 47.

31. See Uchida Yoshiaki, *Vēbā to Marukusu: Nihon shakai kagaku no shisō kōzō* (Tokyo: Iwanami Shoten, 1978), pp. 227–303 passim.

32. Yamada Moritarō, *Bunseki*, p. 3, emphasis added.

33. Yamada Moritarō, *Saiseisan katei: hyōshiki bunseki joron* (1931) (hereafter *Joron*), *YMCS*, vol. 1, pp. 111f; Yamazaki, "Hihanshi," p. 186f.

34. "Simple reproduction" denotes a process in which the entire surplus product is consumed by the capitalist rather than being turned to accumulation; an equilibrium rather than expansive state. See the review of criticisms of Yamada's use of the reproduction schema in Yamazaki, "Hihanshi," pp. 226–31; also Iwasaki Chikatsugu, *Nihon marukusushugi tetsugakushi josetsu* (Tokyo: Miraisha, 1984), pp. 353–61.

35. This particular formulation comes from a postwar text, but in essence restates Yamada's original position: Yamada Moritarō, "Saiseisan hyōshiki" (1955), as cited in Yamazaki, "Hihanshi," p. 189.

36. Yamada Moritarō, *Joron*, pp. 55–56; see also Yamazaki, "Hihanshi," p. 232.

37. M. C. Howard and J. E. King, *A History of Marxian Economics*, vol. 1 (Princeton: Princeton University Press, 1989), chs. 11 and 13 (quote from p. 206).

38. Yamada Moritarō, "Saiseisan hyōshiki to chidai hanchū—Nihon keizai saiken no hōshiki to nōgyō kaikaku no hōkō o kimeru tame no ichi kijun" (1947), *YMCS*, vol. 3, pp. 3–48, esp. pp. 36–38 (quote from p. 41); longer quote from Yamada Moritarō, *Bunseki*, p. 166. See also Yamazaki, "Hihanshi," pp. 176–83, 198–99.

39. See also Ōshima Mario, "A Distant View of the Debate on Japanese Capitalism," *Osaka City University Economic Review* 26, no. 2 (July 1991): 23–34; and Ōshima Mario, "Kakuritsuki Nihon shihonshugi no kōzō," in *Kindai Nihon keizaishi: Kokka to keizai*, ed. Yamamoto Yoshihiko (Kyoto: Mineruva Shobō, 1992), pp. 29–64.

40. Iwasaki, *Nihon marukusushugi tetsugakushi josetsu*, pp. 351, 355, 359. On Bukharin, see also Stephen Cohen, *Bukharin and the Bolshevik Revolution* (New York: Oxford University Press, 1980), pp. 87–98, 107–22; Kenneth Tarbuck, *Bukharin's Theory of Equilibrium* (London: Pluto Press, 1989).

41. Sakisaka Itsurō, *Nihon shihonshugi no shomondai*, p. 17.

42. Uchida Yoshihiko (pseud. "NNN"), " 'Shijō no ronri' to 'chidai hanchū no kiki,' " *Keizai hyōron*, nos. 3, 4, 6 (1949). Repr. in *Uchida Yoshihiko chosakushū*, vol. 10 (Tokyo: Iwanami Shoten, 1989), pp. 143–79.

43. Yamazaki, "Hihanshi," pp. 235–36.

44. Yamada Moritarō, *Bunseki*, p. 151.

CHAPTER 4. THINKING THROUGH "CAPITAL"

An earlier version of this chapter appeared as "Thinking through *Capital*: Uno Kōzō and Marxian Political Economy in Modern Japan," in *Osaka City University Economic Review* 35, no. 1 (Oct. 1999): 23–52. Used here with permission.

1. Uno Kōzō, *Principles of Political Economy*, trans. Thomas T. Sekine (London and Atlantic Highlands, N.J.: Harvester/Humanities Press, 1980), pp. xxii–xxiv, 126. Sekine's translation is based on the 1964 edition of Uno's *Keizai genron*. The original text of the statement on "abolishing capitalism" as it appears in that edition reads "provide scientific grounds for the assertion that the object [of political economy, that is, capitalist society] can be changed." See the reprint of

the 1964 edition in *Uno Kōzō chosakushū* (hereafter *UKCS*), vol. 2 (Tokyo: Iwanami Shoten, 1974), p. 163. Sekine's translation is thus an interpolation.

2. Colin A. M. Duncan, "Under the Cloud of *Capital*: History vs. Theory," *Science and Society* 47, no. 3 (fall 1983): 301.

3. See the appendix to Uno, *Keizai seisakuron* (1971), in *UKCS*, vol. 7, p. 246.

4. Uno Kōzō, *Shihonron gojūnen* (hereafter *SGN*) (Tokyo: Hōsei Daigaku Shuppankai, 1981).

5. See Uno, "Nihon shihonshugi ronsō to wa nani ka" (1950): "Although the task—in some respects excessive"—of turning "political economy" from "money making" or "bringing wealth to the nation," into a real social science "was gradually, hand in hand with the study of *Capital* during this period, set on the road to fulfillment, in the end a scientific solution convincing to all parties proved to lie beyond reach. And at the same time, the impression was left that no solution independent of a partisan viewpoint was even to be expected." *UKCS*, supp. vol., pp. 11–15. On Uno's approach as the solution to the impasse in the capitalism debate, see Ōuchi Hideaki, "Uno keizaigaku no keisei," in *Kōza Sengo Nihon no shisō*, vol. 2, *Keizaigaku*, ed. Hidaka Hiroshi (Tokyo: Gendai Shichōsha, 1962), pp. 108, 124, 138–39, 142; Sekine, translator's introduction to *Principles*, pp. xi–xiii; Shibagaki Kazuo, "Studies in Japanese Capitalism: A Survey with Emphasis on the Contribution of the Marx-Uno School," *Annals of the Institute of Social Science*, no. 30 (1988): 37.

6. Gareth Stedman Jones, "Anglo-Marxism, Neo-Marxism, and the Discursive Approach to History," in *Was bleibt von marxistischen Perspektiven in der Geschichtsforschung?* ed. Alf Lüdtke (Göttingen: Wallstein Verlag, 1997), esp. pp. 207–8.

7. Uno, *SGN*, p. 337.

8. Ibid., p. 470.

9. Ibid., p. 531.

10. For Uno's arrest, "recantation" *(tenkō jōshinsho)*, and trial, see *SGN*, ch. 10 passim. For commentary on the prison poem, see Ōshima Kiyoshi, "Ningen Uno Kōzō," in *Omoigusa*, ed. Uno Maria (privately published, 1979), esp. pp. 45–46. The translation of Bashō's verse comes from R. H. Blyth, *Haiku* (Tokyo: Hokuseidō Press, 1981), p. 896.

11. On Uno's wartime work, see Sugiyama Mitsunobu, "Nihon shakai kagaku no sekai ninshiki: Kōza-ha, Ōtsuka shigaku, Uno keizaigaku o megutte," in *Nihon shakai kagaku no shisō*, vol. 3 of *Iwanami kōza: Shakai kagaku no hōhō*, ed. Yamanouchi Yasushi et al. (Tokyo: Iwanami Shoten, 1993), pp. 196–245; texts in *UKCS*, vol. 8; and Uno's own remarks in "Keizaigaku yonjūnen," interview in *Shakai kagaku kenkyū* 9, nos. 4–5 (1958).

12. Uno's major writings from these years include: *Nōgyō mondai joron* (1947, *UKCS*, vol. 8), *Kachiron* (1947, *UKCS*, vol. 3), *Shihonron no kenkyū* (1948, but composed largely of writings from 1930 to 1937; *UKCS*, vol. 3), *Keizai genron* (1st ed., 1950–52), *Kyōkōron* (1953, *UKCS*, vol. 5), *Keizai seisakuron* (1954; revised ed., 1971; *UKCS*, vol. 7).

13. Uno Kōzō, "Shihonron no kakushin" (1956), in *UKCS*, supp. vol., pp. 32–34. See also *Principles*, p. 51 *(UKCS*, vol. 2, p. 74), and *SGN*, p. 373.

14. *SGN*, pp. 312, 477.

15. Marx, *Grundrisse: Foundations of the Critique of Political Economy* (*Rough Draft*) trans. Martin Nicolaus (Harmondsworth: Penguin, 1973), pp. 100–101. See also Sekine's "Essay on Uno's Dialectic of Capital," appended to the *Principles*, esp. pp. 139–44; Duncan, "Under the Cloud," pp. 309–10.

16. Uno, *SGN*, pp. 50–56; see also his comment that "I always believed that the actual [workers'] movement could succeed even without a complete theory" (p. 107). He also recalled that workers protecting Ōsugi at meetings voiced resentment at his making them "stepping stones," quoting the Chinese proverb, "Thousands die to raise one hero to fame," to make their point (p. 58).

17. See Uno, *SGN*, ch. 2, esp. pp. 82, 102, 107.

18. For Uno's life in Germany, see *SGN*, ch. 4. On one occasion, the socialist writer Max Beer, who was Jewish, visited Uno's rented rooms. After he left, the landlady "acted as if the place had been contaminated by 'that horrible man.' Frau von Stosz was married to a Junker military man. She was hell on Jews" (p. 206). (Note also the two interviewers' questions: "Did she know him, this Max Beer? Or maybe she could tell he was Jewish from his face?") Among Uno's fellow passengers on the return voyage was the Communist leader Fukumoto Kazuo; they argued heatedly and endlessly, but Uno was impressed.

19. See Uno, *SGN*, pp. 258, 344ff, 438; for more developed treatments, see "Furīdorihhi Risuto [Friedrich List] no *Keizaigaku*" (1934), in *UKCS*, vol. 7, pp. 457–99; and "Shakai kagaku no kyakkansei" (1948), in *UKCS*, vol. 10, pp. 358–81; and more compactly in *Keizai seisakuron* (1954; rev. ed., 1971), in *UKCS*, vol. 7, pp. 21–29, 34–35, 42–47. For an overview of the Japanese reception of List, see Kobayashi Noboru, "Hanseiki no Risuto juyō," in *Juyō to hen'yō: Nihon kindai keizai to shisō*, ed. Nakamura Katsumi (Tokyo: Misuzu Shobō, 1989), pp. 173–238.

20. For an exhaustive consideration of the role of stage theory in Uno's system, see Nitta Shigeru, *Dankairon no kenkyū* (Tokyo: Ochanomizu Shobō, 1998).

21. Uno, *SGN*, pp. 439–40.

22. Sekine, translator's introduction to *Principles*, pp. xiii–xiv; Uno's critique of Hilferding is among his earliest published works: "'Kahei no hitsuzensei': Hirufadingu [Hilferding] no kahei riron saikōsatsu" (1930), in *UKCS*, vol. 3, pp. 54–75. See also M. C. Howard and J. E. King, *A History of Marxian Economics*, vol. 1 (Princeton: Princeton University Press, 1989), chs. 5, 11, and 13.

23. Uno, *Keizai seisakuron* (1st ed., 1936), in *UKCS*, vol. 7, pp. 259–60.

24. See Saitō Haruzō, commentary on *Keizai seisakuron*, *UKCS*, vol. 7, pp. 504; *SGN*, p. 285.

25. Uno Kōzō, "Shihonshugi no seiritsu to nōson bunkai no katei," *Chūō kōron* (Nov. 1935) (hereafter "Nōson bunkai"), repr. in *UKCS*, vol. 8, pp. 22–42; also in *Senjika no teikō to jiritsu: Sōzōteki sengo e no taidō*, ed. Furihata Setsuo (Tokyo: Shakai Hyōronsha, 1989), pp. 151–74.

26. Uno, "Nōson bunkai," p. 22; and *SGN*, pp. 352–68; on "noneconomic coercion" see "Iwayuru keizaigai kyōsei ni tsuite" (1947), in *UKCS*, vol. 8, pp. 66–84. See also discussion in Ōuchi, "Uno keizaigaku," pp. 127–28, 138–41. Uno had some choice words for Yamada's famous characterization of Japan's

"sub-Indian" industrial wages: "Even a person who didn't who know the ABC's of economics couldn't have written *that*" (*SGN*, p. 360; emphasis in original).

27. Uno, "Nōson bunkai," pp. 23–33. See also Nitta, *Dankairon*, pp. 27–29.

28. An interesting exchange in *SGN*: Uno: "Before the war I remained in the grip of the idea that I shouldn't take even a step away from *Capital* . . . and I tried to confine my analyses to its categories." Question: "So this was a kind of false obedience [*menjū fukuhai*]?" Uno: "I wouldn't go that far. But still I felt that there was something that just didn't work" *(SGN*, p. 414).

29. Uno, "Nōson bunkai," p. 38.

30. Ibid., pp. 33–35; see also *SGN*, p. 374.

31. Uno, "Nōson bunkai," pp. 35, 37–38. See also Nitta, *Dankairon*, p. 54.

32. Uno, "Nōson bunkai," pp. 39–40.

33. Ibid., p. 41.

34. Ibid., p. 40.

35. Uno, *SGN*, pp. 367–68.

36. See Nitta, *Dankairon*, p. 22. Another interpreter of Uno's work has estimated that of the three levels of analysis in his system—basic principles, stage theory, and concrete analysis—Uno completed 80 percent of the first, 60 percent of the second, and 30 percent of the third. Shohken Mawatari, "The Uno School: A Marxian Approach in Japan," *History of Political Economy* 17, no. 3 (1985): 408.

37. Sekine, translator's introduction to *Principles*, p. xiv.

38. Uno, *SGN*, pp. 589, 610–11.

39. Uno, "Shihonshugi no soshikika to minshushugi," in *Sekai* (May 1946), repr. in *UKCS*, vol. 8, pp. 277–91; quote, p. 278. See also the discussion in Wada Haruki, "Sengo Nihon ni okeru Shakai Kagaku Kenkyūjo no shuppatsu," *Shakai kagaku kenkyū* 32, no. 2 (Aug. 1980): 229–31. Lenin was (predictably?) critical of the notion of "organized capitalism": see *Imperialism* and *Notebooks on Imperialism*, vols. 22 and 39 of his *Collected Works* (Moscow: Progress Publishers, 1968).

40. Uno, *Principles*, pp. xxvi, 17 (*UKCS*, vol. 2, pp. 9, 35).

41. Uno, *Principles*, pp. xix, 16, 25 (*UKCS*, vol. 2, pp. 5, 35–36, 41); see also Sekine, "Essay on Uno's Dialectic," p. 150.

42. See Derek Sayer, *Capitalism and Modernity: An Excursus on Marx and Weber* (London: Routledge, 1991), pp. 3–4: "As Marx said, to write 'the real history' of capitalism is 'a work in its own right'—a work he did not, incidentally, undertake."

43. Sekine, "Essay on Uno's Dialectic," pp. 144–45; economic as "Other": Duncan, "Under the Cloud," p. 302. I will leave aside discussion of the unmistakable correspondences between Uno's *Principles* and Hegel's *Logic*, but note Nitta's comment (*Dankairon*, pp. 46–47):

> When Uno says that 'the system of the basic principles *is* the concretization of the dialectic,' this is limited only to the aspect of the dialectic that, transcending what for Kant is unknowable, is capable of grasping the thing-in-itself; but it is not, in my opinion, a continuation of Hegel's logical manipulations. Here, the traces of dialectic as the inversion of the antinomies—which Marx used in his account of the value form, of the evolution in laws of possession of property, and of the tendencies of

history—were positively effaced. Ultimately, it is entirely unclear what Uno meant by 'dialectic'; as it remains unclear what it was he saw as being inverted materialistically through 'reality copying method.'

See also Sekine, "Essay on Uno's Dialectic," pp. 147–50, and Brian Maclean, "Kōzō Uno's *Principles of Political Economy,*" *Science and Society* 45, no. 2 (1981): 220–22. For general background, see Fred Moseley, ed., *Marx's Method in Capital: A Reexamination* (Atlantic Highlands, N.J.: Humanities Press, 1993).

44. Mawatari, "The Uno School," p. 408.

45. Duncan, "Under the Cloud," p. 315

46. Quote is from Maclean, " Uno's *Principles,*" pp. 213–14. This suggests a comparison with the "absurdist" postulation by the Ukranian economist Mikhail Tugan-Baranovsky (1865–1919) of a capitalism without workers—without consumption requirements. See Howard and King, *History,* vol. 1, pp. 169–70; Richard Kindersley, *The First Russian Revisionists* (Oxford: Clarendon Press, 1962), ch. 5.

47. See esp. *Principles,* pp. 54, 88–89 (*UKCS,* vol. 2, pp. 84, 123–27); also Sekine's glossary, *Principles,* pp. 192–93, 200–01; and Uno, "Shihonron no kakushin," pp. 33–34.

48. Uno, "Shihonron no kakushin," p. 32. See *Principles,* pp. 223–24, for a useful list of these divergences; on his "clarifications," see commentary by Hidaka Hiroshi on successive editions of *Keizai genron* in *UKCS,* vol. 2, p. 468; on the profit rate, see Sekine, glossary, pp. 199–200.

49. Maclean, "Uno's *Principles,*" pp. 214–15.

50. Robert Heilbroner, *The Nature and Logic of Capitalism* (New York: W. W. Norton, 1985), p. 105.

51. Uno, *Keizai seisakuron* (1971 ed.), in *UKCS,* vol. 7, p. 241.

52. Ibid., pp. 28, 241.

53. Duncan, "Under the Cloud," p. 305. We should note here that Hilferding (*Finance Capital,* ch. 25), and Uno emulating him, did not restrict the term "policy" to the state. The proletariat also had its policy. In this sense policy veers in meaning toward "praxis."

54. Uno, *Keizai seisakuron, UKCS,* vol. 7, p.74n1; emphasis mine.

55. Uno's oeuvre contains little about transitions between dominant modes of capital accumulation, but see "Katoki no toriatsukai ni tsuite," *Shisō,* no. 325 (July 1951), repr. in *UKCS,* vol. 9, pp. 358–68, which is his critique of the Sweezy-Dobb debate; see also Duncan's comments in "Under the Cloud," pp. 317–18.

56. Uno, *Keizai seisakuron, UKCS,* vol. 7, p. 19; commentary, pp. 502–3; *Principles,* p. xxv; Duncan, "Under the Cloud," p. 320.

57. Uno, *Keizai seisakuron,* vol. 7, p. 240.

58. The original terms are "*noveishii etap*" (following Hilferding's usage of the German, "*jüngste*") versus "*vysshaya stadiya.*" The original title page is reproduced in V. I. Lenin, *Polnoe sobranie sochinenii,* vol. 27, 5th ed. (Moscow: Gosudarstvennoe Izdatel'stvo Politicheskoi Literatury, 1962). The editors record the change in title but do not comment on it (vol. 27, pp. 519–21). Perhaps to eliminate any confusion, later Soviet editions added "and final" (*i poslednaya*) to the subtitle.

59. Uno, *Keizai seisakuron, UKCS,* vol. 7, pp. 244–48.

60. "It has been a disappointment to me that so few readers have appreciated my work on stage theory. Perhaps they feel it's beneath their dignity to take over what I've done as is. But how can you be a scholar with such a petty mentality? If something in Marx's work is unconvincing, it's perfectly fine to correct it, and if mine *is* convincing, there's nothing at all to be ashamed about in accepting it" *(SGN,* p. 464).

61. Sekine, translator's introduction, p. xv. See also J. Victor Koschmann, "Mao Zedong and the Postwar Japanese Left," in *Critical Perspectives on Mao Zedong's Thought,* ed. Arif Dirlik et al. (Atlantic Highlands, N.J.: Humanities Press, 1997), esp. pp. 347–49, on the impact of Mao and the success of the Chinese Revolution on the Japan Communist Party; under such circumstances, Uno's approach must have appeared as the rankest form of bourgeois quietism.

62. Matsushita Keiichi, "Taishū kokka no seiritsu to sono mondaisei" (1956) in id., *Sengo seiji no rekishi to shisō* (Tokyo: Chikuma Shobō, 1994), pp. 44, 60.

63. The issue of the more recent awareness of Uno's thought among Marxian economists outside Japan, particularly in Canada and Britain, is beyond my considerations here. Thomas Sekine (Sekine Tomohiko), Itō Makoto, and Robert Albritton are the key figures. See, for example, Robert Albritton and Thomas T. Sekine, ed., *A Japanese Approach to Political Economy: Unoist Variations* (New York: St. Martin's Press, 1996).

64. Umemoto Katsumi, statement in Maruyama Masao, Umemoto Katsumi, and Satō Noboru, *Sengo Nihon no kakushin shisō* (Tokyo: Gendai no Rironsha, 1983), p. 70.

65. See the very interesting remarks in Karl Polanyi, *The Great Transformation* (Boston: Beacon Press, 1957), concerning the early envy of natural science for the achievements of social science:

> Unbelievable though it may seem to our generation, the standing of natural science greatly gained by its association with the human sciences. The discovery of economics was an astounding revelation which hastened greatly the transformation of society and the establishment of a market system, while decisive machines had been the inventions of uneducated artisans some of whom could hardly read or write. It was thus both just and appropriate that not the natural but the social sciences should rank as the intellectual of the mechanical revolution which subjected the powers of nature to man.

66. Uno, *Principles,* pp. 125–26n15 (*UKCS,* vol. 2, pp. 163–64). See also Marx, *Capital,* vol. 3 (Harmondsworth: Penguin, 1991), p. 275, for a similar assertion. See also Uno's debate with the philosopher Umemoto Katsumi in Uno and Umemoto, *Shakai kagaku to benshōhō* (Tokyo: Iwanami Shoten, 1976), ch. 1; and Nitta, *Dankairon,* pp. 43ff.

67. See Marx, *Capital,* vol. 1 (Harmondsworth, U.K.: Penguin, 1990), pp. 618, 927–30.

68. Uno develops this theme at length in *Shihonron no keizaigaku* (1969), in *UKCS,* vol. 6, p. 40.

69. See Sekine, "Essay on Uno's Dialectic," passim; "ill-advised actions" *(muyō na bōkō): Principles,* p. 126 (*UKCS,* vol. 2, p. 163).

70. Uno Kōzō, *Shihonron to shakaishugi* (1958), in *UKCS*, vol. 10, p. 11. Although Uno here speaks of dialectical rather than historical materialism, I believe that the relation of the philosophical to the scientific domains remains the same. So too does the problem of practice by the working class in its relation to the scientific achievement of *Capital*.

71. Maruyama, Umemoto, and Satō, *Sengo Nihon no kakushin shisō*, pp. 261–303 passim.

72. Sekine, "Essay on Uno's Dialectic," p. 158. Uno's writings on socialism (as opposed to Marxian economics) form only a small portion of his collected writings. See *Shihonron to shakaishugi* (1958), pp. 3–183; for further commentary, see Nitta, *Dankairon*, pp. 44–45, 48–49.

CHAPTER 5. SCHOOL'S OUT?

1. See editor's annotations to Uno Kōzō, "Shihonshugi no seiritsu to nōson bunkai no katei," *Chūō kōron* (Nov. 1935), in *Senjika no teikō to jiritsu: Sōzōteki sengo e no taidō*, ed. Furihata Setsuo (Tokyo: Shakai Hyōronsha, 1989), pp. 152–53.

2. See Hidaka Hiroshi, ed., *Keizaigaku*, vol. 2 of *Kōza Sengo Nihon no shisō* (Tokyo: Gendai Shichōsha, 1962).

3. Hidaka, "Marukusushugi no senzen to sengo," in ibid., pp. 40–44.

4. Text in *The Essential Stalin*, ed. Bruce Franklin (London: Croom Helm, 1973), pp. 448–89. See discussion in Andrzej Walicki, *Marxism and the Leap to the Kingdom of Freedom* (Stanford: Stanford University Press, 1995), pp. 446–52. "Ideological testament" is Walicki's phrase.

5. Uno Kōzō, "Keizai hōsoku to shakaishugi—Sutārin shosetsu ni taisuru gimon," *Shisō* (Oct. 1953), repr. as ch. 7 of *Shihonron to shakaishugi* (1958); text in *Uno Kōzō chosakushū* (hereafter *UKCS*), vol. 10, pp. 115–40. Quotations from pp. 119, 122, 127, 128, 132–33, 135, 139–40. For contemporary reactions to Stalin's essay among Marxian economists elsewhere, see M. C. Howard and J. E. King, *A History of Marxian Economics*, vol. 2 (Princeton: Princeton University Press, 1992), pp. 35–38.

6. Ōuchi Hideaki, "Uno keizaigaku no keisei," in *Keizaigaku*, vol. 2 of *Kōza Sengo Nihon no shisō*, ed. Hidaka Hiroshi (Tokyo: Gendai Shichōsha, 1962), pp. 108–9.

7. Uno Kōzō, *Principles of Political Economy*, trans. Thomas T. Sekine (London and Atlantic Highlands, N.J.: Harvester/Humanities Press, 1980), pp. xxii–xxiii, xxvii. See also original text of *Keizai genron* (1964 ed.) in *Uno Kōzō chosakushū* (hereafter *UKCS*), vol. 2 (Tokyo: Iwanami Shoten, 1974), pp. 13–14.

8. The significance of Marxian economics having "been there first" in Japan, so to speak, is stressed by Makoto Itoh, *Value and Crisis: Essays on Marxian Economics in Japan* (New York: Monthly Review Press, 1980), p. 45.

9. Karatani Kōjin, " Uno riron to Bunto [Bund]," *Chūō kōron* (Nov. 1981): 178–79. This reference courtesy Yuji Oniki. Karatani did resign his teaching position at the Japan Medical College (Nihon Igaku Daigaku) in 1970 amid the

anti-Security Treaty (Anpo) protests of that year. For detail on the Bund, see Shakai Mondai Kenkyūkai, comp., *Zengakuren kakuha—gakusei undō jiten* (Tokyo: Futabasha, 1969); and Kazuko Tsurumi, *Social Change and the Individual* (Princeton: Princeton University Press, 1969), ch. 9, esp. pp. 331–34.

10. "Thirty percent" is Shohken Mawatari's estimate; "negative heuristic" is his term. See Mawatari, "The Uno School: A Marxian Approach in Japan," *History of Political Economy* 17, no. 3 (1985): 408. On Uno's sense of obligation to answer his critics, see his remarks in "Keizai hōsoku to shakaishugi," p. 116. Sugihara Shirō, the eminent historian of Japanese economic thought, remarks that Uno differed greatly in this respect from what he views as the more authoritarian stance of refusal to engage taken by scholars in the Kōza-ha line, including Yamada Moritarō, Ōtsuka Hisao—and Maruyama Masao. Sugihara, personal communication, Nov. 1996.

11. For a lucid overview of the Uno-school approach to value theory, see Itoh, *Value and Crisis*, and Robert Albritton and Thomas T. Sekine, eds., *A Japanese Approach to Political Economy: Unoist Variations* (London: Macmillan, 1995), chs. 2–4. On hermeticism in the later Uno school, see the remarks in Tessa Morris-Suzuki, *A History of Japanese Economic Thought* (London: Routledge, 1989), p. 121. On the impact of Stalinism, see Helena Sheehan, *Marxism and the Philosophy of Science* (Atlantic Highlands, N.J.: Humanities Press, 1985), ch. 4.

12. Ōuchi Hideaki, "Uno keizaigaku," p. 149.

13. It is also important to remember that for Japan, the end of the Cold War coincided not only with the collapse of the bubble economy, but with the end of an entire epoch of unprecedented growth. Key institutions such as government ministries, major corporations, and especially banks—in short, much of the infrastructure of accumulation—face the specter of failure, yet are resistant to neoliberal recipes for restructuring insofar as they threaten the social contract. Even if (as seems impossible) the future is defined in terms of a transition to socialism, capitalism—the social rule of the market—remains just as much a question to be answered as the answer to a question.

14. Uno Kōzō, "Sekai keizairon no hōhō to mokuhyō" (1950), in *UKCS*, vol. 9, pp. 345–57; quotes from pp. 352–53, 356. On the relationship between the "national economy" and the "world economy" in the Uno school, see Nitta, *Dankairon*, ch. 3; I will return to this point in the section on Baba Hiroji, below. See also the useful amplification in Ōuchi Tsutomu, *Sekai keizairon*, vol. 6 of *Ōuchi Tsutomu keizaigaku taikei* (Tokyo: Tokyo Daigaku Shuppankai, 1991), pp. 37–38. Ōuchi's work is considered in the following section of this chapter.

15. Uno Kōzō, "Shihonshugi no soshikika to minshushugi," *Sekai* (May 1946), in *UKCS*, vol. 8, pp. 277–91; inset quote from p. 291. In speaking of the organization of capitalism, Uno does not quote Hilferding directly, only Bukharin; interestingly, both Bukharin and Lenin were critical of Hilferding's argument for exaggerating the capacity of capitalism to stabilize. In general, Uno's stance owes much to Hilferding.

16. Ōuchi Hideaki, "Uno keizaigaku," p. 152.

17. Uno, "Sekai keizairon," p. 350.

18. Wada Haruki, "Sengo Nihon ni okeru Shakai Kagaku Kenkyūjo no shuppatsu," *Shakai kagaku kenkyū* 32, no. 2 (Aug. 1980): 230–31.

19. I could not resist the temptation here to imitate the phrasing of Maruyama Masao in *Studies in the Intellectual History of Tokugawa Japan* (Princeton: Princeton University Press; Tokyo: Tokyo University Press, 1974), p. 184.

20. Baba Hiroji, *Shin shihonshugiron—Shikaku tenkan no keizaigaku* (Nagoya: Nagoya Daigaku Shuppankai, 1997), p. 10n3. I am grateful to Hiwatari Nobuhiro (Institute of Social Science, Tokyo University) for introducing me to this work.

21. See Ōuchi Tsutomu, "Notes on the Theory of State Monopoly Capitalism," *Annals of the Institute of Social Science*, no. 23 (1982): 1–21; quote from p. 16. Originally published in 1962, it was appended to Ōuchi, *Kokka dokusen shihonshugi* (Tokyo: Tokyo Daigaku Shuppankai, 1970). See also Shibagaki Kazuo, "Studies in Japanese Capitalism: A Survey with Emphasis on the Contributions of the Marx-Uno School," *Annals of the Institute of Social Science*, no. 30 (1988): 29–56. Shibagaki equates "stamocap" with the more familiar "mixed economy" (pp. 40–41).

22. Ōuchi Tsutomu, *Ōuchi Tsutomu keizaigaku taikei* (hereafter OTKT), 8 vols. (Tokyo: Tokyo Daigaku Shuppankai, 1980–91).

23. Ōuchi Tsutomu, *Keizaigaku hōhōron*, in OTKT, vol. 1, pp. i–ii.

24. The key works here are Ōuchi Tsutomu, *Nihon shihonshugi no nōgyō mondai* (Tokyo: Nihon Hyōronsha, 1948) and a companion commentary, id., *Nihon nōgyō no ronri* (Tokyo: Nihon Hyōronsha, 1949). Taken together, these texts set the direction for all of Ōuchi's subsequent work. One authoritative commentator remarks that they constitute both a point of departure and a "summary written in advance" of fifty years of scholarship. See Kase Kazutoshi, "Nihon nōgyō ron no sengo 50-nen: Ōuchi Tsutomu-shi no baai," *Shakai kagaku kenkyū* 48, no. 4 (Jan. 1997): 3–36; quote from p. 6. See also Ōuchi, *Nihon keizairon* (Tokyo Daigaku Shuppankai, 1962–63), vol. 1, ch. 2, and vol. 2, ch. 5. My discussion here is heavily indebted to Kase's comprehensive treatment.

25. Kase, "Nihon nōgyō," pp. 6–8.

26. See Ōuchi Tsutomu, *Nihon shihonshugi no nōgyō mondai*; and *Nihon nōgyō no zaiseigaku* (Tokyo: Tokyo Daigaku Shuppankai, 1950); the influential term for this trend, coined by Kurihara Hyakuju, was *"shōnō hyōjunka"*; see Kurihara, *Nihon nōgyō no kiso kōzō* (1942; reprint, Tokyo: Nōsangyoson Bunka Kyōkai, 1979), esp. pp. 72, 84–85. Like Kurihara, Ōuchi recognized instances of expansion, but the weight of his analysis was on the upward limits to the development of the *shōnō*. See also Ōuchi Tsutomu, *Teikokushugiron*, OTKT, vol. 5, p.322n74; also Kase, "Nihon nōgyō," pp. 9, 28, 31n6.

27. Ōuchi, *Nihon shihonshugi no nōgyō mondai*, p. 14; see Kase, "Nihon nōgyō," pp. 8–9.

28. Ōuchi, *Nōgyō kyōkō* (Tokyo: Yūhikaku, 1954), p. 296; see Kase, "Nihon nōgyō," p. 11; also Ōuchi, *Nihon keizairon*, vol. 2. Is it possible that the conceptual shift from "early versus late" development to "imperialism" also reflects the heightened militancy on the Japanese left in the early 1950s? Kase makes no mention of it.

29. On postwar apprehensions over the scale of holdings, see Nakamura

Takafusa, *The Postwar Japanese Economy* (Tokyo: University of Tokyo Press, 1983), p. 193ff.

30. Kase, "Nihon nōgyō," pp. 12–13.

31. Ōuchi Tsutomu, *Amerika nōgyō ron* (Tokyo: Tokyo Daigaku Shuppankai, 1965), preface and pp. 8–10.

32. Kase, "Nihon nōgyō," p. 14.

33. Kase, "Nihon nōgyō," pp. 14–15. Stolypin quote from G. T. Robinson, *Rural Russia under the Old Regime* (Berkeley and Los Angeles: University of California Press, 1960), p. 194; see also Esther Kingston-Mann, *In Search of the True West: Culture, Economics, and the Problems of Russian Development* (Princeton: Princeton University Press, 1999), pp. 171–78; and the comparative discussion in D. A. Low, *The Egalitarian Moment: Asia and Africa, 1950–1980* (Cambridge: Cambridge University Press, 1996), pp. 63–68.

34. Ōuchi, *Nihon keizairon*, vol. 2, ch. 5, esp. p. 653; the situation in the United States, Ōuchi argued, was similar. Inset quote from Kase, "Nihon nōgyō," p. 17.

35. Kase, "Nihon nōgyō," p. 16. See Ōuchi, *Nihon keizairon*, vol. 1, ch. 5, esp. pp. 282–302; also Nakamura Takafusa, *Postwar Japanese Economy*, p. 199, for a similar point. The "upward shift in the axis of rural differentiation" that brought the *shōnō* into a position of "dependent viability" on the state was also, from the landlord point of view, a "downward shift" as well.

36. Ōuchi, *Kokka dokusen shihonshugi*, p. 151.

37. See discussion and references in Morris-Suzuki, *A History of Japanese Economic Thought*, pp. 122–25; and Shibagaki, "Studies in Japanese Capitalism," pp. 38–46, both of whom note critiques of Ōuchi's argument by his fellow Marxists. See also Baba Hiroji, "Changing the Paradigm of Japanese Marx Economics," *Annals of the Institute of Social Science*, no. 27 (1985): 26–63, esp. pp. 32, 38–39.

38. See Ōuchi Tsutomu, *Atarashii shakaishugizō no tankyū* (Tokyo: Rōdō Shakai Mondai Kenkyū Sentā, 1979); Ogura Toshimaru, *Nettowāku shihai kaitai no senryaku* (Tokyo: Kage Shobō, 1986), pp. 139–47. It should be added that Ōuchi regarded Japan's economic growth in the 1980s as essentially a speculative bubble, and hardly as the vindication of a resurgent Japanese stamocap.

39. Kase, "Nihon nōgyō," pp. 16–18.

40. Ibid., pp. 23–24. Kase (p. 28) raises an interesting question in this connection. Apart from (Chayanovian?) "intensification of self-exploitation," Ōuchi offers no "positive" foundation for the expansion of scale among ultrasmall cultivators. How then, in relation to his initial image of a "passive smallholder" on one hand, and "enterprising agriculturalist" on the other, is the "upward shift" among the *shōnō* to be theorized?

41. Kase, "Nihon nōgyō," pp. 24–26, 30. As Kase notes, Ōuchi and his fellow erstwhile modernists were not spared withering criticisms for their embrace of environmentalism or regionalism, since it was they who had pressed for the exclusion of petty rice farming from unfavorable mountain and woodlands in favor of developing large-scale cultivation (p.34n25).

42. See Kase, "Nihon nōgyō," p. 21. For Wendell Berry see, for example, "Failing Our Farmers," *New York Times*, July 6, 1999, op-ed page.

43. For Ōuchi's self-critical assessment of his work on agriculture and the change in his views, see Ōuchi Tsutomu, *Nōgyō no kihonteki kachi* (Tokyo: Ie no Hikari Kyōkai, 1990).

44. Ōuchi Tsutomu, "Tsuitō Uno Kōzō sensei," in *Omoigusa*, ed. Uno Maria (privately published, 1979), pp. 53–66; quotes from pp. 54, 66. One notes also that Ōuchi was the first of Uno's students asked to speak at the memorial symposium held shortly after his death *(Omoigusa*, pp. 229–72).

45. In the discussion that follows, I refer particularly to Baba Hiroji, "Changing the Paradigms"; *Shin shihonshugiron; Fuyūka to kin'yū shihon* (Kyoto: Mineruva Shobō, 1986); "Kaishashugi no puroburematīku," in *Gendai shisō*, special issue: *Hōjin shihonshugi)* (Dec. 1993): 136–51; Sugiyama Mitsunobu, "Nihon shakai kagaku no sekai ninshiki: Kōza-ha, Ōtsuka shigaku, Uno keizaigaku o megutte," in *Nihon shakai kagaku no shisō*, vol. 3 of *Iwanami kōza: Shakai kagaku no hōhō*, ed. Yamanouchi Yasushi et al. (Tokyo: Iwanami Shoten, 1993), esp. pp. 238–42.

46. Quotes from Baba, "Changing the Paradigms," pp. 29, 45; and *Shin shihonshugiron*, p.345n12.

47. Baba Hiroji, "Sekai keizairon no taishō" (1968), in id., *Sekai keizai— Kijiku to shūhen* (Tokyo: Tokyo Daigaku Shuppankai, 1973), esp. pp. 19–21; and discussion in Nitta, *Dankairon*, pp. 121–23.

48. Nitta, *Dankairon*, p. 121; Sugiyama, "Nihon shakai kagaku no sekai ninshiki," esp. pp. 231–38.

49. Baba, "Changing the Paradigms," p. 26. Apart from the reference to Japan, Baba's points here resonate nicely with the judicious concluding remarks in Howard and King, *History of Marxian Economics*, vol. 2, pp. 387–95: To be sure, "for the most part the capitalist mode of production has continued to deliver the goods"; but the "inescapable reality of the *class* nature of capitalist society," the continuing need for economists to analyze the processes of *social reproduction*, the salience of *contradictions* in those processes, and the necessarily *uneven* character of capitalist development constitute a "hard core" of issues that will continue to demand that "other types of economics . . . be revised in the direction of Marx."

50. A bit of *petite histoire:* I remember vividly my shocked discovery, on reading Makoto Itoh's *The World Economic Crisis and Japanese Capitalism* (New York: St. Martin's Press, 1990), that the world economy in the 1970s had undergone a depression.

51. Baba, "Changing the Paradigms," pp. 33.

52. Ibid., p. 31.

53. Ibid., p. 35.

54. Baba, "Changing the Paradigms," pp. 40–42; "Fordist linkage" comes from Sugiyama, "Nihon shakai kagaku no sekai ninshiki," pp. 239–40.

55. On Japanese capitalism as a "second-and-a-half" stage, see Baba, "Changing the Paradigms," pp. 40–43; Baba, *Fuyūka to kin'yū shihon*, pp. 194–212, esp. 208–9; by the time he published *Shin shihonshugiron*, that notion seems to disappear. See also *Shin shihonshugiron*, pp. 312–20. Baba feels that ingrained prejudice among Western analysts, as well as an unbecoming dependency among Japanese scholars on external validation, prevented earlier recogni-

tion that something of significance in the history of capitalism was occurring in Japan. *Shin shihonshugiron*, p. 310.

56. See the references in Baba, *Shin shihonshugiron*, p.328n10, for the successive presentations of this notion.

57. "Governing ideology": Baba, "Changing the Paradigms," p. 43; "transformation of workers": Baba, *Shin shihonshugiron*, p. 321.

58. Baba, "Changing the Paradigms," pp. 40, 43.

59. Baba, *Shin shihonshugiron*, pp. 325–26. For a somewhat more critical perspective on this process, see Shibagaki Kazuo, "The Welfare State, Japanese Management, and Socialism: The *Aufhebung* of Commoditized Labor Power," *Annals of the Institute of Social Science*, no. 33 (1991):112–35.

60. Baba, *Shin shihonshugiron*, p. 325.

61. As Sugiyama points out, the much-vaunted methods of production control, along with the so-called Ōnoist style of worker mobilization associated with Toyota, came after the political defeat—that is, co-optation into a position of permanent subordination—of the labor movement (Sugiyama, "Nihon shakai kagaku no sekai ninshiki," pp. 240–41). See also Yagi Kiichirō, "The Age of Toyotism: A Transitional Period to Civil Society?," unpublished paper (Dec. 1999); and Yamada Toshio, "Nihongata shihonshugi to kigyōshugiteki chōsei," *Gendai shisō*, special issue: *Hōjin shihonshugi* (Dec. 1993): 166–75.

62. Baba, *Shin shihonshugiron*, pp. 319–20.

63. In Bernstein's version, "peasants do not sink; the middle class does not disappear; crises do not grow ever larger; misery and serfdom do not increase." The more realistic political stance, Bernstein held, was that "there is increase in insecurity, dependence, social distance, social character of production, functional superfluity of property owners." For Bernstein's comments and Hilferding's views, see entries in Tom Bottomore, ed., *Dictionary of Marxist Thought*, 2nd ed. (Oxford: Blackwell, 1991), esp. "Finance Capital," "Revisionism," etc.

64. Baba, "Changing the Paradigms," pp. 36–37.

65. Ibid.

66. Baba, *Shin shihonshugiron*, p. 306.

67. For a similar treatment of culture as the necessary obstacle to unconstrained growth under capitalism (or "economic renovation"), see Shibagaki Kazuo, "Studies in Japanese Capitalism: A Survey with Emphasis on the Contributions of the Marx-Uno School," *Annals of the Institute of Social Science*, no. 30 (1988), esp. pp. 51–52.

68. Baba, "Changing the Paradigms," pp. 43–47. Baba has been justly criticized for ignoring the segmented character of the workforce in Japan; in general, although he gets at the habitus of the representative firm, Yamada Toshio argues, there is a "fatal absence" of any linkage between it and the macrostructures of accumulation (see Yamada, "Nihongata shihonshugi," p. 169). In focusing on the dominant or representative form of capital, Baba is in a sense consistent with the Uno school's methodology. So the issue becomes whether a new methodology is now called for.

69. Baba, "Changing the Paradigms," pp. 46, 49–50; see also Shibagaki, "Studies in Japanese Capitalism."

70. On the timber issue, see Peter Dauvergne, *Shadows in the Forest: Japan*

and the Politics of Timber in Southeast Asia (Cambridge, Mass.: MIT Press, 1997). This is hardly to single out Japan, of course. The historian David Landes writes of an economist who has proposed that "rich nations dump unwanted [nuclear] wastes in poor places such as Africa—all that sand, and the Africans need the money." "The very idea," Landes adds with less than his usual precision, "is symbolically unacceptable." *The Wealth and Poverty of Nations* (New York: W. W. Norton, 1999), p. 516n.

71. Baba, *Shin shihonshugiron*, p. 344.

72. See John Cassidy, "Wall Street Follies," *New Yorker*, Sept. 13, 1999, p. 32, summarizing the results of a joint study by the Institute for Policy Studies (Washington, D.C.) and the advocacy group, United for a Fair Economy.

73. Nitta, *Dankairon*, p. 480.

74. See the following chapters in Hirata Kiyoaki et al., *Gendai shimin shakai to kigyō kokka* (Tokyo: Ochanomizu Shobō, 1994): Yamada Toshio, "Kigyō kokka to shimin shakai" (pp. 47–73, esp. pp. 61–72) and Katō Tetsurō, "Karōshi to sābisu zangyō no seiji keizaigaku—shimin shakai no kiso wa rōdō jikan ka jiyū jikan ka" (pp. 75–126, esp. pp. 84–86, 95, 113–16).

75. In addition to the works by Tamanoi cited in succeeding notes, my discussion draws upon the following critical essays appended to *Keizaigaku no isan* (hereafter *KI*), vol. 1 of *Tamanoi Yoshirō chosakushū* (Tokyo: Gakuyō Shobō, 1990): Kabayama Kōichi, "Chiseishi toshite no 'Tamanoi-gō'" (pp. 3–19); Yoshitomi Masaru, "Henkaku no shisō toshite no keizaigaku" (pp. 316–33); Yagi Kiichirō, "Keizaigakushi ni okeru kyūshin to enshin" (pp. 334–42); and Sekine Tomohiko, "Keizaigaku ni okeru paradaimu tenkan" (pp. 343–59). I have also consulted Nakamura Hisashi, "Nihon ni okeru seimeikei no keizaigaku: Tamanoi Yoshirō no shigoto ni manabu," in *Kakutō suru gendai shisō: Toransumodan e no kokoromi*, ed. Imamura Hitoshi (Tokyo: Kōdansha Gendai Shinsho, 1991), pp. 119–33; and Thomas T. Sekine, "Socialism as a Living Idea," in *Socialist Dilemmas*, ed. Thomas Sekine and Henryk Flakierski (Armonk, N.Y.: M. E. Sharpe, 1990), pp. 128–51.

76. Tamanoi Yoshirō, "Gakumon o aisuru mono e no kitai" (1978), in id., *Ekonomī to ekorojī* (hereafter *EE*) (Tokyo: Misuzu Shobō, 1985), pp. 349–51.

77. See Nakamura Hisashi, "Nihon ni okeru seimeikei no keizaigaku," pp. 119–20.

78. In the preface to *Shin shihonshugiron* (p. iii), Baba Hiroji notes that it was not until he wrote his conclusion that he read Tamanoi's *Ekonomī to ekorojī;* it had no influence whatever on the body of his argument. One suspects that his dismissal of "dime-a-dozen" calls for "regional economic communities" as "well-intentioned foolishness" was aimed at Tamanoi, among others.

79. Tamanoi Yoshirō, *Rikādō kara Marukusu e* (Tokyo: Shin Hyōronsha, 1954); *Keizaigaku no shuyō isan* (1956; reprint, Tokyo: Kōdansha Gakujutsu Bunko, 1980).

80. See Tamanoi, *Keizaigaku no shuyō isan*, in his *Keizaigaku no isan*, pp. 28–32, 150–51; Uno Kōzō, *Keizaigaku hōhōron* (1958), in *UKCS*, vol. 9, p. 8. Note also Kabayama's remark that "one can clearly recognize in Tamanoi a 'scientism' in the sense that—so long as it carried no derogatory connotations—in

his estimation, theoretical transparency took precedence over concrete social processes" (Kabayama, "Chiseishi toshite no 'Tamanoi-gō,'" p. 18).

81. Tamanoi Yoshirō, "Uno keizaigaku no kōseki to genkai," orig. in *Ekonomisuto,* Mar. 29, 1977, in *EE,* pp. 289–309; also in *Keizaigaku no isan,* pp. 293–314. Quote from *EE,* pp. 291–92.

82. Tamanoi, "Uno keizaigaku," pp. 294–96. Uno, "'Kahei no hitsuzensei': Hirufadingu [Hilferding] no kahei riron saikōsatsu" (1930), *UKCS,* vol. 3, esp. pp. 60, 62, 64, 65–7; Rudolf Hilferding, *Finance Capital* (1910), trans. Tom Bottomore (Routledge and Kegan Paul, 1985), ch. 1, esp. pp. 29–35. In his analysis, Uno plays on two terms for necessity: *hitsuyō(sei)* vs. *hitsuzensei;* only the latter seems to convey a sense of inevitability.

83. Itoh, *Value and Crisis,* p. 43.

84. Tamanoi, "Uno keizaigaku," p. 294.

85. Ibid., pp. 297–98; Uno Kōzō and Umemoto Katsumi, *Shakai kagaku to benshōhō* (Tokyo: Iwanami Shoten, 1976), pp. 61–62; "entrusts its destiny": Hilferding, *Finance Capital,* p. 32.

86. Tamanoi Yoshirō, "Shakai kagaku ni okeru seimei no sekai—hiseimeikei kara seimeikei e" (1977), in *EE,* pp. 2–40; quote from p. 19.

87. See Sekine, "Socialism as a Living Idea," p. 130; and Sekine, "Keizaigaku ni okeru paradaimu tenkan," esp. pp. 350–53.

88. See Yoshitomi, "Henkaku no shisō toshite no keizaigaku," pp. 320, 322; Yagi, "Keizaigakushi ni okeru kyūshin to enshin," p. 336; *tenkan* vs. *tenkō:* Kabayama, "Chiseishi toshite no 'Tamanoi-gō,'" p. 15.

89. For this reason, Tamanoi eventually was unmoved by Uno's assertion (voiced in the spirit of the *German Ideology*) that "with the abolition of the commodity form, labor power would be capable of making anything it wished." Tamanoi, "Uno keizaigaku," p. 306; see Marx and Engels, *German Ideology,* in *The Marx-Engels Reader,* R. Tucker ed. (New York: W. W. Norton, 1978), p. 160.

90. Kabayama, "Chiseishi toshite no 'Tamanoi-gō,'" p. 10.

91. This came via his student Kumon Shunpei. Then a graduate student at Indiana University, Kumon went on to collaborate with Tamanoi on some of his comparative inquiries into economic systems, but is best known as one of the most energetic propagators of the notion that Japan's "household" *(ie)* system has created in Japan a distinct form—and model—of industrial organization. See Nakamura Hisashi, "Nihon ni okeru seimeikei no keizaigaku," p. 124.

92. Tamanoi, "Shakai kagaku ni okeru seimei no sekai," in *EE,* p. 21.

93. For this reason, as Sekine points out, when Tamanoi criticized Uno's theory as incapable of "grasping social substance," he was missing the point. For Uno, the *muri* of capitalist society was that it could only construct social relations in commodified form, and never as substance. See Sekine, "Keizaigaku ni okeru paradaimu tenkan," p. 346.

94. Interestingly, this also meant substituting "real" for "empty and reversible Newtonian time." Tamanoi did not oppose space to *time* but to unilinear *history.* See Sekine, "Socialism as a Living Idea," pp. 131–39.

95. Tamanoi, "Kokka to keizai—chiiki bunken o motomete" (1973), in *EE,*

pp. 252–88. Originally published in *Bunmei toshite no keizai,* ed. Tamanoi Yoshirō, vol. 6 of *Ningen no seiki* (Tokyo: Ushio Shuppansha, 1973).

96. Tamanoi, "Kokka to keizai," in *EE,* pp. 255–57, 263–68, 276–86.

97. Ibid., pp. 269–79; see also Uno Kōzō, "Chitsuroku shobun ni tsuite" (1958), *UKCS,* vol. 8, pp. 120–51.

98. Tamanoi, "Kokka to keizai," *EE,* pp. 286–88; Tamanoi, *Keizai taisei* (1975), in *KI,* pp. 265–78.

99. Tamanoi, *Keizai taisei, KI,* pp. 272–73. The "continental pattern" culture referred to here forms one part of a dyad with the "coastal." Weber had argued that latter, as in the Mediterranean, had given way to the former north of the Alps and gone on to generate both markets and an organic relation between city and agriculture. Tamanoi modifies Weber's argument, pointing out the important role of riverine systems and inland port towns as mediators of the market economy (*KI,* pp. 267–68).

100. On the Great Leap Forward, see the following works by Maurice Meisner: *Marxism, Maoism, and Utopianism* (Madison: University of Wisconsin Press, 1982), pp. 67–71, 190–96; *Mao's China and After* (New York: Free Press, 1977), chaps. 12–14; *The Deng Xiaoping Era* (New York: Hill and Wang, 1996), pp. 40–48.

101. Tamanoi, "Shakai kagaku ni okeru seimei no sekai," in *EE,* p. 29; also "Chūgoku zakkan" (1977), in *EE,* pp. 338–48.

102. Tamanoi, "Kokka to keizai," pp. 287–88; "Shakai kagaku ni okeru seimei no sekai," in *EE,* pp. 12–15. "Centripetal" and "centrifugal" are Yagi's terms. See also Yoshitomi, "Henkaku no shisō toshite no keizaigaku," pp. 328, 331.

103. See Kabayama, "Chiseishi toshite no 'Tamanoi-gō,'" p. 11; Yagi, "Keizaigakushi ni okeru kyūshin to enshin," p. 334.

104. Nakamura Hisashi, "Nihon ni okeru seimeikei no keizaigaku," pp. 127–30.

105. See Sekine, "Socialism as a Living Idea," pp. 135–39.

106. Tamanoi, "Shakai kagaku ni okeru seimei no sekai," *EE,* pp. 23–29, 31.

107. Tamanoi, Tsuchida, and Murota, "Towards an entropic theory of economy and ecology," *Economie appliquée* 37, no. 2 (1984): 279–94, esp. pp. 285ff. Tamanoi's major reference here was Nicholas Georgescu-Roegen, *The Entropy Law and the Economic Process* (Cambridge, Mass.: Harvard University Press, 1971) and subsequent works. See also Tamanoi, *EE,* chaps. 2–3, and Sekine, "Socialism as a Living Idea," pp. 131–35.

108. Tamanoi, "Shakai kagaku ni okeru seimei no sekai," *EE,* pp. 36–37.

109. Quotes from Kabayama, "Chiseishi toshite no 'Tamanoi-gō,'" p. 14; Yagi, "Keizaigakushi ni okeru kyūshin to enshin," pp. 340–41; Yoshitomi, "Henkaku no shisō toshite no keizaigaku," pp. 332–33.

110. There are five references to Japan over the three volumes, the most substantive of which is the well-known remark that "Japan, with its purely feudal organization of landed property and its developed small-scale agriculture, gives a much truer picture of the European Middle Ages than all our history books, dic-

tated as these are, for the most part, by bourgeois prejudices." *Capital,* vol. 1, p. 878n.

111. See John Lie, "Reactionary Marxism: the End of Ideology in Japan?" *Monthly Review* 38 (Apr. 1987): 45–51, and Baba's reply, "Revolution and Counterrevolution in Marxian Economics," *Monthly Review* 40 (June 1989): 52–58, and a longer version, "*Fuyūka to kin'yū shihon o megutte,*" *Shakai kagaku kenkyū* 40, no. 3 (Sept. 1988): 51–62.

112. See Ogura Toshimaru, *Shihai no "keizaigaku"* (Tokyo: Renga Shobō, 1985), and his *Nettowāku shihai kaitai no senryaku* (Tokyo: Kage Shobō, 1986) for two attempts to develop a post-Uno critique of capitalism.

113. See the incisive discussion by Simon Clarke, "The Basic Theory of Capitalism: A Critical Review of Itoh and the Uno School," *Capital and Class* 37 (1989): 133–49. This reference courtesy Endō Kōshi.

114. Colin A. M. Duncan, "Under the Cloud of *Capital:* History vs. Theory," *Science and Society* 47, no. 3 (fall 1983), esp. pp. 301–310; inset quote from pp. 301, 307.

115. Had he tried to do so, his system might have ended up looking like that of the later Parsons—another inveterate theorist—in his work on religion. Here was an ever-expanding system whose vast network of cells could accommodate any phenomenon, and therefore precluded disagreement. I owe these points to discussions with Clifford Geertz and Ogura Toshimaru.

CHAPTER 6. SOCIAL SCIENCE AND ETHICS

An earlier version of this chapter appeared as "Capitalism and Civil Society in Modern Japan: Perspectives from Intellectual History," in *The State of Civil Society in Japan,* ed. Frank Schwartz and Susan Pharr (Cambridge, U.K.: Cambridge University Press, 2003). Used here with permission.

1. *Kōjien,* ed. Shinmura Izuru (Tokyo: Iwanami Shoten, 1977), p. 1017.

2. See Irwin Scheiner, *Christian Converts and Social Protest in Meiji Japan* (Berkeley and Los Angeles: University of California Press, 1970), esp. pp. 188–224.

3. Kawakami Hajime, "Nihon dokutoku no kokkashugi" (1911), quoted in Uchida Yoshihiko, *Sakuhin toshite no shakai kagaku* (Tokyo: Iwanami Dōjidai Raiburarī, 1993), pp. 217–18.

4. Antonio Gramsci, *Selections from the Prison Notebooks,* trans. Quintin Hoare and Geoffrey Nowell Smith (New York: International Publishers, 1971), p. 238. On interwar civil society, see Sheldon Garon, *Molding Japanese Minds: The State in Everyday Life* (Princeton: Princeton University Press, 1998).

5. Yamada Toshio, "Kigyō shakai to shimin shakai," in Hirata Kiyoaki et al., *Gendai shimin shakai to kigyō kokka* (Tokyo: Ochanomizu Shobō, 1994), p. 69.

6. See transcript of tributes delivered at memorial, March 30, 1989: Hirata Kiyoaki, "Keizaigakusha Uchida Yoshihiko—sono fūkaku to sakuhin," in *Watakushi no naka no Uchida Yoshihiko* (Tokyo: Iwanami Shoten, 1989), pp. 3–10.

7. Sugiyama Mitsunobu, "Nihon shakai kagaku no sekai ninshiki—Kōza-ha, Ōtsuka shigaku, Uno keizaigaku o megutte." In *Nihon shakai kagaku no shisō,* vol. 3 of *Iwanami kōza: Shakai kagaku no hōhō,* ed. Yamanouchi Yasushi et al. (Tokyo: Iwanami Shoten, 1993), pp. 215–17.

8. Ibid., pp. 217–20.

9. See Sugiyama Mitsunobu, " 'Shimin shakai' ron to senji dōin—Uchida Yoshihiko no shisō keisei o megutte," in *Sōryokusen to gendaika,* ed. Yamanouchi Yasushi et al. (Tokyo: Kashiwa Shobō, 1995), esp. p. 148. Sugiyama's paraphrase here makes explicit an argument that Yamada was compelled to couch in coded terms. See Yamada Moritarō, *Nihon shihonshugi bunseki* (1934), in *Yamada Moritarō chosakushū,* vol. 2 (Tokyo: Iwanami Shoten, 1982), p. 140.

10. Compare Hirano Yoshitarō, *Nihon shihonshugi shakai no kikō* (1934; reprint, Tokyo: Iwanami Shoten, 1949), esp. p. 156, with his *Minzoku seiji no kihon mondai* (Tokyo: Koyama Shoten, 1944); see also Sugiyama Mitsunobu, "Nihon shakai kagaku no sekai ninshiki: Kōza-ha, Ōtsuka shigaku, Uno keizaigaku o megutte," in *Nihon shakai kagaku no shisō,* vol. 3 of *Iwanami kōza: Shakai kagaku no hōhō,* ed. Yamanouchi Yasushi et al. (Tokyo: Iwanami Shoten, 1993), esp. pp. 207–20.

11. See Sugiyama, " 'Shimin shakai' ron to senji dōin," pp. 146–50.

12. Uchida Yoshihiko, "Senji keizaigaku no mujunteki tenkai to keizai riron" (Jan. 1948), in *Uchida Yoshihiko chosakushū,* vol. 10 (Tokyo: Iwanami Shoten, 1989), pp. 109–18.

13. See Uchida Yoshihiko, *Keizaigaku no seitan* (1953), in *Uchida Yoshihiko chosakushū,* vol. 1. This is generally regarded as Uchida's masterpiece, albeit a flawed one (compare Hirata, "Keizaigakusha Uchida Yoshihiko," pp. 7–8). Of this work, Hirata writes:

> The era in which *The Birth of Economics* appeared was one in which workers carried out factory control, and people's control in the railways, in which managers formed Keidanren and other organizations in order to establish managerial rights, and various efforts were made to speed the process leading to the alliance of conservative forces. Articles reporting that Tokyo University graduates were becoming union officials appeared in the papers; at Hitotsubashi—I graduated from there—there were even those who burst out, determined to become revolutionaries. That was the age in which *The Birth* was written" (p. 6).

14. It is to be recalled that the German empire was regarded as combining advanced industrial capitalism (to its west, along the Rhine) with a highly backward agrarian form (to the east, particularly in Prussia).

15. Sugiyama, " 'Shimin shakai' ron to senji dōin," pp. 151–54. On the *narodniki,* see Uchida Yoshihiko, "Narōdoniki to marukusushugi—Rēnin riron seiritsu no ichi sōwa" (Sept. 1946), in *Uchida Yoshihiko chosakushū,* vol. 10, p. 79.

16. See Uchida Yoshihiko, *Nihon shihonshugi no shisōzō* (Tokyo: Iwanami Shoten, 1967), pp. 81, 96.

17. John Bennett and Iwao Ishino, *Paternalism in the Japanese Economy: Anthropological Studies of Oyabun-Kobun Patterns* (Minneapolis: University of

Minnesota Press, 1955); Kawashima Takeyoshi, *Nihon shakai no kazokuteki kōsei* (Tokyo: Gakusei Shobō, 1948).

18. Uchida, *Nihon shihonshugi no shisōzō*, pp. 92–93. Emphases in original.

19. See Takabatake Michitoshi, "Citizens' Movements: Organizing the Spontaneous," *Japan Interpreter* 9, no. 3 (winter 1975): 315–23; Kitazawa Masakuni, "Ningen—sono botsuraku to saisei: Kyūshinteki kōzōshugi no ningenkan," *Tenbō*, no. 111 (Mar. 1968): 16–36; id., "Militarism under the Cloak of Management Society," *Japan Intepreter* 9, no. 3 (winter 1975): 324–30; and Wesley Sasaki-Uemura, *Organizing the Spontaneous: Citizen Protest in Postwar Japan* (Honolulu: University of Hawai'i Press, 2001).

20. Sugiyama, " 'Shimin shakai' ron to senji dōin," p. 160.

21. See Uchida Yoshihiko, *Shihonron no sekai* (Tokyo: Iwanami Shoten, 1966).

22. Uchida Yoshihiko, "Japan Today and *Das Kapital*," in *Japan Interpreter* 6, no. 1 (spring 1970): 14–16. The English version is a considerable abridgment of "*Shihonron* to gendai—Meiji hyakunen to *Shihonron* hyakunen," published in *Sekai* (Sept. 1967): 33–53, and reprinted in Uchida, *Nihon shihonshugi no shisōzō*, pp. 315–60.

23. See Karl Marx, *Grundrisse: Foundations of the Critique of Political Economy (Rough Draft)* (1857–58), trans. Martin Nicolaus (Harmondsworth, U.K.: Penguin, 1973), p. 158; Derek Sayer, *Capitalism and Modernity: An Excursus on Marx and Weber* (London: Routledge, 1991), pp. 13–14.

24. Uchida, "Japan Today and *Das Kapital*," pp. 19–25. Uchida might have linked the antinomy between these two sanctities to the contrast between the "pseudo-Darwinian" right to live and Weber's notion of a "chance to live."

25. Ibid., pp. 15–16; emphasis in original.

26. Yamada Toshio, "Les Tendances du marxisme japonais contemporain," in *Actuel Marx*, no. 2, special issue: *Le Marxisme au Japon* (1987): 40.

27. See also Yamada Toshio, "Kigyō shakai to shimin shakai," p. 49; Sugiyama, " 'Shimin shakai' ron to senji dōin," p. 144.

28. Hirata Kiyoaki, "Shimin shakai to shakaishugi," in id., *Shimin shakai to shakaishugi* (Tokyo: Iwanami Shoten, 1969), pp. 73–125. Quote from p. 75.

29. Ibid., pp. 73, 74, 76, 79.

30. Karl Marx, *Capital*, vol. 1 (Harmondsworth, U.K.: Penguin, 1990), p. 929.

31. Hirata, "Shimin shakai to shakaishugi," pp. 76, 86.

32. Marx, *Capital*, vol. 1, p. 929.

33. Hirata, "Shimin shakai to shakaishugi," p. 93.

34. Ibid., pp. 110–25 passim.

35. See Michael Kenny, "Marxism and Regulation Theory," in *Marxism and Social Science*, ed. Andrew Gamble, David Marsh, and Tony Tant (Urbana and Chicago: University of Illinois Press, 1999).

36. Yamada Toshio, "Kigyō shakai to shimin shakai," p. 69.

37. Hirata Kiyoaki et al., *Gendai shimin shakai to kigyō kokka* (Tokyo: Ochanomizu Shobō, 1994).

38. Yamada Toshio, "Kigyō shakai to shimin shakai," pp. 51–58.

39. Hirata, "Gendai shimin shakai to kigyō kokka," in Hirata et al., *Gendai shimin shakai to kigyō kokka*, p. 33.

40. Yamada Toshio, "Kigyō shakai to shimin shakai," p. 70.

41. Katō Tetsurō, "Karōshi to sābisu zangyō no keizaigaku—Shimin shakai no kiso wa rōdōjikan ka, jiyū jikan ka?" in Hirata et al., *Gendai shimin shakai to kigyō kokka*, pp. 75–126.

42. Maruyama Masao, *Jikonai taiwa* (Tokyo: Misuzu Shobō, 1998), p. 127. The note is dated 1954.

43. Hirata, "Gendai shimin shakai to kigyō kokka," pp. 41–43; Yamada, "Kigyō shakai to shimin shakai," pp. 66, 70–73.

44. Takashima Zen'ya, "Shakai kagaku to wa nani ka," in *Shakai kagaku no kiso riron* (Tokyo: Kōbundō, 1950), pp. 1–22; Hirata, "Gendai shimin shakai to kigyō kokka," pp. 21–22.

45. Maruyama Masao, "Sei'ō bunka to kyōsanshugi no taiketsu," in id., *Gendai seiji no shisō to kōdō*, exp. ed. (Tokyo: Miraisha, 1966), p. 222; Maruyama Masao, Umemoto Katsumi, and Satō Noboru, *Sengo Nihon no kakushin shisō* (Tokyo: Gendai no Rironsha, 1983), pp. 142–43.

46. See Maruyama Masao, *Nihon no shisō* (Tokyo: Iwanami Shinsho, 1961), esp. pp. 179–80 and afterword.

47. Ishida Takeshi and Kang Sangjung, *Maruyama Masao to shimin shakai* (Yokohama: Seori Shobō, 1997), esp. pp. 11–37, 68–76, 98. See also Hiraishi Naoaki, "Maruyama Masao no 'shimin shakai' ron" (paper presented to the twelfth international symposium, Japan Research Center, Fudan University [Shanghai], Apr. 2002), esp. pp. 4–7.

CHAPTER 7. IMAGINING DEMOCRACY IN POSTWAR JAPAN

An earlier version of this chapter appeared as "Imagining Democracy in Postwar Japan: Reflections on Maruyama Masao and Modernism," in *Journal of Japanese Studies* 18, no. 2 (summer 1992): 365–406. Used here with permission.

1. John Dunn, *Western Political Theory in the Face of the Future* (Cambridge: Cambridge University Press, 1979), pp. 1–27; quotes from pp. 1, 9, 27.

2. For book-length treatments of Maruyama's work see Sasakura Hideo, *Maruyama Masao ron nōto* (Tokyo: Misuzu Shobō, 1988); Tsuzuki Tsutomu, *Sengo Nihon no chishikijin: Maruyama Masao to sono jidai* (Yokohama: Seori Shobō, 1995); Rikki Kersten, *Democracy in Postwar Japan: Maruyama Masao and the Search for Autonomy* (London: Routledge, 1996). For details on the reception of Maruyama's early postwar work, including articles about, and interviews with, Maruyama, see Imai Juichirō and Kawaguchi Shigeo, *Maruyama Masao chosaku nōto*, exp. ed. (Tokyo: Gendai no Rironsha, 1987).

3. The term was not a self-designation but a somewhat pejorative and reductionist Marxist label; the Communist Party journal *Zen'ei* (Aug. 1948) was devoted to the critique of modernism. The label stuck, however, as witnessed by the collection edited by Hidaka Rokurō: *Kindaishugi*, vol. 34 of *Gendai Nihon shisō taikei* (Tokyo: Chikuma Shobō, 1966). *Kindai(shugi)* is historically distinct from *modan(izumu)*, a coinage of the post–World War I era. While overlapping in some respects, *kindaishugi* was concerned with the social transition from something other than and prior to modernity, and it held modernity out as a goal to be attained; *modan* pertained to a mode of life claimed to be already actualized

within Japan's urban spaces, and potentially realizable beyond them. *Modani-zumu* was its cultural articulation.

4. See Hidaka Rokurō's introductory essay in ibid., esp. pp. 10f.

5. Yoshida Masatoshi, *Sengo shisō ron* (Tokyo: Aoki Shoten, 1984), pp. 22–23, 30–31.

6. See Maruyama's afterword to "Kindaiteki shii" (1945), in his *Senchū to sengo no aida* (Tokyo: Misuzu Shobō, 1976), p. 190, for a discussion of the intellectual atmosphere of the Seinen Bunka Kaigi.

7. On Etō Jun, see Yoshida, *Sengo shisō ron*, pp. 134–61. See also Shimizu Ikutarō, *Sengo o utagau* (Tokyo: Kōdansha, 1980), pp. 7–61.

8. See Byron K. Marshall, *Academic Freedom and the Japanese Imperial University, 1868–1939* (Berkeley and Los Angeles: University of California Press, 1992).

9. The phrase "Quest for a science of society" is taken from Alexander Vucinich, *Social Thought in Tsarist Russia: The Quest for a General Science of Society* (Chicago: University of Chicago Press, 1976).

10. See M. Rainer Lepsius, "Sociology in the Interwar Period: Trends in Development and Criteria for Evaluation," in *Modern German Sociology*, ed. Volker Meja, Dieter Misgeld, and Nico Stehr (New York: Columbia University Press, 1987), p. 49.

11. The value and status distinctions between "insiders" and "outsiders" within the public sphere of imperial Japan are explored in Andrew E. Barshay, *State and Intellectual in Imperial Japan: The Public Man in Crisis* (Berkeley and Los Angeles: University of California Press, 1988), esp. pp. 1–33. The argument, in essence, is that the state successfully hegemonized the public sphere. Thus state service, and by extension "service to the nation" via large-scale bureaucratic organizations, tended to enjoy higher status as insider public activity than would outsider activities such as independent scholarship, journalism, labor union work, etc. See also Maruyama Masao, "Kindai Nihon no chishiki-jin," in his *Kōei no ichi kara* (Tokyo: Miraisha, 1982).

12. On socialists as metaphorical foreigners see Carol Gluck, *Japan's Modern Myths: Ideology in the Late Meiji Period* (Princeton: Princeton University Press, 1985), esp. pp. 38–39, 135, 174–77. On the early development of sociology in Japan see Kawamura Nozomu, *Nihon shakaigakushi kenkyū*, vol. 1 (Tokyo: Ningen no Kagakusha, 1975), pp. 164–232, and his "Interwar Sociology and Socialism," in *Culture and Identity: Japanese Intellectuals during the Interwar Years*, ed. J. Thomas Rimer (Princeton: Princeton University Press, 1990), esp. pp. 63–69.

13. Umemoto Katsumi, "Marukusushugi to kindai seijigaku: Maruyama Masao no tachiba o chūshin toshite," in *Kōza gendai no ideorogī*, vol. 5 of *Gendai Nihon no shisō to kōdō*, ed. Ikumi Takuichi et al. (Tokyo: San'ichi Shobō, 1962); Uno Kōzō, "Nihon shihonshugi ronsō to wa nani ka" (1950), in *Uno Kōzō chosakushū*, suppl. vol. (Tokyo: Iwanami Shoten, 1974), pp. 11–15; Maruyama, *Nihon no shisō* (Tokyo: Iwanami Shinsho, 1961), pp. 55–62.

14. On social science as a movement see Morito Tatsuo, *Shisō tōsōshijō ni okeru shakai kagaku undō no jūyōsei* (Tokyo: Kaizōsha, 1926).

15. Maruyama, "Kindai Nihon no chishikijin," pp. 107–8; Maruyama

Masao's introduction to his *Studies in the Intellectual History of Tokugawa Japan* (Princeton: Princeton University Press; Tokyo: Tokyo University Press, 1974), p. xxiv. Emphasis in original. As noted in ch. 2 of this book, various social science disciplines developed in Japan as discrete sciences, and in contrast to Europe, Japan had not experienced the crisis and collapse of general sociology à la Comte and Spencer. Under these circumstances the impact of Marxism was all the more profound. See J. K. Fairbank and Masataka Banno, intro. to *Japanese Studies of Modern China* (Cambridge, Mass.: Harvard University Press, 1955), pp. xiv–xv.

16. Ishida Takeshi, *Nihon no shakai kagaku* (Tokyo: Tokyo Daigaku Shuppankai, 1984) pp. 141–48; Kawamura, *Nihon shakaigakushi kenkyū*, vol. 2, pp. 211–82.

17. Sakuta Keiichi, "The Controversy over Community and Autonomy," in *Authority and the Individual in Japan*, ed. J. Victor Koschmann (Tokyo: Tokyo University Press, 1974); Fujita Shōzō, *Tennōsei kokka no shihai genri* (Tokyo: Miraisha, 1959). On Takata see the lengthy exposition in Harry Harootunian, *Overcome by Modernity: History, Culture, and Community in Interwar Japan* (Princeton: Princeton University Press, 2000), pp. 402–13; and Kawamura, *Nihon shakaigakushi kenkyū*, vol. 2, pp. 22–43, 242–55.

18. Ishida, *Nihon no shakai kagaku*, p. 147.

19. Lepsius, "Sociology in the Interwar Period," pp. 43, 47–48, 49–50; Mannheim is quoted on p. 43.

20. See Maruyama Masao, "Politics as a Science in Japan" (1947), in his *Thought and Behavior in Modern Japanese Politics* (hereafter *Thought and Behavior*) (New York: Oxford University Press, 1969), pp. 225–44; and the statement of purpose submitted to the Ministry of Education by the founding committee of the Institute of Social Science, Tokyo University, in April 1946, repr. in *Shakai Kagaku Kenkyūjo no sanjūnen* (Tokyo: Shakai Kagaku Kenkyūjo, 1977), pp. 43–44. This does not mean that empirical research was neglected; see Kawamura, *Nihon shakaigakushi kenkyū*, vol. 2, pp. 137–211; on the "sublimation" or denial of politics, see Bernard Silberman, "The Bureaucratic State in Japan: The Problem of Authority and Legitimacy," in *Conflict in Modern Japanese History: The Neglected Tradition*, ed. Tetsuo Najita and J. Victor Koschmann (Princeton: Princeton University Press, 1982).

21. Eliza Marian Butler, *The Tyranny of Greece over Germany: A Study of the Influence Exercised by Greek Art and Poetry over the Great German Writers of the Eighteenth, Nineteenth, and Twentieth Centuries* (Cambridge: Cambridge University Press, 1935).

22. Kurt Lenk, "The Tragic Consciousness of German Sociology," in *Modern German Sociology*, ed. Volker Meja, Dieter Misgeld, and Nico Stehr (New York: Columbia University Press, 1987), pp. 57–75, esp. pp. 68, 71.

23. See comments of Karl Löwith in "Japan's Westernization and Moral Foundation" (1942–43), in *Sämtliche Schriften*, vol. 2 (Stuttgart: J. B. Metzler, 1983), pp. 541–55, esp. p. 545.

24. Maruyama, *Studies in the Intellectual History of Tokugawa Japan*, esp. pp. 26–31, 195–205. Maruyama explores the conflation of value and reality in his *Nihon no shisō*, part 1, passim.

25. Maruyama Masao, "Thought and Behavior Patterns of Japan's Wartime Leaders" (1949), in his *Thought and Behavior,* pp. 107, 114. On the "Ideas of 1914," see Harry Liebersohn, *Fate and Utopia in German Sociology, 1870–1923* (Cambridge, Mass.: MIT Press, 1988), esp. pp. 74–75, on Ernst Troeltsch. Compare with remarks made by the critic Kawakami Tetsutarō at the conclusion of the Overcoming the Modern Conference in July 1942 (" 'Kindai no chōkoku' ketsugo," in *Kindai no chōkoku,* ed. Kawakami Tetsutarō [Tokyo: Fuzanbō, 1979], esp. p. 166).

26. Emil Lederer and Emy Seidler-Lederer, *Japan in Transition* (New Haven: Yale University Press, 1938), p. xi.

27. See the philosopher Tanabe Hajime's agonized preface to his *Zangedō toshite no tetsugaku,* translated by Takeuchi Yoshinori as *Philosophy as Metanoetics* (Berkeley and Los Angeles: University of California Press, 1986).

28. Note that "absolute negativity" does not equal radical evil, but rather an all-productive emptiness.

29. See Takeuchi Yoshimi, "Kindai no chōkoku" (1959), in his *Kindai no chōkoku* (Tokyo: Chikuma Shobō, 1983), esp. pp. 109–111.

30. See Tsurumi Shunsuke, in appx. I to *Nationalism and the Right Wing in Japan: A Study of Post-war Trends,* by Ivan Morris (Oxford: Oxford University Press, 1960), pp. 426–27.

31. The term "substantialist view of concepts" was used self-critically by Maruyama *(Thought and Behavior,* p. xv) but was eminently applicable to Marxists.

32. This information comes from author's notes on Maruyama's oral account, taken at the first of a series of talks at the University of California, Berkeley, May 1983.

33. Maruyama Masao, Nishida Toshiyuki, and Uete Michiari, "Kindai Nihon to Kuga Katsunan" (1968), roundtable discussion, in *Gyakusetsu toshite no gendai,* ed. *Misuzu* (Tokyo: Misuzu Shobō, 1983), pp. 149–87; Maruyama Masao, "Nyozekan to chichi to watakushi," in *Hasegawa Nyozekan: Hito; jidai; shisō to chosaku mokuroku,* ed. Sera Masatoshi et al. (Tokyo: Chūō Daigaku Shuppanbu, 1986), pp. 267–317.

34. Basic texts are collected in *Ōtsuka Hisao chosakushū* (Tokyo: Iwanami Shoten, 1969); see esp. "Kindaiteki ningen ruikei no sōshutsu" (1946) and "Jan Karuvan [Jean Calvin]" (1947), in vol. 8, pp. 169–75, 404–20. Also essential is Otsuka's *Kyōdōtai no kiso riron* (1955) (Tokyo: Iwanami Shoten, 1984). An important discussion is Uchida Yoshiaki, *Vēbā to Marukusu: Nihon shakai kagaku no shisō kōzō* (Tokyo: Iwanami Shoten, 1972), esp. part 2. As suggested in chapter 2, something of a controversy has developed in recent years over the interpretation of Ōtsuka's postwar work: How far did he merely transpose his wartime writings on "productivity" as the essence of modern and rational imperial subjecthood to suit the "democratic" postwar milieu? Conversely, how far did Uchimura's insistence on the ultimate value of individual conscience shape Ōtsuka's interventions? See Yasushi Yamanouchi, J. Victor Koschmann, and Narita Ryūichi, eds., *Total War and 'Modernization'* (Ithaca: East Asia Program, Cornell University, 1998), particularly the essays by Yamanouchi, Koschmann,

Sugiyama Mitsunobu, and Iwasaki Minoru. As should be clear, my own sense is that, in Ōtsuka's case, the force of conscience is not to be underestimated. Ultimately, wartime mobilization was underlain by coercion and violence to a qualitatively different extent than it was during the postwar period.

35. On Nanbara, see Barshay, *State and Intellectual,* pp. 36–122 passim.

36. The choice to do so, Maruyama claims, came at Nanbara's instance; it was Nanbara's belief that Japanese tradition could not be confronted effectively except via scientific analysis and on its own grounds. See Maruyama Masao, "Nihon shisōshi ni okeru 'kosō' no mondai" (1979) in *Maruyama Masao shū,* vol. 11 (Tokyo: Iwanami Shoten, 1995), pp. 158–59.

37. This paragraph draws upon Maruyama Masao, "Shisōshi no hōhō o mosaku shite—hitotsu no kaisō," *Nagoya daigaku hōsei ronshū* no. 77 (Sept. 1978): 1–31, esp. pp. 6–9.

38. Maruyama, *Studies in the Intellectual History of Tokugawa Japan,* pp. xxvii–xxviii, 192.

39. Karl Mannheim, *Ideology and Utopia* (1936; reprint, New York: Harcourt Brace Jovanovich ed., n.d.), p. 259.

40. Maruyama, "Shisōshi no hōhō o mosaku shite," p. 18.

41. Ibid., p. 20.

42. Mannheim, *Ideology and Utopia,* pp. 1–13, esp. pp. 8–9.

43. I use the term "nonsensification" to suggest the essential gutting of the intellectual content of public discourse by means of slogans backed with force. Simone Weil considered "nonsensification" to be characteristic of fascist regimes. See esp. "The Power of Words" (1937), in *Selected Essays,* ed. Richard Rees (Oxford: Oxford University Press, 1963). In *Being and Time* (1927), Martin Heidegger provides a virtually self-fulfilling prophecy of this process. See his condemnation of *Gerede* ("mere talk") as characteristic of the discourse of "the they" who make up the "public," "the glare of which obscures everything." See his *Being and Time* (New York: Random House, 1962), pp. 165, 213; also Hannah Arendt, preface to *Men in Dark Times* (New York: Harcourt Brace Jovanovich, 1968).

44. Maruyama, *Studies in the Intellectual History of Tokugawa Japan,* pp. 222, 238.

45. Maruyama Masao, "Asō Yoshiteru, *Kinsei Nihon tetsugakushi* o yomu," in his *Senchū to sengo no aida,* esp. pp. 119, 127–32. See also Karl Löwith, "Der europäische Nihilismus" (1940), in *Sämtliche Schriften,* vol. 2, pp. 473–540, esp. pp. 532–40.

46. Maruyama, "Kindaiteki shii," pp. 188–90.

47. See Maruyama's dialogue with Tsurumi Shunsuke, in Tsurumi Shunsuke and Maruyama Masao, "Fuhen genri no tachiba," in *Kataritsugu sengoshi,* vol. 1, ed. Tsurumi Shunsuke (Tokyo: Shisō no Kagakusha, 1969), pp. 80–107; quote from p. 93.

48. As Maruyama puts it, "*'uchi'-teki de nai nashonarizumu.*" Ibid., p. 95.

49. Maruyama, *Studies in the Intellectual History of Tokugawa Japan,* pp. xxxiv–xxxv; Klaus Kracht, "Traditional and Modern Thought in Japan: Some Notes on the Problem of Continuity and Its Meaning," in *Tradition and Modern Japan,* ed. P. G. O'Neill (Tenterden, Kent: Paul Norbury, 1981), pp. 54–59.

50. Robert Bellah, review of Maruyama's *Studies in the Intellectual History of Tokugawa Japan,* in *Journal of Japanese Studies* 3, no. 1 (winter 1977).

51 On the revival and reorientation of publications, see *Nihon shuppan nenkan* (Tokyo: Kyōdō Shuppansha, 1943–48) volumes for 1944–46 and 1947–48, esp. the overview of trends (part 1 of each volume) and the statistical tables that follow; on reforms of higher education and expansion of the university system, see Michio Nagai, *Higher Education in Japan: Its Take-Off and Crash* (Tokyo: University of Tokyo Press, 1971), part 1, esp. pp. 45–54.

52. Maruyama Masao, "Nationalism in Japan: Its Theoretical Background and Prospects" (1951), in *Thought and Behavior,* p. 152. See also *Gendai seiji no shisō to kōdō* (Tokyo: Miraisha, 1966), p. 168.

53. Fujita, *Tennōsei kokka no shihai genri,* p. 189. Emphasis added.

54. Maruyama Masao, "Theory and Psychology of Ultranationalism" (1946), in *Thought and Behavior,* pp. 1–23. In the English edition, the title is mistakenly translated as "theory and psychology"; the proper rendering of *ronri* should be "logic," which is something less explicit and harder to get at. For reactions to the article, see Matsumoto Sannosuke et al., "Maruyama riron to genzai shisō jōkyō," in *Gendai no riron,* ed. Andō Jinbei (Tokyo: Gendai no Rironsha, 1978), pp. 74–75; also Takahashi Saburō, sociology department, Kyoto University, personal communication.

55. Yoshimoto Takaaki, "Maruyama Masao ron" in *Yoshimoto Takaaki zenchosakushū,* vol. 12 (Tokyo: Keisō Shobō, 1969), pp. 5–96, esp. pp. 23–26.

56. Yoshimoto, "Maruyama Masao ron," p. 26. That it should have come from the masses, however, seems an unwarranted expectation to begin with.

57. See Alfred Schutz, "Common-Sense and Scientific Intepretation of Human Action," in id., *Collected Papers,* vol. 1 (The Hague: Martinus Nijhoff, 1967), pp. 43–44: "Each term in a scientific model of human action must be constructed in such a way that a human act performed within the life-world by an individual actor . . . would be understandable for the actor himself as well as for his fellow-men in terms of common-sense interpretation of everyday life."

58. For contemporary analyses of fascism, see Barshay, *State and Intellectual,* pp. 191–202; and Tanaka Hiroshi, *Hasegawa Nyozekan kenkyū josetsu* (Tokyo: Miraisha, 1990), pp. 76–96.

59. The term "reactionary modernism" is drawn from Jeffrey Herf, *Reactionary Modernism: Technology, Culture, and Politics in Weimar and the Third Reich* (Cambridge: Cambridge University Press, 1984). For relevant work on Japan in this connection, see Miles Fletcher, *The Search for a New Order* (Chapel Hill: University of North Carolina Press, 1982).

60. Note, however, that Maruyama never called for the destruction of the monarchy (Iizuka Kōji, *Nihon no guntai* [1958], as quoted in Yoshimoto, "Maruyama Masao ron," pp. 16–17). See also Maruyama Masao, "Shōwa tennō o meguru kiregire no kaisō" (1989) in *Maruyama Masao shū,* vol. 15 (Tokyo: Iwanami Shoten, 1996), pp. 13–36, esp. p. 33.

61. One's freedom of expression was obviously more circumscribed about the occupied present, but it would be a distortion to equate this censorship with the repressive apparatus of the imperial state.

62. Stanley Cavell, *The Claim of Reason: Wittgenstein, Skepticism, Morality, Tragedy* (Oxford: Oxford University Press, 1979), p. xvi.

63. Maruyama Masao, "The Ideology and Dynamics of Japanese Fascism" (1947), in *Thought and Behavior*, p. 63.

64. Maruyama, "Thought and Behavior Patterns," pp. 84–134.

65. Leszek Kolakowski, "The Concept of the Left," in his *Toward a Marxist Humanism* (New York: Grove Press, 1968), p. 68.

66. Maruyama Masao, "Nihon ni okeru jiyū ishiki no keisei to tokushitsu" (Aug. 1947), in id., *Senchū to sengo no aida*, p. 305.

67. See Imai and Kawaguchi, *Maruyama Masao chosaku nōto*, pp. 12–68, for the years from 1945 through 1960. Ishida, *Nihon no shakai kagaku*, pp. 176, 274.

68. On "class subjectivity," see J. Victor Koschmann, *Revolution and Subjectivity in Postwar Japan* (Chicago: University of Chicago Press, 1996), ch. 3. For Maruyama's characterization of "old liberalism," see his comments on Fukai Eigo in *Thought and Behavior*, p. 109n; on his attitude toward the early postwar left, see Tsurumi and Maruyama, "Fuhen genri no tachiba," pp. 84–85.

69. Maruyama Masao, "Aru jiyūshugisha e no tegami" (1950), in id., *Gendai seiji no shisō to kōdō*, exp. ed. (Tokyo: Miraisha, 1966), pp. 131–51, 511–16.

70. Ibid., p. 513, with emphasis in original.

71. "Gendai ni okeru taido kettei," *Sekai*, no. 175 (July 1960): 175–84; quote from p. 182. Also reprinted in Maruyama, *Gendai seiji*, pp. 446–61.

72. Ishida, *Nihon no shakai kagaku*, p. 198.

73. Maruyama Masao, *Nihon no shisō* (Tokyo: Iwanami Shinsho ed., 1961). The texts that make up this book were initially published between 1957 and 1959.

74. Ibid., pp. 11–12, 14, 20–21, 52–62; the "mother's nostalgia" formulation comes from Nakajima Makoto, *Sengo shisōshi nyūmon* (Tokyo: Ushio Shuppansha, 1968), p. 84.

75. Maruyama, *Nihon no shisō*, pp. 176–80. "Genji": Maruyama, *Thought and Behavior*, p. 310.

76. Maruyama, *Nihon no shisō*, pp. 44–52.

77. Maruyama, statement in Maruyama Masao, Umemoto Katsumi, and Satō Noboru, *Sengo Nihon no kakushin shisō* (Tokyo: Gendai no Rironsha, 1983), pp. 48–49.

78. Irokawa Daikichi, *The Culture of the Meiji Period*, translation ed. Marius Jansen (Princeton: Princeton University Press, 1986), p. 246.

79. Maruyama, *Nihon no shisō*, part 3, esp. pp. 129–34.

80. Ibid., pp. 179–80 and afterword.

81. Maruyama Masao, "Politics and Man in the Contemporary World," in *Thought and Behavior*, p. 347.

82. For a discussion of "irrationalization," see Maruyama, "Nationalism in Japan," p. 152.

83. The theme of "complacent spirit" (*tarunda seishin*) and "blind faith" (*wakudeki*) in institutions derives from Fukuzawa Yukichi. See Umemoto,

"Marukusushugi to kindai seijigaku," pp. 54f, and J. Victor Koschmann, "Maruyama Masao and the Incomplete Project of Modernity," in *Postmodernism and Japan*, ed. H. D. Harootunian and Masao Miyoshi (Durham: Duke University Press, 1989) for discussion of this key aspect of Maruyama's work.

84. Maruyama, *Gendai seiji*, p. 574; longer quote is Matsumoto Sannosuke's paraphrase, see Matsumoto et al., "Maruyama riron," p. 88.

85. Maruyama, *Gendai seiji*, p. 585.

86. Maruyama, *Thought and Behavior*, p. xvii.

87. Maruyama Masao, "Meiji kokka no shisō" (1946), in id., *Senchū to sengo no aida*, p. 243.

88. Maruyama, "Theory and Psychology of Ultranationalism," pp. 4–5. Emphasis in original.

89. Maruyama, "Aru jiyūshugisha e no tegami," p. 144. Note, however, Yoshimoto's comment that he found more to respect in Maruyama's account than in the work of postwar scholars who are driven to look to "graffiti on bathroom walls" for examples of popular resistance to war (Yoshimoto, "Maruyama Masao ron," p. 78).

90. In addition to items cited in notes 81–87 above, the foregoing paragraphs have drawn upon the following: Maruyama, "Nihon ni okeru jiyū ishiki no keisei to tokushitsu," pp. 297–306; "From Carnal Literature to Carnal Politics" (1949), in *Thought and Behavior*, pp. 245–67, and "Kaikoku" (1959), in *Kindaishugi*, vol. 34 of *Gendai Nihon shisō taikei* (Tokyo: Chikuma Shobō, 1964), pp. 282–312.

91. Maruyama, "Politics as a Science in Japan," p. 233.

92. Maruyama, "Kindai Nihon no chishikijin," esp. pp. 113–25.

93. Maruyama Masao, "Sensō sekinin ron no mōten" (1956), in id., *Senchū to sengo no aida*, pp. 596–602.

94. Maruyama, "Politics as a Science in Japan," p. 232. I have modified the translation slightly.

95. Ibid., pp. 238–39; see also Umemoto, "Marukusushugi to kindai seijigaku," pp. 29–30, 34, 52.

96. Maruyama, "Kindai Nihon no chishikijin," pp. 117–18; Watanabe Yoshimichi, *Shisō to gakumon no jiden* (1974), quoted in Ishida, *Nihon no shakai kagaku*, pp. 178–79.

97. Fujita Shōzō, "Shakai kagakusha no shisō," in *Sengo Nihon no shisō* by Kuno Osamu, Tsurumi Shunsuke, and Fujita Shōzō (Tokyo: Keisō Shobō, 1966), pp. 37–38, 40, 47; Maruyama Masao, "A Critique of De-Stalinization" (1956) in *Thought and Behavior*, pp. 177–224.

98. Maruyama Masao, "Seijigaku nyūmon" (1949) in *Senchū to sengo no aida*, pp. 421–49; "A Critique of De-Stalinization," p. 185.

99. Maruyama, "Shisōshi no hōhō o mosaku shite," p. 27.

100. Maruyama Masao, "Rekishi ishiki no 'kosō,'" in *Rekishi shisō shū*, ed. id. (Tokyo: Chikuma Shobō, 1972); id., "Genkei/kosō/shitsuyō tei'on: Nihon shisōshi hōhōron ni tsuite no watakushi no ayumi," in *Nihon bunka no kakureta kata*, ed. Takeda Kiyoko (Tokyo: Iwanami Shoten, 1984); id., "Matsurigoto no kōzō: Seiji ishiki no shitsuyō tei'on" (1985), in id., *Maruyama Masao shū*, vol. 12 (Tokyo: Iwanami Shoten, 1996).

101. Mitani Taichirō, *Futatsu no sengo: Kenryoku to chishikijin* (Tokyo: Chikuma Shobō, 1988), esp. pp. 239–40; Maruyama, "Kindai Nihon no chishikijin," pp. 127–30.

102. Maruyama, *Nihon no shisō*, p. 56.

103. Umemoto, "Marukusushugi to kindai seijigaku," p. 13.

104. Takeuchi Yoshimi, "Kindaishugi to minzoku no mondai" (1951), in id., *Kindai no chōkoku* (Tokyo: Chikuma Shobō, 1983), esp. pp. 239–40; Andrew E. Barshay, "Imagining Democracy in Postwar Japan: Reflections on Maruyama Masao and Modernism," *Journal of Japanese Studies* 18, no. 2 (summer 1992), p. 403.

105. See Maruyama's postscript to his *Nihon seiji shisōshi kenkyū* (Tokyo: Tokyo Daigaku Shuppankai, 1952), esp. p. 7.

106. Yoshida, *Sengo shisō ron*, pp. 30–31.

107. Murakami Yasusuke, "The Japanese Model of Political Economy," in *The Domestic Transformation*, vol. 1 of *The Political Economy of Japan*, ed. Kozo Yamamura and Yasukichi Yasuba (Stanford: Stanford University Press, 1987), pp. 33–90.

108. Ibid., pp. 35–43, 46–47, 56–71 passim; long quote from p. 61.

109. Ibid., pp. 57, 62, 597 n24.

110. Ibid., pp. 58–61, 85ff.

CONCLUSION

1. Dōgen, *Shōbōgenzō*, vol. 2 (Tokyo: Iwanami Bunko, 1999), p. 118; Tosaka Jun, *Sekai no ikkan toshite no Nihon* (1937), in *Tosaka Jun zenshū*, vol. 5 (Tokyo: Keisō Shobō, 1967).

2. "The Meiji Restoration, as it is called, not only overthrew the Tokugawa, as China's revolutionaries overthrew the Manchus nearly fifty years later, but also brought to power a group of men who were dedicated to the aim of expanding the country's wealth and strength. What they meant by this was to combine government and military structures in the western manner with modern industry, traditional ideology and a minimum of social change. It proved to be a durable formula." W. G. Beasley, *The Japanese Experience* (Berkeley and Los Angeles: University of California Press, 1999), p. xvii.

3. See Maruyama Masao, "Politics and Man in the Contemporary World" (1961), in id., *Thought and Behavior in Modern Japanese Politics* (New York: Oxford University Press, 1969), p. 348.

4. Uno Kōzō, *Shihonron gojūnen* (Tokyo: Hōsei Daigaku Shuppankyoku, 1981), pp. 367–68.

5. Uno himself was spared attack, not because he was in the least sympathetic, but (probably) because he was too old; Uno's close disciple, Ōuchi Tsutomu (b. 1918), by contrast, was treated in a manner similar to Maruyama—physically trapped and harangued with demands that he carry out a self-criticism.

6. See the discussion of this and the related notion of "faith in lived experience," taken from Maruyama's *Nihon no shisō*, in chapter 7. The particular point about "modern economics" subsisting on a "faith in theory" is owed to

Sawa Takamitsu, "Nihon shihonshugi to *Nihon no shisō*," *Sekai* (Nov. 1995): 49–56.

7. Yamamoto Yoshitaka, *Chisei no hanran: Tōdai kaitai made* (Tokyo: Zen'eisha, 1969), pp. 22–31.

8. As Maruyama stressed, he had begun to think about the problems associated with these notions in the years after 1958, when he wrote his essay on the "Opening of the Country" ("Kaikoku"). "Prototype" was used in lecture presentations after 1963; "ancient substrate" after 1972; and "basso ostinato" after 1975. The turn to the ancient past, he emphasized, was not a *tenkō*, or flight, from unpalatable political reality after being attacked. Nevertheless, the coincidence is striking, and understandable. See Maruyama, "Genkei/kosō/shitsuyō tei'on: Nihon shisōshi hōhōron ni tsuite no watakushi no ayumi," in *Nihon bunka no kakureta kata*, ed. Takeda Kiyoko (Tokyo: Iwanami Shoten, 1984), esp. pp. 94, 139–52.

9. Maruyama Masao, "Rekishi ishiki no 'kosō,'" in *Rekishi shisō shū*, ed. Maruyama Masao, vol. 6 of *Nihon no shisō* (Tokyo: Chikuma Shobō, 1972), pp. 19, 35. This essay is reprinted in Maruyama, *Chūsei to hangyaku* (Tokyo: Chikuma Shobō, 1992); and in *Maruyama Masao shū* (Tokyo: Iwanami Shoten, 1996), vol. 10.

10. Maruyama Masao, "The Structure of Matsurigoto: The Basso Ostinato of Japanese Political Life," in *Themes and Theories in Modern Japanese History*, ed. Jean-Pierre Lehmann and Sue Henny (London: Athlone Press, 1988); quote from p. 43.

11. Maruyama, "Rekishi ishiki no 'kosō,'" p. 41.

12. Maruyama Masao, *Bunmeiron no gairyaku o yomu*, 3 vols. (Tokyo: Iwanami Shoten, 1986).

13. See Yamanouchi Yasushi, "Sengo hanseiki no shakai kagaku to rekishi ninshiki," *Rekishigaku kenkyū* no. 689 (Oct. 1996): 32–43, esp. p. 41.

14. Maruyama, statement in Maruyama Masao, Umemoto Katsumi, and Satō Noboru, *Sengo Nihon no kakushin shisō* (Tokyo: Gendai no Rironsha, 1983), p. 148.

15. "For me the world since the Renaissance and the Reformation is a story of the revolt of man against nature, of the revolt of the poor against privilege, of the revolt of the 'undeveloped' against the 'West,' now one emerging, now the other, each evoking the other and forming in the modern world a composition of harmony and dissonance on the grandest scale." Maruyama, *Thought and Behavior*, preface to English edition, p. xvi.

16. Maruyama Masao, "The Changing Images of *Model* States: Modern Japan and Utopia" (unpublished MS, Jan. 20, 1962), p. 16. I am grateful to Robert Bellah for making this essay available to me.

17. Beasley, *The Japanese Experience*, p. xviii.

18. Marx, *Capital*, vol. 1 (Harmondsworth, U.K.: Penguin, 1990), p.878n; Marc Bloch, *Feudal Society* (Chicago: University of Chicago Press, 1974), pp. 446–47; on Umesao, see Andrew E. Barshay, "Postwar Social and Political Thought, 1945–90," in *Modern Japanese Thought*, ed. Bob Tadashi Wakabayashi (Cambridge: Cambridge University Press, 1998), pp. 317–19; quote is

from Perry Anderson, *Lineages of the Absolutist State* (London: Verso, 1986), p. 413.

19. Anderson, *Lineages*, p. 417.

20. Thomas C. Smith, *Nakahara: Family Farming and Population in a Japanese Village, 1717–1830* (Stanford: Stanford University Press, 1977), p. 2:

> Western countries . . . appear to have been rich, by global standards, even before the miracle of modern industry appeared. And that miracle may have been as much the result of wealth as a new source of it. Instead of asking, 'How did poor Western countries industrialize?' we ought perhaps to ask, 'How did poor Western countries become rich enough to industrialize?' The answer would not seem to be the obvious one: that Western economies expanded output in an unparalleled way before industrializing. Other parts of the world have enjoyed great periods of expansion. China, for instance, almost certainly stood for many centuries on a higher technological and organizational level than Europe. Yet something must have gone 'wrong' in this case. Somehow gains in output were not translated into gains in per capita income as they were in the West.

21. See Maruyama Masao, "An Approach to the History of Thought," *Asian Cultural Studies* 5 (Oct. 1966), esp. pp. 10–11; Jacques Maritain, *On the Use of Philosophy* (New York: Atheneum, 1969), p. 5.

Bibliography

Akamatsu Katsumaro. "The Russian Impact on the Early Japanese Social Movement." In *The Russian Impact on Japan: Literature and Social Thought*, ed. and trans. Peter Berton, Paul Langer, and George O. Totten. Los Angeles: University of Southern California Press, 1981.

Albritton, Robert, and Thomas T. Sekine, eds. *A Japanese Approach to Political Economy: Unoist Variations*. New York: St. Martin's Press, 1996.

Anderson, Perry. *Lineages of the Absolutist State*. London: Verso, 1986.

———. Preface to *Marxism, Wars, and Revolutions: Essays from Four Decades*, by Isaac Deutscher. London: Verso, 1984.

Aoki Tamotsu. *"Nihon bunkaron" no hen'yō*. Tokyo: Chūō Kōronsha, 1990.

Arendt, Hannah. *Men in Dark Times*. New York: Harcourt Brace Jovanovich, 1968.

Ariès, Philippe. *Centuries of Childhood: A Social History of Family Life*. New York: Vintage, 1962.

Arkush, David. *Fei Xiaotong and Sociology in Revolutionary China*. Cambridge, Mass.: Council on East Asian Studies, Harvard University, 1981.

Baba Hiroji. "Changing the Paradigm of Japanese Marx Economics." In *Annals of the Institute of Social Science*, no. 27 (1985): 26–63.

———. *Fuyūka to kin'yū shihon*. Kyoto: Mineruva Shobō, 1986.

———. *"Fuyūka to kin'yū shihon o megutte." Shakai kagaku kenkyū* 40, no. 3 (Sept. 1988): 51–62.

———. "Kaishashugi no puroburematīku." *Gendai shisō*, special issue: *Hōjin shihonshugi* (Dec. 1993): 136–51.

———. "Revolution and Counterrevolution in Marxian Economics." *Monthly Review* 40 (June 1989): 52–58.

———. "Sekai keizairon no taishō" (1968). In id., *Sekai keizai—Kijiku to shūhen*. Tokyo: Tokyo Daigaku Shuppankai, 1973.

———. *Shin shihonshugiron—Shikaku tenkan no keizaigaku.* Nagoya: Nagoya Daigaku Shuppankai, 1997.

Barshay, Andrew E. "Postwar Social and Political Thought, 1945–90." In *Modern Japanese Thought,* ed. Bob Tadashi Wakabayashi. Cambridge: Cambridge University Press, 1998.

———. *State and Intellectual in Imperial Japan: The Public Man in Crisis.* Berkeley and Los Angeles: University of California Press, 1988.

Bauman, Zygmunt. *Legislators and Interpreters: On Modernity, Post-Modernity, and Intellectuals.* Ithaca: Cornell University Press, 1987.

Beasley, W G. *The Japanese Experience.* Berkeley and Los Angeles: University of California Press, 1999.

Beckmann, George, and Genji Okubo. *The Japanese Communist Party, 1922–1945.* Stanford: Stanford University Press, 1969.

Bellah, Robert. Review of *Studies in the Intellectual History of Tokugawa Japan,* by Maruyama Masao. *Journal of Japanese Studies* 3, no. 1 (winter 1977).

Benedict, Ruth. *The Chrysanthemum and the Sword.* Boston: Houghton Mifflin, 1946.

Bennett, John, and Iwao Ishino. *Paternalism in the Japanese Economy: Anthropological Studies of Oyabun-Kobun Patterns.* Minneapolis: University of Minnesota Press, 1955.

Bergner, Jeffrey. *The Origin of Formalism in Social Science.* Chicago: University of Chicago Press, 1981.

Berlin, Isaiah. *The Hedgehog and the Fox* (1953). New York: Touchstone Books, n.d.

Berman, Marshall. *All That Is Solid Melts into Air: The Experience of Modernity.* New York: Penguin, 1988.

Berry, Wendell. "Failing Our Farmers." *New York Times,* July 6, 1999, final ed.: A17.

Bienkowski, Wladyslaw. *Theory and Reality.* London: Busby and Allen, 1982.

Bloch, Marc. *Feudal Society.* Chicago: University of Chicago Press, 1974.

Blyth, R. H. *Haiku.* Tokyo: Hokuseidō Press, 1981.

Bottomore, Tom, ed. *Dictionary of Marxist Thought.* 2nd ed. Oxford: Blackwell, 1991.

Bukharin, Nikolai. *Historical Materialism—A System of Sociology* (1921). Ann Arbor: University of Michigan Press, 1969.

Bukharin, Nikolai, and Evgenii Preobrazhensky. *The ABC of Communism* (1919). Ed. E. H. Carr. Harmondsworh, U.K.: Penguin, 1969.

Butler, Eliza Marian. *The Tyranny of Greece over Germany: A Study of the Influence Exercised by Greek Art and Poetry over the Great German Writers of the Eighteenth, Nineteenth, and Twentieth Centuries.* Cambridge: Cambridge University Press, 1935.

Cassidy, John. "Wall Street Follies." *New Yorker,* Sept. 13, 1999.

Cavell, Stanley. *The Claim of Reason: Wittgenstein, Skepticism, Morality, Tragedy.* Oxford: Oxford University Press, 1979.

Chayanov, A. V. *The Theory of Peasant Economy.* Madison, Wisc.: University of Wisconsin Press, 1986.

Clarke, Simon. "The Basic Theory of Capitalism: A Critical Review of Itoh and the Uno School." *Capital and Class* 37 (1989): 133–49.

Cohen, Stephen. *Bukharin and the Bolshevik Revolution.* New York: Oxford University Press, 1980.

Dahrendorf, Ralf. *Life Chances: Approaches to Social and Political Theory.* Chicago: University of Chicago Press, 1979.

Dauvergne, Peter. *Shadows in the Forest: Japan and the Politics of Timber in Southeast Asia.* Cambridge, Mass.: MIT Press, 1997.

Dōgen. *Shōbōgenzō.* Vol. 2. Tokyo: Iwanami Bunko, 1999.

Dore, Ronald P. *Shinohata: Portrait of a Japanese Village.* New York: Pantheon, 1978.

Duncan, Colin A. M. "Under the Cloud of *Capital:* History vs. Theory." *Science and Society* 47, no. 3 (fall 1993): 300–320.

Dunn, John. *Western Political Theory in the Face of the Future.* Cambridge: Cambridge University Press, 1979.

Duus, Peter. "Liberal Intellectuals and Social Conflict in Taishō Japan." In *Conflict in Modern Japanese History,* ed. J. Victor Koschmann and Tetsuo Najita. Princeton: Princeton University Press, 1982.

Edwards, Walter. "Buried Discourse: The Toro Archaeological Site and Japanese National Identity in the Early Postwar Period." *Journal of Japanese Studies* 17, no. 1 (winter 1991): 1–23.

Fairbank, J. K. and Masataka Banno. *Japanese Studies of Modern China.* Cambridge, Mass.: Harvard University Press, 1955.

Fletcher, Miles. *The Search for a New Order.* Chapel Hill: University of North Carolina Press, 1982.

Fujita Shōzō. "Shakai kagakusha no shisō." In *Sengo Nihon no shisō* by Kuno Osamu, Tsurumi Shunsuke, and Fujita Shōzō. Tokyo: Keisō Shobō, 1966.

———. *Tennōsei kokka no shihai genri.* Tokyo: Miraisha, 1959.

Fukuda Tokuzō. *Shakai seisaku to kaikyū tōsō.* Tokyo: Ōkura Shoten, 1922.

Fukutake Tadashi, *Chūgoku nōson shakai no kōzō.* Rev. ed. Tokyo: Yūhikaku, 1951.

Fukuzawa Yukichi. "Datsu-A ron" (Mar. 1885). In *Fukuzawa Yukichi zenshū.* Vol. 10. Tokyo: Iwanami Shoten, 1960.

Gao, Bai. "Arisawa Hiromi and His Theory for a Managed Economy." *Journal of Japanese Studies* 20, no. 1 (winter 1994): 115–53.

Garon, Sheldon. *Molding Japanese Minds: The State in Everyday Life.* Princeton: Princeton University Press, 1998.

Geertz, Clifford. *Local Knowledge: Further Essays in Interpretive Anthropology.* New York: Basic Books, 1983.

Georgescu-Roegen, Nicholas. *The Entropy Law and the Economic Process.* Cambridge, Mass.: Harvard University Press, 1971.

Gerschenkron, Alexander. *Economic Backwardness in Historical Perspective.* Cambridge, Mass.: Harvard University Press, 1962.

———. *Europe in the Russian Mirror.* Cambridge: Cambridge University Press, 1970.

Gluck, Carol. *Japan's Modern Myths: Ideology in the Late Meiji Period*. Princeton: Princeton University Press, 1985.

Gramsci, Antonio. *Selections from the Prison Notebooks*. Trans. Quintin Hoare and Geoffrey Nowell Smith. New York: International Publishers, 1971.

Harootunian, Harry. *Overcome by Modernity: History, Culture, and Community in Interwar Japan*. Princeton: Princeton University Press, 2000.

Hashikawa Bunzō. "The 'Civil Society' Ideal and Wartime Resistance." In *Authority and the Individual in Japan*, ed. J. Victor Koschmann. Tokyo: Tokyo University Press, 1978.

Havens, Thomas R. H. *Valley of Darkness: The Japanese People and World War Two*. New York: W. W. Norton, 1978.

Heidegger, Martin. *Being and Time*. New York: Random House, 1962.

Heilbroner, Robert. *The Nature and Logic of Capitalism*. New York: W. W. Norton, 1985.

Hein, Laura. "In Search of Peace and Democracy: Postwar Japanese Economic Thought in Political Context." *Journal of Asian Studies* 53, no. 3 (Aug. 1994): 752–78.

Heine, Heinrich. *Religion and Philosophy in Germany* (1833–52). Trans. J. Snodgrass. Boston: Beacon Press, 1959.

Herf, Jeffrey. *Reactionary Modernism: Technology, Culture, and Politics in Weimar and the Third Reich*. Cambridge: Cambridge University Press, 1984.

Herzen, Alexander. *My Past and Thoughts: The Memoirs of Alexander Herzen*. Berkeley and Los Angeles: University of California Press, 1982.

Hidaka Hiroshi. Commentary on Uno Kōzō, *Keizai genron*. In *Uno Kōzō chosakushū*. Vol. 2. Tokyo: Iwanami Shoten, 1974.

———, ed. *Kōza Sengo Nihon no shisō*. Vol. 2, *Keizaigaku*. Tokyo: Gendai Shichōsha, 1962.

———. "Marukusushugi no senzen to sengo." In *Kōza Sengo Nihon no shisō*. Vol. 2, *Keizaigaku*. Tokyo: Gendai Shichōsha, 1962.

Hidaka Rokurō, ed. *Kindaishugi*. Vol. 34 of *Gendai Nihon shisō taikei*. Tokyo: Chikuma Shobō, 1966.

Hilferding, Rudolf. *Finance Capital: A Study of the Latest Phase of Capitalist Development* (1910). Trans. Tom Bottomore. London: Routledge and Kegan Paul, 1985.

Hinada Shizuma. Review of Kojima Shūichi, *Roshia nōgyō shisōshi no kenkyū*. In *Acta Slavica Iaponica*, Tomus VI (1988): 109–12.

Hirano Yoshitarō. *Minzoku seiji no kihon mondai*. Tokyo: Koyama Shoten, 1944.

———. *Nihon shihonshugi shakai no kikō*. 1934. Repr., Tokyo: Iwanami Shoten, 1949.

Hiraishi Naoaki. "Maruyama Masao no 'shimin shakai' ron." Paper presented at the twelfth International Symposium, Japan Research Center, Fudan University (Shanghai). April 2002.

Hirata Kiyoaki. "Gendai shimin shakai to kigyō kokka." In Hirata Kiyoaki et al., *Gendai shimin shakai to kigyō kokka*. Tokyo: Ochanomizu Shobō, 1994.

———. "Keizaigakusha Uchida Yoshihiko—sono fūkaku to sakuhin." In *Watakushi no naka no Uchida Yoshihiko.* Tokyo: Iwanami Shoten, 1989.

———. "Shimin shakai to shakaishugi." In id., *Shimin shakai to shakaishugi.* Tokyo: Iwanami Shoten, 1969.

———. "La Société civile japonaise contemporaine." *Actuel Marx,* no. 2, special issue: *Le marxisme au Japon* (1987): 65–71.

Hirata Kiyoaki et al. *Gendai shimin shakai to kigyō kokka.* Tokyo: Ochanomizu Shobō, 1994.

Hiromatsu Wataru. "Tōhoku Ajia ga rekishi no shuyaku ni; Ōbei chūshin no sekaikan wa hōkai e." *Asahi shinbun,* Mar. 16, 1994.

Hoston, Germaine. *Marxism and the Crisis of Development in Prewar Japan.* Princeton: Princeton University Press, 1986.

Howard, M. C., and J. E. King. *A History of Marxian Economics.* 2 vols. Princeton: Princeton University Press, 1989–92.

Hozumi Nobushige. *Ancestor Worship and Japanese Law.* Tokyo: Z. P. Maruya, 1901.

Iida Taizō. *Hihan seishin no kōseki.* Tokyo: Chikuma Shobō, 1997.

Iikura Shōhei, ed. *Yanagita Kunio/Minakata Kumagusu ōfuku shokanshū.* 2 vols. Tokyo: Heibonsha, 1994.

Imai Juichirō and Kawaguchi Shigeo. *Maruyama Masao chosaku nōto.* Exp. ed. Tokyo: Gendai no Rironsha, 1987.

Irokawa Daikichi. *The Culture of the Meiji Period.* Translation ed. Marius Jansen. Princeton: Princeton University Press, 1986.

Ishida Takeshi. *Nihon no shakai kagaku.* Tokyo: Tokyo Daigaku Shuppankai, 1984.

———. *Shakai kagaku saikō.* Tokyo: Tokyo Daigaku Shuppankai, 1995.

Ishida Takeshi and Kang Sangjung. *Maruyama Masao to shimin shakai.* Yokohama: Seori Shobō, 1997.

Isobe Toshihiko. "Chayanovu riron to Nihon ni okeru shōnō keizai kenkyū no kiseki." *Nōgyō keizai kenkyū* 62, no. 3 (1990): 153–65.

Itō Hirobumi. "Some Reminiscences of the Grant of the New Constitution." In *Fifty Years of New Japan,* vol. 1, ed. Ōkuma Shigenobu. New York: Dutton, 1909.

Itoh, Makoto. *Value and Crisis: Essays on Marxian Economics in Japan.* New York: Monthly Review Press, 1980.

———. *The World Economic Crisis and Japanese Capitalism.* New York: St. Martin's Press, 1990.

Iwasaki Chikatsugu. *Nihon marukusushugi tetsugakushi josetsu.* Tokyo: Miraisha, 1984.

Jay, Martin. *Marxism and Totality: The Adventures of a Concept from Lukács to Habermas.* Berkeley and Los Angeles: University of California Press, 1984.

Jones, Gareth Stedman. "Anglo-Marxism, Neo-Marxism, and the Discursive Approach to History." In *Was bleibt von marxistischen Perspektiven in der Geschichtsforschung?* Ed. Alf Lüdtke. Göttingen: Wallstein Verlag, 1997.

Kabayama Kōichi. "Chiseishi toshite no 'Tamanoi-gō.'" In *Keizaigaku no isan.* Vol. 1 of *Tamanoi Yoshirō chosakushū.* Tokyo: Gakuyō Shobō, 1990.

Kagawa Toyohiko. *Hinmin shinri no kenkyū* (1915). In *Kagawa Toyohiko zen-shū*. Vol. 8. Tokyo: Kirisuto Shinbunsha, 1973.

———. *Ningenku to ningen kenchiku* (1920). In *Kagawa Toyohiko zenshū*. Vol. 9. Tokyo: Kirisuto Shinbunsha, 1973.

Kajiki Gō. *Yanagita Kunio no shisō*. Tokyo: Keisō Shobō, 1990.

Karatani Kōjin. "Uno riron to Bunto [Bund]." *Chūō kōron* (Nov. 1981): 178–79.

Kase Kazutoshi. "Nihon nōgyō ron no sengo 50-nen: Ōuchi Tsutomu-shi no baai." *Shakai kagaku kenkyū* 48, no. 4 (Jan. 1997): 3–36.

Katō Shūichi. "Taishō Democracy as the Pre-Stage for Japanese Militarism." In *Japan in Crisis: Essays in Taishō Democracy*, ed. Bernard Silberman and H. D. Harootunian. Princeton: Princeton University Press, 1974.

Katō Tetsurō. "Karōshi to sābisu zangyō no seiji keizaigaku—Shimin shakai no kiso wa rōdō jikan ka, jiyū jikan ka?" In Hirata Kiyoaki et al., *Gendai shimin shakai to kigyō kokka*. Tokyo: Ochanomizu Shobō, 1994.

Kawada Minoru. *Yanagita Kunio no shisōshiteki kenkyū*. Tokyo: Miraisha, 1985.

Kawakami Hajime. "Nihon dokutoku no kokkashugi" (1911). In *Kawakami Hajime hyōronshū*. Ed. Sugihara Shirō. Tokyo: Iwanami Bunko, 1999.

Kawakami Tetsutarō. " 'Kindai no chōkoku' ketsugo." In *Kindai no chōkoku*, ed. id. Tokyo: Fuzanbō, 1979.

Kawamura Nozomu. "Interwar Sociology and Socialism." In *Culture and Identity: Japanese Intellectuals during the Interwar Years*, ed. J. Thomas Rimer. Princeton: Princeton University Press, 1990.

———. *Nihon shakaigakushi kenkyū*. 2 vols. Tokyo: Ningen no Kagakusha, 1973–75.

———. *Sociology and Society of Japan*. London: Kegan Paul International, 1994.

Kawashima Takeyoshi. " 'Kindaika' no imi." *Shisō*, no. 473 (Nov. 1963): 2–8.

———. *Nihon shakai no kazokuteki kōsei*. Tokyo: Gakusei Shobō, 1948.

Kenny, Michael. "Marxism and Regulation Theory." In *Marxism and Social Science*, ed. Andrew Gamble, David Marsh, and Tony Tant. Urbana and Chicago: University of Illinois Press, 1999.

Kersten, Rikki. *Democracy in Postwar Japan: Maruyama Masao and the Search for Autonomy*. London: Routledge, 1996.

Keynes, John Maynard. *The General Theory of Employment, Interest, and Money* (1936). Repr., London: Macmillan and Co., 1961.

Kindersley, Richard. *The First Russian Revisionists*. Oxford: Clarendon Press, 1962.

Kingston-Mann, Esther. *In Search of the True West: Culture, Economics, and the Problems of Russian Development*. Princeton: Princeton University Press, 1999.

Kirisuto Shinbunsha, ed. *Shiryōshū—Kagawa Toyohiko zenshū to buraku sabetsu*. Tokyo: Kirisuto Shinbunsha, 1991.

Kitazawa Masakuni. "Militarism under the Cloak of Management Society." *Japan Interpreter* 9, no. 3 (winter 1975): 324–30.

———. "Ningen—sono botsuraku to saisei: Kyūshinteki kōzōshugi no nin-genkan." *Tenbō*, no. 111 (Mar. 1968): 16–36.

Kobayashi Noboru. "Hanseiki no Risuto juyō." In *Juyō to hen'yō—Nihon kindai keizai to shisō*, ed. Nakamura Katsumi. Tokyo: Misuzu Shobō, 1989.

Kōjien. Ed. Shinmura Izuru. Tokyo: Iwanami Shoten, 1977.

Kojima Shūichi. *Roshia nōgyō shisōshi no kenkyū*. Kyoto: Mineruva Shobō, 1987.

Kolakowski, Leszek. "The Concept of the Left." In id., *Toward a Marxist Humanism*. New York: Grove Press, 1968.

Koschmann, J. Victor. "Mao Zedong and the Postwar Japanese Left." In *Critical Perspectives on Mao Zedong's Thought*, ed. Arif Dirlik et al. Atlantic Highlands, N.J.: Humanities Press, 1997.

———. "Maruyama Masao and the Incomplete Project of Modernity." In *Postmodernism and Japan*, ed. H. D. Harootunian and Masao Miyoshi. Durham, N.C.: Duke University Press, 1989.

———. *Revolution and Subjectivity in Postwar Japan*. Chicago: University of Chicago Press, 1996.

Kracht, Klaus. "Traditional and Modern Thought in Japan: Some Notes on the Problem of Continuity and Its Meaning." In *Tradition and Modern Japan*, ed. P. G. O'Neill. Tenterden, Kent: Paul Norbury, 1981.

Kuribayashi Teruo. *Keikan no shingaku*. Tokyo: Shinkyō Shuppansha, 1993.

Kurihara Hyakuju. *Nihon nōgyō no kiso kōzō*. 1942. Repr., Tokyo: Nōsangyoson Bunka Kyōkai, 1979.

Landes, David. *The Wealth and Poverty of Nations*. New York: W. W. Norton, 1999.

Lavrov, P. L. (Pyotr Lavrovich). *Historical Letters* (1869). Trans. J. P. Scanlan. Berkeley and Los Angeles: University of California Press, 1967.

———. *Iz istorii sotsial'nykh uchenii (From the history of social doctrines)*. Petrograd: Kolos', 1919.

Lederer, Emil, and Emy Seidler-Lederer. *Japan in Transition*. New Haven: Yale University Press, 1938.

Lenin, V. I. "The Fall of Port Arthur" (Jan. 1905). In *Collected Works*. Vol. 8. London: Lawrence and Wishart, 1962.

———. *Imperialism* (1917). In *Collected Works*. Vol. 22. Moscow: Progress Publishers, 1968.

———. *Notebooks on Imperialism*. In *Collected Works*. Vol. 39. Moscow: Progress Publishers, 1968.

———. *Polnoe sobranie sochinenii*. 5th ed. Vol. 27. Moscow: Gosudarstvennoe Izdatel'stvo Politicheskoi Literatury, 1962.

Lenk, Kurt. "The Tragic Consciousness of German Sociology." In *Modern German Sociology*, ed. Volker Meja, Dieter Misgeld, and Nico Stehr. New York: Columbia University Press, 1987.

Lepsius, M. Rainer. "Sociology in the Interwar Period: Trends in Development and Criteria for Evaluation." In *Modern German Sociology*, ed. Volker Meja, Dieter Misgeld, and Nico Stehr. New York: Columbia University Press, 1987.

Levitskii, N. A. *Russko-Yaponskaya voina*. Moscow: Gosudarstvennoe Voennoe Izdatel'stvo, 1935.

Lie, John. "Reactionary Marxism: the End of Ideology in Japan?" *Monthly Review* 38 (Apr. 1987): 45–51.

Liebersohn, Harry. *Fate and Utopia in German Sociology, 1870–1923.* Cambridge, Mass.: MIT Press, 1988.

Low, D. A. *The Egalitarian Moment: Asia and Africa, 1950–1980.* Cambridge: Cambridge University Press, 1996.

Löwith, Karl. "Der europäische Nihilismus" (1940). In *Sämtliche Schriften.* Vol. 2. Stuttgart: J. B. Metzler, 1983.

———. "Japan's Westernization and Moral Foundation" (1942–43). In *Sämtliche Schriften.* Vol. 2. Stuttgart: J. B. Metzler, 1983.

Macdonald, Dwight. "Appendix: Marx vs. Herzen," in *My Past and Thoughts: The Memoirs of Alexander Herzen.* Berkeley and Los Angeles: University of California Press, 1982.

Maclean, Brian. "Kōzō Uno's *Principles of Political Economy.*" *Science and Society* 45, no. 2 (1981): 212–27.

Mannheim, Karl. *Ideology and Utopia.* 1936. Repr., New York: Harcourt Brace Jovanovich, n.d.

Maritain, Jacques. *On the Use of Philosophy.* New York: Atheneum, 1969.

Marshall, Byron K. *Academic Freedom and the Japanese Imperial University, 1868–1939.* Berkeley and Los Angeles: University of California Press, 1992.

Maruyama Masao. "An Approach to the History of Thought." *Asian Cultural Studies* 5 (Oct. 1966): 1–18.

———. "Aru jiyūshugisha e no tegami" (1950). In id., *Gendai seiji no shisō to kōdō.* Tokyo: Miraisha, 1966.

———. "Asō Yoshiteru, *Kinsei Nihon tetsugakushi* o yomu." In id., *Senchū to sengo no aida.* Tokyo: Misuzu Shobō, 1976.

———. *Bunmeiron no gairyaku o yomu,* 3 vols. Tokyo: Iwanami Shoten, 1986.

———. "The Changing Images of *Model* States: Modern Japan and Utopia." Unpublished manuscript, Jan. 20, 1962.

———. *Chūsei to hangyaku.* Tokyo: Chikuma Shobō, 1992.

———. "A Critique of De-Stalinization" (1956). In id., *Thought and Behavior in Modern Japanese Politics.* New York: Oxford University Press, 1969.

———. "From Carnal Literature to Carnal Politics" (1949). In id., *Thought and Behavior in Modern Japanese Politics.* New York: Oxford University Press, 1969.

———. "Gendai ni okeru taido kettei." *Sekai,* no. 175 (July 1960).

———. *Gendai seiji no shisō to kōdō.* Exp. ed. Tokyo: Miraisha, 1966.

———. "Genkei/kosō/shitsuyō tei'on: Nihon shisōshi hōhōron ni tsuite no watakushi no ayumi." In *Nihon bunka no kakureta kata,* ed. Takeda Kiyoko. Tokyo: Iwanami Shoten, 1984.

———. "The Ideology and Dynamics of Japanese Fascism" (1947). In id., *Thought and Behavior in Modern Japanese Politics.* New York: Oxford University Press, 1969.

———. *Jikonai taiwa.* Tokyo: Misuzu Shobō, 1998.

———. "Kaikoku" (1959). In *Kindaishugi.* Vol. 34 of *Gendai Nihon shisō taikei,* ed. Hidaka Rokurō. Tokyo: Chikuma Shobō, 1966.

———. "Kindai Nihon no chishikijin." In id., *Kōei no ichi kara.* Tokyo: Miraisha, 1982.

———. "Kindaiteki shii" (1945). In id., *Senchū to sengo no aida*. Tokyo: Misuzu Shobō, 1976.

———. "Matsurigoto no kōzō—Seiji ishiki no shitsuyō tei'on" (1985). In id., *Maruyama Masao shū*. vol. 12. Tokyo: Iwanami Shoten, 1996.

———. "Meiji kokka no shisō" (1946). In id., *Senchū to sengo no aida*. Tokyo: Misuzu Shobō, 1976.

———. *Maruyama Masao shū*. 16 vols. Tokyo: Iwanami Shoten, 1995–96.

———. "Nationalism in Japan: Its Theoretical Background and Prospects" (1951). In id., *Thought and Behavior in Modern Japanese Politics*. New York: Oxford University Press, 1969.

———. "Nihon ni okeru jiyū ishiki no keisei to tokushitsu" (Aug. 1947). In id., *Senchū to sengo no aida*. Tokyo: Misuzu Shobō, 1976.

———. *Nihon no shisō*. Tokyo: Iwanami Shinsho, 1961.

———. *Nihon seiji shisōshi kenkyū*. Tokyo: Tokyo Daigaku Shuppankai, 1952.

———. "Nihon shisōshi ni okeru 'kosō' no mondai" (1979). In *Maruyama Masao shū*. Vol. 11. Tokyo: Iwanami Shoten, 1995.

———. "Nyozekan to chichi to watakushi." In *Hasegawa Nyozekan—Hito; jidai; shisō to chosaku mokuroku*, ed. Sera Masatoshi et al. Tokyo: Chūō Daigaku Shuppanbu, 1986.

———. "Politics and Man in the Contemporary World." In id., *Thought and Behavior in Modern Japanese Politics*. New York: Oxford University Press, 1969.

———. "Politics as a Science in Japan" (1947). In id., *Thought and Behavior in Modern Japanese Politics*. New York: Oxford University Press, 1969.

———. "Rekishi ishiki no 'kosō.'" In *Rekishi shisō shū*, ed. id. Vol. 6 of *Nihon no shisō*. Tokyo: Chikuma Shobō, 1972.

———. "Seijigaku nyūmon" (1949). In id., *Senchū to sengo no aida*. Tokyo: Misuzu Shobō, 1976.

———. "Sei'ō bunka to kyōsanshugi no taiketsu" (1946). In id., *Gendai seiji no shisō to kōdō*. Exp. ed. Tokyo: Miraisha, 1966.

———. "Sensō sekinin ron no mōten" (1956). In id., *Senchū to sengo no aida*. Tokyo: Misuzu Shobō, 1976.

———. "Shisōshi no hōhō o mosaku shite—hitotsu no kaisō." *Nagoya daigaku hōsei ronshū*, no. 77 (Sept. 1978): 1–31.

———. "Shōwa tennō o meguru kiregire no kaisō" (1989). In *Maruyama Masao shū*. Vol. 15. Tokyo: Iwanami Shoten, 1996.

———. "The Structure of Matsurigoto: The Basso Ostinato of Japanese Political Life." In *Themes and Theories in Modern Japanese History*, ed. Jean-Pierre Lehmann and Sue Henny. London: Athlone Press, 1988.

———. *Studies in the Intellectual History of Tokugawa Japan*. Princeton: Princeton University Press; Tokyo: Tokyo University Press, 1974.

———. "Theory and Psychology of Ultranationalism" (1946). In id., *Thought and Behavior in Modern Japanese Politics*. New York: Oxford University Press, 1969.

———. *Thought and Behavior in Modern Japanese Politics*. New York: Oxford University Press, 1969.

———. "Thought and Behavior Patterns of Japan's Wartime Leaders" (1949). In id., *Thought and Behavior in Modern Japanese Politics*. New York: Oxford University Press, 1969.

Maruyama Masao and Katō Shūichi. *Honyaku to Nihon no kindai*. Tokyo: Iwanami Shinsho, 1998.

Maruyama Masao, Nishida Toshiyuki, and Uete Michiari. "Kindai Nihon to Kuga Katsunan" (1968). In *Gyakusetsu toshite no gendai*, ed. *Misuzu*. Tokyo: Misuzu Shobō, 1983.

Maruyama Masao, Umemoto Katsumi, and Satō Noboru. *Sengo Nihon no kakushin shisō*. Tokyo: Gendai no Rironsha, 1983.

Marx, Karl. *Capital*. 3 vols. Harmondsworth, U.K.: Penguin, 1990–92.

———. *The Eighteenth Brumaire of Louis Bonaparte* (1852). In *The Marx-Engels Reader*, ed. Robert Tucker. New York: W. W. Norton, 1978.

———. *The First International and After*. In *Political Writings*, Vol. 3. New York: Penguin, 1992.

———. *Grundrisse: Foundations of the Critique of Political Economy* (1857–58). Trans. Martin Nicolaus. Harmondsworth, U.K.: Penguin, 1973.

Marx, Karl, and Friedrich Engels. *The German Ideology: Part I* (1846). In *The Marx-Engels Reader*, ed. Robert Tucker. New York: W. W. Norton, 1978.

Masamura Kimihiro. "Shakaiteki kōka kara mita Nihon no shakai kagaku." In *Shakai kagaku no genba*. Vol. 4 of *Iwanami kōza: Shakai kagaku no hōhō*, ed. Yamanouchi Yasushi et al. Tokyo: Iwanami Shoten, 1993.

Matsumoto Sannosuke et al. "Maruyama riron to genzai shisō jōkyō." In *Gendai no riron*, ed. Andō Jinbei. Tokyo: Gendai no Rironsha, 1978.

Matsushita Keiichi. "Taishū kokka no seiritsu to sono mondaisei" (1956). In id., *Sengo seiji no rekishi to shisō*. Tokyo: Chikuma Shobō, 1994.

Mawatari, Shohken. "The Uno School: A Marxian Approach in Japan." *History of Political Economy* 17, no. 3 (1985): 403–18.

Meisner, Maurice. *The Deng Xiaoping Era*. New York: Hill and Wang, 1996.

———. *Mao's China and After*. New York: Free Press, 1977.

———. *Marxism, Maoism, and Utopianism*. Madison: University of Wisconsin Press, 1982.

Meja, Volker, Dieter Misgeld, and Nico Stehr, eds. *Modern German Sociology*. New York: Columbia University Press, 1987.

Miki Kiyoshi. *Shakai kagaku gairon* (1932). In *Miki Kiyoshi zenshū*. Vol 6. Tokyo: Iwanami Shoten, 1967.

———. *Shakai kagaku no yobi gainen* (1929). In *Miki Kiyoshi zenshū*. Vol 3. Tokyo: Iwanami Shoten, 1967.

———. *Shin Nihon no shisō genri* (1939). In *Miki Kiyoshi zenshū*. Vol 17. Tokyo: Iwanami Shoten, 1967.

Miki Kiyoshi, Nagata Kiyoshi, and Nakayama Ichirō, eds. *Shakai kagaku shin-jiten*. Tokyo: Kawade Shobō, 1941.

Minami Hiroshi. *Nihonjin no shinri*. Tokyo: Iwanami Shinsho, 1953.

Minobe Tatsukichi. *Kenpō kōwa*. Tokyo: Yūhikaku, 1912; 1918.

———. *Kenpō satsuyō*. Tokyo: Yūhikaku, 1923.

———. *Nihon kenpō*. Tokyo: Yūhikaku, 1921.

Mitani Taichirō. *Futatsu no sengo — Kenryoku to chishikijin*. Tokyo: Chikuma Shobō, 1988.

Moore, Barrington. *Social Origins of Dictatorship and Democracy: Lord and Peasant in the Making of the Modern World.* Boston: Beacon Press, 1966.

Morishima, Michio. *Why Has Japan "Succeeded"?* Cambridge: Cambridge University Press, 1982.

Morito Tatsuo. *Shisō tōsōshijō ni okeru shakai kagaku undō no jūyōsei.* Tokyo: Kaizōsha, 1926.

Morris-Suzuki, Tessa. *A History of Japanese Economic Thought.* London: Routledge, 1989.

Moseley, Fred, ed. *Marx's Method in Capital: A Reexamination.* Atlantic Highlands, N.J.: Humanities Press, 1993.

Murakami Yasusuke. *An Anticlassical Political-Economic Analysis: A Vision for the Next Century.* Trans. Kozo Yamamura. Stanford: Stanford University Press, 1996.

———. "The Japanese Model of Political Economy." In *The Domestic Transformation.* Vol. 1 of *The Political Economy of Japan,* ed. Kozo Yamamura and Yasukichi Yasuba. Stanford: Stanford University Press, 1987.

Nagai, Michio. *Higher Education in Japan: Its Take-Off and Crash.* Tokyo: Tokyo University Press, 1971.

Nagazumi Akira. "The Diffusion of the Idea of Social Darwinism in East and Southeast Asia." *Historia Scientiarum* 24 (1983).

Najita, Tetsuo. *Visions of Virtue: The Kaitokudō Merchant Academy in Tokugawa Japan.* Chicago: University of Chicago Press, 1987.

Nakajima Makoto. *Sengo shisōshi nyūmon.* Tokyo: Ushio Shuppansha, 1968.

Nakamura Hisashi. "Nihon ni okeru seimeikei no keizaigaku: Tamanoi Yoshirō no shigoto ni manabu." In *Kakutō suru gendai shisō—Toransumodan e no kokoromi,* ed. Imamura Hitoshi. Tokyo: Kōdansha/Gendai Shinsho, 1991.

Nakamura Takafusa. "Nihon shihonshugi ronsō ni tsuite." *Shisō,* no. 624 (June 1976): 185–97.

———. *The Postwar Japanese Economy.* Tokyo: University of Tokyo Press, 1983.

———. *Shōwa shi.* Tokyo: Tōyō Keizai Shinpōsha, 1993.

Nanbara Shigeru et al., eds. *Yanaihara Tadao—Shinkō, gakumon, shōgai.* Tokyo: Iwanami Shoten, 1969.

Nihon shuppan nenkan. Tokyo: Kyōdō Shuppansha, 1943–48.

Nishida Yoshiaki. "Growth of the Meiji Landlord System and Tenancy Disputes after World War I: A Critique of Richard Smethurst, *Agricultural Development and Tenancy Disputes in Japan, 1870–1940.*" *Journal of Japanese Studies* 15, no. 2 (summer 1989): 389–415.

Nitta Shigeru. *Dankairon no kenkyū.* Tokyo: Ochanomizu Shobō, 1998.

Noro Eitarō, ed. *Nihon shihonshugi hattatsushi kōza* (1932). 7 vols. Tokyo: Iwanami Shoten, 1982.

Ogura Toshimaru. *Nettowāku shihai kaitai no senryaku.* Tokyo: Kage Shobō, 1986.

———. *Shihai no "keizaigaku."* Tokyo: Renga Shobō, 1985.

Ōkita Saburō et al. *Postwar Reconstruction of the Japanese Economy* (Ministry of Foreign Affairs, 1946). Tokyo: University of Tokyo Press, 1992.

Ōshima Kiyoshi. *Takano Iwasaburō den.* Tokyo: Iwanami Shoten, 1968.

———. "Ningen Uno Kōzō." In *Omoigusa — Uno Kōzō tsuitō bunshū*, ed. Uno Maria. Privately published, 1979.

Ōshima Mario. "A Distant View of the Debate on Japanese Capitalism." *Osaka City University Economic Review* 26, no. 2 (July 1991): 23–34.

———. "Kakuritsuki Nihon shihonshugi no kōzō." In *Kindai Nihon keizaishi — Kokka to keizai*, ed. Yamamoto Yoshihiko. Kyoto: Mineruva Shobō, 1992.

Ōshima Sadamasu. *Jōseiron* (1896). In *Meiji bunka zenshū*, ed. Yoshino Sakuzō. Vol. 9. Tokyo: Nihon Hyōronsha, 1929.

Ōtsuka Hisao. "Jan Karuvan [Jean Calvin]" (1947). In *Ōtsuka Hisao chosakushū*. Vol. 8. Tokyo: Iwanami Shoten, 1969.

———. "Kindaiteki ningen ruikei no sōshutsu" (1946). In *Ōtsuka Hisao chosakushū*. Vol. 8. Tokyo: Iwanami Shoten, 1969.

———. *Kyōdōtai no kiso riron.* (1955). Tokyo: Iwanami Shoten, 1984.

Ōuchi Hideaki. "Uno keizaigaku no keisei." In *Keizaigaku*. Vol. 2 of *Kōza Sengo Nihon no shisō*, ed. Hidaka Hiroshi. Tokyo: Gendai Shichōsha, 1962.

Ōuchi Tsutomu. *Amerika nōgyō ron.* Tokyo: Tokyo Daigaku Shuppankai, 1965.

———. *Atarashii shakaishugizō no tankyū.* Tokyo: Rōdō Shakai Mondai Kenkyū Sentā, 1979.

———. *Keizaigaku hōhōron.* Vol. 1 of *Ōuchi Tsutomu keizaigaku taikei.* Tokyo: Tokyo Daigaku Shuppankai, 1980–91.

———. *Kokka dokusen shihonshugi.* Tokyo: Tokyo Daigaku Shuppankai, 1970.

———. *Nihon keizairon.* 2 vols. Tokyo: Tokyo Daigaku Shuppankai, 1962–63.

———. *Nihon nōgyō no ronri.* Tokyo: Nihon Hyōronsha, 1949.

———. *Nihon nōgyō no zaiseigaku.* Tokyo: Tokyo Daigaku Shuppankai, 1950.

———. *Nihon shihonshugi no nōgyō mondai.* Tokyo: Nihon Hyōronsha, 1948.

———. *Nōgyō kyōkō.* Tokyo: Yūhikaku, 1954.

———. *Nōgyō no kihonteki kachi.* Tokyo: Ie no Hikari Kyōkai, 1990.

———. "Notes on the Theory of State Monopoly Capitalism." *Annals of the Institute of Social Science*, no. 23 (1982): 1–21.

———. *Ōuchi Tsutomu keizaigaku taikei.* 8 vols. Tokyo: Tokyo Daigaku Shuppankai, 1980–91.

———. *Sekai keizairon.* Vol. 6 of *Ōuchi Tsutomu keizaigaku taikei.* Tokyo: Tokyo Daigaku Shuppankai, 1991.

———. *Teikokushugiron.* Vols. 4–5 of *Ōuchi Tsutomu keizaigaku taikei.* Tokyo: Tokyo Daigaku Shuppankai, 1980–91.

———. "Tsuitō Uno Kōzō sensei." In *Omoigusa*, ed. Uno Maria. Privately published, 1979.

Palat, Madhavan K. "What is Left of Marxism in Russian History." In *Was bleibt von marxistischen Perspektiven in der Geschichtsforschung?* ed. Alf Lüdtke. Göttingen: Wallstein Verlag, 1997.

Peattie, Mark. "Japanese Attitudes Toward Colonialism, 1895–1945." In *The Japanese Colonial Empire, 1895–1945,* ed. Ramon Myers and Mark Peattie. Princeton: Princeton University Press, 1984.

Piovesana, Gino. *Contemporary Japanese Philosophical Thought.* New York: St. John's University Press, 1969.

Polanyi, Karl. *The Great Transformation.* Boston: Beacon Press, 1957.

Pollard, Sidney. *Peaceful Conquest: The Industrialization of Europe, 1760–1970.* Oxford: Oxford University Press, 1992.

Pyle, Kenneth. "The Advantages of Followership: German Economics and Japanese Bureaucrats, 1890–1925." *Journal of Japanese Studies* 1, no. 1 (fall 1974): 127–64.

———. *The New Generation in Meiji Japan.* Stanford: Stanford University Press, 1969.

Read, Christopher. *From Tsar to Soviets: The Russian People and Their Revolution.* Oxford: Oxford University Press, 1996.

Robinson, G. T. *Rural Russia under the Old Regime.* Berkeley and Los Angeles: University of California Press, 1960.

Rōyama Masamichi. *Nihon ni okeru kindai seijigaku no hattatsu.* 1949. Repr., Tokyo: Shinsensha, 1971.

Saitō Haruzō. Commentary on *Keizai seisakuron.* In *Uno Kōzō chosakushū.* Vol. 7. Tokyo: Iwanami Shoten, 1974.

Sakisaka Itsurō. *Nihon shihonshugi no shomondai.* Tokyo: Shiseidō, 1958.

Sakuta Keiichi. "The Controversy over Community and Autonomy." In *Authority and the Individual in Japan,* ed. J. Victor Koschmann. Tokyo: University of Tokyo Press, 1974.

Sasaki-Uemura, Wesley. *Organizing the Spontaneous: Citizen Protest in Postwar Japan.* Honolulu: University of Hawaii Press, 2001.

Sasakura Hideo. *Maruyama Masao ron nōto.* Tokyo: Misuzu Shobō, 1988.

Sawa Takamitsu. "Nihon shihonshugi to *Nihon no shisō.*" *Sekai* (Nov. 1995): 49–56.

Sayer, Derek. *Capitalism and Modernity: An Excursus on Marx and Weber.* London: Routledge, 1991.

Scheiner, Irwin. *Christian Converts and Social Protest in Meiji Japan.* Berkeley and Los Angeles: University of California Press, 1970.

Schumpeter, Joseph. *A History of Economic Analysis.* New York: Oxford University Press, 1954.

Schutz, Alfred. "Common-Sense and Scientific Interpretation of Human Action." In id., *Collected Papers.* Vol. 1. The Hague: Martinus Nijhoff, 1967.

Sekine, Thomas [Tomohiko]. "Essay on Uno's Dialectic of Capital." Appended to Uno Kōzō, *Principles of Political Economy,* trans. Thomas Sekine. London and Atlantic Highlands, N.J.: Harvester/Humanities Press, 1980.

———. "Keizaigaku ni okeru paradaimu tenkan." In *Keizaigaku no isan.* Vol. 1 of *Tamanoi Yoshirō chosakushū.* Tokyo: Gakuyō Shobō, 1990.

———. "Socialism as a Living Idea." In *Socialist Dilemmas,* ed. Thomas Sekine and Henryk Flakierski. Armonk, N.Y.: M. E. Sharpe, 1990.

Shakai Kagaku Kenkyūjo no sanjūnen. Tokyo: Shakai Kagaku Kenkyūjo, 1977.

Shakai Mondai Kenkyūkai, comp. *Zengakuren kakuha—gakusei undō jiten.* Tokyo: Futabasha, 1969.

Sheehan, Helena. *Marxism and the Philosophy of Science.* Atlantic Highlands, N.J.: Humanities Press, 1985.

Shibagaki Kazuo. "Studies in Japanese Capitalism: A Survey with Emphasis on the Contribution of the Marx-Uno School." *Annals of the Institute of Social Science,* no. 30 (1988): 29–56.

———. "The Welfare State, Japanese Management, and Socialism: The *Aufhebung* of Commoditized Labor Power." *Annals of the Institute of Social Science,* no. 33 (1991): 112–35.

Shimizu Ikutarō. *Sengo o utagau*. Tokyo: Kōdansha, 1980.

Šik, Ota. *The Third Way: Marxist Leninist Theory and Modern Industrial Society*. Trans. Marian Sling. London: Wildwood House, 1976.

Silberman, Bernard. "The Bureaucratic State in Japan: The Problem of Authority and Legitimacy." In *Conflict in Modern Japanese History: The Neglected Tradition*, ed. Tetsuo Najita and J. Victor Koschmann. Princeton: Princeton University Press, 1982.

Smethurst, Richard. "A Challenge to Orthodoxy and Its Orthodox Critics: A Reply to Nishida Yoshiaki." *Journal of Japanese Studies* 15, no. 2 (summer 1989): 417–37.

Smith, Thomas C. *Nakahara: Family Farming and Population in a Japanese Village, 1717–1830*. Stanford: Stanford University Press, 1977.

———. *Native Sources of Japanese Industrialization*. Berkeley and Los Angeles: University of California Press, 1988.

———. *Political Change and Industrial Development in Japan: Government Enterprise, 1868–1880*. Stanford: Stanford University Press, 1965.

Sōda Kiichirō. "Bunkashugi no ronri." In id., *Bunka kachi to kyokugen gainen* (1922). Tokyo: Iwanami Shoten, 1972.

Soviak, Eugene. "Tsuchida Kyōson and the Sociology of the Masses." In *Culture and Identity: Japanese Intellectuals in the Interwar Years*. Ed. J. Thomas Rimer. Princeton: Princeton University Press, 1990.

Stalin, Joseph. *Economic Problems of Socialism in the USSR* (1952). In *The Essential Stalin*. Ed. Bruce Franklin. London: Croom Helm, 1973.

Sugiyama Mitsunobu. "Nihon shakai kagaku no sekai ninshiki: Kōza-ha, Ōtsuka shigaku, Uno keizaigaku o megutte." In *Nihon shakai kagaku no shisō*. Vol. 3 of *Iwanami kōza: Shakai kagaku no hōhō*, ed. Yamanouchi Yasushi et al. Tokyo: Iwanami Shoten, 1993.

———. " 'Shimin shakai' ron to senji dōin—Uchida Yoshihiko no shisō keisei o megutte." In *Sōryokusen to gendaika*, ed. Yamanouchi Yasushi et al. Tokyo: Kashiwa Shobō, 1995.

Sumiya Mikio. *Kagawa Toyohiko*. Tokyo: Iwanami Dōjidai Raiburarī, 1995.

Taguchi Fukuji. *Sengo Nihon seijigaku shi*. Tokyo: Tokyo Daigaku Shuppankai, 2000.

Takabatake Michitoshi. "Citizens' Movements: Organizing the Spontaneous." *Japan Interpreter* 9, no. 3 (winter 1975): 324–30.

Takahashi Sadaki. *Hisabetsu buraku issennenshi* (1924). Tokyo: Iwanami Bunko, 1996.

Takashima Zen'ya. "Shakai kagaku to wa nani ka." In *Shakai kagaku no kiso riron*. Tokyo: Kōbundō, 1950.

Takeuchi Kei. "Nihon shakai kagaku no chiteki kankyō." In *Shakai kagaku no genba*. Vol. 4 of *Iwanami Kōza: Shakai kagaku no hōhō*, ed. Yamanouchi Yasushi et al. Tokyo: Iwanami Shoten, 1993.

Takeuchi Yoshimi. "Kindai no chōkoku" (1959). In id., *Kindai no chōkoku*. Tokyo: Chikuma Shobō, 1983.

———. "Kindaishugi to minzoku no mondai" (1951). In id., *Kindai no chōkoku*. Tokyo: Chikuma Shobō, 1983.

Tamanoi Yoshirō. "Chūgoku zakkan" (1977). In id., *Ekonomī to ekorojī*. Tokyo: Misuzu Shobō, 1985.

———. *Ekonomī to ekorojī*. Tokyo: Misuzu Shobō, 1985.

———. "Gakumon o aisuru mono e no kitai" (1978). In id., *Ekonomī to ekoroī*. Tokyo: Misuzu Shobō, 1985.

Tamanoi Yoshirō. *Keizaigaku no isan*. Vol. 1 of *Tamanoi Yoshirō chosakushū*. Tokyo: Gakuyō Shobō, 1990.

———. *Keizaigaku no shuyō isan* (1956). Tokyo: Kōdansha Gakujutsu Bunko, 1980.

———. *Keizai taisei* (1975). In id., *Keizaigaku no isan*. Tokyo: Gakuyō Shobō, 1990.

———. "Kokka to keizai—chiiki bunken o motomete" (1973). In *Bunmei toshite no keizai*. Vol. 6 of *Ningen no seiki*, ed. Tamanoi Yoshirō. Tokyo: Ushio Shuppansha, 1973. Repr. in id., *Ekonomī to ekorojī*. Tokyo: Misuzu Shobō, 1985.

———. *Rikādō kara Marukusu e*. Tokyo: Shin Hyōronsha, 1954.

———. "Shakai kagaku ni okeru seimei no sekai—hiseimeikei kara seimeikei e" (1977). In id., *Ekonomī to ekorojī*. Tokyo: Misuzu Shobō, 1985.

———. "Uno keizaigaku no kōseki to genkai." *Ekonomisuto*, Mar. 29, 1977. Repr. in id., *Ekonomī to ekorojī*. Tokyo: Misuzu Shobō, 1985.

Tamanoi Yoshirō, Tsuchida Atsushi and Murota Takeshi "Towards an entropic theory of economy and sociology." *Economie appliquée* 37, no. 2 (1984): 279–94.

Tanabe Hajime. *Philosophy as Metanoetics [Zangedō toshite no tetsugaku]*. Trans. Takeuchi Yoshinori with Valdo Viglielmo and James W. Heisig. Berkeley and Los Angeles: University of California Press, 1986.

Tanaka Hiroshi. *Hasegawa Nyozekan kenkyū josetsu*. Tokyo: Miraisha, 1990.

Tarbuck, Kenneth. *Bukharin's Theory of Equilibrium*. London: Pluto Press, 1989.

Tolstoy, L. N. *Anna Karenin*. Trans. Rosemary Edmonds. Harmondsworth, U.K.: Penguin, 1978.

———. *Tolstoy's Letters*. Ed. R. F. Christian. 2 vols. New York: Scribner's, 1978.

Tominaga Kenichi. "Sengo Nihon no shakai kagaku ni okeru paradaimu no sōkoku to sono shūen." In *Yuragi no naka no shakai kagaku*. Vol. 3 of *Iwanami Kōza: Shakai kagaku no hōhō*, ed. Yamanouchi Yasushi et al. Tokyo: Iwanami Shoten, 1993.

Tosaka Jun. *Sekai no ikkan toshite no Nihon* (1937). In *Tosaka Jun zenshū*. Vol. 5. Tokyo: Keisō Shobō, 1967.

Touraine, Alain. *Return of the Actor: Social Theory in Postindustrial Society.* Minneapolis: University of Minnesota Press, 1988.

Tsuru, Shigeto. *Japan's Capitalism: Creative Defeat and Beyond*. Cambridge: Cambridge University Press, 1993.

Tsurumi, Kazuko. *Social Change and the Individual*. Princeton: Princeton University Press, 1969.

Tsurumi, Shunsuke. Appx. I, *Nationalism and the Right Wing in Japan: A Study of Post-war Trends* by Ivan Morris. Oxford: Oxford University Press, 1960.

Tsurumi Shunsuke and Maruyama Masao. "Fuhen genri no tachiba." In *Kataritsugu sengoshi,* vol. 1, ed. Tsurumi Shunsuke. Tokyo: Shisō no Kagakusha, 1969.

Tsuzuki Tsutomu. *Sengo Nihon no chishikijin — Maruyama Masao to sono jidai*. Yokohama: Seori Shobō, 1995.

Uchida Yoshiaki. *Vēbā to Marukusu — Nihon shakai kagaku no shisō kōzō*. Tokyo: Iwanami Shoten, 1978.

Uchida Yoshihiko. "Japan Today and *Das Kapital*." *Japan Interpreter* 6, no. 1 (spring 1970): 8–28.

———. *Keizaigaku no seitan* (1953). In *Uchida Yoshihiko chosakushū*. Vol. 1. Tokyo: Iwanami Shoten, 1989.

———. "Narōdoniki to marukusushugi—Rēnin riron seiritsu no ichi sōwa" (1946). In *Uchida Yoshihiko chosakushū*. Vol. 10. Tokyo: Iwanami Shoten, 1989.

———. *Nihon shihonshugi no shisōzō*. Tokyo: Iwanami Shoten, 1967.

———. *Sakuhin toshite no shakai kagaku*. Tokyo: Iwanami Dōjidai Raiburarī, 1993.

———. "Senji keizaigaku no mujunteki tenkai to keizai riron" (1948). In *Uchida Yoshihiko chosakushū*. Vol. 10. Tokyo: Iwanami Shoten, 1989.

——— (pseud. "NNN"). " 'Shijō no ronri' to 'chidai hanchū no kiki.' " *Keizai hyōron*, nos. 3, 4, 6 (1949). In *Uchida Yoshihiko chosakushū*. Vol. 10. Tokyo: Iwanami Shoten, 1989.

———. *Shihonron no sekai*. Tokyo: Iwanami Shoten, 1966.

———. "*Shihonron* to gendai—Meiji hyakunen to *Shihonron* hyakunen." *Sekai* (Sept. 1967).

Umemoto Katsumi. "Marukusushugi to kindai seijigaku: Maruyama Masao no tachiba o chūshin toshite." In *Kōza gendai no ideorogī*. Vol. 5 of *Gendai Nihon no shisō to kōdō*, ed. Ikumi Takuichi et al. Tokyo: San'ichi Shobō, 1962.

Uno Kōzō. "Chitsuroku shobun ni tsuite" (1958). In *Uno Kōzō chosakushū*. Vol. 8. Tokyo: Iwanami Shoten, 1974.

———. "Furīdorihhi Risuto [Friedrich List] no *Keizaigaku*" (1934). In *Uno Kōzō chosakushū*. Vol. 7. Tokyo: Iwanami Shoten, 1974.

———. "Iwayuru keizaigai kyōsei ni tsuite" (1947). In *Uno Kōzō chosakushū*. Vol. 8. Tokyo: Iwanami Shoten, 1974.

———. *Kachiron* (1947). In *Uno Kōzō chosakushū*. Vol. 3. Tokyo: Iwanami Shoten, 1974.

———. " 'Kahei no hitsuzensei': Hirufadingu [Hilferding] no kahei riron saikōsatsu" (1930). In *Uno Kōzō chosakushū*. Vol. 3. Tokyo: Iwanami Shoten, 1974.

———. "Katoki no toriatsukai ni tsuite." *Shisō*, no. 325 (July 1951). Repr. in *Uno Kōzō chosakushū*. Vol. 9. Tokyo: Iwanami Shoten, 1974.

———. *Keizaigaku hōhōron* (1958). In *Uno Kōzō chosakushū*. Vol. 9. Tokyo: Iwanami Shoten, 1974.

———. "Keizaigaku yonjūnen." Interview in *Shakai kagaku kenkyū* 9, nos. 4–5 (1958).

———. *Keizai genron*. 2 vols. 1st ed. Tokyo: Iwanami Shoten, 1950–52.

———. *Keizai genron*. 2nd ed. Tokyo: Iwanami Shoten, 1964.

———. "Keizai hōsoku to shakaishugi—Sutārin shosetsu ni taisuru gimon," *Shisō* (Oct. 1953). Repr. as ch. 7 of *Shihonron to shakaishugi* (1958). In *Uno Kōzō chosakushū*. Vol. 10. Tokyo: Iwanami Shoten, 1974.

——. *Keizai seisakuron* (1st ed., 1936). In *Uno Kōzō chosakushū*. Vol. 7. Tokyo: Iwanami Shoten, 1974.

——. *Keizai seisakuron* (1954; 1971). In *Uno Kōzō chosakushū*. Vol. 7. Tokyo: Iwanami Shoten, 1974.

——. *Kyōkōron* (1953). In *Uno Kōzō chosakushū*. Vol. 5. Tokyo: Iwanami Shoten, 1974.

——. "Nihon shihonshugi ronsō to wa nani ka." In *Uno Kōzō chosakushū*. Supp. vol. Tokyo: Iwanami Shoten, 1974.

——. *Nōgyō mondai joron* (1947). In *Uno Kōzō chosakushū*. Vol. 8. Tokyo: Iwanami Shoten, 1974.

——. *Principles of Political Economy*. Trans. Thomas T. Sekine. London and Atlantic Highlands, N.J.: Humanities Press, 1980.

——. "Sekai keizairon no hōhō to mokuhyō" (1950). In *Uno Kōzō chosakushū*. Vol. 9. Tokyo: Iwanami Shoten, 1974.

——. "Shakai kagaku no kyakkansei" (1948). In *Uno Kōzō chosakushū*. Vol. 10. Tokyo: Iwanami Shoten, 1974.

——. *Shihonron gojūnen* Tokyo: Hōsei Daigaku Shuppankyoku, 1981.

——. "*Shihonron* no kakushin" (1956). In *Uno Kōzō chosakushū*. Supp. vol. Tokyo: Iwanami Shoten, 1974.

——. *Shihonron no keizaigaku* (1969). In *Uno Kōzō chosakushū*. Vol. 6. Tokyo: Iwanami Shoten, 1974.

——. *Shihonron no kenkyū* (1948). In *Uno Kōzō chosakushū* Vol. 3. Tokyo: Iwanami Shoten, 1974.

——. *Shihonron to shakaishugi* (1958). *Uno Kōzō chosakushū*. Vol. 10. Tokyo: Iwanami Shoten, 1974.

——. "Shihonshugi no seiritsu to nōson bunkai no katei," *Chūō kōron* (Nov. 1935). In *Senjika no teikō to jiritsu — Sōzōeki sengo e no taidō*, ed. Furihata Setsuo. Tokyo: Shakai Hyōronsha, 1989. Also in *Uno Kōzō chosakushū*. Vol. 8. Tokyo: Iwanami Shoten, 1974.

——. *Uno Kōzō chosakushū*. 10 vols. plus suppl. Tokyo: Iwanami Shoten, 1974.

Uno Kōzō and Umemoto Katsumi. *Shakai kagaku to benshōhō*. Tokyo: Iwanami Shoten, 1976.

Unoura Hiroshi. "Kindai Nihon ni okeru shakai dāwinizumu no juyō to tenkai." In *Kōza: Shinka*. Vol. 2 of *Shinka shisō to shakai*, ed. Shibatani Atsuhiro et al. Tokyo: Tokyo Daigaku Shuppankai, 1991.

Uzawa Hirofumi. *Uzawa Hirofumi chosakushū*. Tokyo: Iwanami Shoten, 1994–96.

Vlastos, Stephen, ed. *Mirror of Modernity: Invented Traditions of Modern Japan*. Berkeley and Los Angeles: University of California Press, 1998.

Vucinich, Alexander. *Social Thought in Tsarist Russia: The Quest for a General Science of Society, 1861–1917*. Chicago: University of Chicago Press, 1976.

Wada, Haruki. "Kindaikaron." In *Nihonshi ronsō*. Vol. 9 of *Kōza Nihonshi*. Ed. Rekishigaku Kenkyūkai and Nihonshi Kenkyūkai. Tokyo: Tokyo Daigaku Shuppankai, 1971.

——. "Nihonjin no Roshia-kan: Sensei, teki; tomo ni kurushimu mono." In *Roshia to Nihon: Nisso rekishigaku shimpojiumu*, ed. Fujiwara Akira. Tokyo: Sairyūsha, 1985.

————. "Sengo Nihon ni okeru Shakai Kagaku Kenkyūjo no shuppatsu." *Shakai kagaku kenkyū* 32, no. 2 (Aug. 1980): 216–32.

Walicki, Andrzej. *A History of Russian Thought: From the Enlightenment to Marxism.* Stanford: Stanford University Press, 1979.

————. *Marxism and the Leap to the Kingdom of Freedom.* Stanford: Stanford University Press, 1995.

————. *The Slavophile Controversy.* South Bend: University of Notre Dame Press, 1989.

Wallerstein, Immanuel. "Culture as the Ideological Battleground of the Modern World System." In *Hitotsubashi Journal of Social Studies*, no. 21 (1989): 5–22.

————. *Unthinking Social Science: The Limits of Nineteenth-Century Paradigms.* London: Polity Press, 1991.

Wallerstein, Immanuel, et al. *Open the Social Sciences.* Stanford: Stanford University Press, 1996.

Wasiolek, Edward. *Tolstoy's Major Fiction.* Chicago: University of Chicago Press, 1978.

Weber, Max. *Economy and Society: Outline of Interpretive Sociology.* Trans. Guenther Roth and Claus Wittich. Berkeley and Los Angeles: University of California Press, 1978.

————. "'Objectivity' in Social Science and Social Policy" (1904). In id., *The Methodology of the Social Sciences,* trans. Edward Shils and H. H. Finch. New York: The Free Press, 1949.

————. "Politics as a Vocation" (1918). In *From Max Weber: Essays in Sociology,* ed. Hans Gerth and C. Wright Mills. New York: Oxford University Press, 1958.

————. *The Protestant Ethic and the Spirit of Capitalism.*1921. Repr., New York: Scribners, 1974.

————. "Science as a Vocation" (1918). In *From Max Weber: Essays in Sociology,* ed. Hans Gerth and C. Wright Mills. New York: Oxford University Press, 1958.

Weil, Simone. "The Power of Words" (1937). In *Selected Essays,* ed. Richard Rees. Oxford: Oxford University Press, 1963.

Windelband, Wilhelm. "Kritische oder genetische Methode?" In id., *Präludien.* 3rd ed. Tübingen: J. C. B. Mohr [Paul Siebeck], 1907.

Yagi Kiichirō. "The Age of Toyotism: A Transitional Period to Civil Society?" Unpublished paper (Dec. 1999).

————. "Keizaigakushi ni okeru kyūshin to enshin." In *Keizaigaku no isan.* Vol. 1 of *Tamanoi Yoshirō chosakushū.* Tokyo: Gakuyō Shobō, 1990.

————. *Nihon no shakai-keizaigaku.* Tokyo: Chikuma Shobō, 1999.

Yamada Moritarō. *Nihon shihonshugi bunseki* (1934). In *Yamada Moritarō chosakushū.* Vol. 2. Tokyo: Iwanami Shoten, 1984.

————. "Nihon nōgyō no tokushusei" (Nov. 1945). In *Yamada Moritarō chosakushū.* Vol. 3. Tokyo: Iwanami Shoten, 1984.

————. "Saiseisan hyōshiki to chidai hanchū—Nihon keizai saiken no hōshiki to nōgyō kaikaku no hōkō o kimeru tame no ichi kijun" (1947). In *Yamada Moritarō chosakushū.* Vol. 3. Tokyo: Iwanami Shoten, 1984.

————. *Saiseisan katei: hyōshiki bunseki joron* (1931). In *Yamada Moritarō chosakushū.* Vol. 1. Tokyo: Iwanami Shoten, 1984.

Yamada Toshio. "Kigyō shakai to shimin shakai." In Hirata Kiyoaki et al., *Gendai shimin shakai to kigyō kokka.* Tokyo: Ochanomizu Shobō, 1994.

————. "Nihongata shihonshugi to kigyōshugiteki chōsei." *Gendai shisō,* special issue: *Hōjin shihonshugi* (Dec. 1993): 166–75.

————. "Les Tendances du marxisme japonais contemporain." In *Actuel Marx,* no. 2, special issue: *Le marxisme au Japon* (1987): 34–44.

Yamamoto Yoshitaka. *Chisei no hanran: Tōdai kaitai made.* Tokyo: Zen'eisha, 1969.

Yamanouchi Yasushi, ed. *Iwanami kōza: Shakai kagaku no hōhō.* 12 vols. Tokyo: Iwanami Shoten, 1993.

————. *Nihon shakai kagaku to Wēbā taiken.* Tokyo: Chikuma Shobō, 1999.

————. "Sengo hanseiki no shakai kagaku to rekishi ninshiki." *Rekishi gaku kenkyū,* no. 689 (Oct. 1996): 32–43.

————. *Shisutemu shakai no gendaiteki isō.* Tokyo: Iwanami Shoten, 1996.

Yamanouchi Yasushi, J. Victor Koschmann, and Narita Ryūichi, eds. *Sōryokusen to gendaika.* Tokyo: Kashiwa Shobō, 1995.

————. *Total War and "Modernization."* Ithaca: East Asia Program, Cornell University, 1998.

Yamazaki Ryūzō. "*Nihon shihonshugi bunseki* no hōhō to sono hihanshi." In id., *Kindai Nihon keizaishi no kihon mondai.* Kyoto: Mineruva Shobō, 1989.

Yanagita Kunio. *Jidai to nōsei* (1910). In *Teihon Yanagita Kunio shū.* Vol. 16. Tokyo: Chikuma Shobō, 1964.

————. *Kyōdo seikatsu no kenkyūhō* (1935). In *Teihon Yanagita Kunio shū.* Vol. 25. Tokyo: Chikuma Shobō, 1964.

————. *Minkan denshō ron* (1934). In *Teihon Yanagita Kunio shū.* Vol. 25. Tokyo: Chikuma Shobō, 1964.

Yanaihara Isaku. *Wakaki hi no nikki.* Tokyo: Gendai Hyōronsha, 1974.

————. *Yanaihara Tadao den.* Tokyo: Misuzu Shobō, 1998.

Yanaihara Tadao. "Kanrika no Nihon—Shūsengo mansannen no zuisō" (Oct. 1948). In *Yanaihara Tadao zenshū.* Vol. 19. Tokyo: Iwanami Shoten, 1964.

————. *Kokka no risō: Senji hyōronshū.* Tokyo: Iwanami Shoten, 1982.

————. *Watakushi no ayunde kita michi.* Tokyo: Tokyo Daigaku Shuppankai, 1975.

————. *Yanaihara Tadao zenshū.* 29 vols. Tokyo: Iwanami Shoten, 1963–65.

Yasuba Yasukichi. "Anatomy of the Debate on Japanese Capitalism." *Journal of Japanese Studies* 2, no. 1 (fall 1975).

Yoshida Masatoshi. *Sengo shisō ron.* Tokyo: Aoki Shoten, 1984.

Yoshimoto Takaaki. "Maruyama Masao ron." In *Yoshimoto Takaaki zenchosakushū.* Vol. 12. Tokyo: Keisō Shobō, 1969.

Yoshino Sakuzō. *Yoshino Sakuzō hyōronshū.* Ed. Oka Yoshitake. Tokyo: Iwanami Bunko, 1975.

Yoshitomi Masaru. "Henkaku no shisō toshite no keizaigaku." In *Keizaigaku no isan.* Vol. 1 of *Tamanoi Yoshirō chosakushū.* Tokyo: Gakuyō Shobō, 1990.

Index

Compositor: BookMatters, Berkeley
Text: 10/13 Sabon
Display: Sabon
Printer and Binder: Odyssey Press